3

My Love Mix-Up!

Art by **Aruko**
Story by **Wataru Hinekure**

Contents

Aoki borrows an eraser from his unrequited crush, Hashimoto. He finds the name "IDA♡" written on the eraser, and his hopes are dashed. Then Ida sees him holding that very eraser and thinks Aoki is in love with him! While attempting to resolve the misunderstanding, Aoki ends up falling for Ida. It turns out Hashimoto's unrequited crush isn't Ida, but Aoki's friend Aida! Aoki and Hashimoto end up cheering each other on. Unaware of Aoki's true feelings, Aida reveals to Ida that Aoki liking him was a misunderstanding. When Ida says he's glad it was just a mix-up, Aoki is heartbroken. Just when Aoki decides to give up, he becomes frazzled when a girl aggressively goes after Ida. Ida, who has never been acquainted with matters of love, starts to show some curiosity when it comes to Aoki. Has Ida started paying more attention to him...?!

Chapter 10

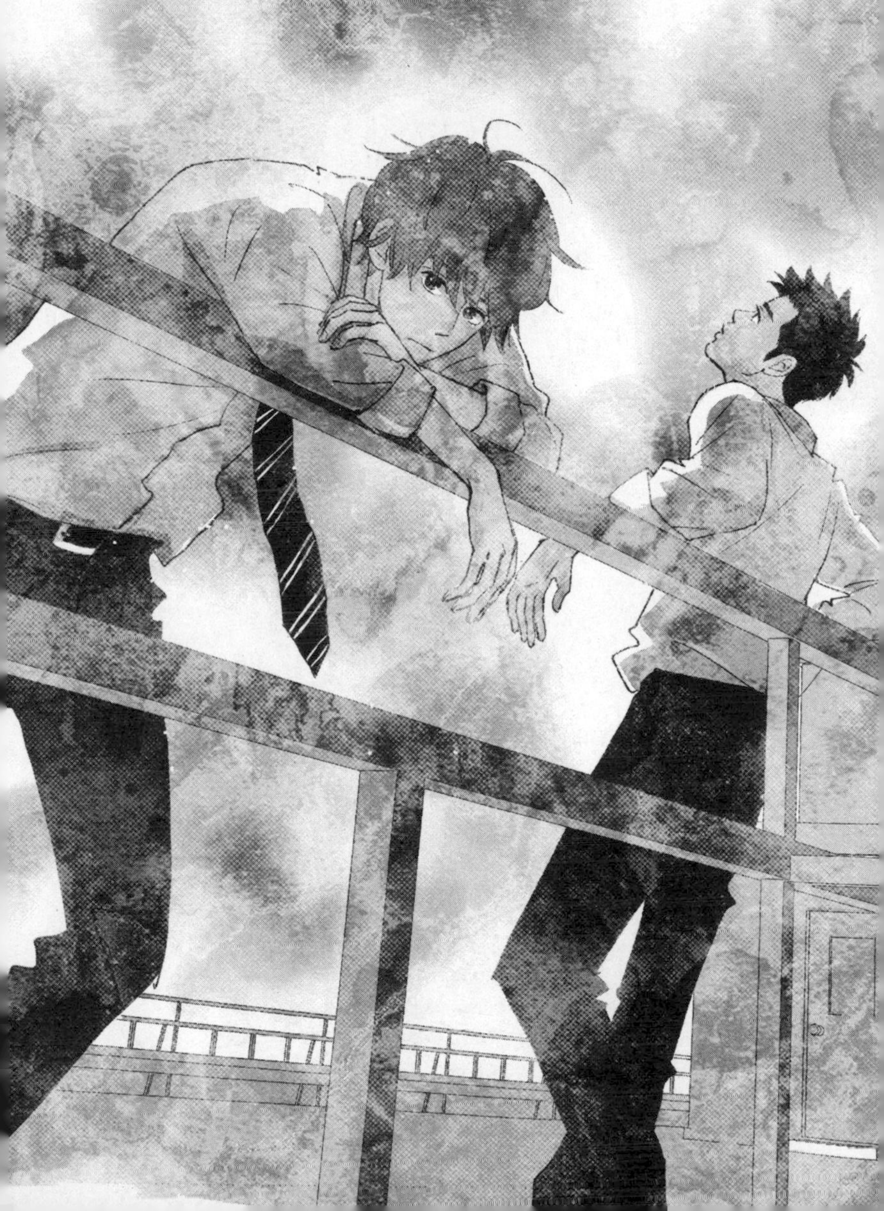

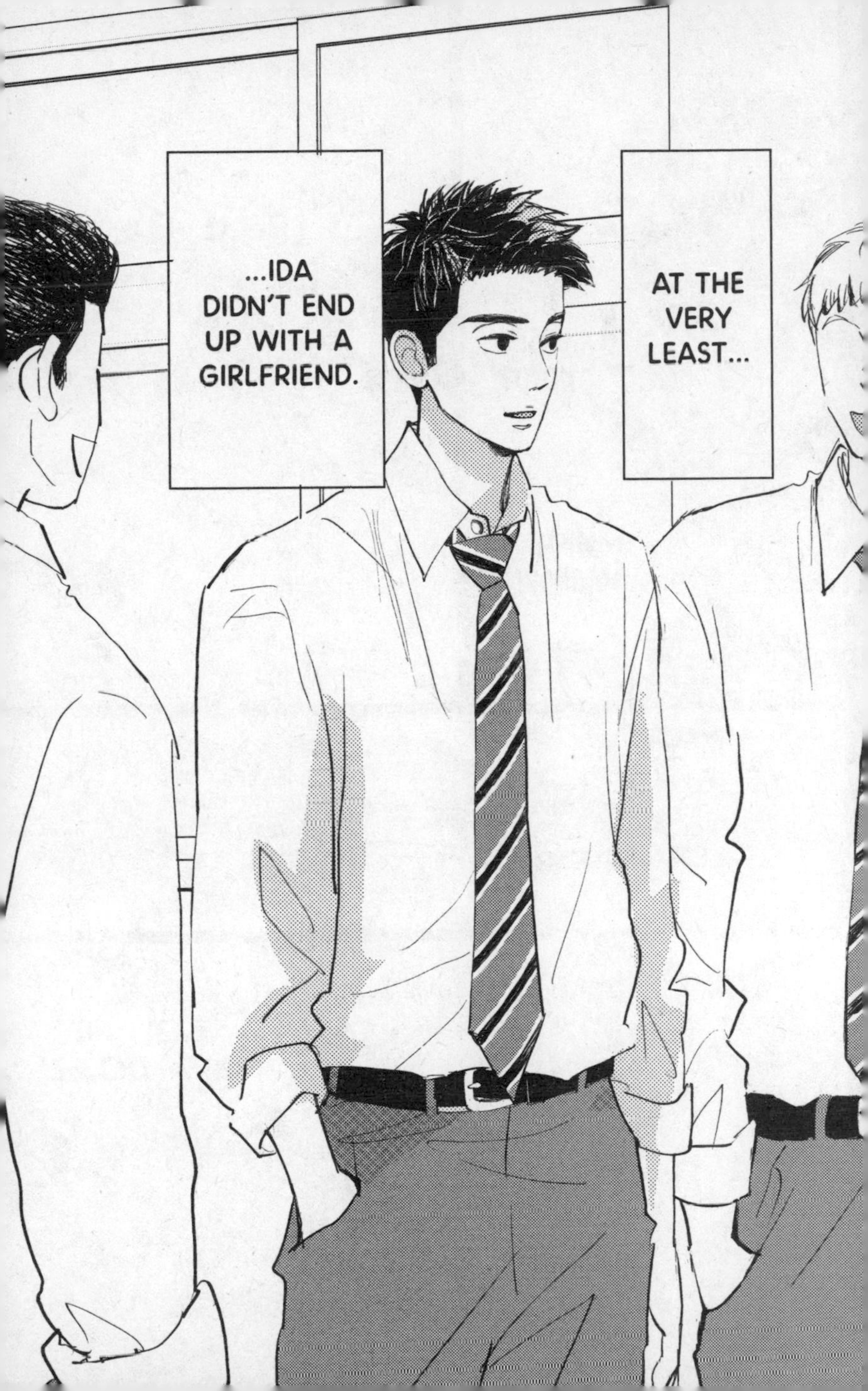
AT THE VERY LEAST...
...IDA DIDN'T END UP WITH A GIRLFRIEND.

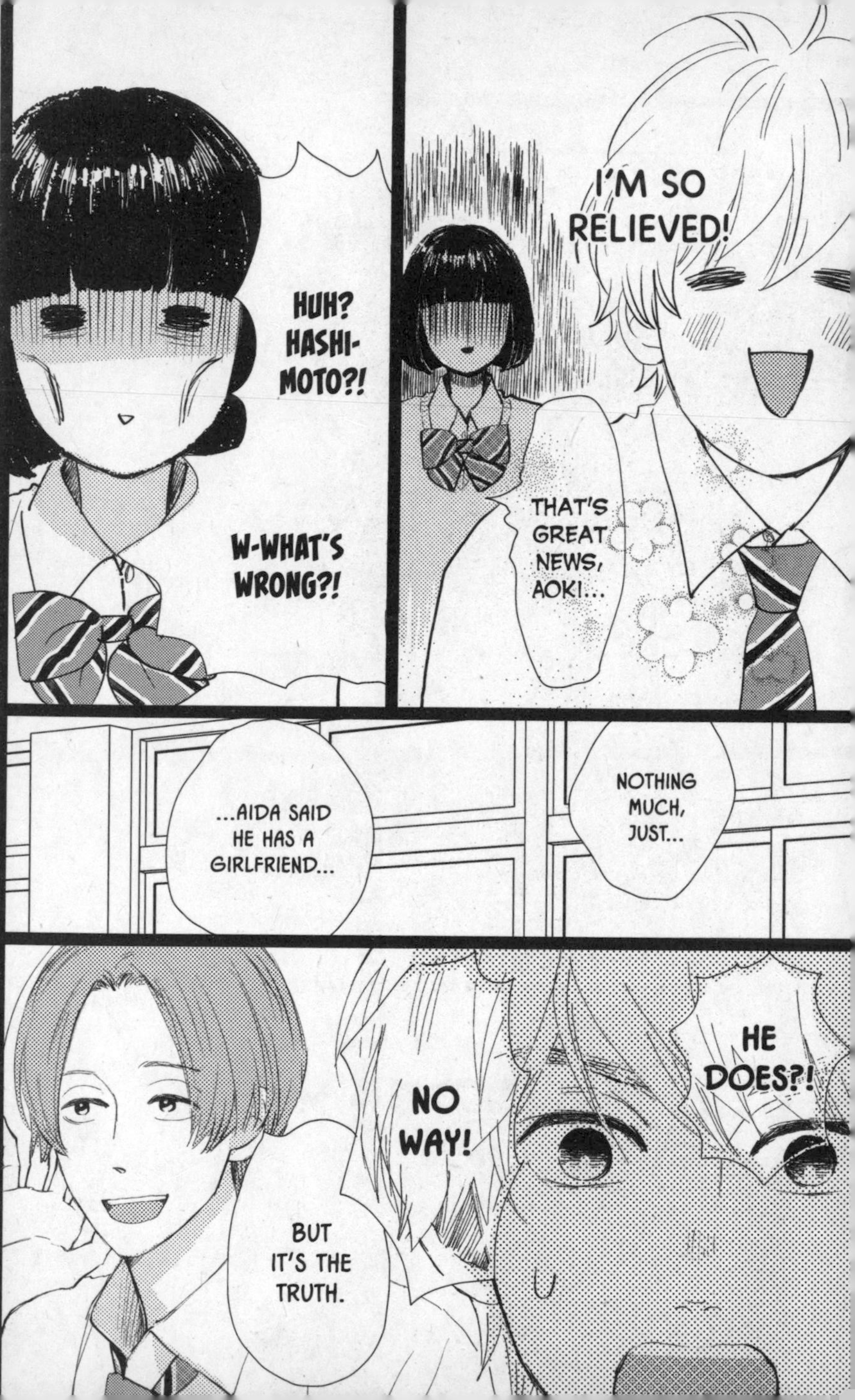
I'M SO RELIEVED!
THAT'S GREAT NEWS, AOKI...
HUH? HASHI-MOTO?!
W-WHAT'S WRONG?!
NOTHING MUCH, JUST...
...AIDA SAID HE HAS A GIRLFRIEND...
HE DOES?!
NO WAY!
BUT IT'S THE TRUTH.

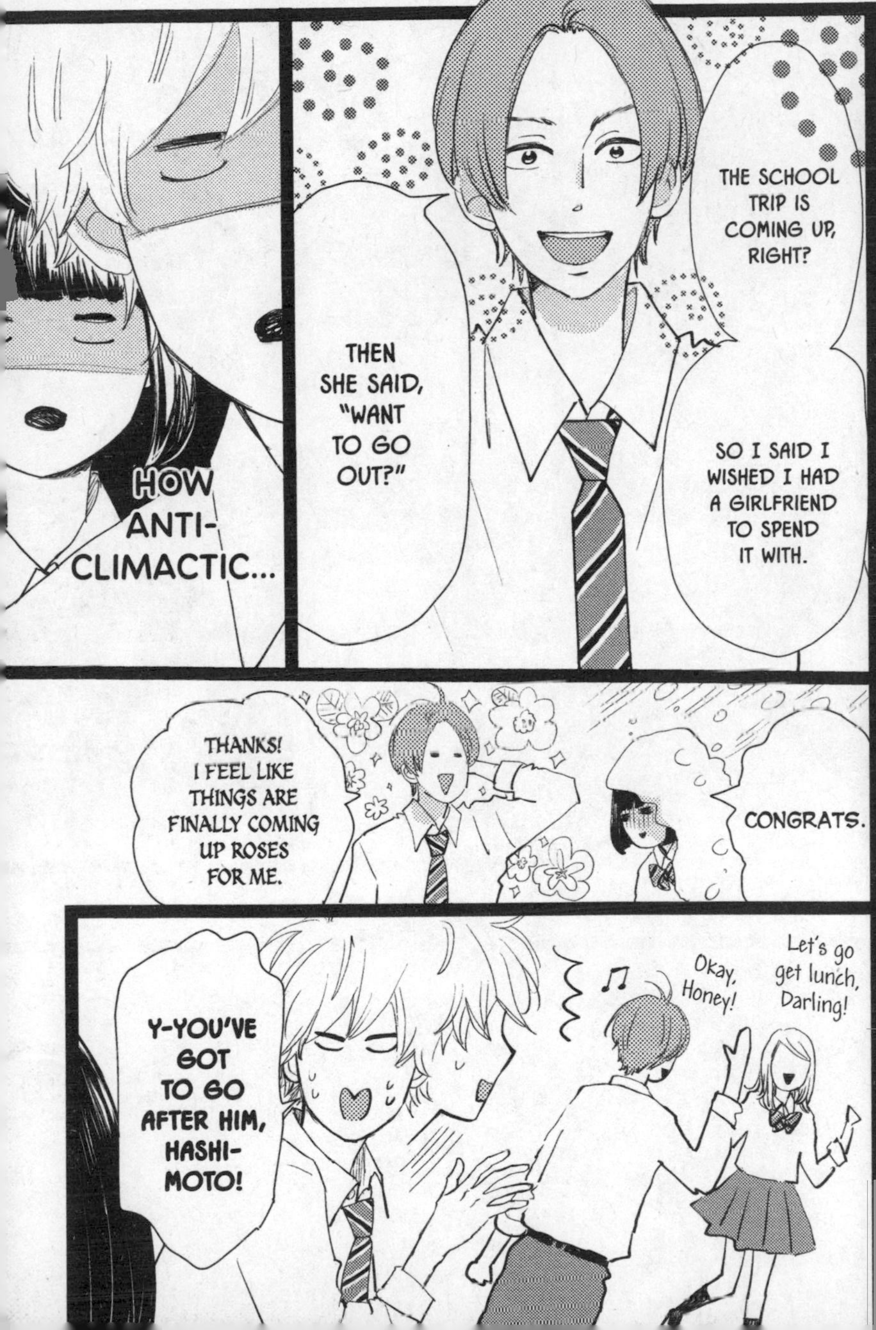
THE SCHOOL TRIP IS COMING UP, RIGHT?
SO I SAID I WISHED I HAD A GIRLFRIEND TO SPEND IT WITH.
THEN SHE SAID, "WANT TO GO OUT?"
HOW ANTI-CLIMACTIC...
CONGRATS.
THANKS! I FEEL LIKE THINGS ARE FINALLY COMING UP ROSES FOR ME.
Let's go get lunch, Darling!
Okay, Honey!
Y-YOU'VE GOT TO GO AFTER HIM, HASHI-MOTO!

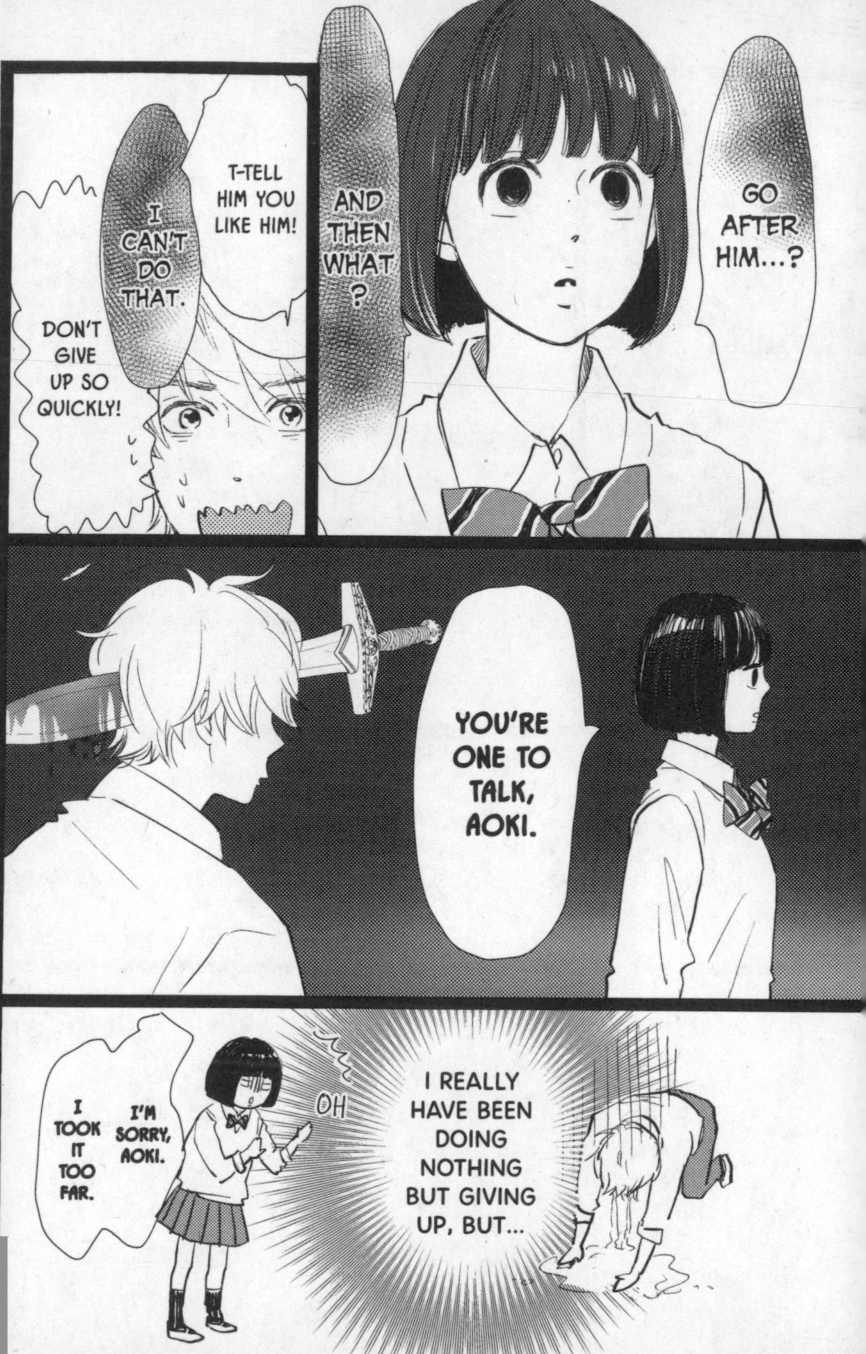
GO AFTER HIM...?
AND THEN WHAT?
T-TELL HIM YOU LIKE HIM!
I CAN'T DO THAT.
DON'T GIVE UP SO QUICKLY!
YOU'RE ONE TO TALK, AOKI.
I REALLY HAVE BEEN DOING NOTHING BUT GIVING UP, BUT...
OH
I'M SORRY, AOKI.
I TOOK IT TOO FAR.

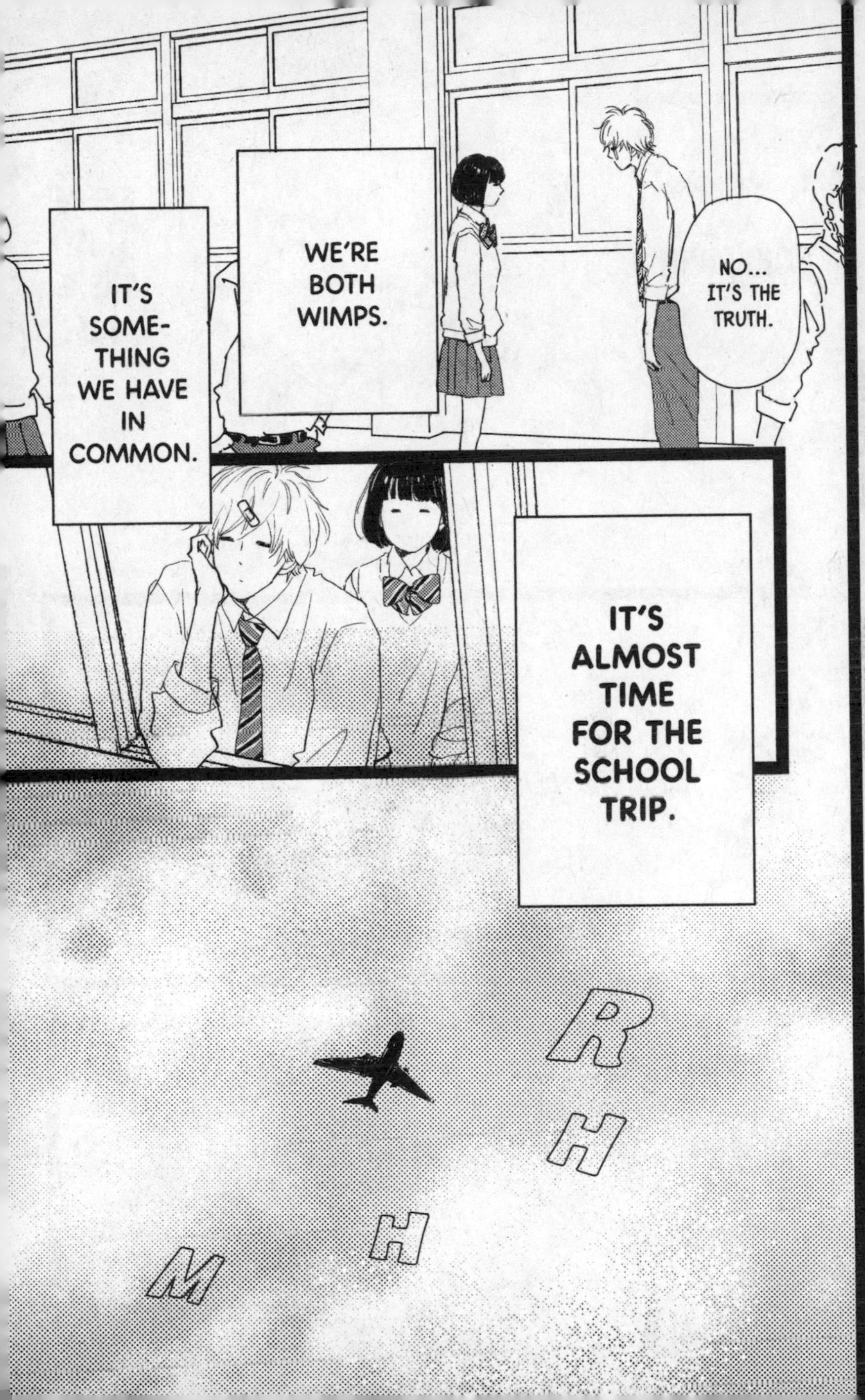
NO... IT'S THE TRUTH.
WE'RE BOTH WIMPS.
IT'S SOME-THING WE HAVE IN COMMON.
IT'S ALMOST TIME FOR THE SCHOOL TRIP.
RHHM

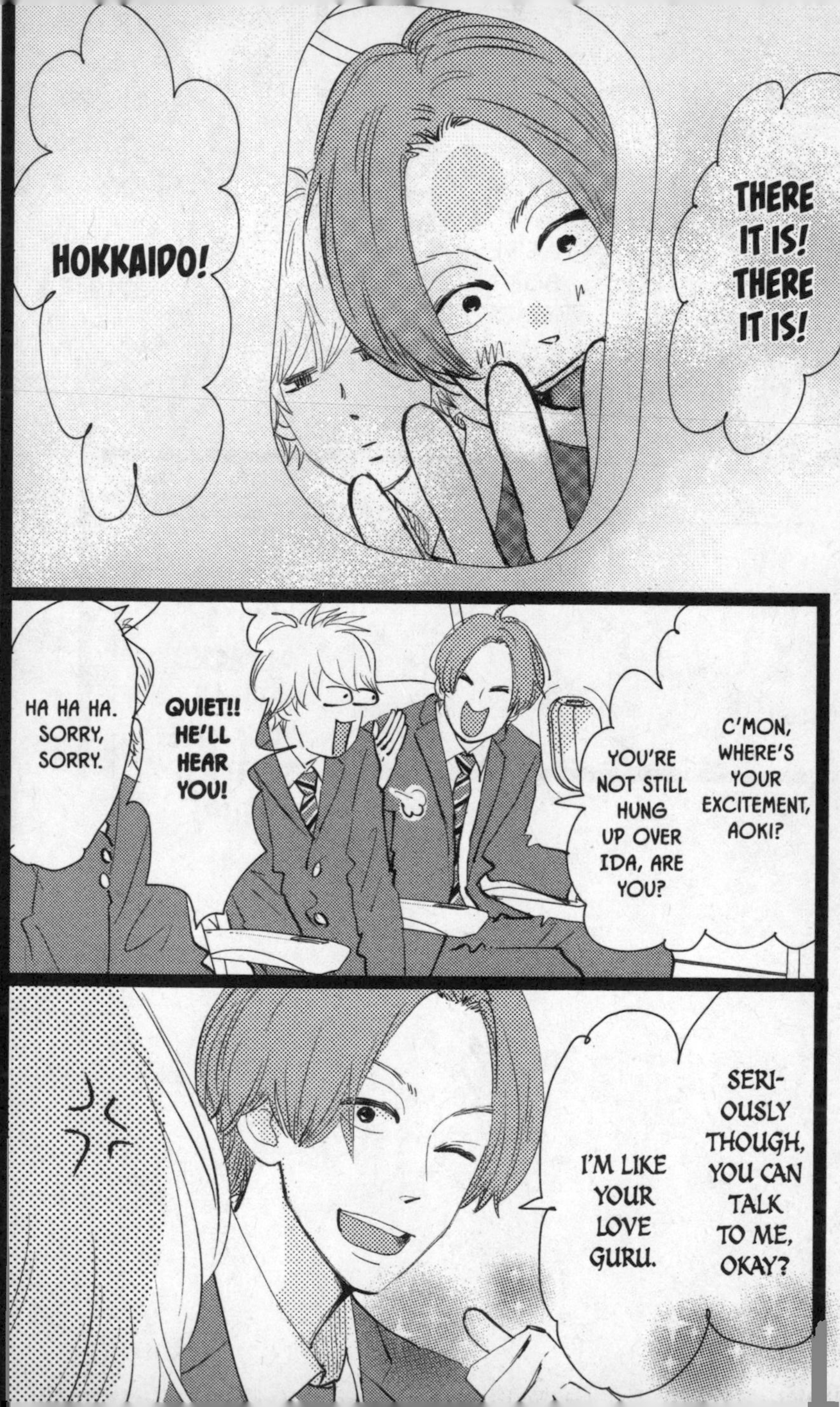
THERE IT IS! THERE IT IS!
HOKKAIDO!
C'MON, WHERE'S YOUR EXCITEMENT, AOKI?
YOU'RE NOT STILL HUNG UP OVER IDA, ARE YOU?
QUIET!! HE'LL HEAR YOU!
HA HA HA. SORRY, SORRY.
SERI-OUSLY THOUGH, YOU CAN TALK TO ME, OKAY?
I'M LIKE YOUR LOVE GURU.

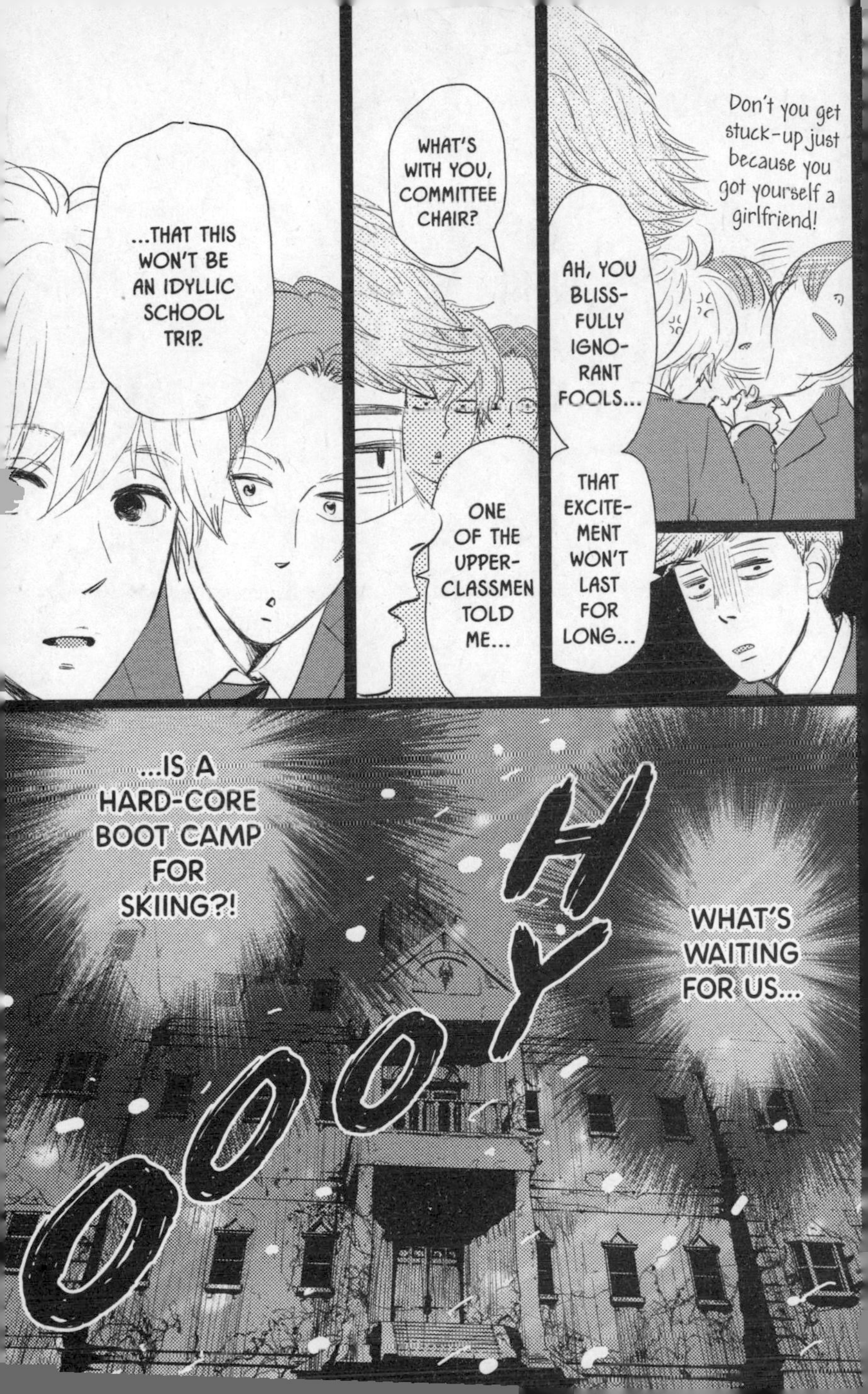
Don't you get stuck-up just because you got yourself a girlfriend!
AH, YOU BLISS-FULLY IGNO-RANT FOOLS...
THAT EXCITE-MENT WON'T LAST FOR LONG...
WHAT'S WITH YOU, COMMITTEE CHAIR?
ONE OF THE UPPER-CLASSMEN TOLD ME...
...THAT THIS WON'T BE AN IDYLLIC SCHOOL TRIP.
WHAT'S WAITING FOR US...
...IS A HARD-CORE BOOT CAMP FOR SKIING?!
HYOOOO

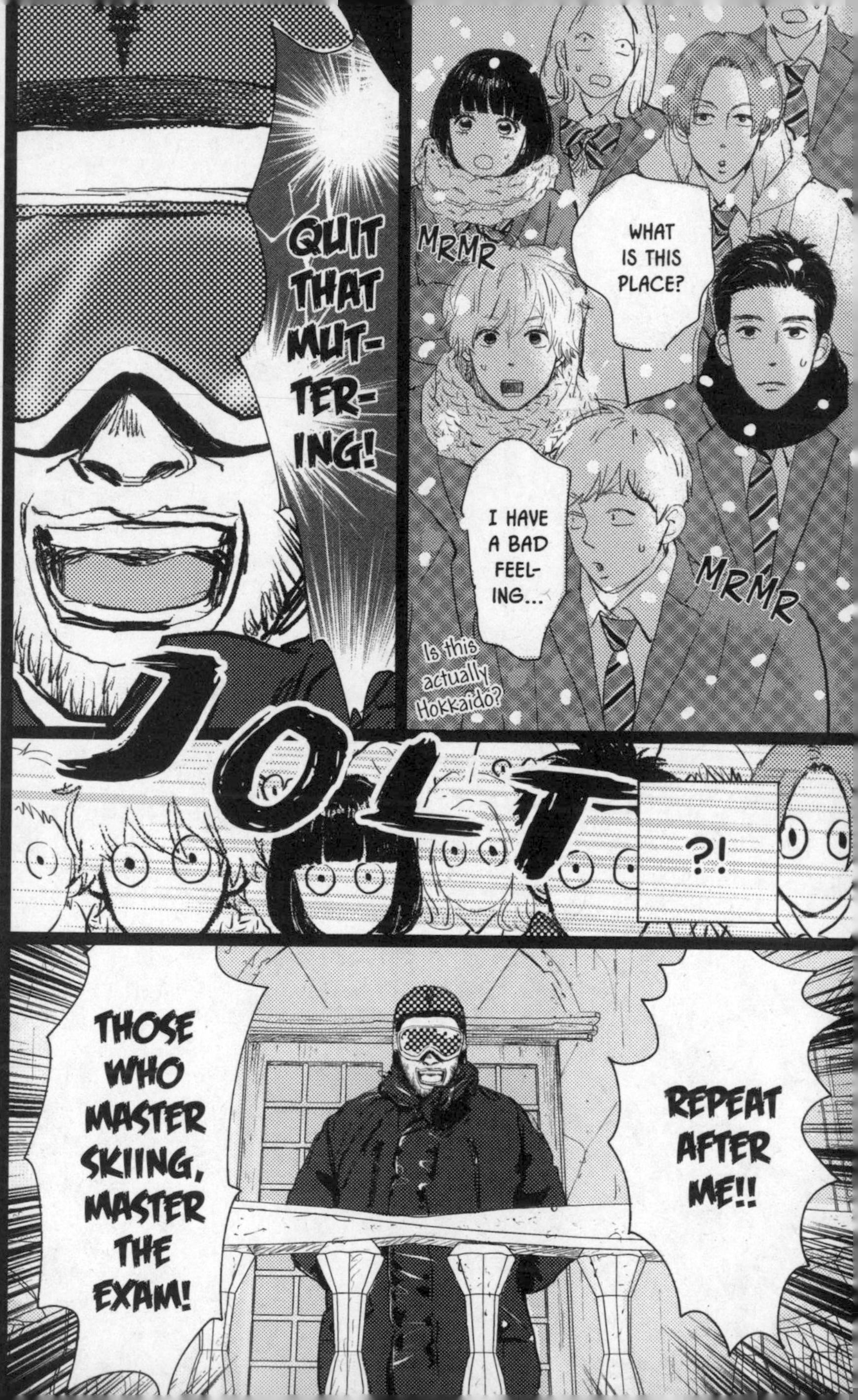
MRMR
WHAT IS THIS PLACE?
I HAVE A BAD FEELING...
MRMR
Is this actually Hokkaido?
QUIT THAT MUTTERING!
JOLT
?!
REPEAT AFTER ME!!
THOSE WHO MASTER SKIING, MASTER THE EXAM!

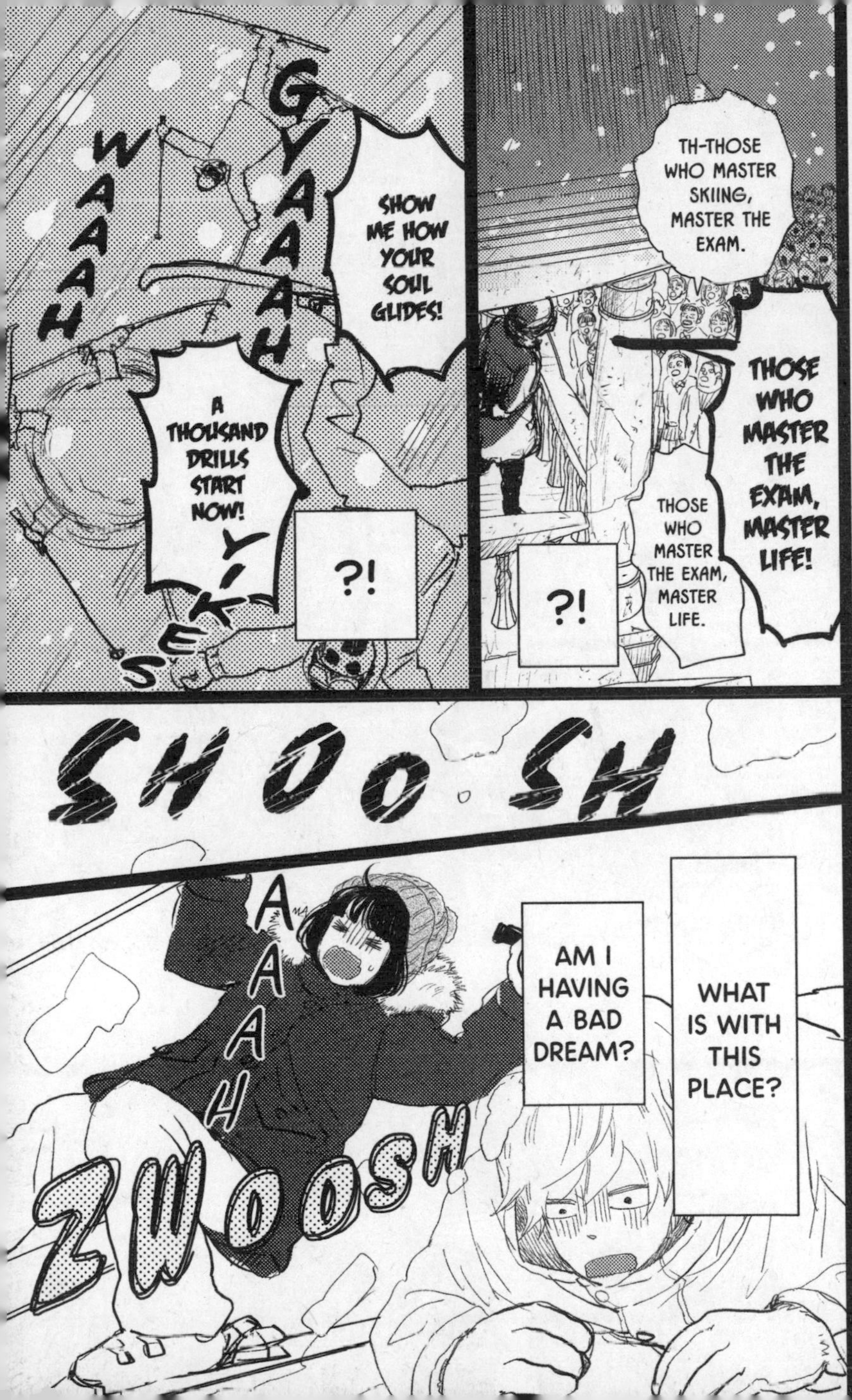
TH-THOSE WHO MASTER SKIING, MASTER THE EXAM.
THOSE WHO MASTER THE EXAM, MASTER LIFE!
THOSE WHO MASTER THE EXAM, MASTER LIFE.
?!
GYAAAAH
SHOW ME HOW YOUR SOUL GLIDES!
WAAAAH
A THOUSAND DRILLS START NOW!
?!
YIKES
SHOOSH
WHAT IS WITH THIS PLACE?
AM I HAVING A BAD DREAM?
AAAAH
ZWOOSH

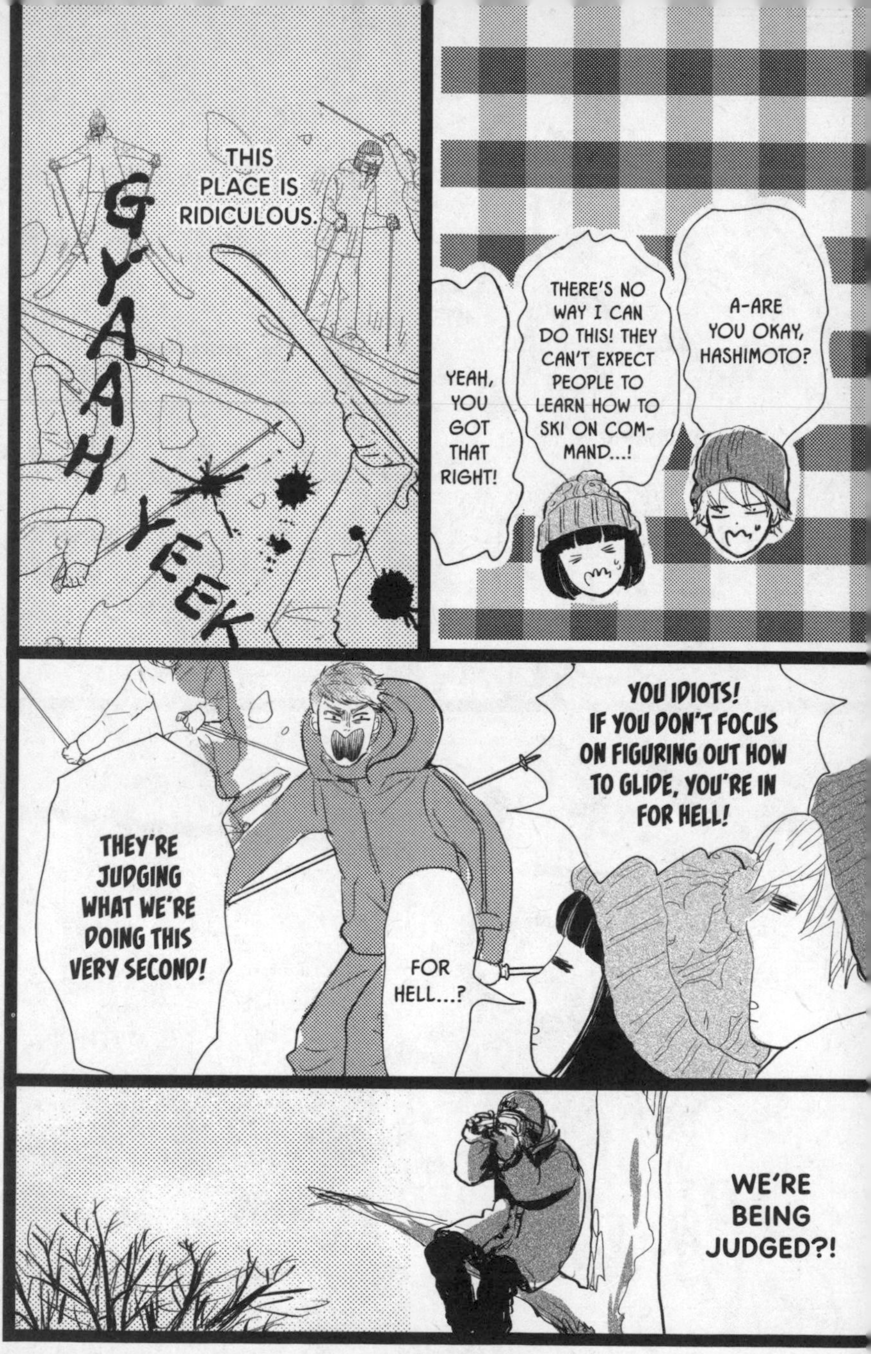
A-ARE YOU OKAY, HASHIMOTO?
THERE'S NO WAY I CAN DO THIS! THEY CAN'T EXPECT PEOPLE TO LEARN HOW TO SKI ON COM-MAND...!
YEAH, YOU GOT THAT RIGHT!
THIS PLACE IS RIDICULOUS.
GYAAH
YEEK
YOU IDIOTS! IF YOU DON'T FOCUS ON FIGURING OUT HOW TO GLIDE, YOU'RE IN FOR HELL!
FOR HELL...?
THEY'RE JUDGING WHAT WE'RE DOING THIS VERY SECOND!
WE'RE BEING JUDGED?!

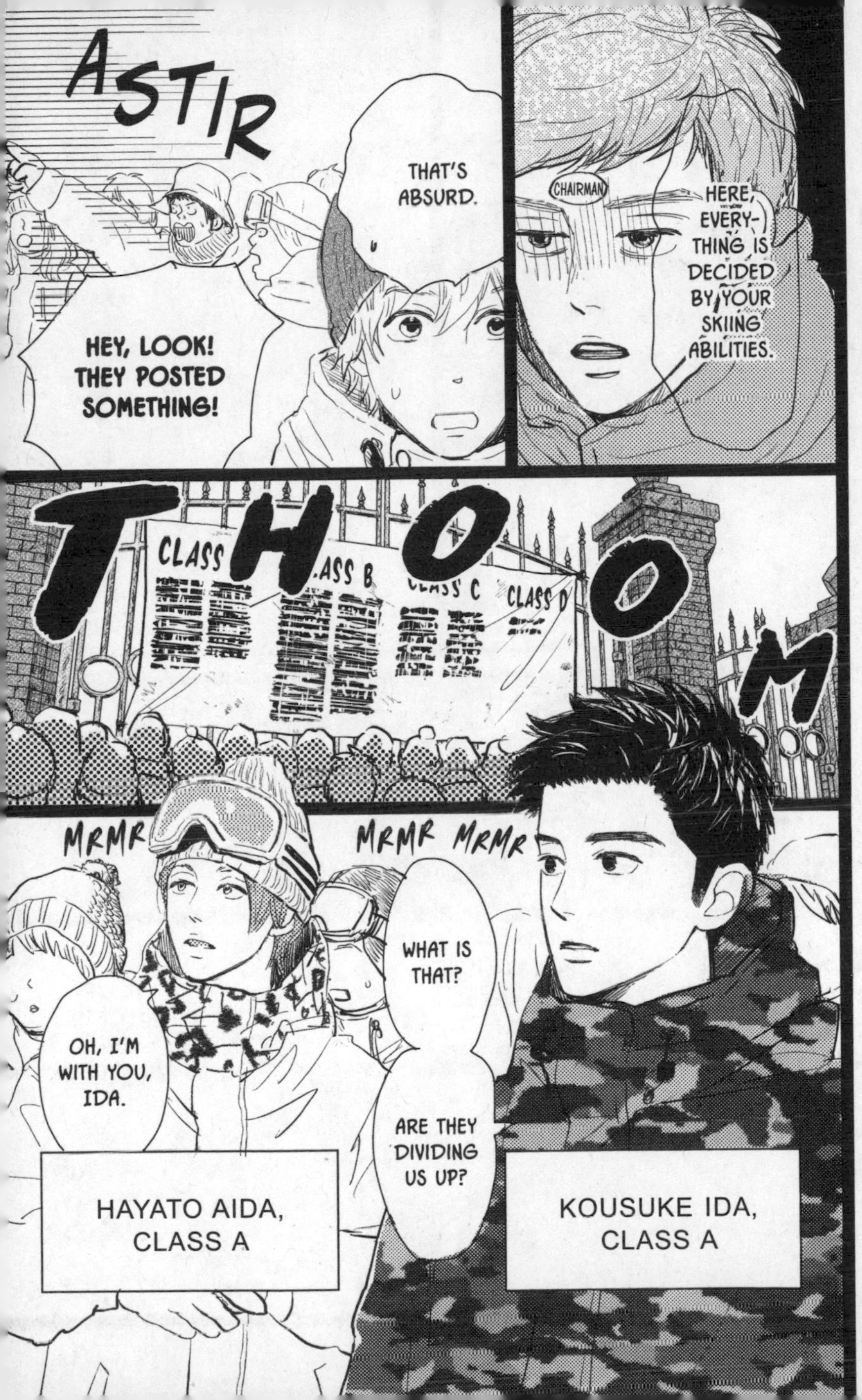
CHAIRMAN
HERE, EVERY-THING IS DECIDED BY YOUR SKIING ABILITIES.
ASTIR
THAT'S ABSURD.
HEY, LOOK! THEY POSTED SOMETHING!
THOOM
CLASS
CLASS C
CLASS D
MRMR MRMR
WHAT IS THAT?
ARE THEY DIVIDING US UP?
KOUSUKE IDA, CLASS A
MRMR
OH, I'M WITH YOU, IDA.
HAYATO AIDA, CLASS A

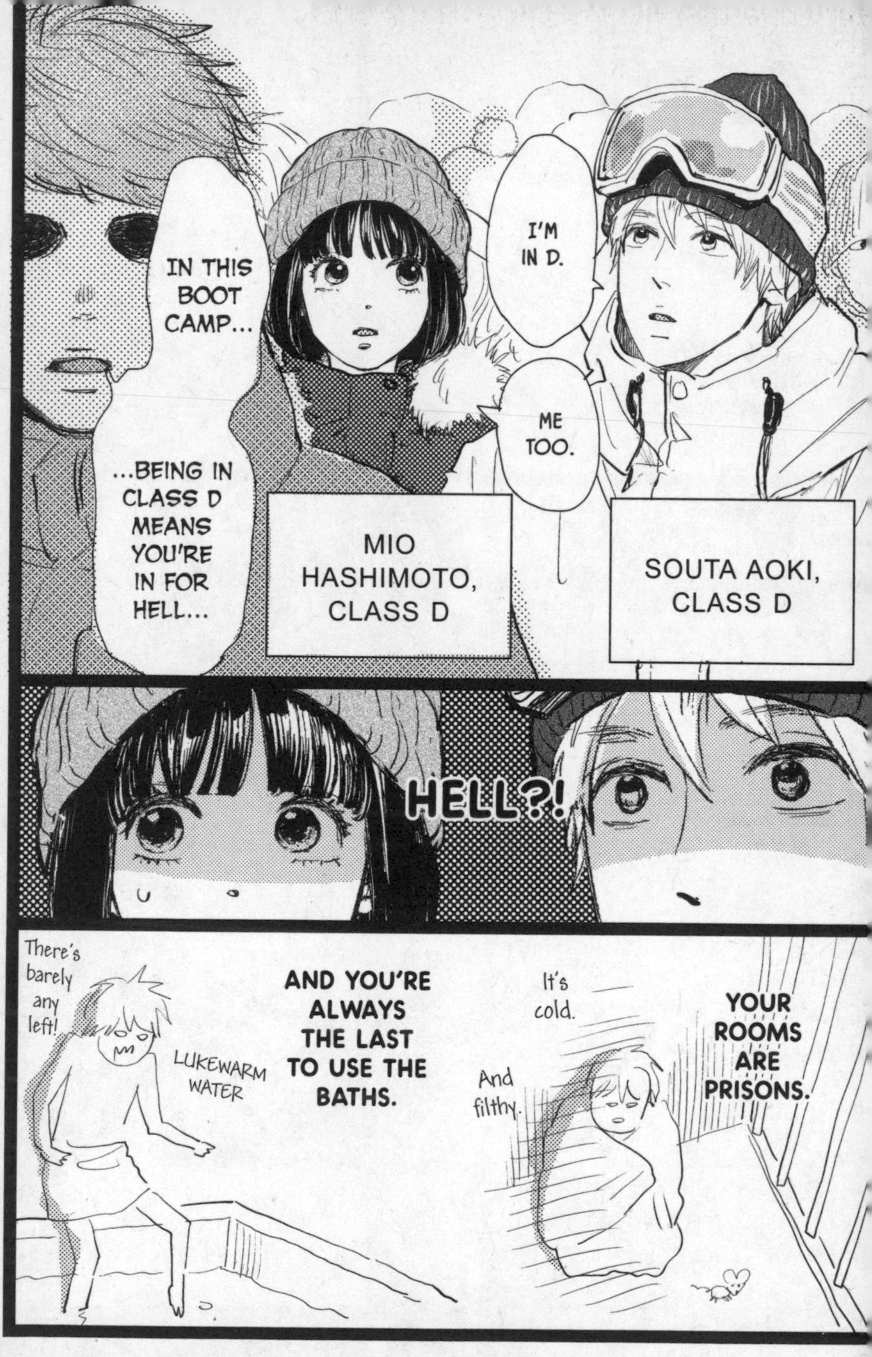

I'M IN D.
ME TOO.
SOUTA AOKI, CLASS D
MIO HASHIMOTO, CLASS D
IN THIS BOOT CAMP...
...BEING IN CLASS D MEANS YOU'RE IN FOR HELL...
HELL?!
YOUR ROOMS ARE PRISONS.
It's cold.
And filthy.
AND YOU'RE ALWAYS THE LAST TO USE THE BATHS.
LUKEWARM WATER
There's barely any left!

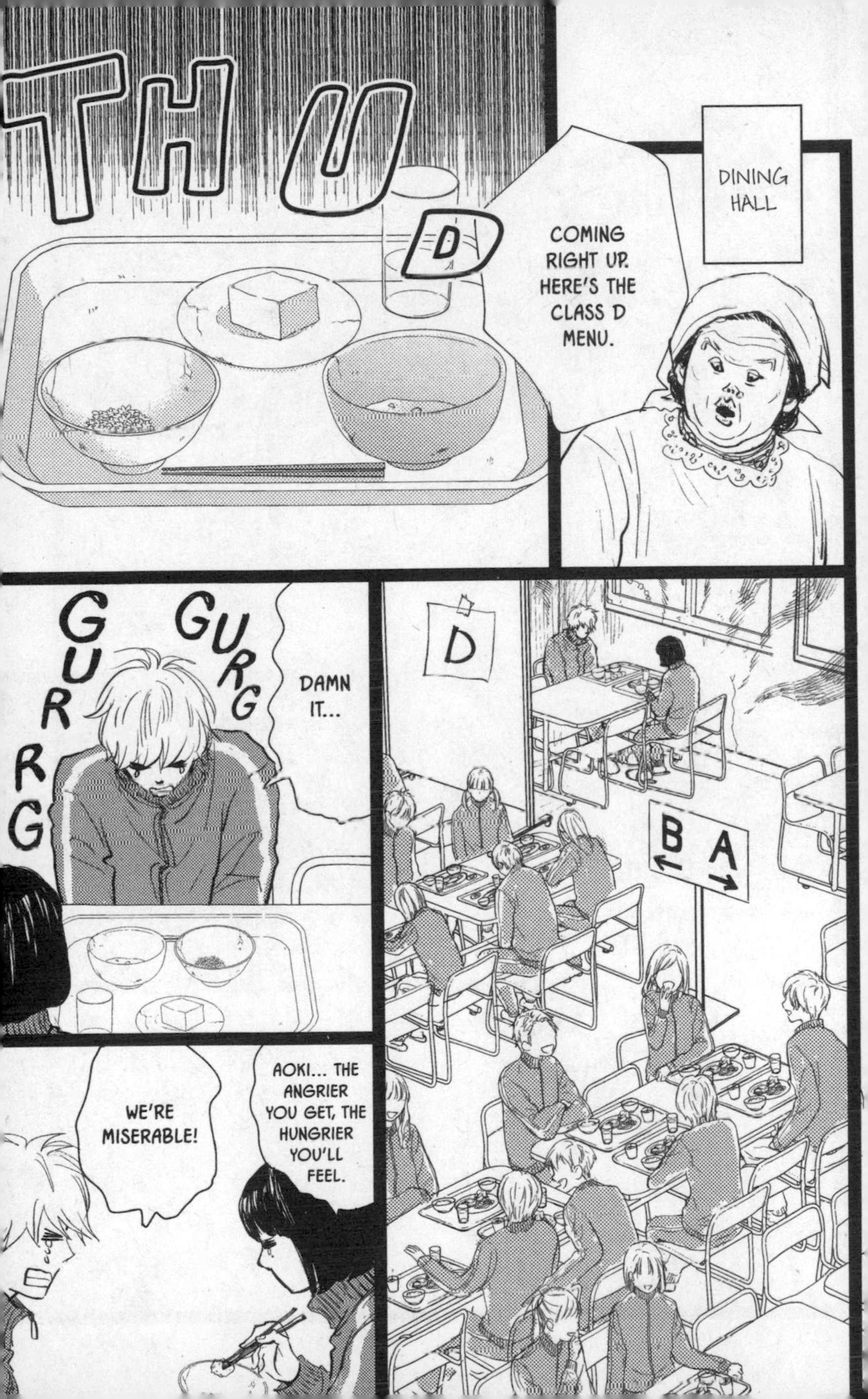
DINING HALL
COMING RIGHT UP. HERE'S THE CLASS D MENU.
THUD
D
B
A
GURG
GURG
DAMN IT...
AOKI... THE ANGRIER YOU GET, THE HUNGRIER YOU'LL FEEL.
WE'RE MISERABLE!

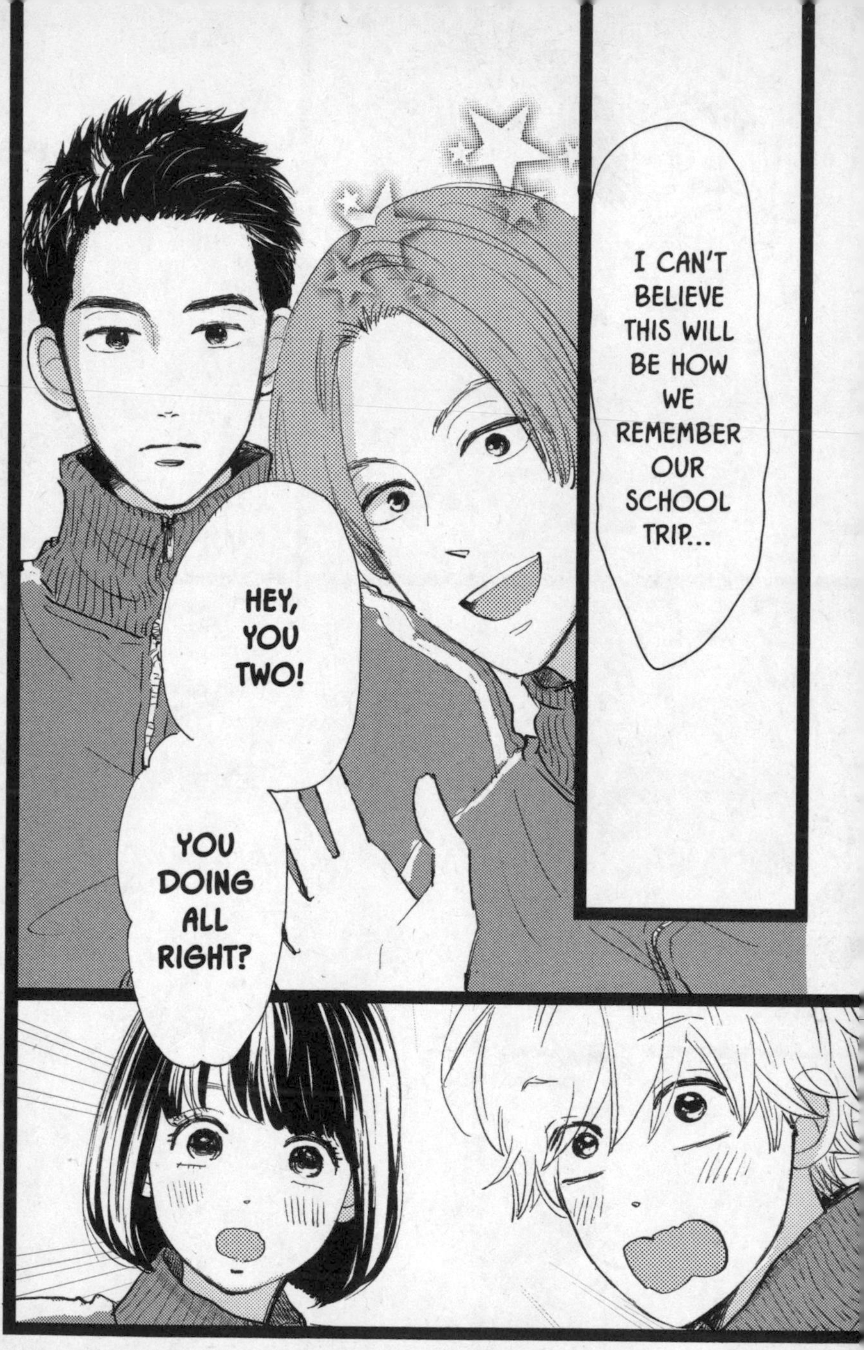
I CAN'T BELIEVE THIS WILL BE HOW WE REMEMBER OUR SCHOOL TRIP...
HEY, YOU TWO!
YOU DOING ALL RIGHT?

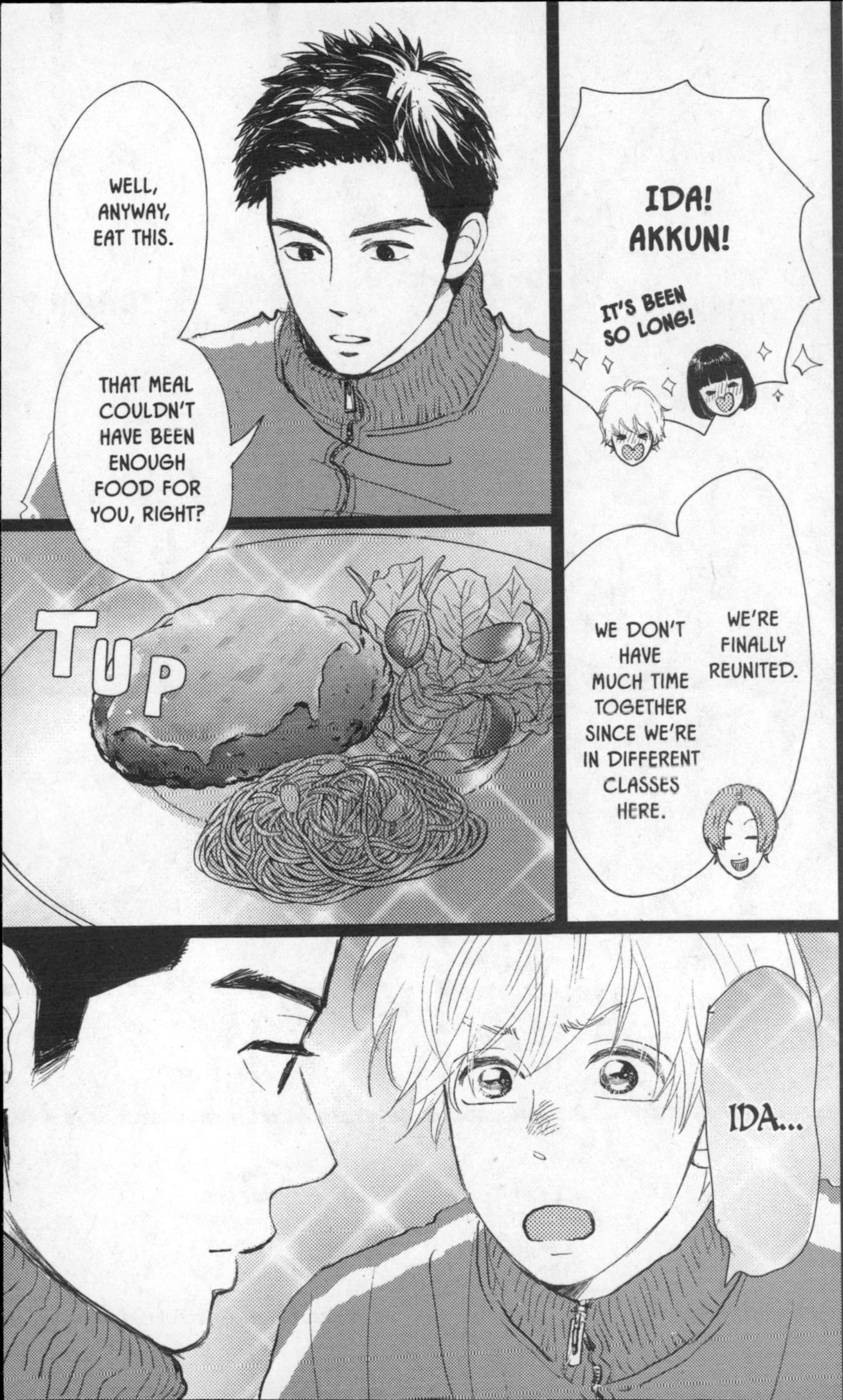
IDA! AKKUN!
IT'S BEEN SO LONG!
WE'RE FINALLY REUNITED.
WE DON'T HAVE MUCH TIME TOGETHER SINCE WE'RE IN DIFFERENT CLASSES HERE.
WELL, ANYWAY, EAT THIS.
THAT MEAL COULDN'T HAVE BEEN ENOUGH FOOD FOR YOU, RIGHT?
TUP
IDA...

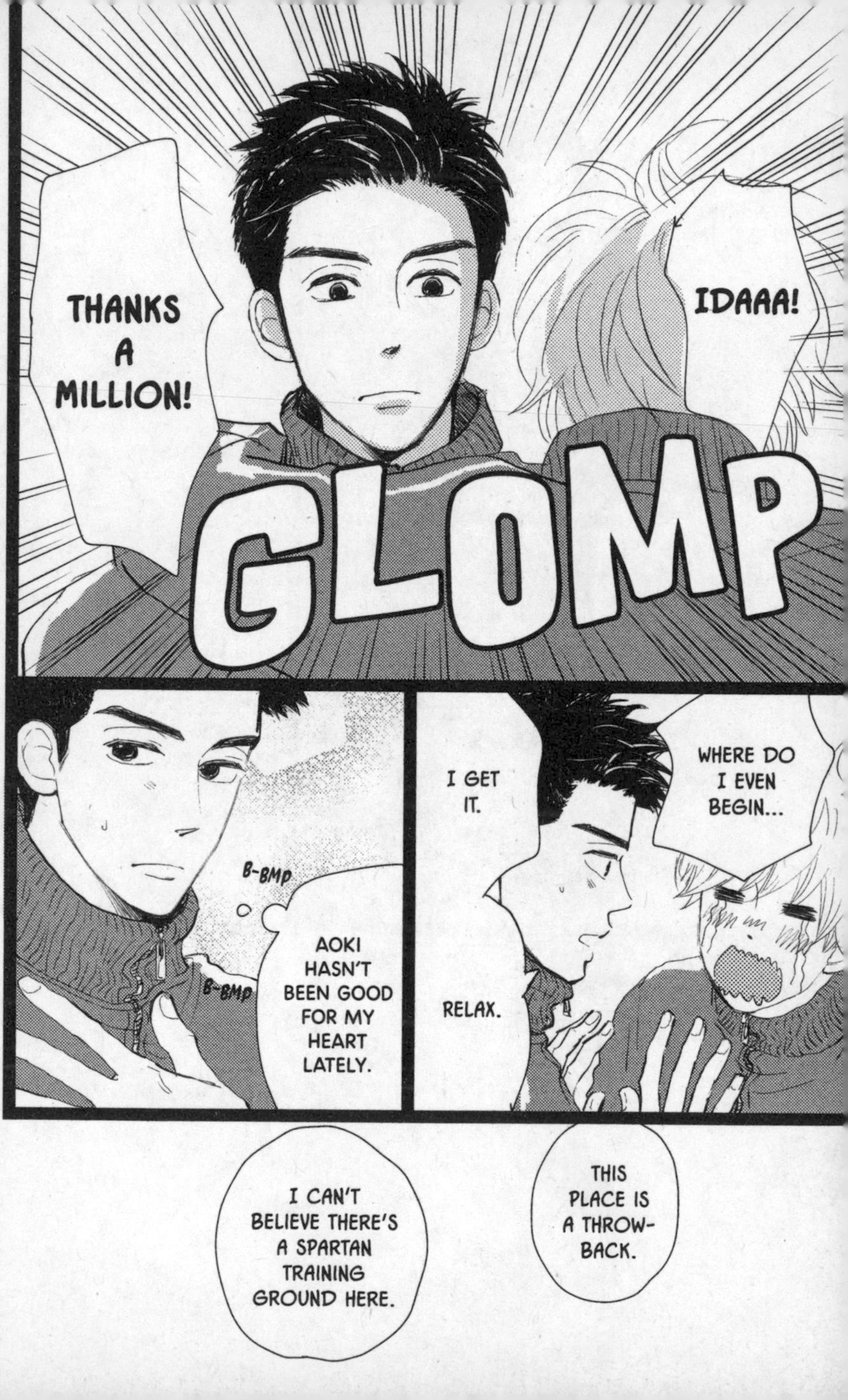
IDAAA!
THANKS A MILLION!
GLOMP
WHERE DO I EVEN BEGIN...
I GET IT.
RELAX.
B-BMP
B-BMP
AOKI HASN'T BEEN GOOD FOR MY HEART LATELY.
THIS PLACE IS A THROW-BACK.
I CAN'T BELIEVE THERE'S A SPARTAN TRAINING GROUND HERE.

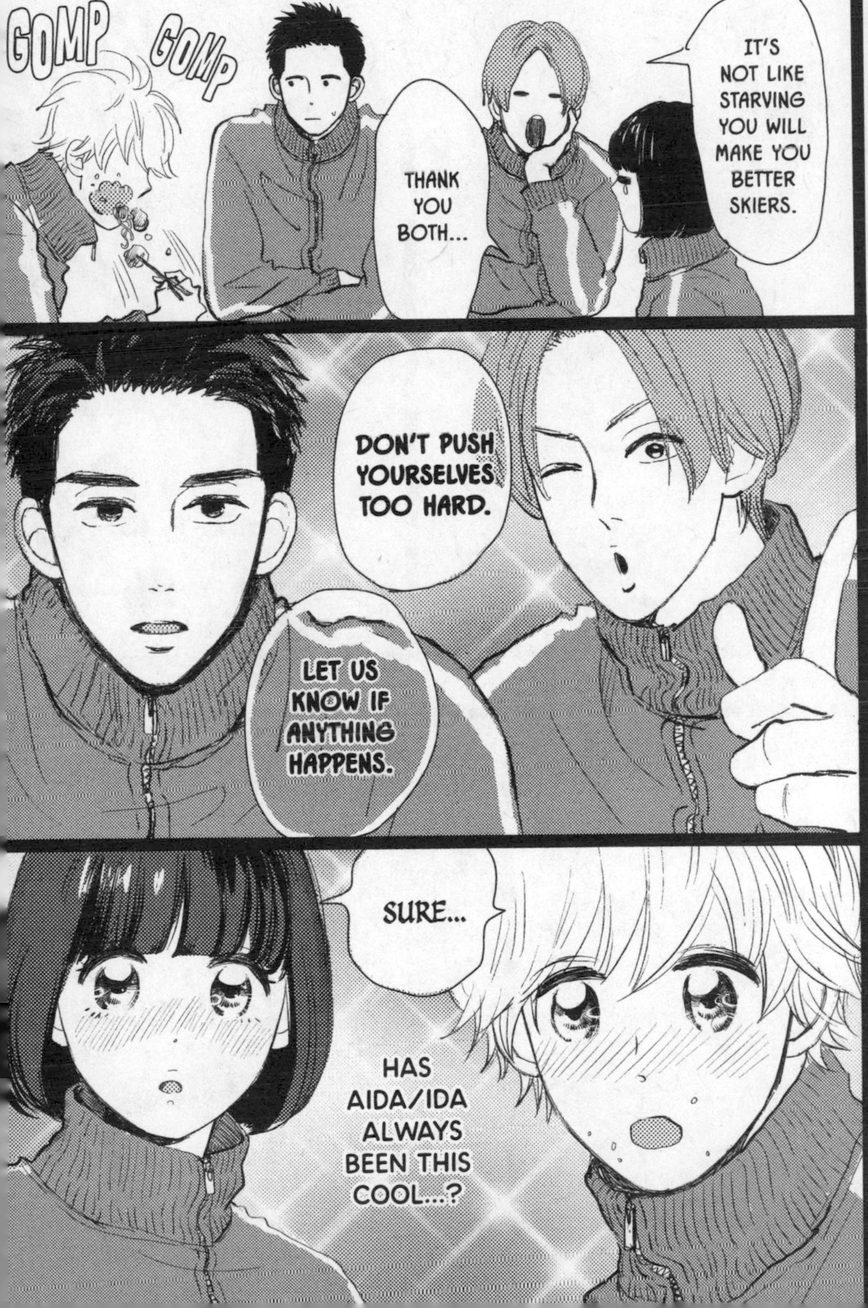
IT'S NOT LIKE STARVING YOU WILL MAKE YOU BETTER SKIERS.
THANK YOU BOTH...
GOMP
GOMP
DON'T PUSH YOURSELVES TOO HARD.
LET US KNOW IF ANYTHING HAPPENS.
SURE...
HAS AIDA/IDA ALWAYS BEEN THIS COOL...?

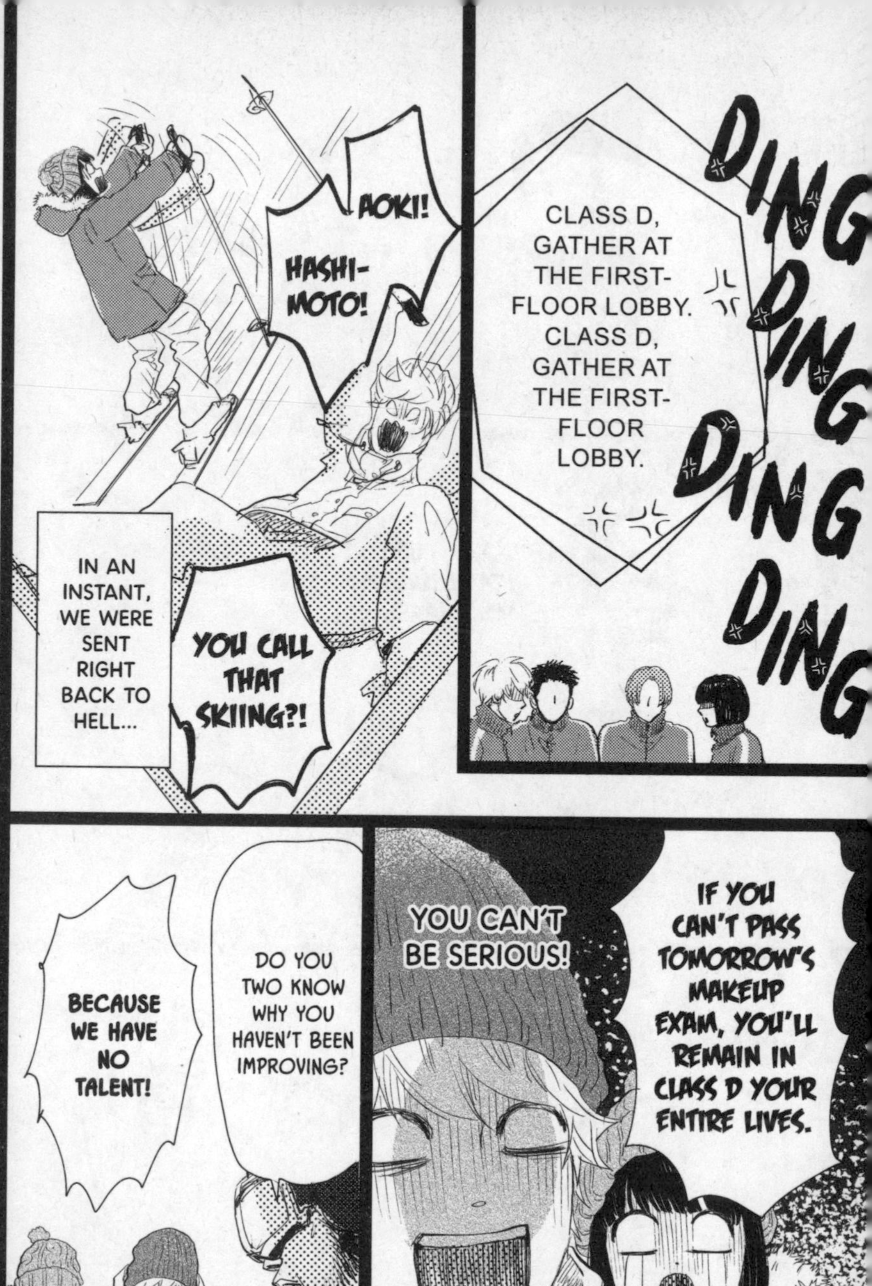
DING DING DING DING DING
CLASS D, GATHER AT THE FIRST-FLOOR LOBBY. CLASS D, GATHER AT THE FIRST-FLOOR LOBBY.
AOKI!
HASHI-MOTO!
YOU CALL THAT SKIING?!
IN AN INSTANT, WE WERE SENT RIGHT BACK TO HELL...
IF YOU CAN'T PASS TOMORROW'S MAKEUP EXAM, YOU'LL REMAIN IN CLASS D YOUR ENTIRE LIVES.
YOU CAN'T BE SERIOUS!
DO YOU TWO KNOW WHY YOU HAVEN'T BEEN IMPROVING?
BECAUSE WE HAVE NO TALENT!

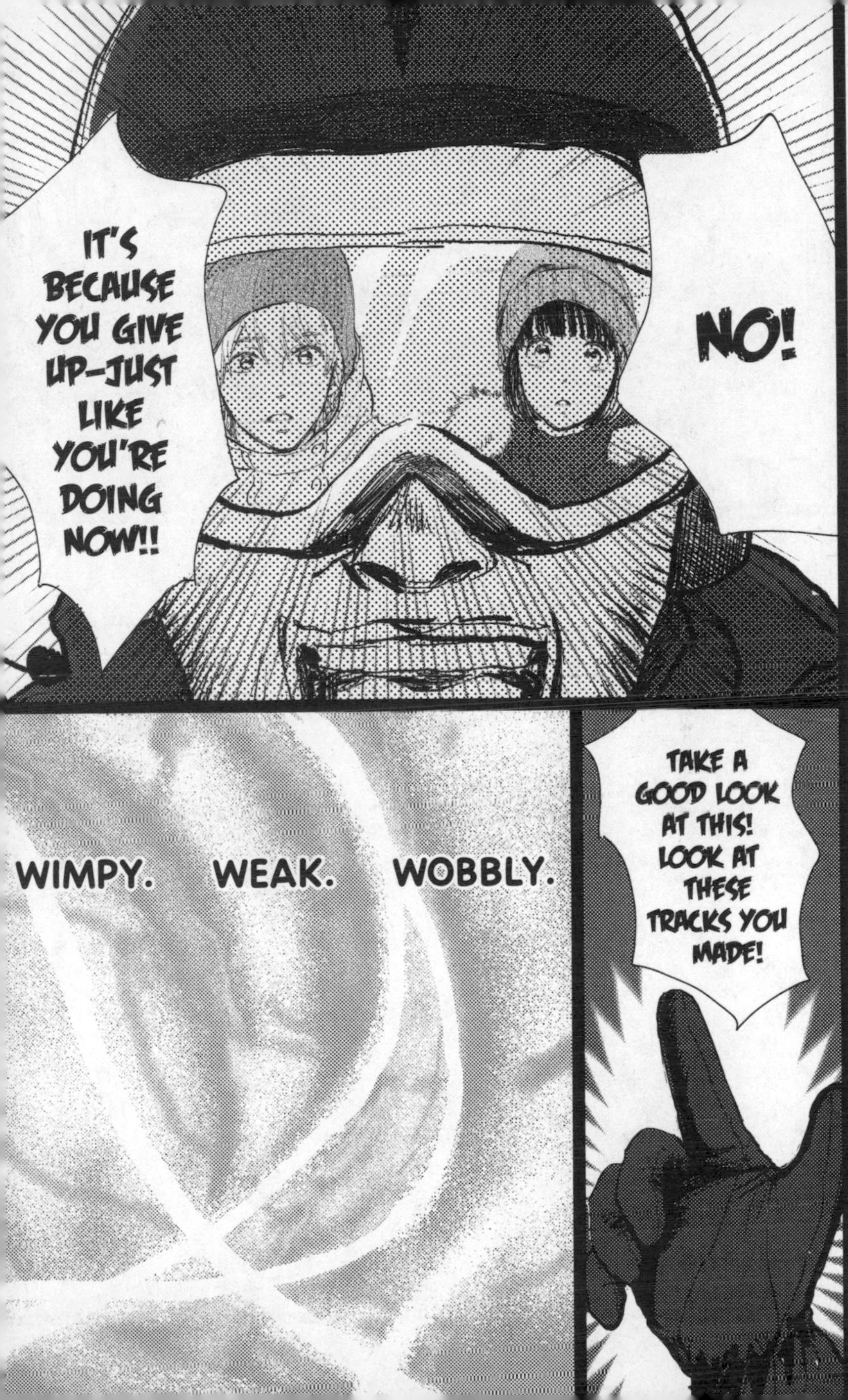
NO!
IT'S BECAUSE YOU GIVE UP—JUST LIKE YOU'RE DOING NOW!!
TAKE A GOOD LOOK AT THIS! LOOK AT THESE TRACKS YOU MADE!
WIMPY. WEAK. WOBBLY.

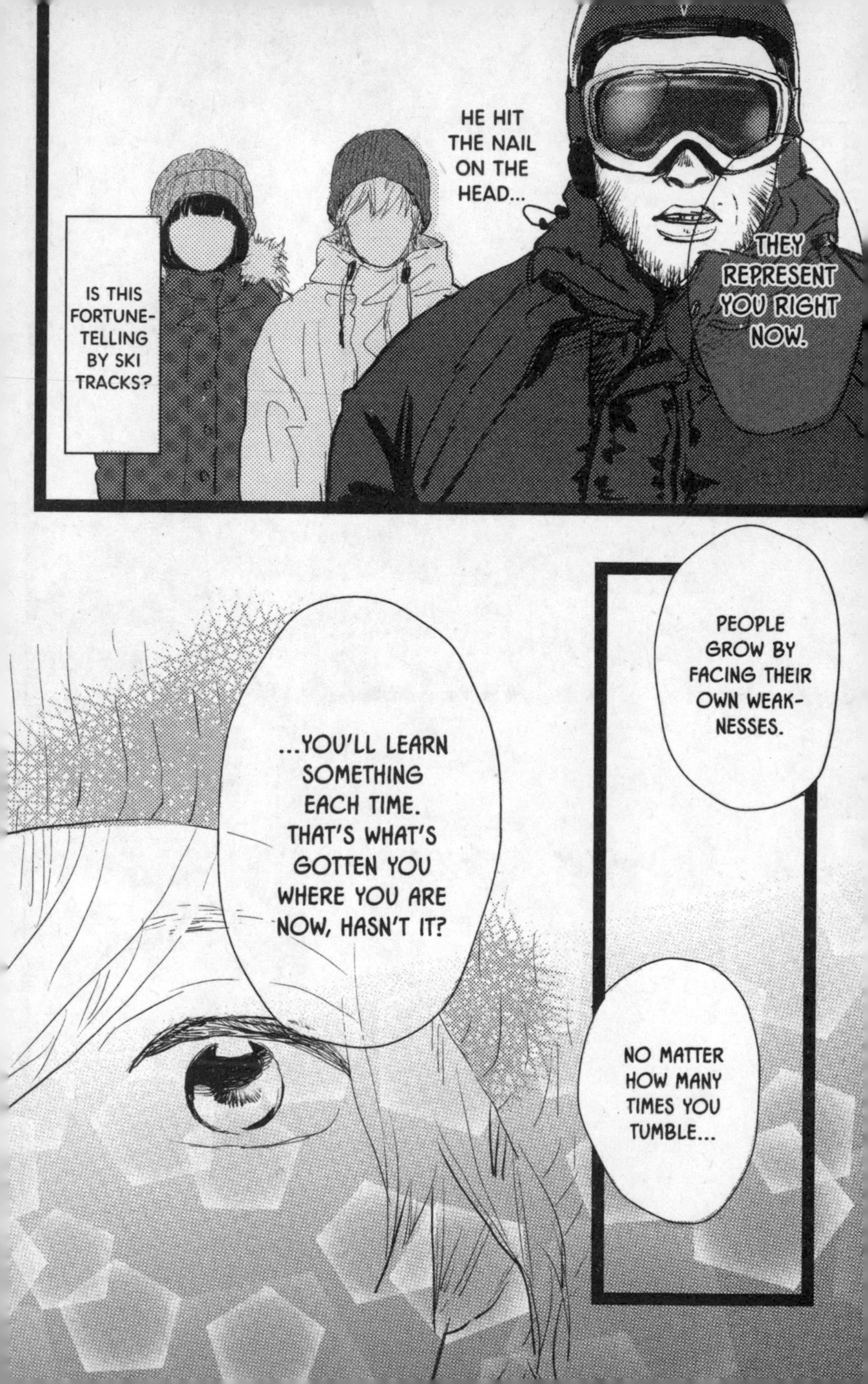
THEY REPRESENT YOU RIGHT NOW.
HE HIT THE NAIL ON THE HEAD...
IS THIS FORTUNE-TELLING BY SKI TRACKS?
PEOPLE GROW BY FACING THEIR OWN WEAK-NESSES.
NO MATTER HOW MANY TIMES YOU TUMBLE...
...YOU'LL LEARN SOMETHING EACH TIME. THAT'S WHAT'S GOTTEN YOU WHERE YOU ARE NOW, HASN'T IT?

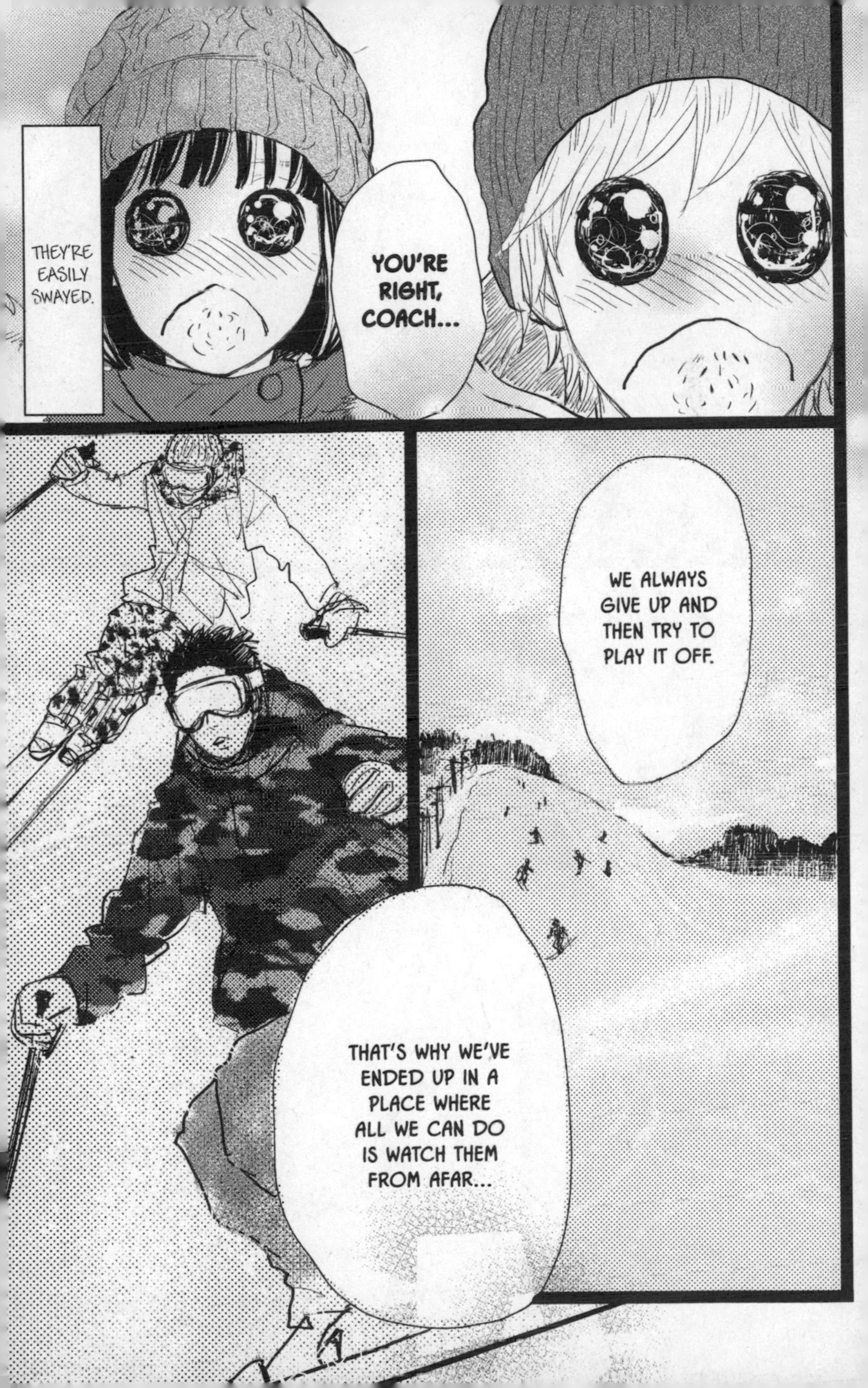
YOU'RE RIGHT, COACH...
THEY'RE EASILY SWAYED.
WE ALWAYS GIVE UP AND THEN TRY TO PLAY IT OFF.
THAT'S WHY WE'VE ENDED UP IN A PLACE WHERE ALL WE CAN DO IS WATCH THEM FROM AFAR...

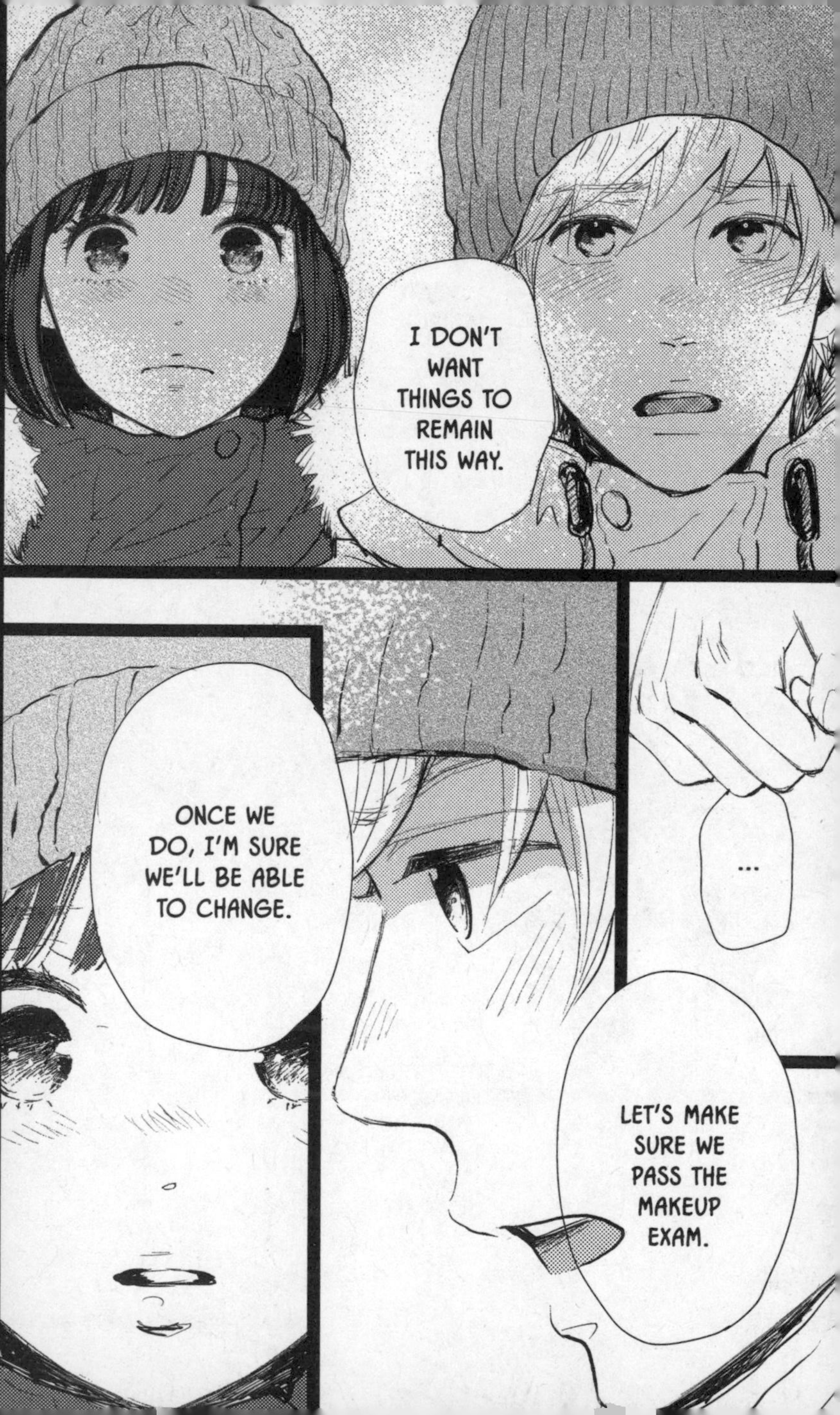
I DON'T WANT THINGS TO REMAIN THIS WAY.
...
LET'S MAKE SURE WE PASS THE MAKEUP EXAM.
ONCE WE DO, I'M SURE WE'LL BE ABLE TO CHANGE.

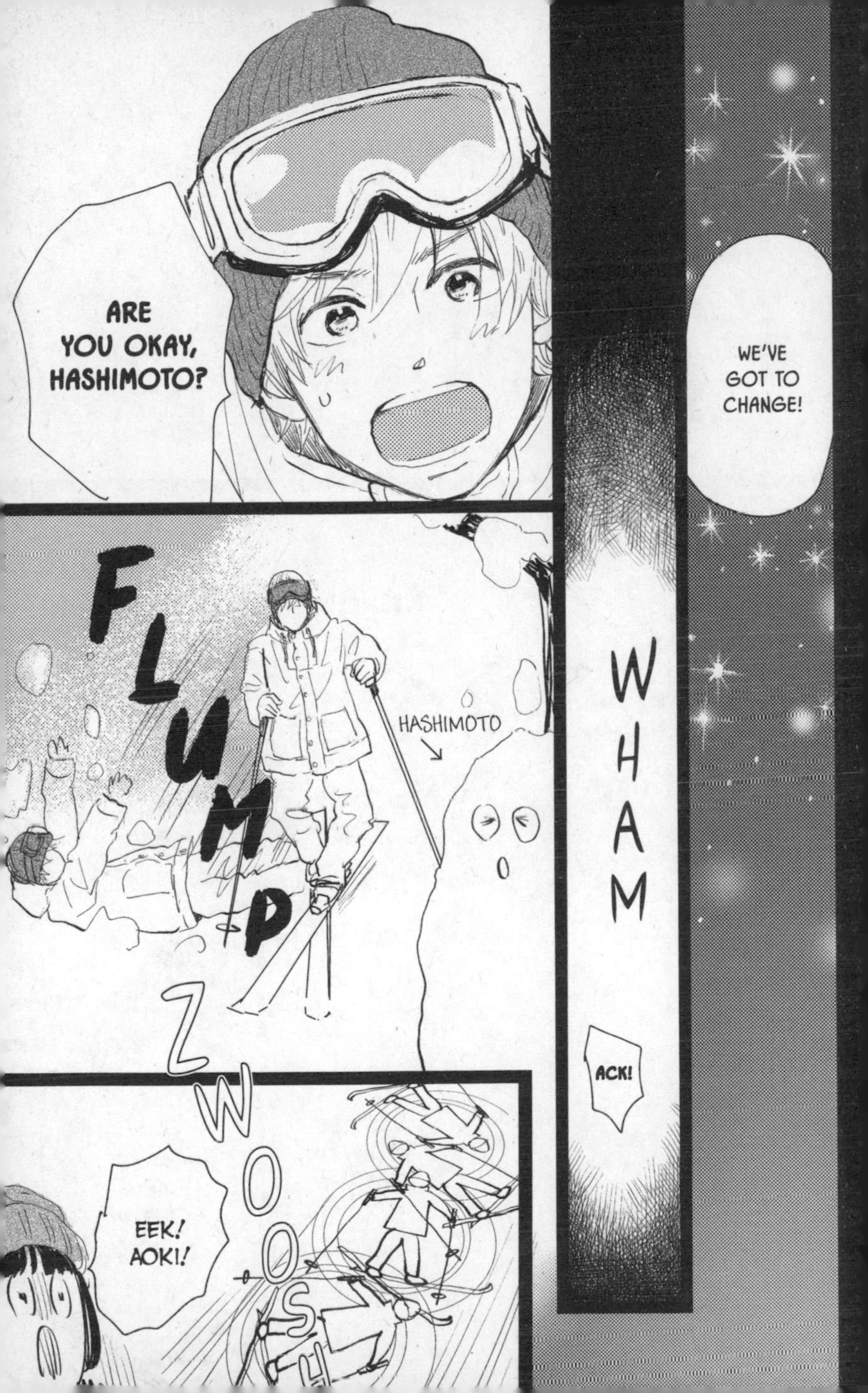
WE'VE GOT TO CHANGE!
WHAM
ACK!
ARE YOU OKAY, HASHIMOTO?
FLUMP
HASHIMOTO
ZWOOSH
EEK! AOKI!

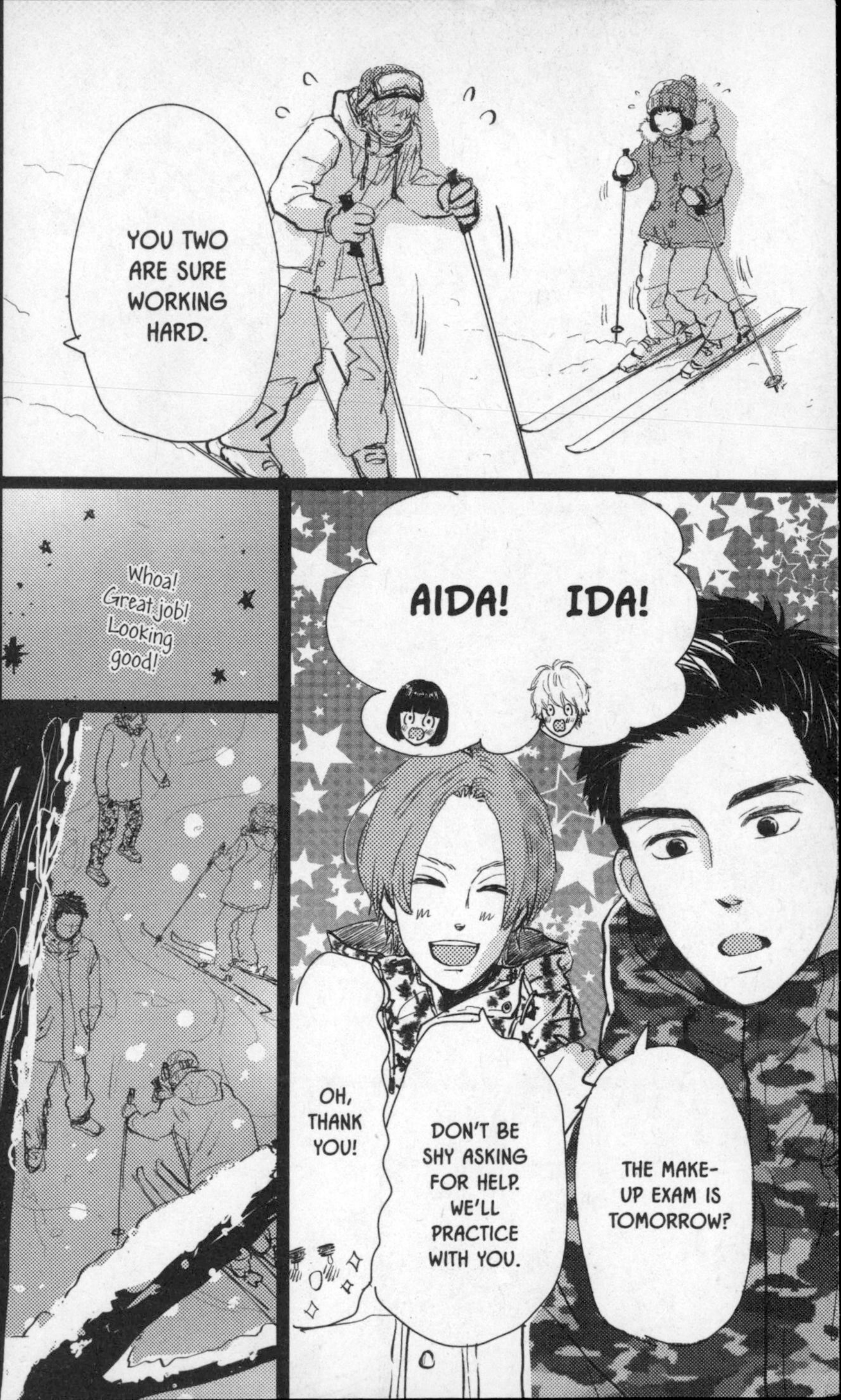
YOU TWO ARE SURE WORKING HARD.
AIDA! IDA!
THE MAKE-UP EXAM IS TOMORROW?
DON'T BE SHY ASKING FOR HELP. WE'LL PRACTICE WITH YOU.
OH, THANK YOU!
Whoa! Great job! Looking good!

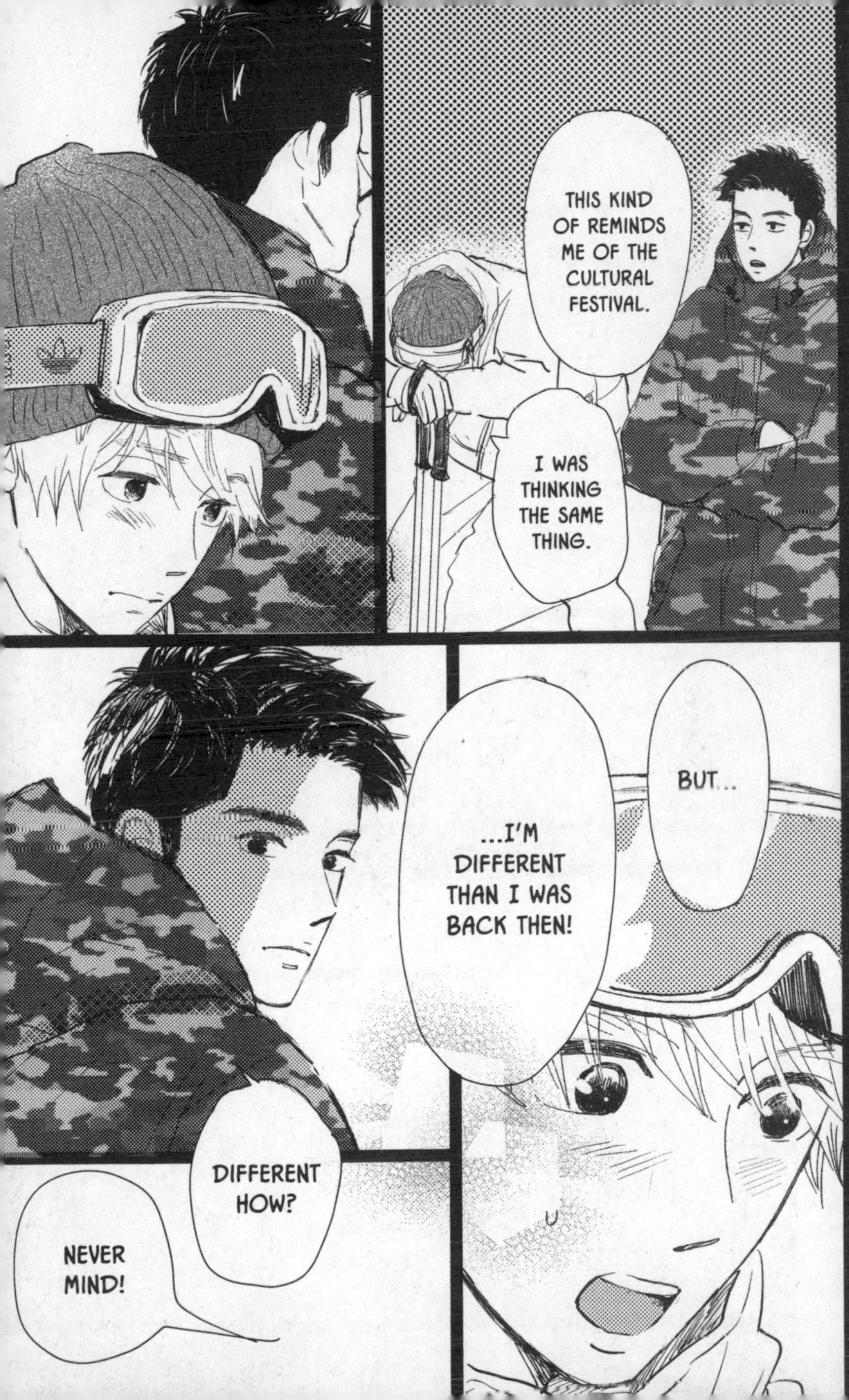
THIS KIND OF REMINDS ME OF THE CULTURAL FESTIVAL.
I WAS THINKING THE SAME THING.
BUT...
...I'M DIFFERENT THAN I WAS BACK THEN!
DIFFERENT HOW?
NEVER MIND!

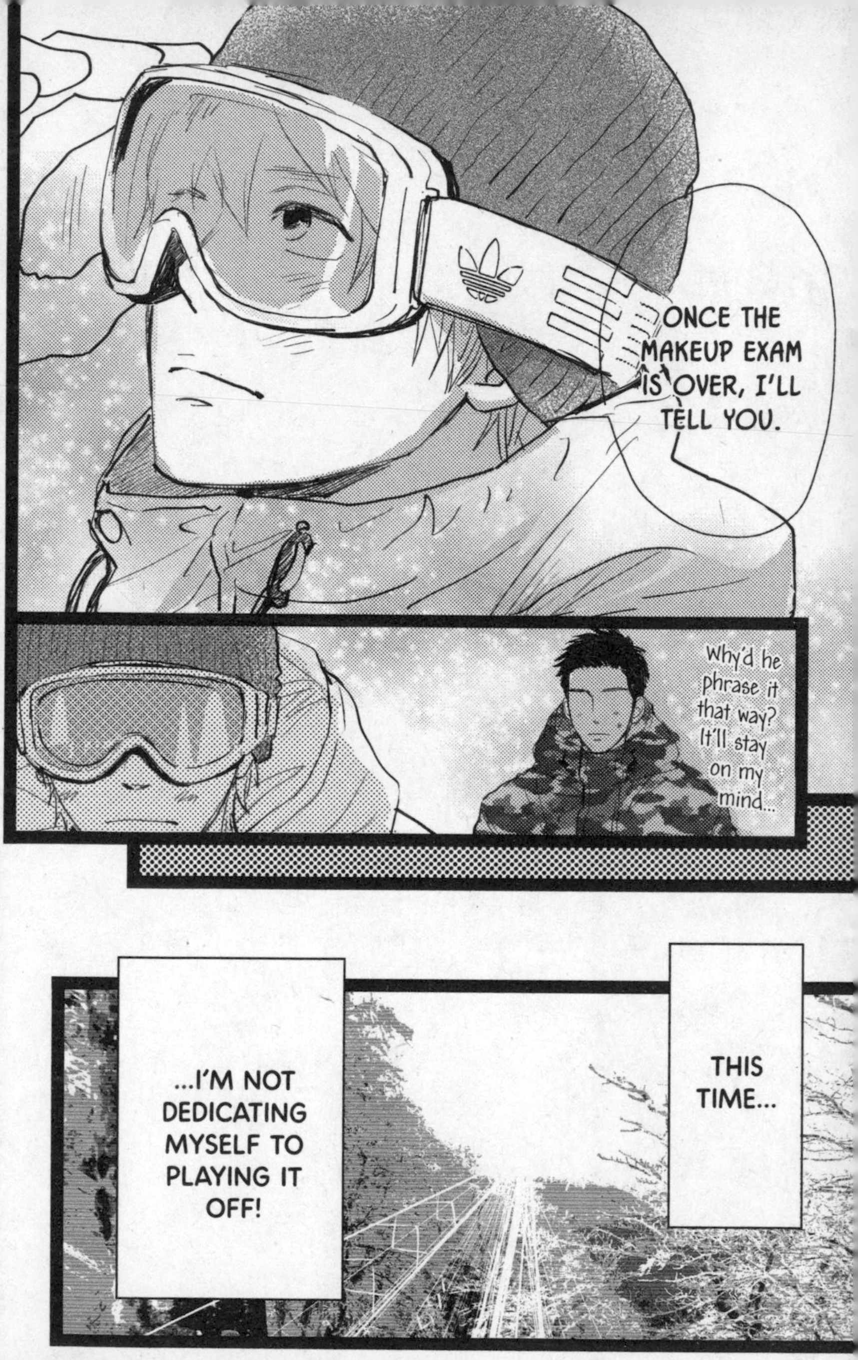
ONCE THE MAKEUP EXAM IS OVER, I'LL TELL YOU.
Why'd he phrase it that way? It'll stay on my mind...
THIS TIME...
...I'M NOT DEDICATING MYSELF TO PLAYING IT OFF!

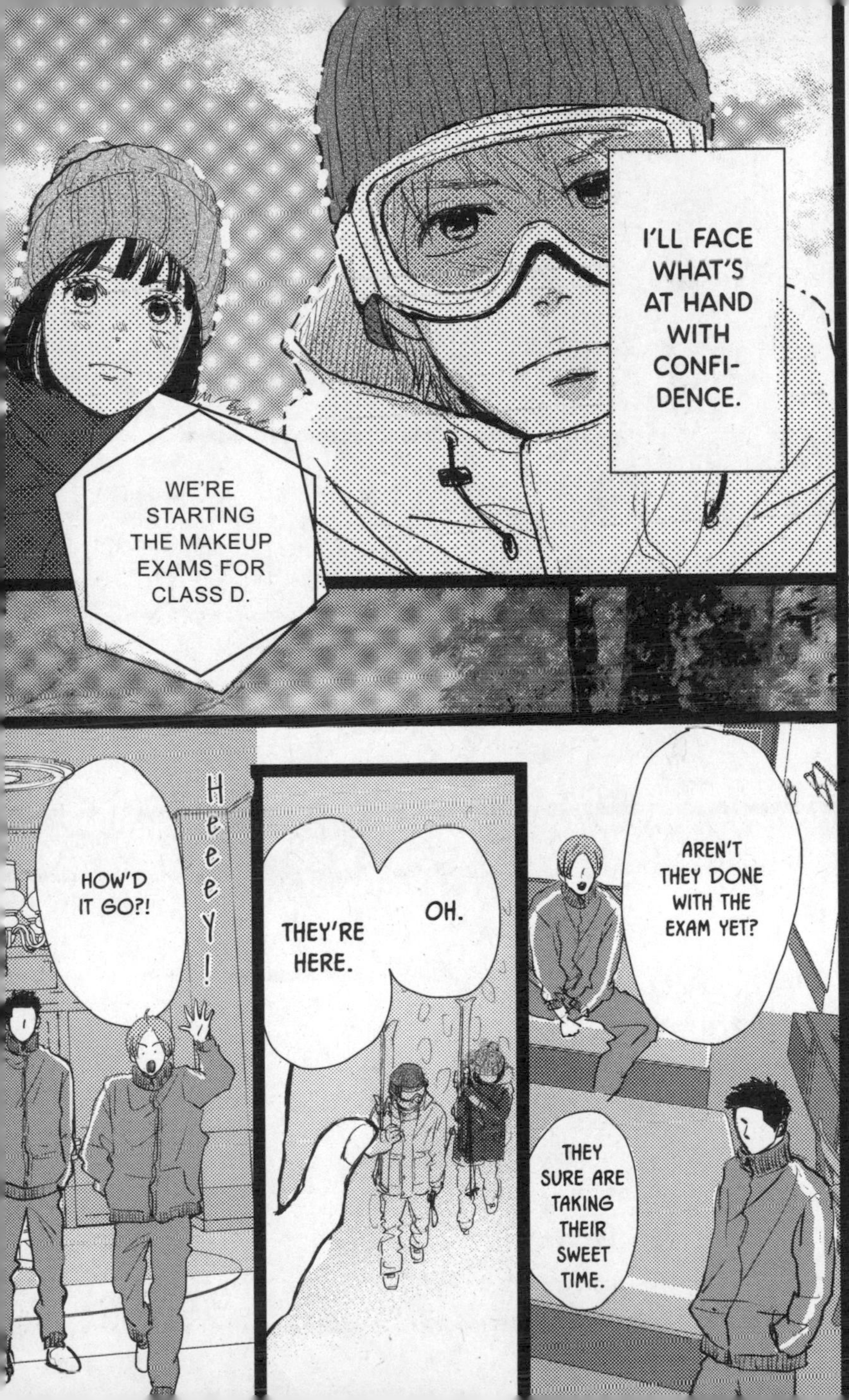
I'LL FACE WHAT'S AT HAND WITH CONFI- DENCE.
WE'RE STARTING THE MAKEUP EXAMS FOR CLASS D.
AREN'T THEY DONE WITH THE EXAM YET?
THEY SURE ARE TAKING THEIR SWEET TIME.
OH.
THEY'RE HERE.
Heeey!
HOW'D IT GO?!

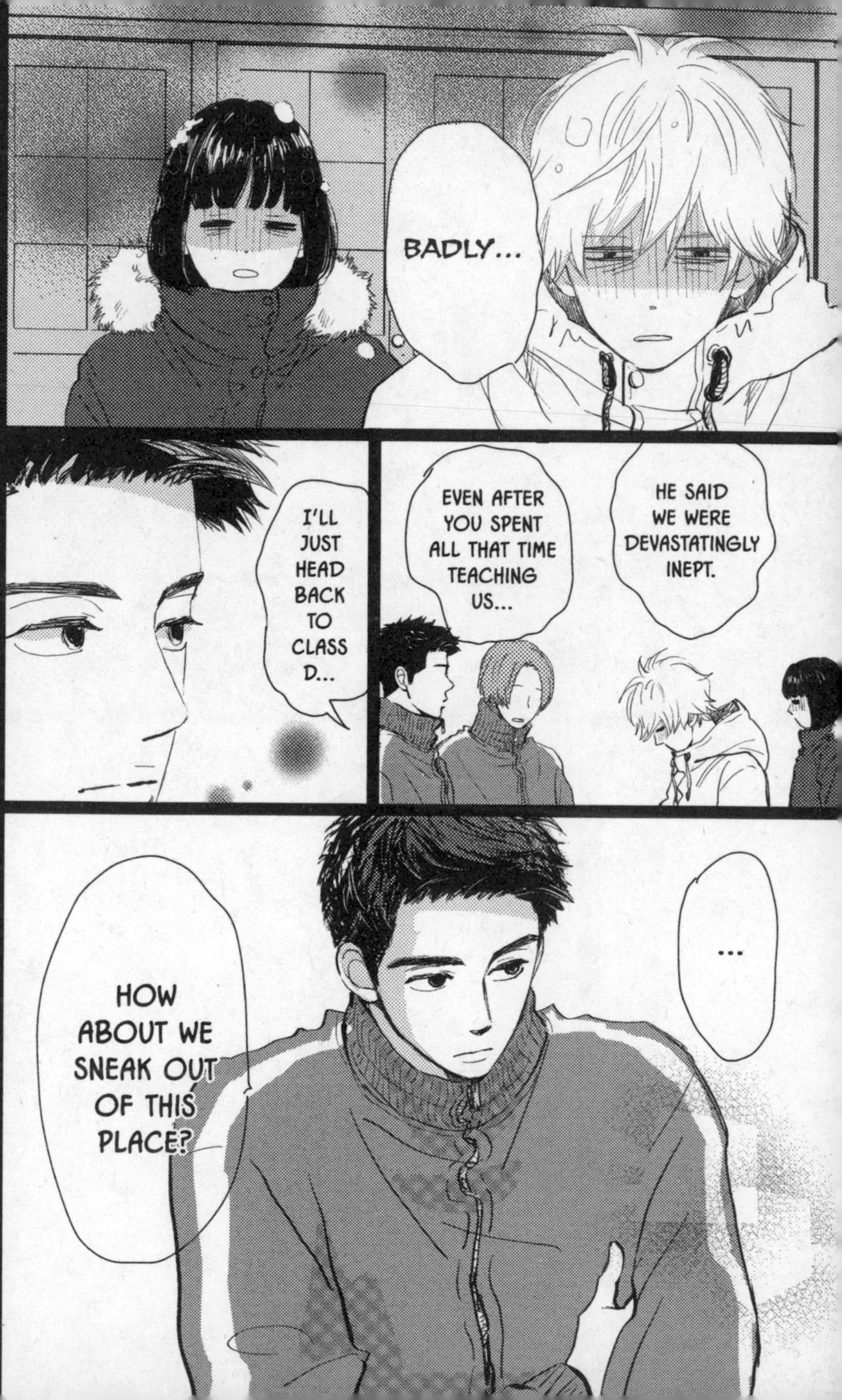
BADLY...
HE SAID WE WERE DEVASTATINGLY INEPT.
EVEN AFTER YOU SPENT ALL THAT TIME TEACHING US...
I'LL JUST HEAD BACK TO CLASS D...
...
HOW ABOUT WE SNEAK OUT OF THIS PLACE?

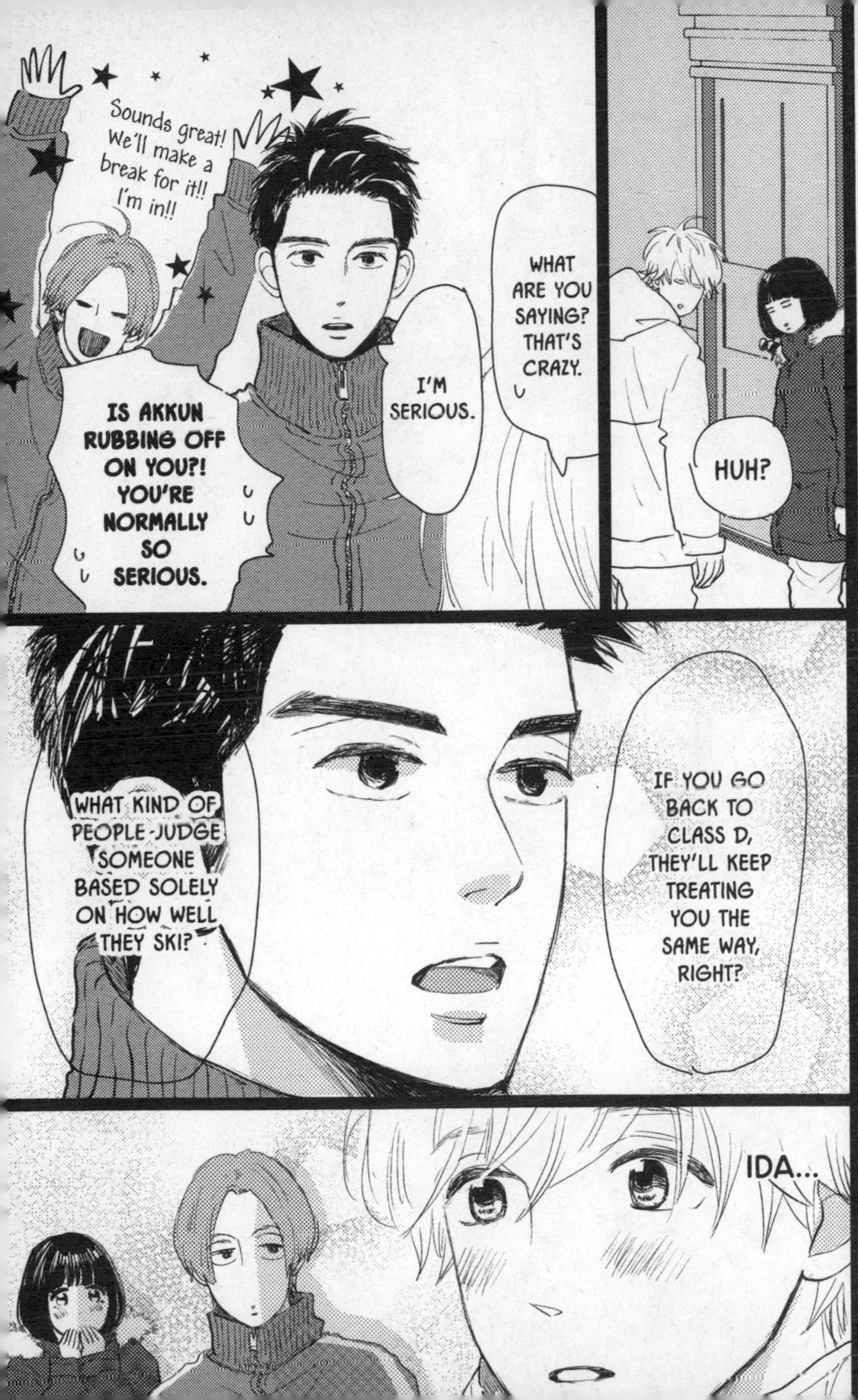
HUH?
WHAT ARE YOU SAYING? THAT'S CRAZY.
I'M SERIOUS.
Sounds great! We'll make a break for it!! I'm in!!
IS AKKUN RUBBING OFF ON YOU?! YOU'RE NORMALLY SO SERIOUS.
IF YOU GO BACK TO CLASS D, THEY'LL KEEP TREATING YOU THE SAME WAY, RIGHT?
WHAT KIND OF PEOPLE JUDGE SOMEONE BASED SOLELY ON HOW WELL THEY SKI?
IDA...

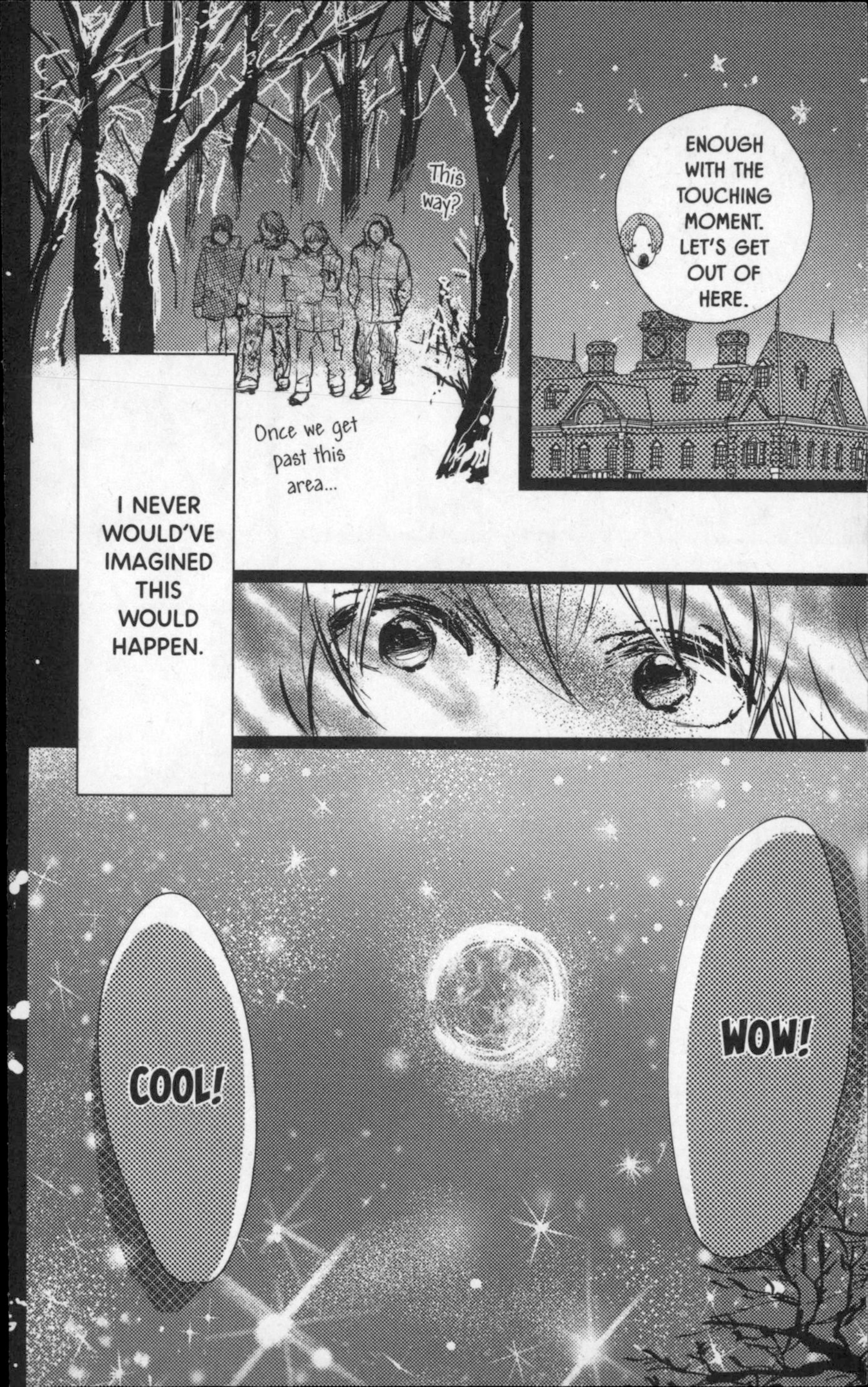
ENOUGH WITH THE TOUCHING MOMENT. LET'S GET OUT OF HERE.
This way?
Once we get past this area...
I NEVER WOULD'VE IMAGINED THIS WOULD HAPPEN.
WOW!
COOL!

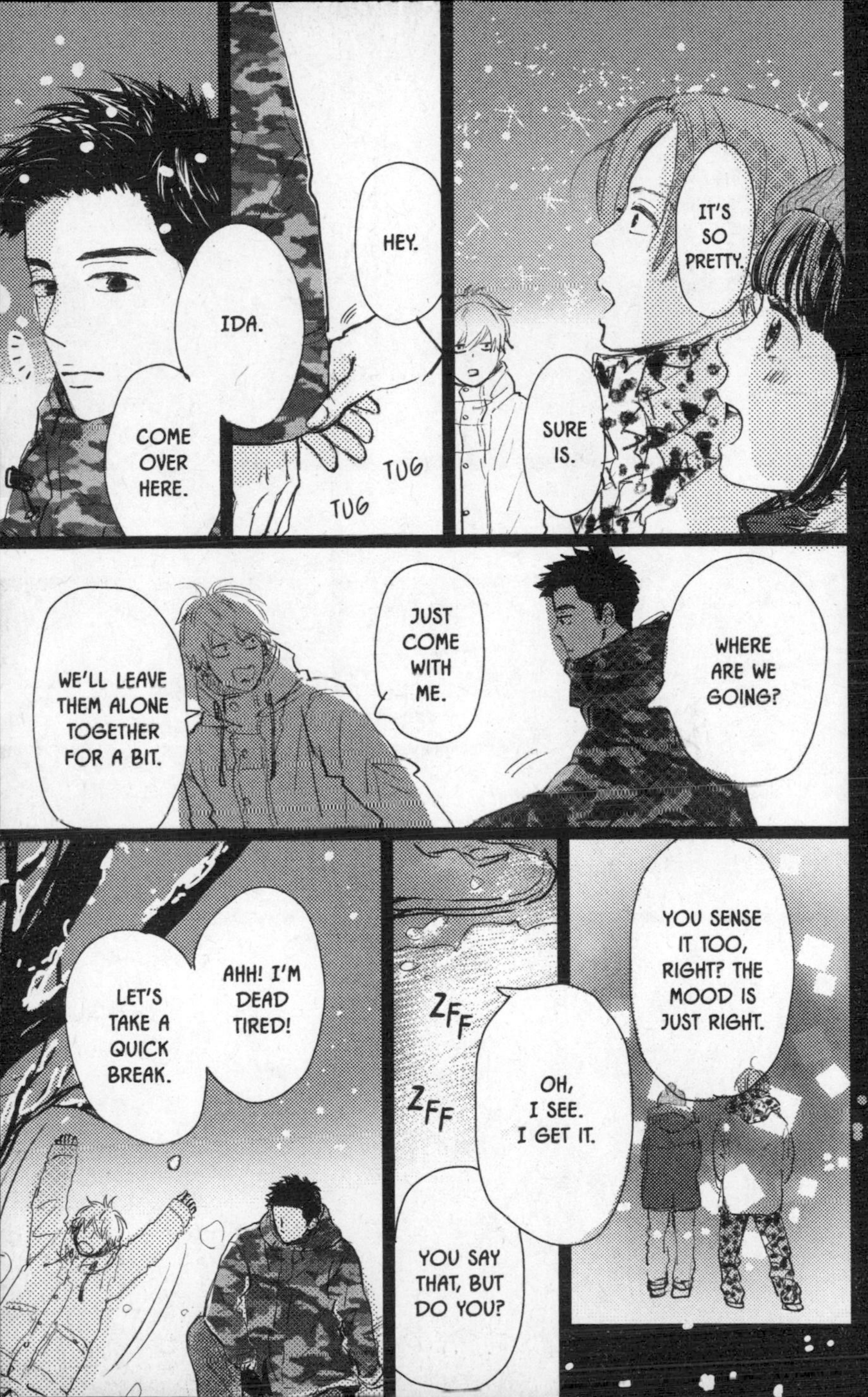
IT'S SO PRETTY.
SURE IS.
HEY.
TUG
TUG
IDA.
COME OVER HERE.
WHERE ARE WE GOING?
JUST COME WITH ME.
WE'LL LEAVE THEM ALONE TOGETHER FOR A BIT.
YOU SENSE IT TOO, RIGHT? THE MOOD IS JUST RIGHT.
OH, I SEE. I GET IT.
YOU SAY THAT, BUT DO YOU?
ZFF
ZFF
AHH! I'M DEAD TIRED!
LET'S TAKE A QUICK BREAK.

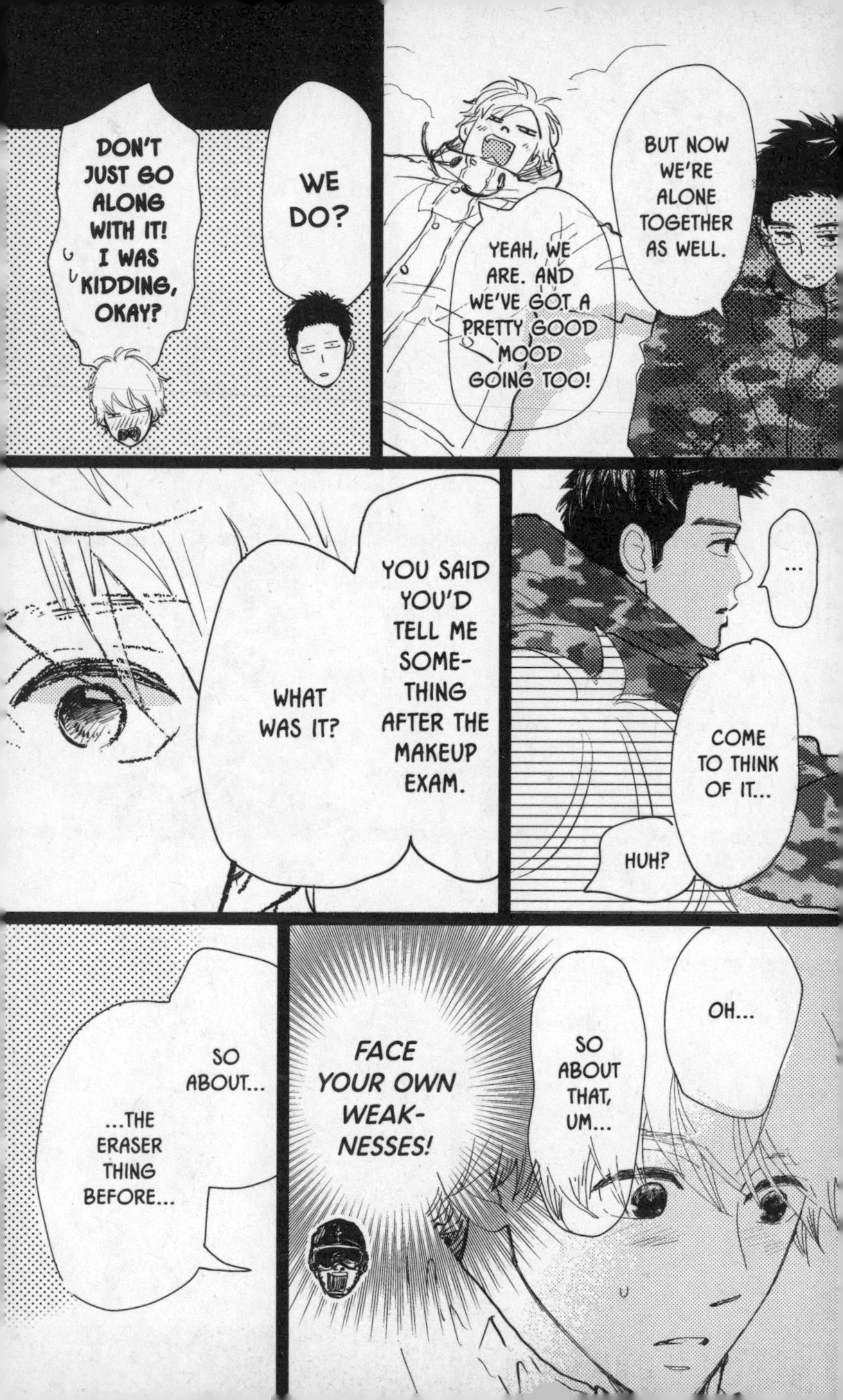
BUT NOW WE'RE ALONE TOGETHER AS WELL.
YEAH, WE ARE. AND WE'VE GOT A PRETTY GOOD MOOD GOING TOO!
WE DO?
DON'T JUST GO ALONG WITH IT! I WAS KIDDING, OKAY?
...
COME TO THINK OF IT...
HUH?
YOU SAID YOU'D TELL ME SOME-THING AFTER THE MAKEUP EXAM.
WHAT WAS IT?
OH...
SO ABOUT THAT, UM...
FACE YOUR OWN WEAK-NESSES!
SO ABOUT...
...THE ERASER THING BEFORE...

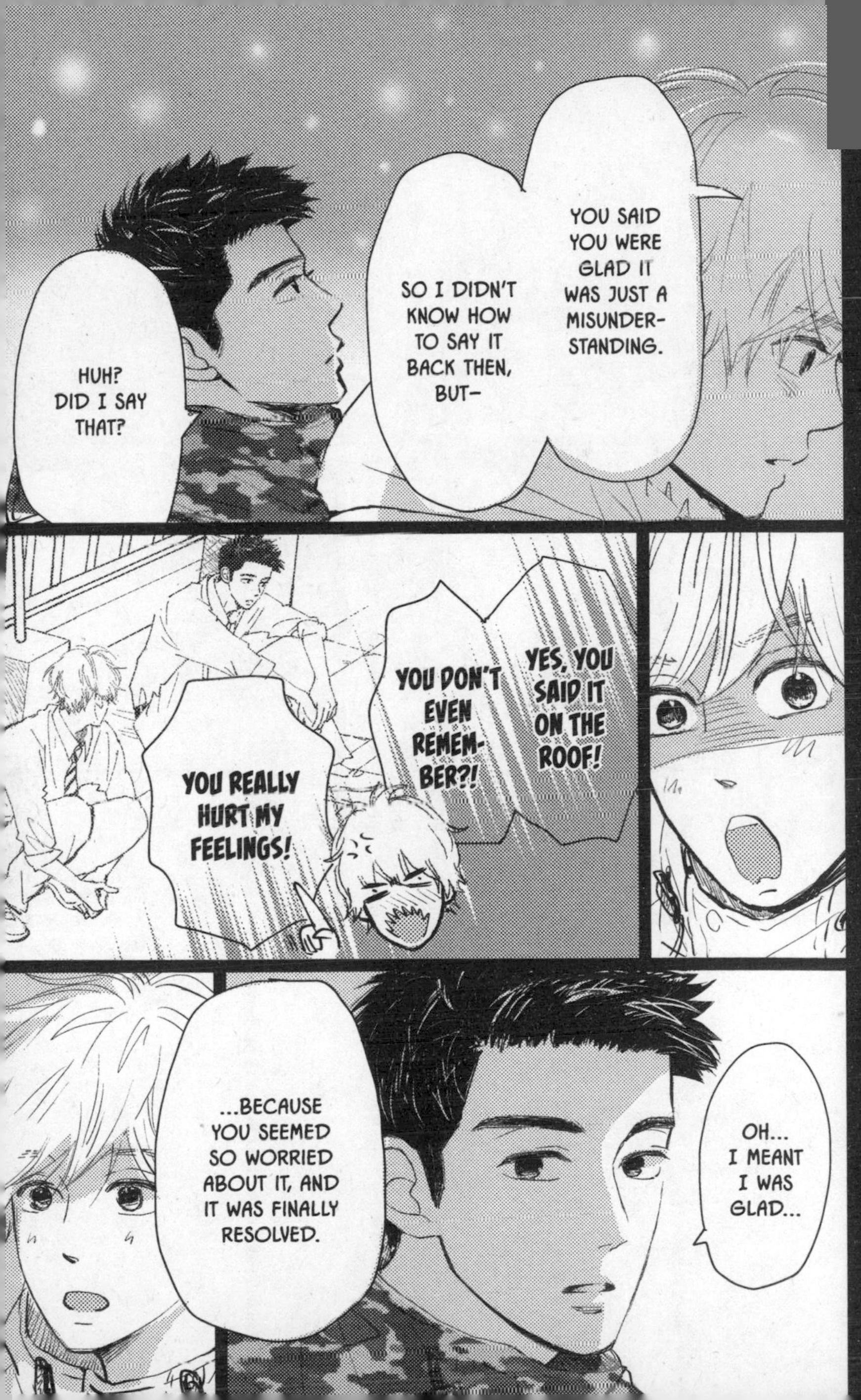
YOU SAID YOU WERE GLAD IT WAS JUST A MISUNDER-STANDING.
SO I DIDN'T KNOW HOW TO SAY IT BACK THEN, BUT–
HUH? DID I SAY THAT?
YES, YOU SAID IT ON THE ROOF!
YOU DON'T EVEN REMEM-BER?!
YOU REALLY HURT MY FEELINGS!
OH... I MEANT I WAS GLAD...
...BECAUSE YOU SEEMED SO WORRIED ABOUT IT, AND IT WAS FINALLY RESOLVED.

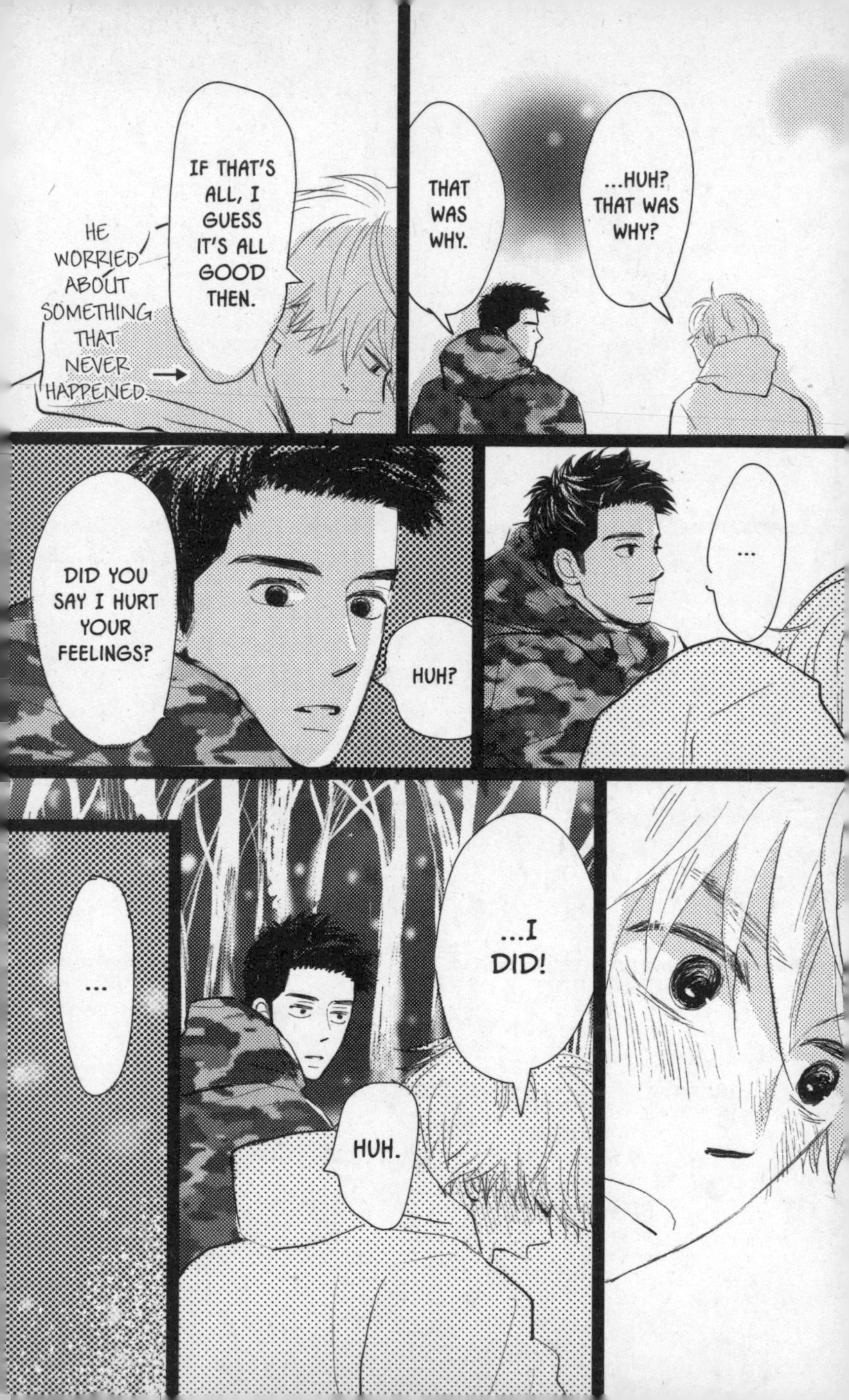
...HUH? THAT WAS WHY?
THAT WAS WHY.
IF THAT'S ALL, I GUESS IT'S ALL GOOD THEN.
HE WORRIED ABOUT SOMETHING THAT NEVER HAPPENED
...
HUH?
DID YOU SAY I HURT YOUR FEELINGS?
...I DID!
HUH.
...

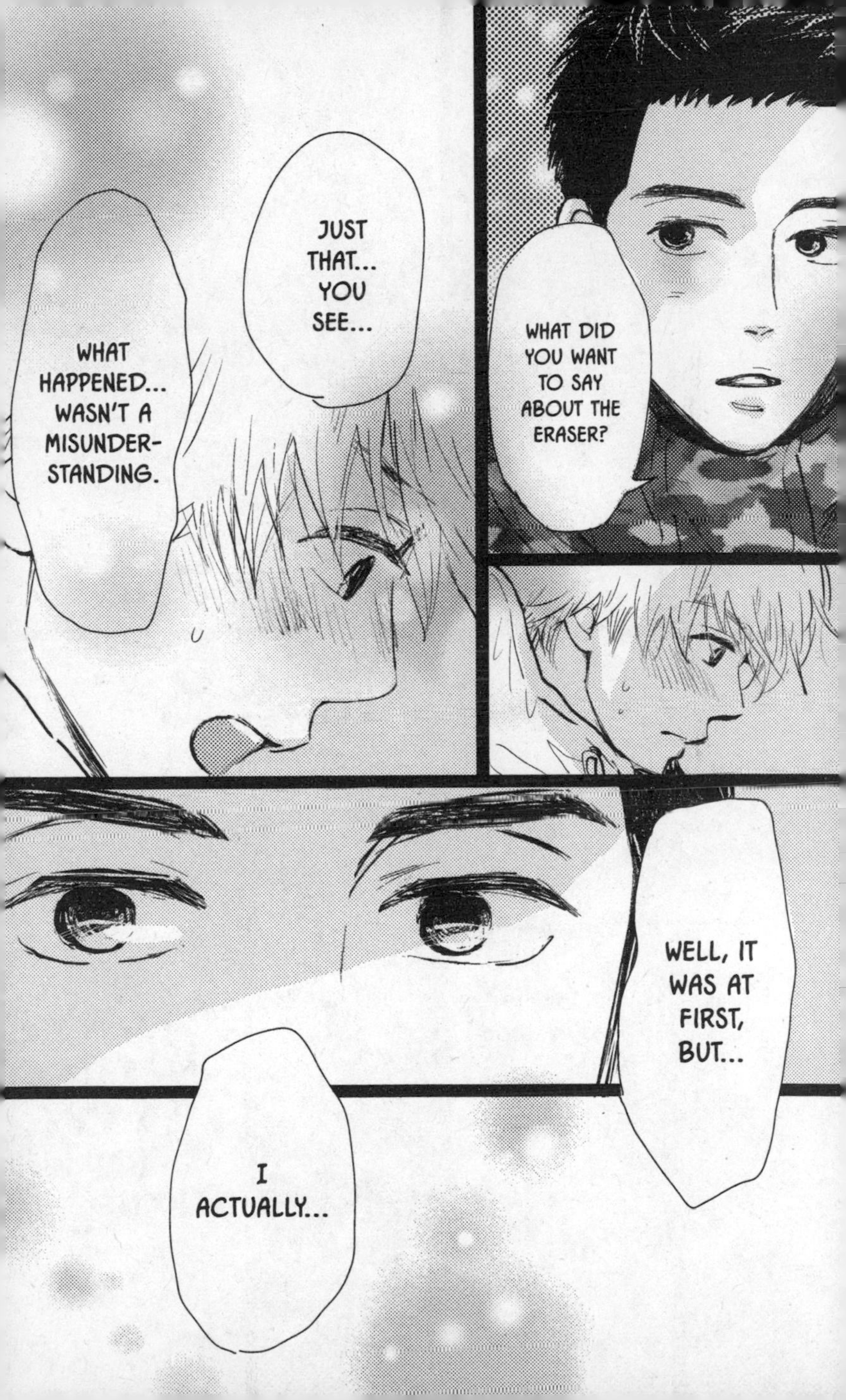
WHAT DID YOU WANT TO SAY ABOUT THE ERASER?
JUST THAT... YOU SEE...
WHAT HAPPENED... WASN'T A MISUNDER-STANDING.
WELL, IT WAS AT FIRST, BUT...
I ACTUALLY...

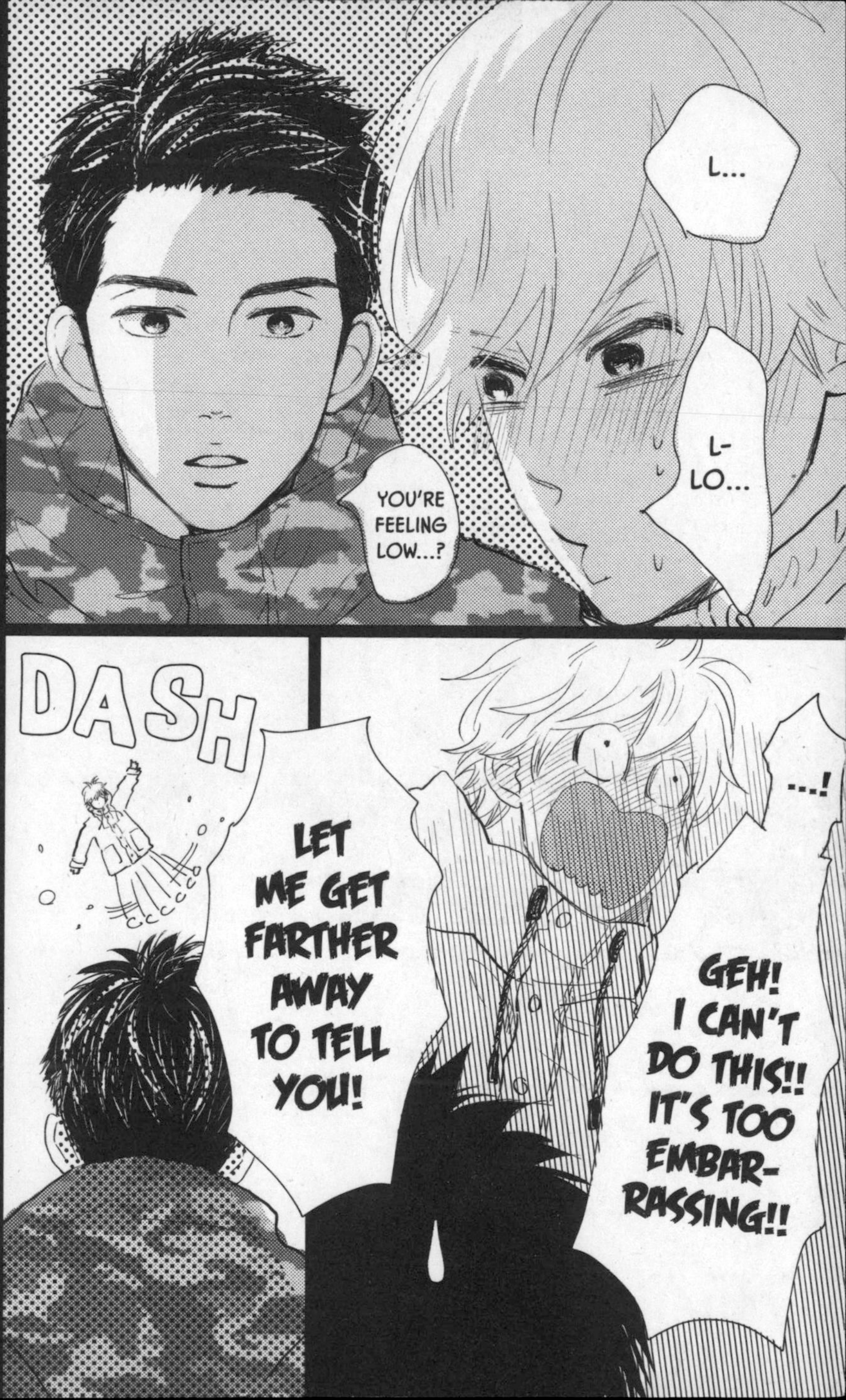
L...
L- LO...
YOU'RE FEELING LOW...?
...!
GEH! I CAN'T DO THIS!! IT'S TOO EMBAR-RASSING!!
DASH
LET ME GET FARTHER AWAY TO TELL YOU!

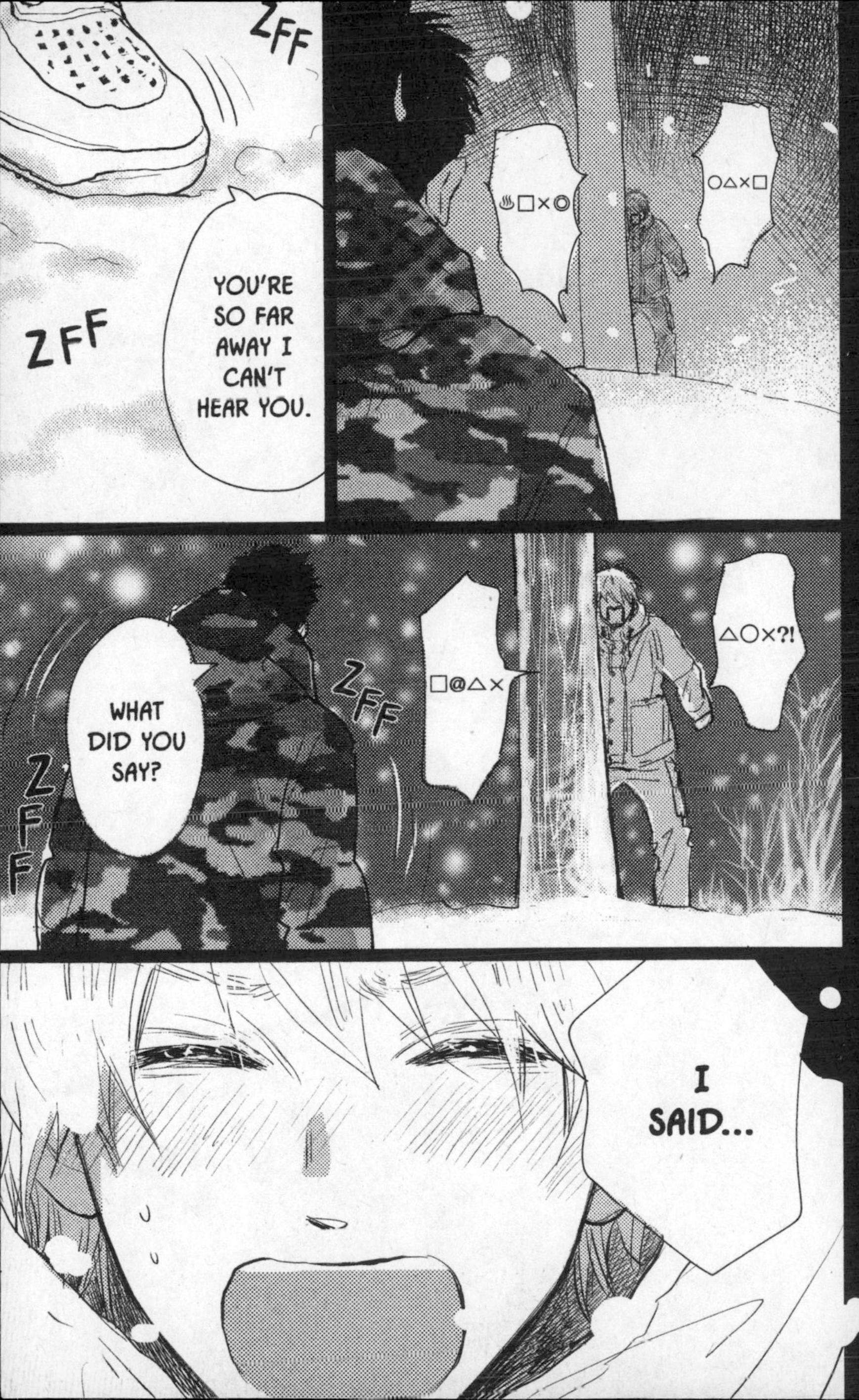
○△×□
♨□×◎
ZFF
YOU'RE SO FAR AWAY I CAN'T HEAR YOU.
ZFF
△○×?!
□@△×
ZFF
WHAT DID YOU SAY?
ZFF
I SAID...

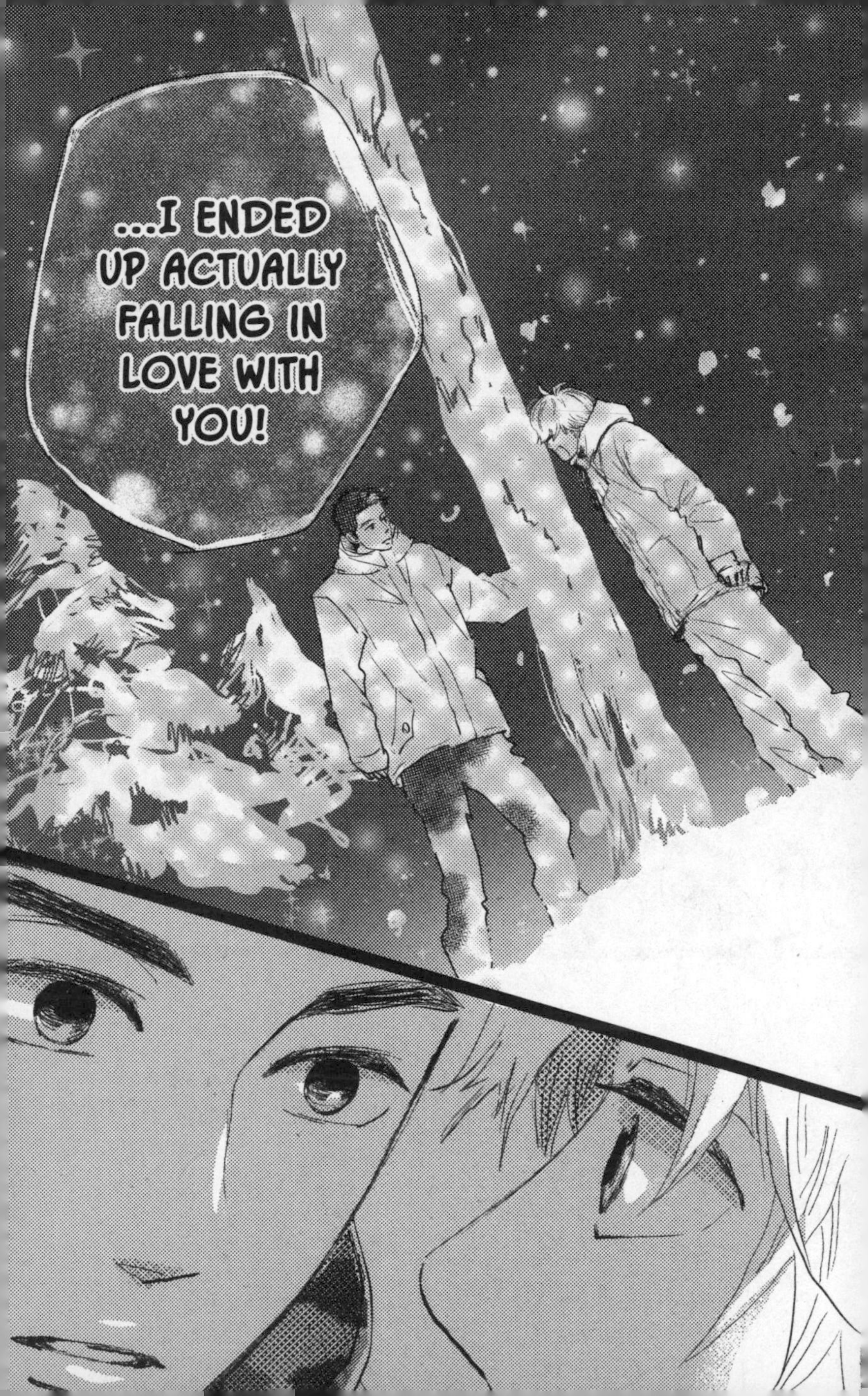
...I ENDED UP ACTUALLY FALLING IN LOVE WITH YOU!

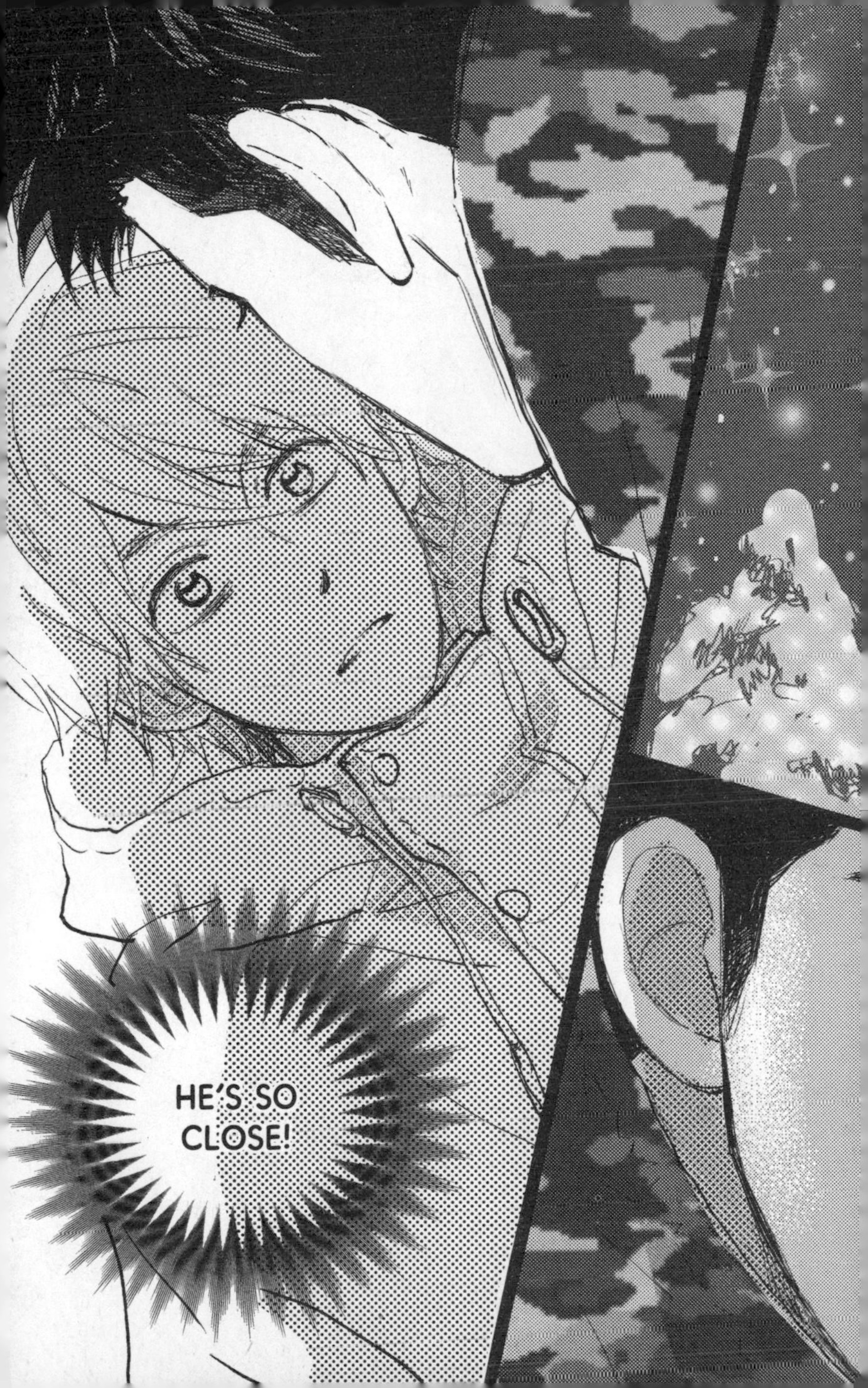
HE'S SO CLOSE!

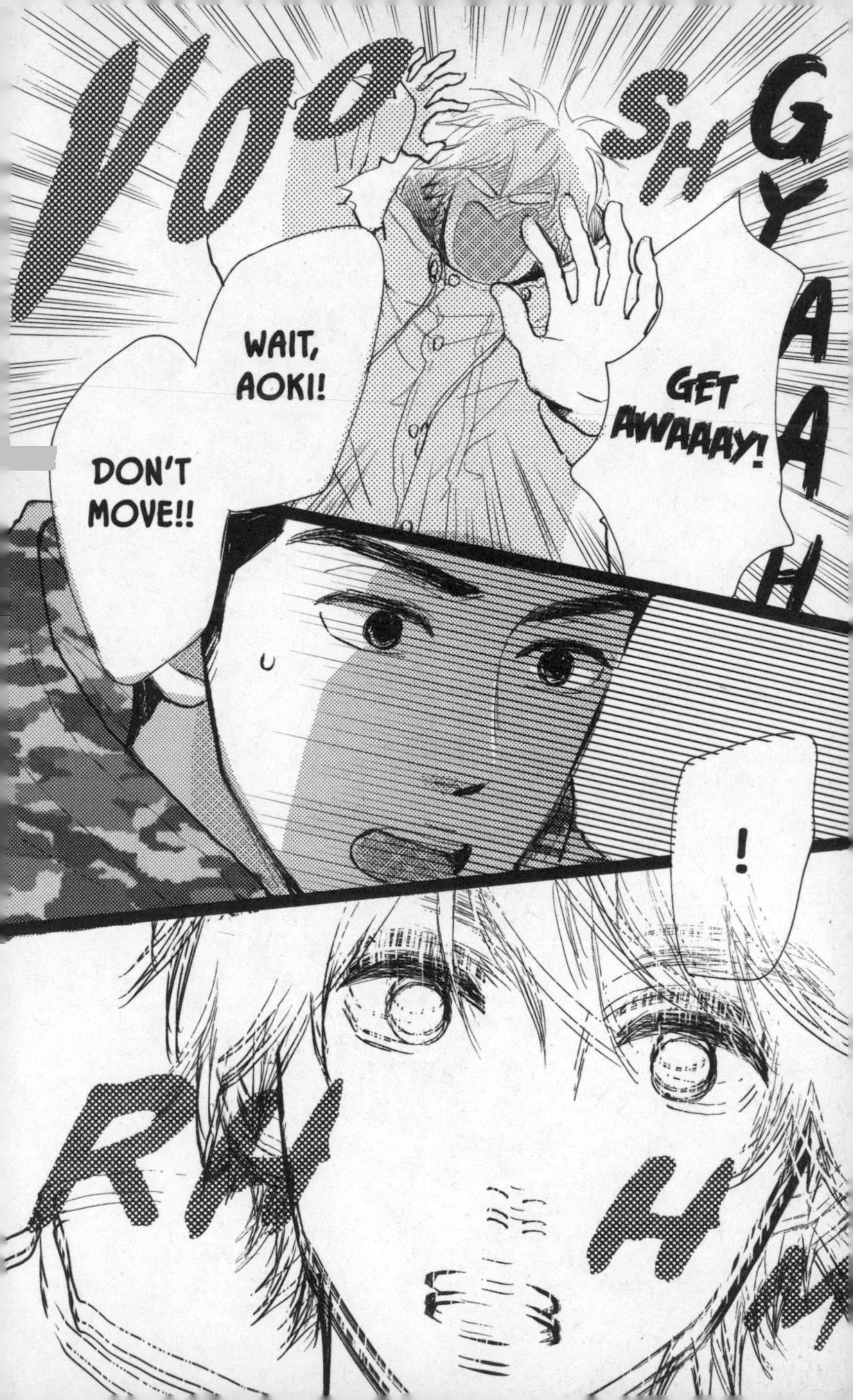
GYAAAH
GET AWAAAY!
VOOSH
WAIT, AOKI!
DON'T MOVE!!
!

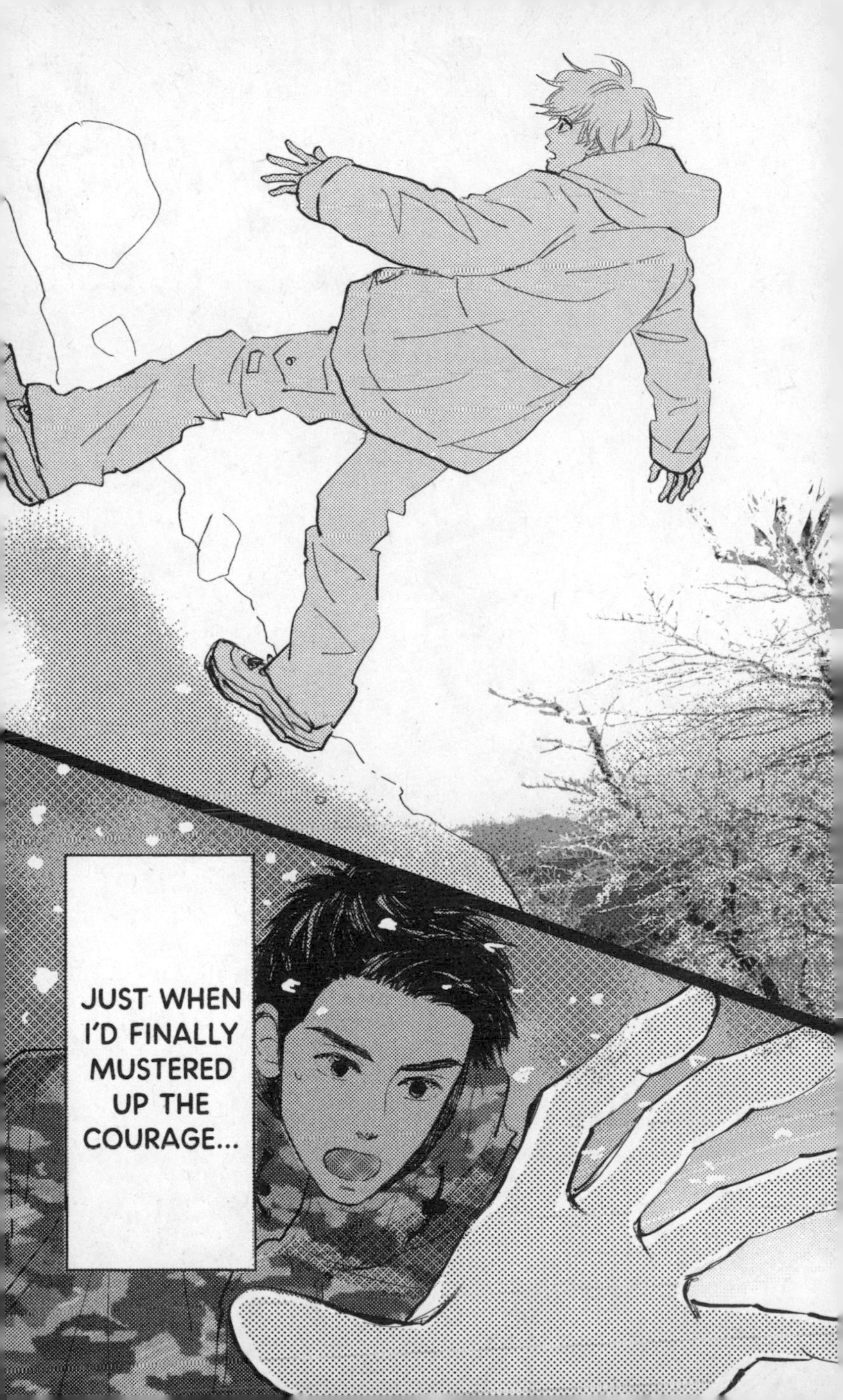
JUST WHEN I'D FINALLY MUSTERED UP THE COURAGE...

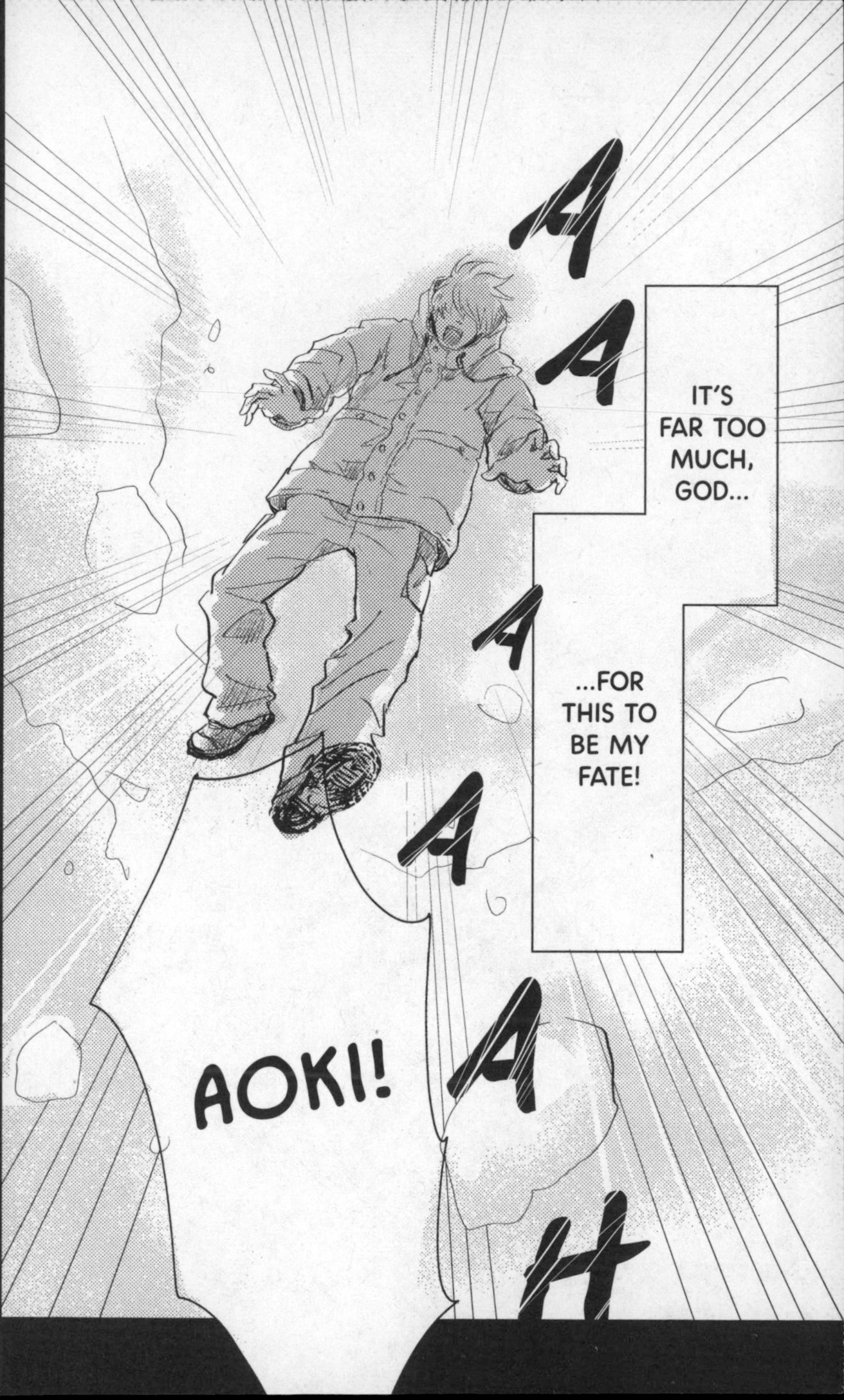

IT'S FAR TOO MUCH, GOD...
...FOR THIS TO BE MY FATE!
AAAAAH
AOKI!

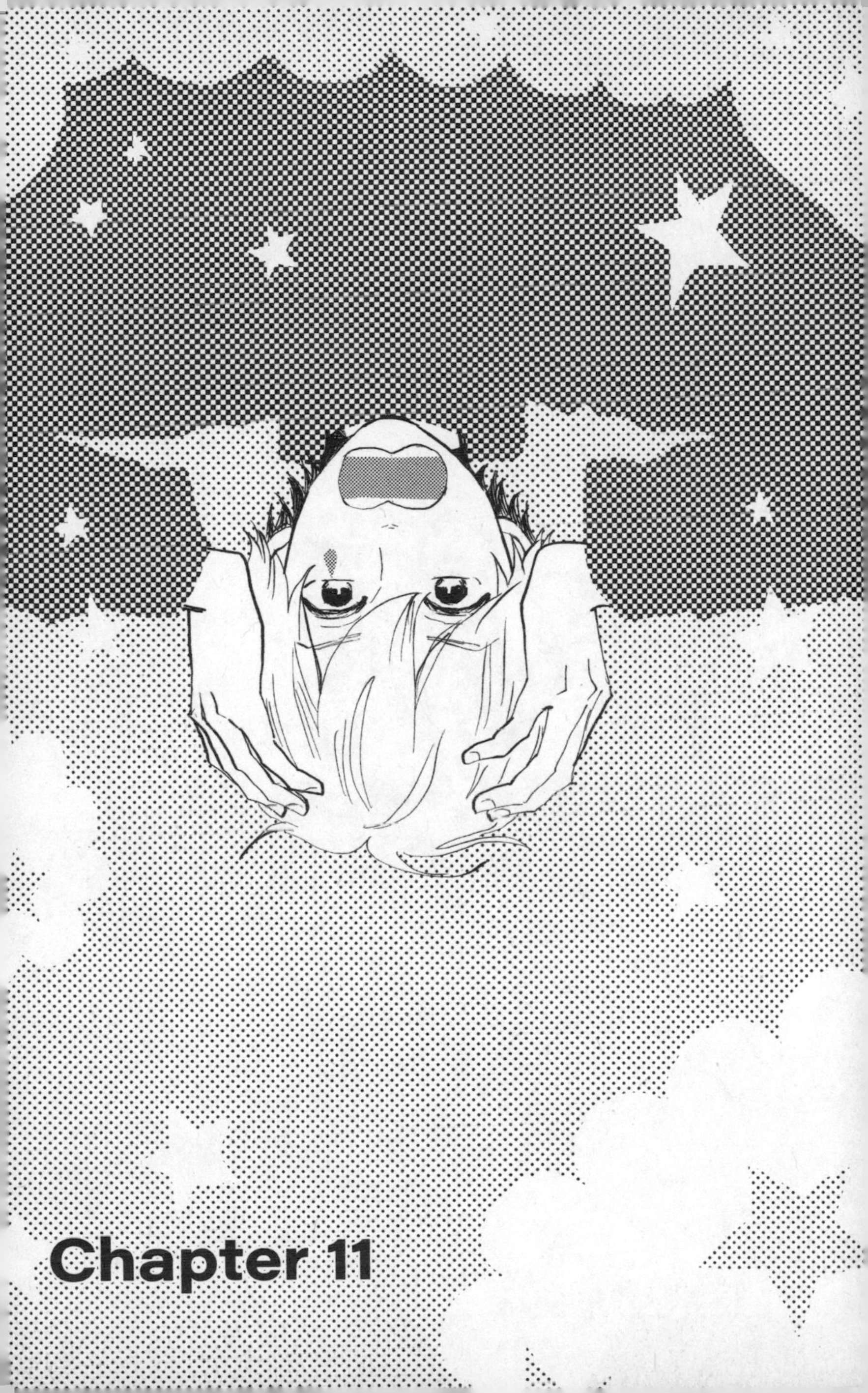

Chapter 11

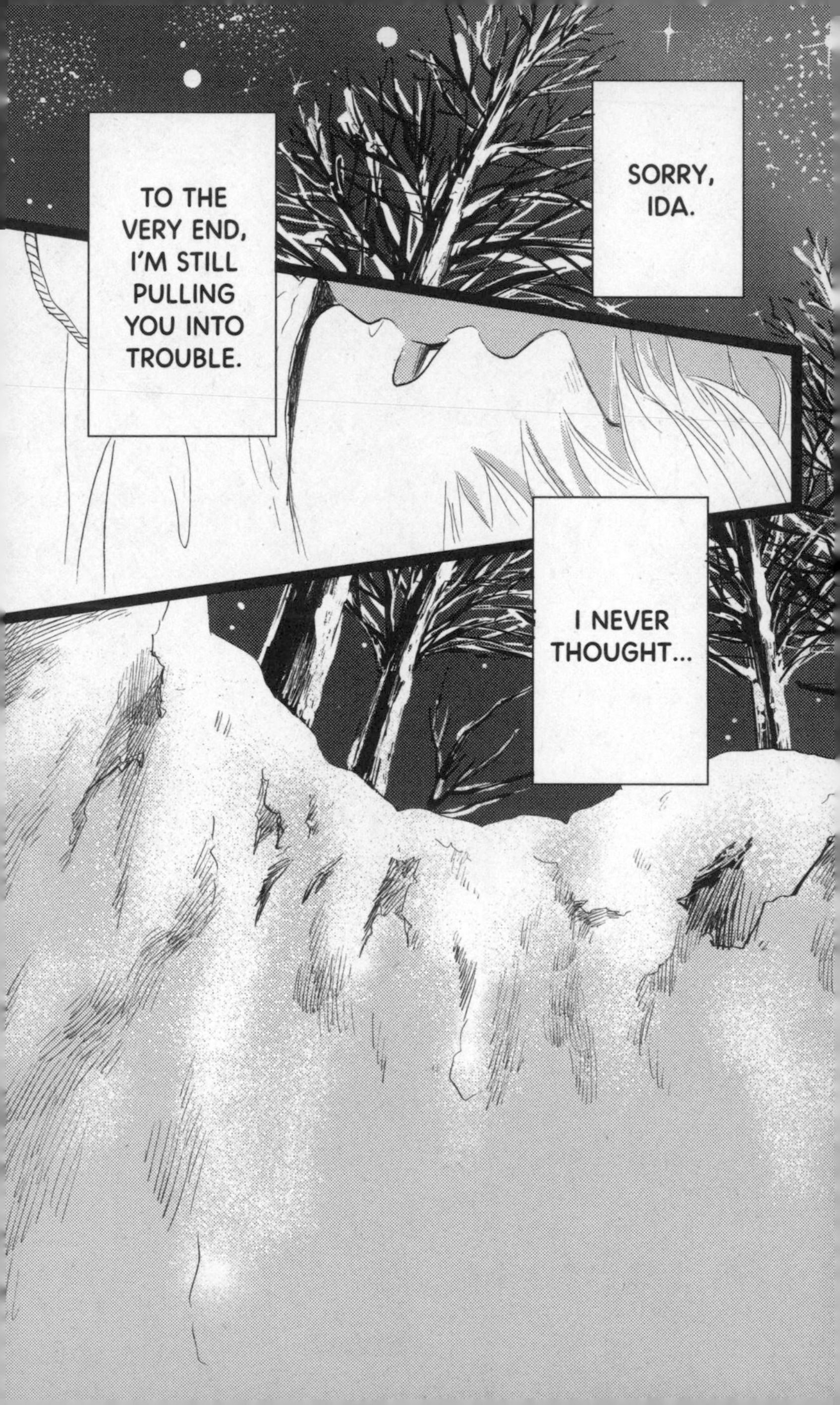
SORRY, IDA.
TO THE VERY END, I'M STILL PULLING YOU INTO TROUBLE.
I NEVER THOUGHT...

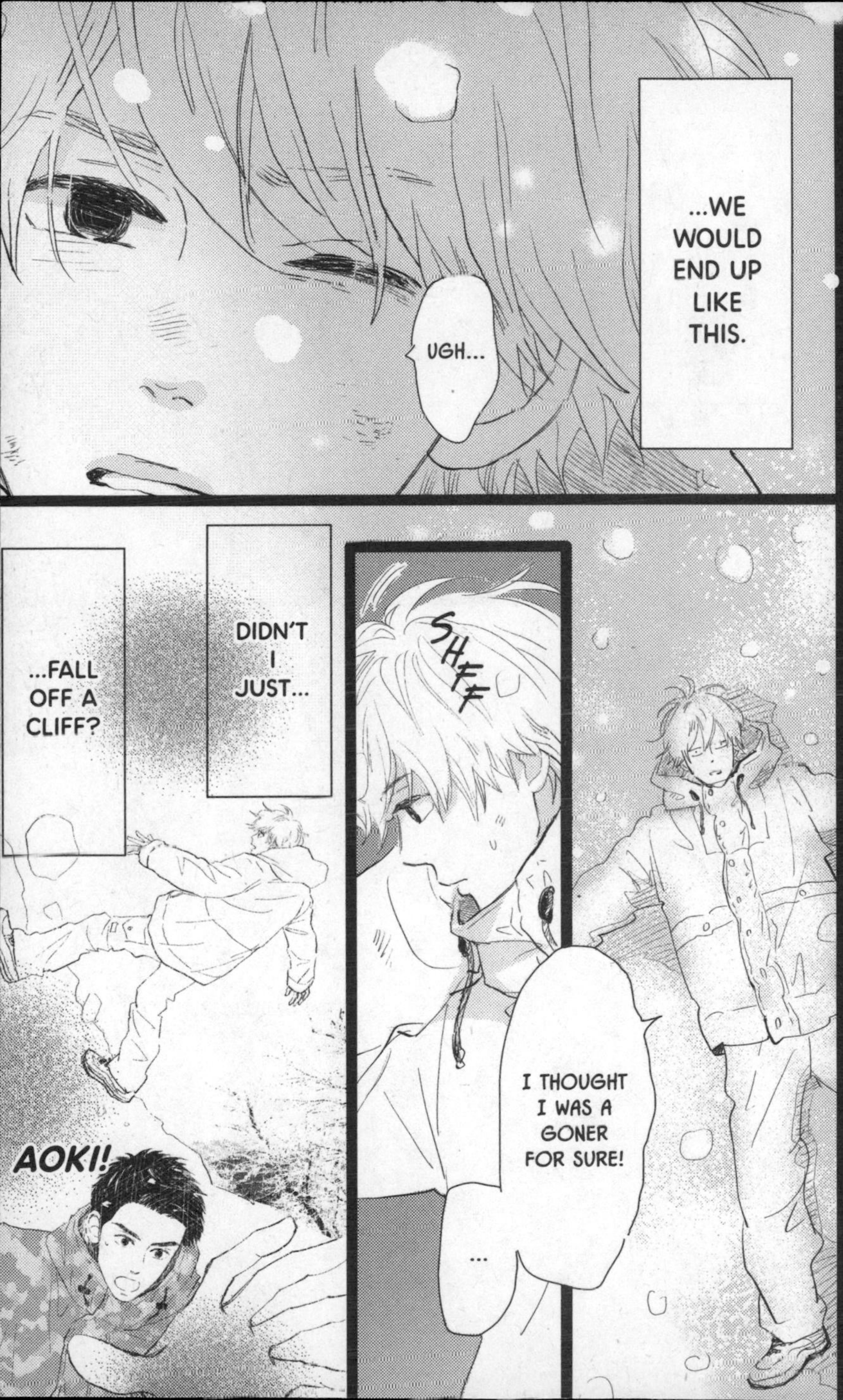
...WE WOULD END UP LIKE THIS.
UGH...
I THOUGHT I WAS A GONER FOR SURE!
SHFF
...
DIDN'T I JUST...
...FALL OFF A CLIFF?
AOKI!

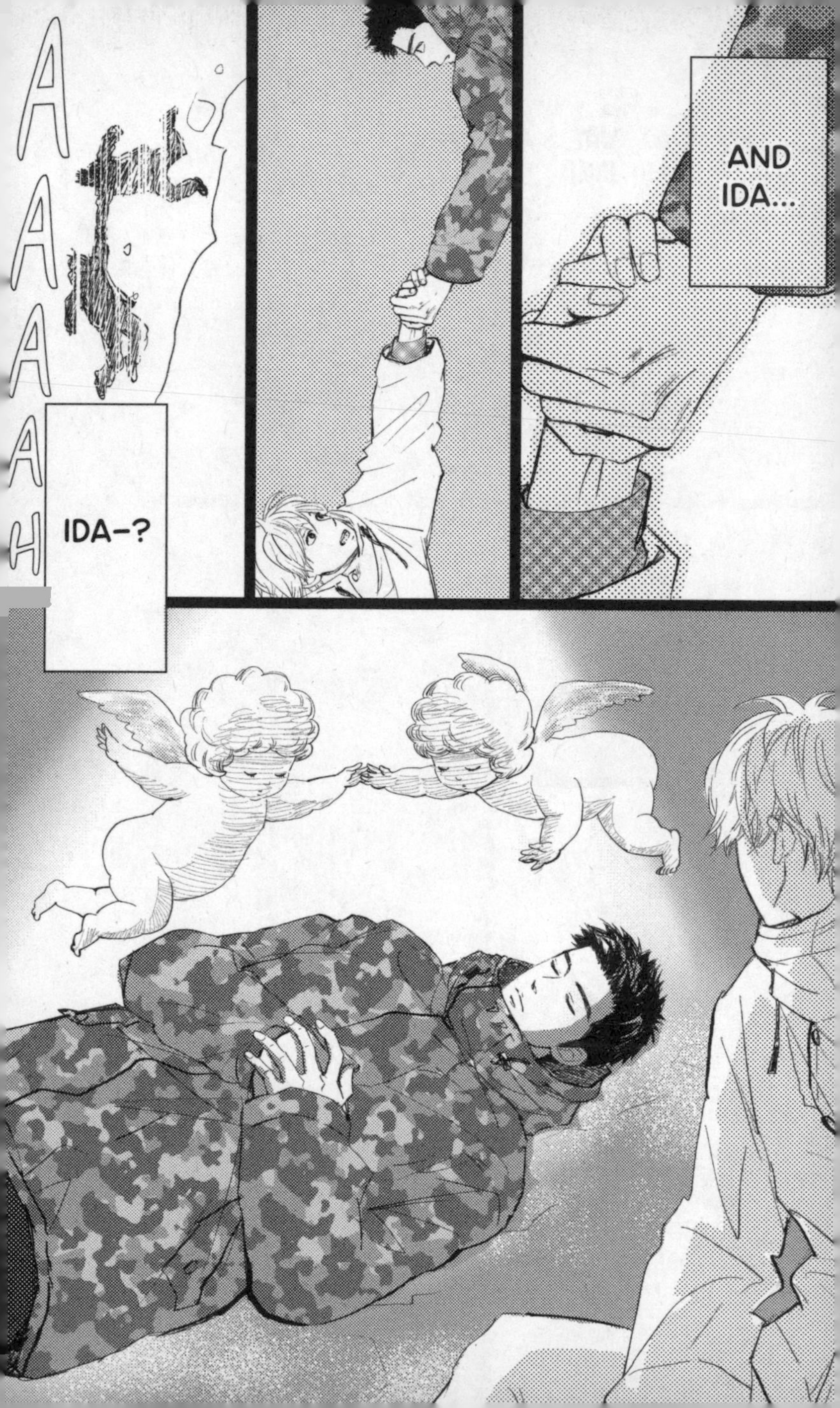
AND IDA...
AAAAAH
IDA-?

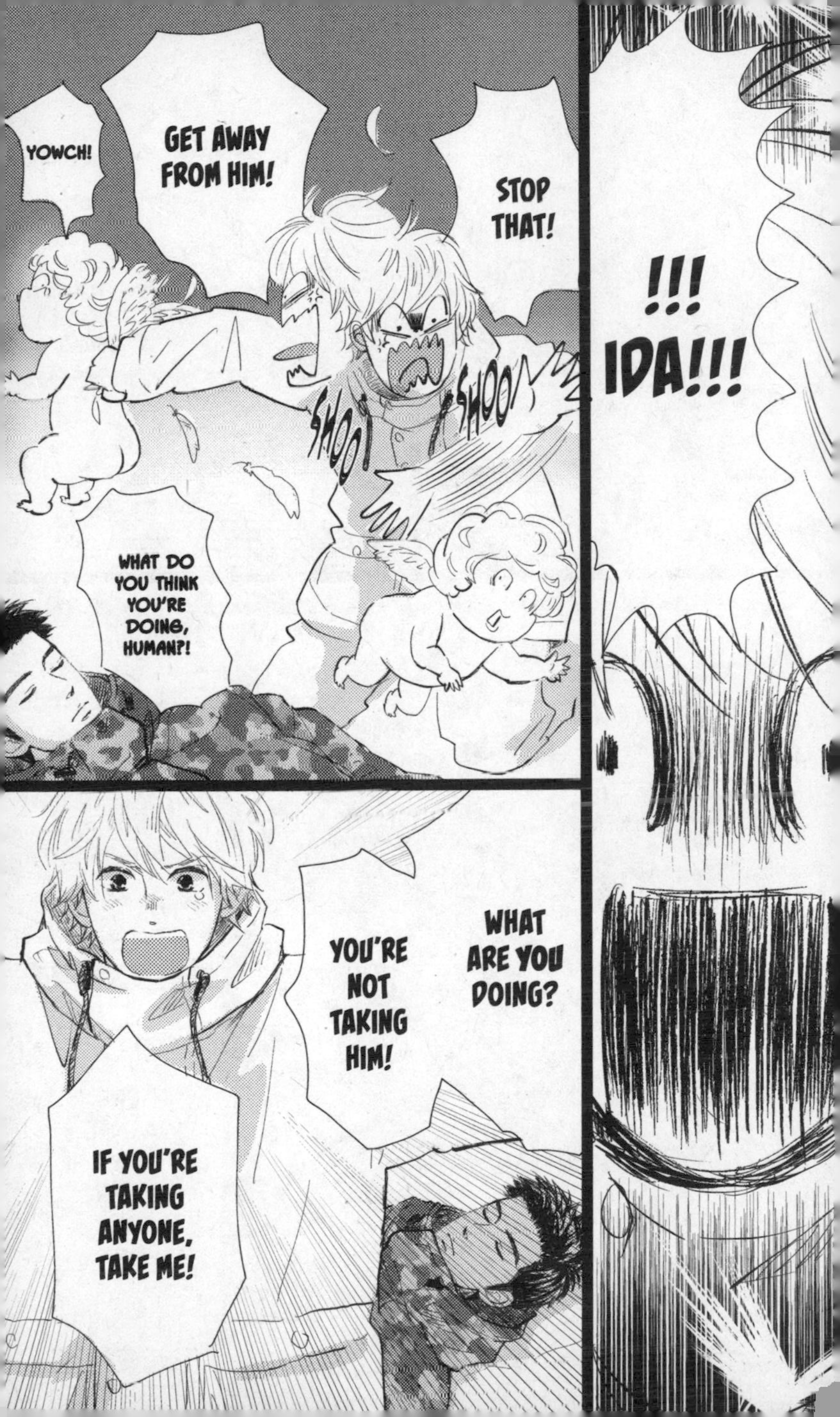
!!!
IDA!!!
STOP THAT!
SHOOM
SHOOM
GET AWAY FROM HIM!
YOWCH!
WHAT DO YOU THINK YOU'RE DOING, HUMAN?!
WHAT ARE YOU DOING?
YOU'RE NOT TAKING HIM!
IF YOU'RE TAKING ANYONE, TAKE ME!

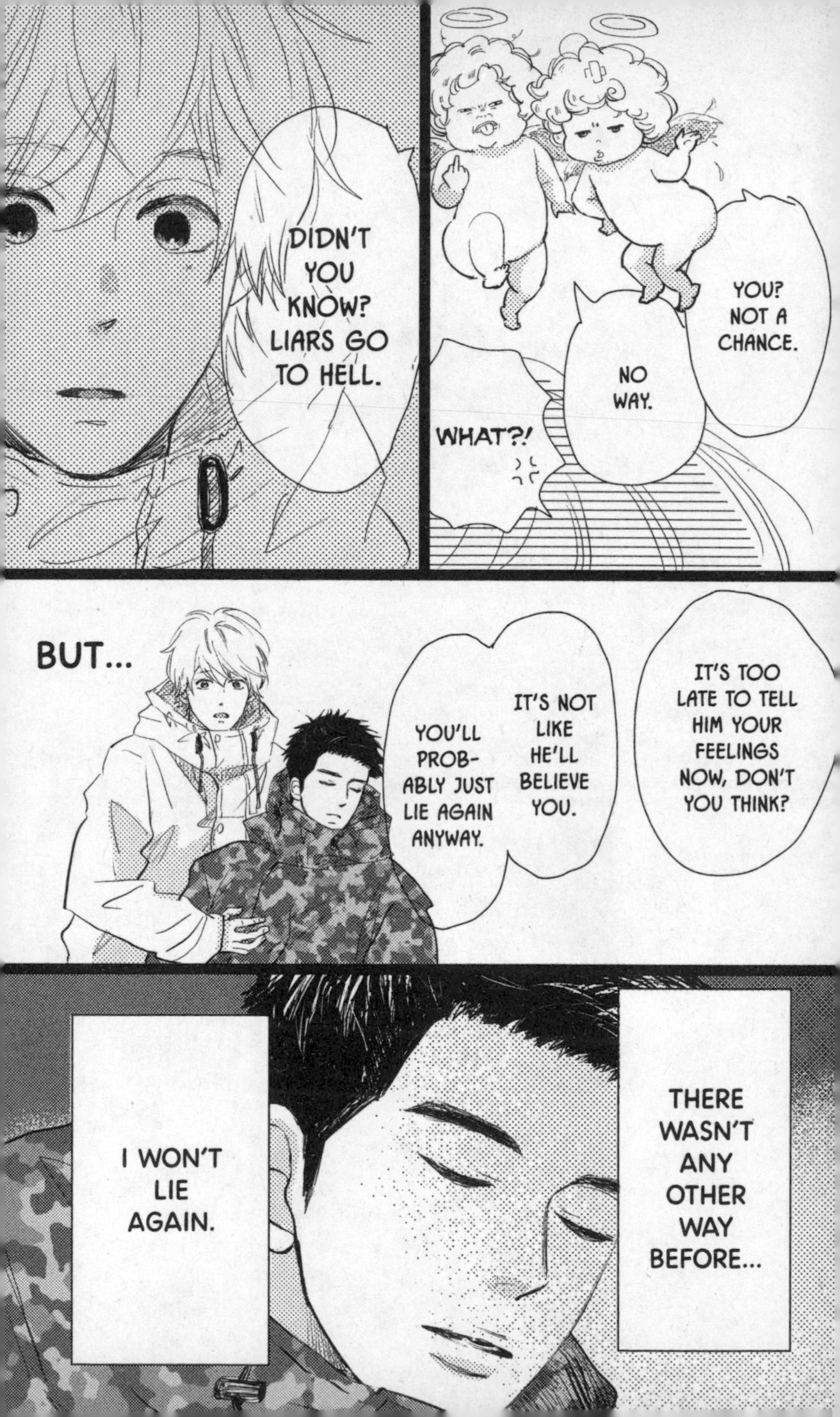
YOU? NOT A CHANCE.
NO WAY.
WHAT?!
DIDN'T YOU KNOW? LIARS GO TO HELL.
IT'S TOO LATE TO TELL HIM YOUR FEELINGS NOW, DON'T YOU THINK?
IT'S NOT LIKE HE'LL BELIEVE YOU.
YOU'LL PROBABLY JUST LIE AGAIN ANYWAY.
BUT...
THERE WASN'T ANY OTHER WAY BEFORE...
I WON'T LIE AGAIN.

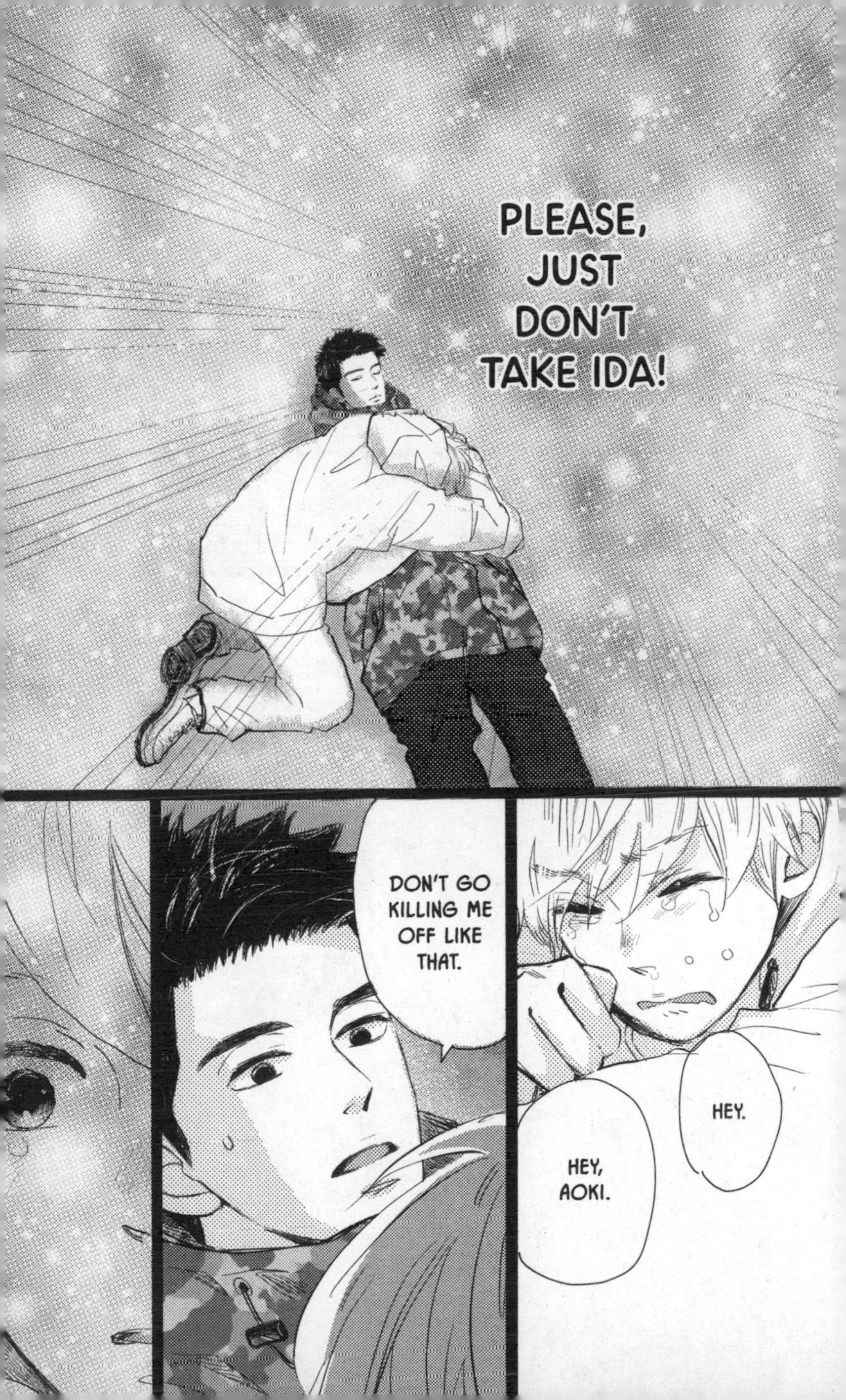
PLEASE, JUST DON'T TAKE IDA!
HEY.
HEY, AOKI.
DON'T GO KILLING ME OFF LIKE THAT.

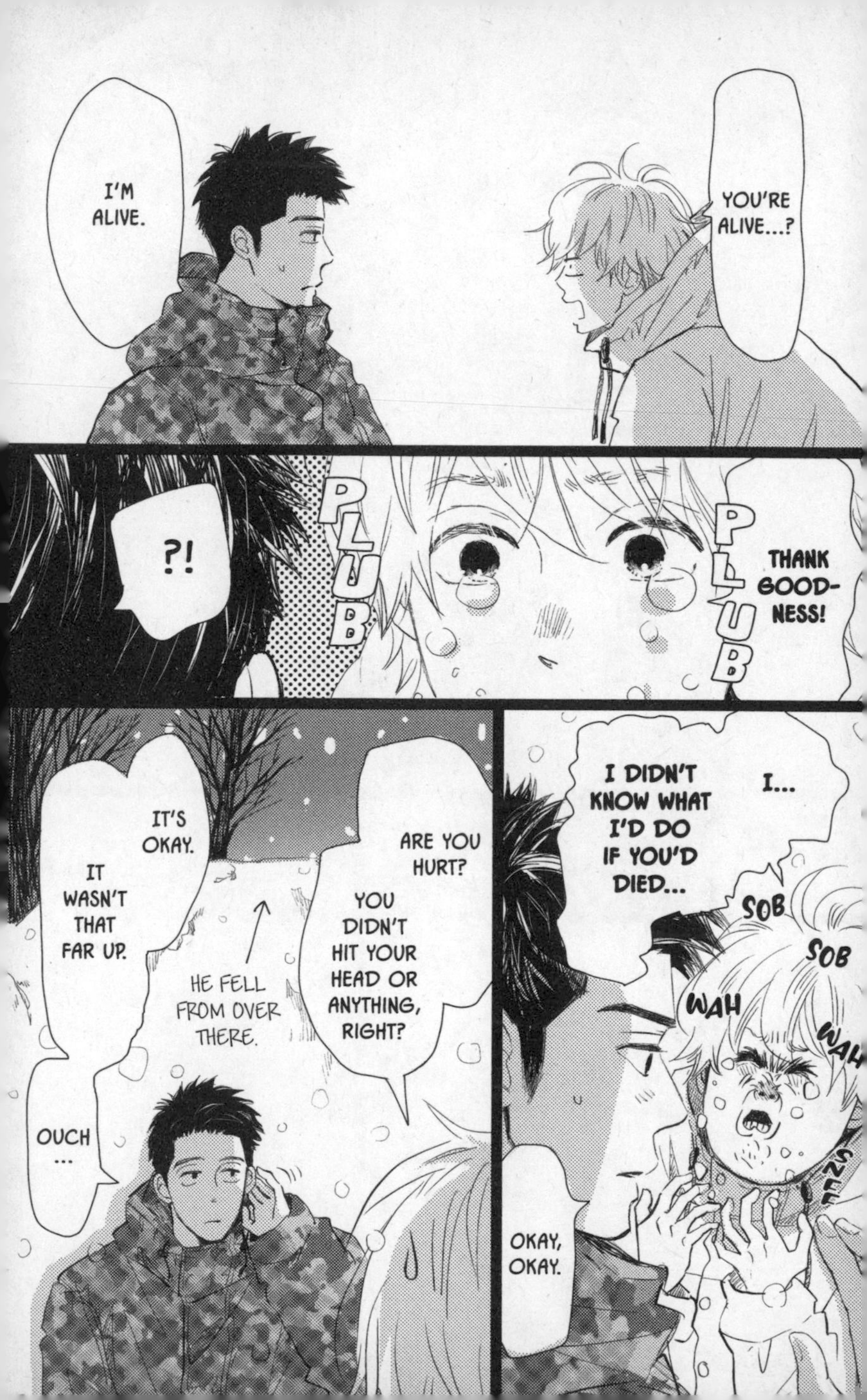
YOU'RE ALIVE...?
I'M ALIVE.
THANK GOODNESS!
PLUB
PLUB
?!
I...
I DIDN'T KNOW WHAT I'D DO IF YOU'D DIED...
SOB
SOB
WAH
WAH
OKAY, OKAY.
ARE YOU HURT?
YOU DIDN'T HIT YOUR HEAD OR ANYTHING, RIGHT?
HE FELL FROM OVER THERE.
IT'S OKAY.
IT WASN'T THAT FAR UP.
OUCH...

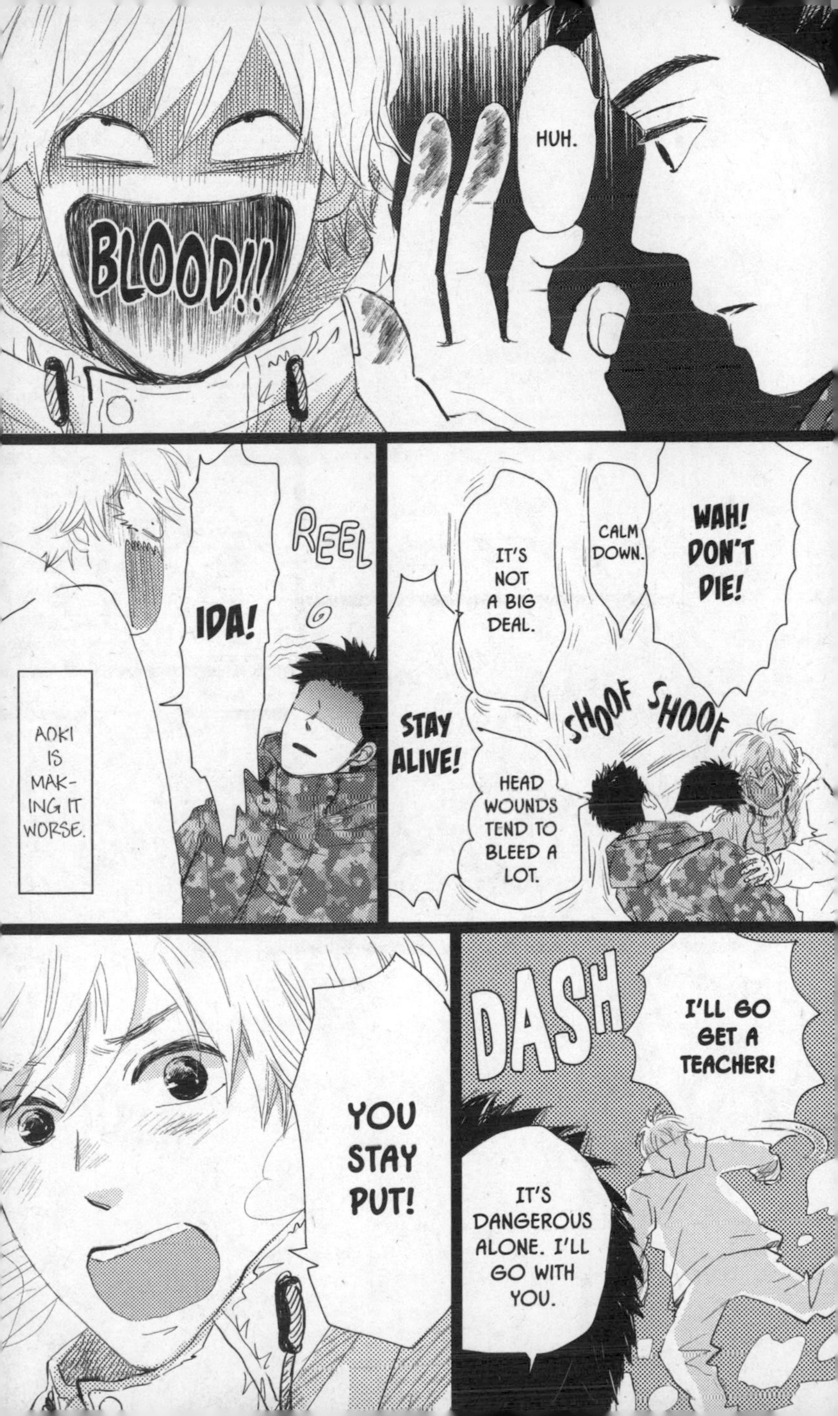
HUH.
BLOOD!!
WAH! DON'T DIE!
CALM DOWN.
IT'S NOT A BIG DEAL.
SHOOF SHOOF
STAY ALIVE!
HEAD WOUNDS TEND TO BLEED A LOT.
REEL
IDA!
AOKI IS MAK-ING IT WORSE.
I'LL GO GET A TEACHER!
DASH
IT'S DANGEROUS ALONE. I'LL GO WITH YOU.
YOU STAY PUT!

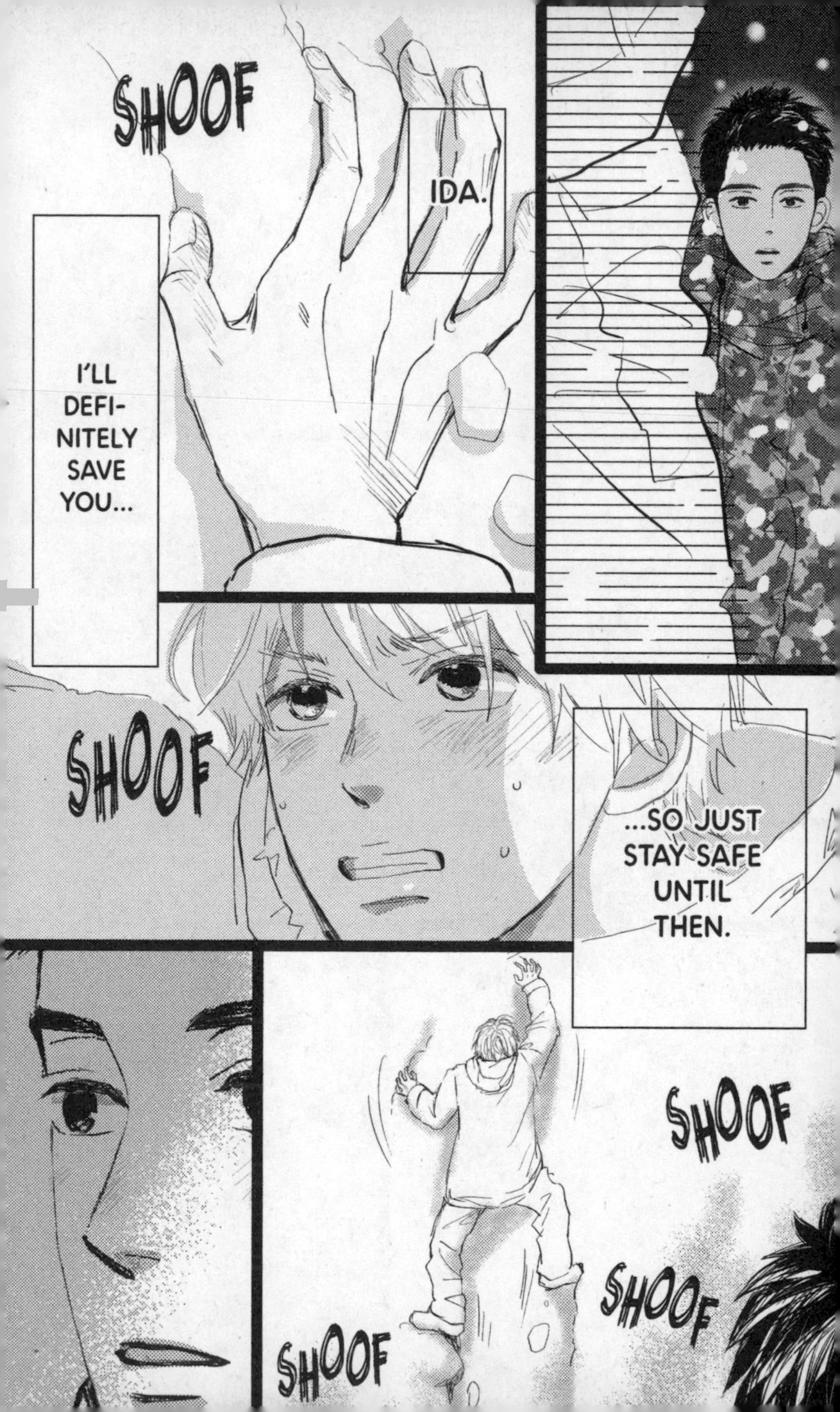
IDA.
SHOOF
I'LL DEFI- NITELY SAVE YOU...
...SO JUST STAY SAFE UNTIL THEN.
SHOOF
SHOOF
SHOOF
SHOOF

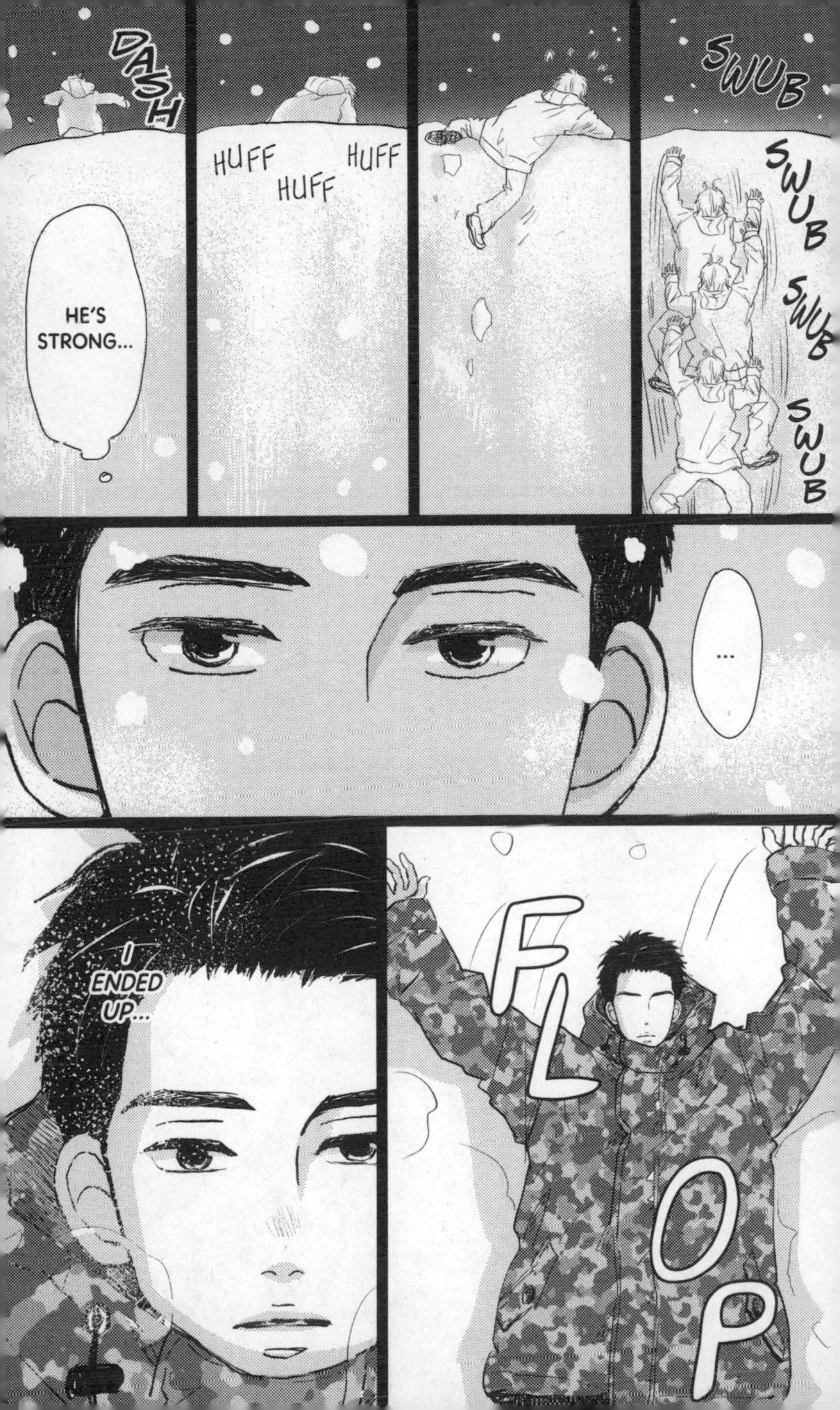
SWUB
SWUB
SWUB
SWUB
HUFF
HUFF
HUFF
DASH
HE'S STRONG...
...
FLOP
I ENDED UP...

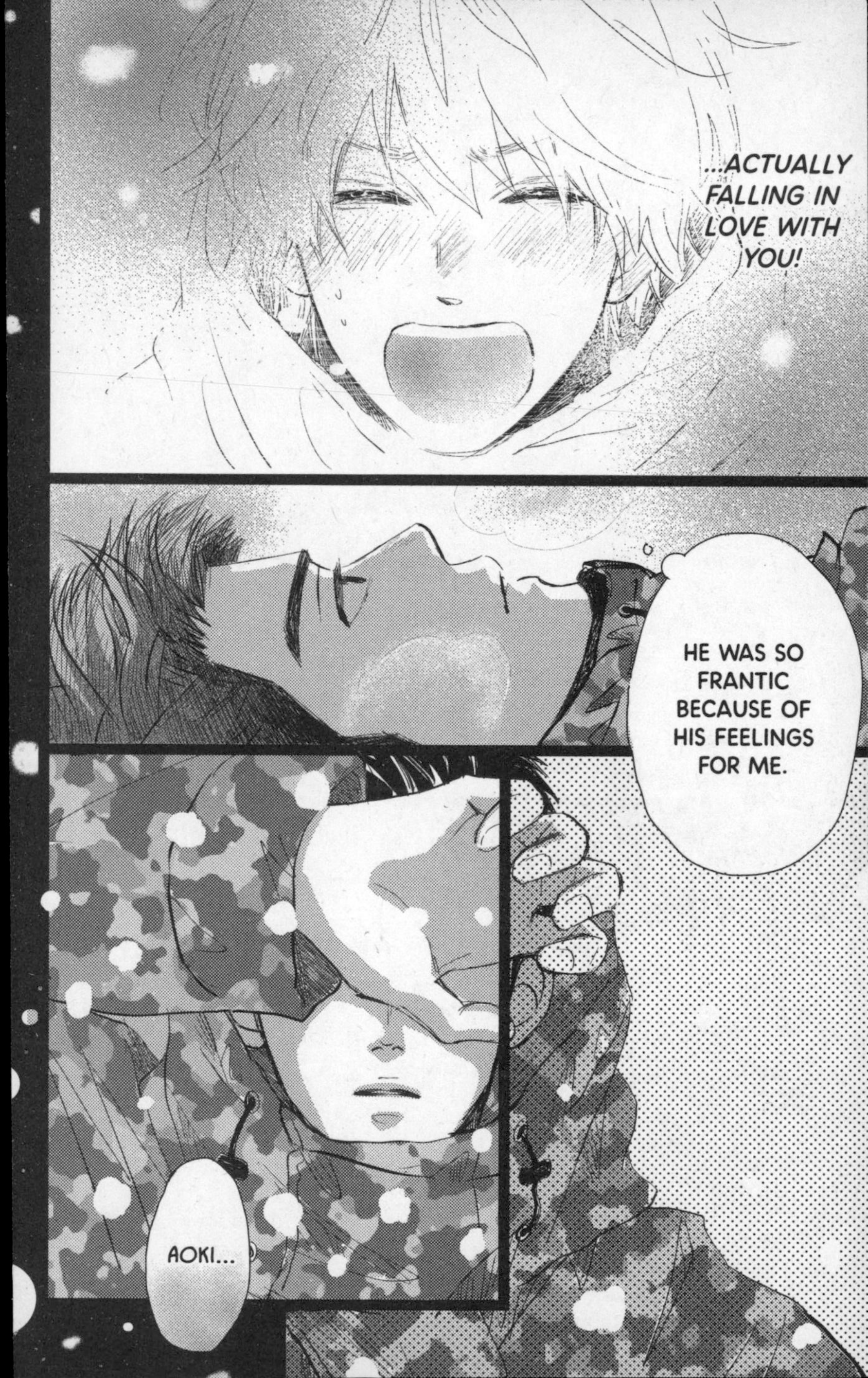
...ACTUALLY FALLING IN LOVE WITH YOU!
HE WAS SO FRANTIC BECAUSE OF HIS FEELINGS FOR ME.
AOKI...

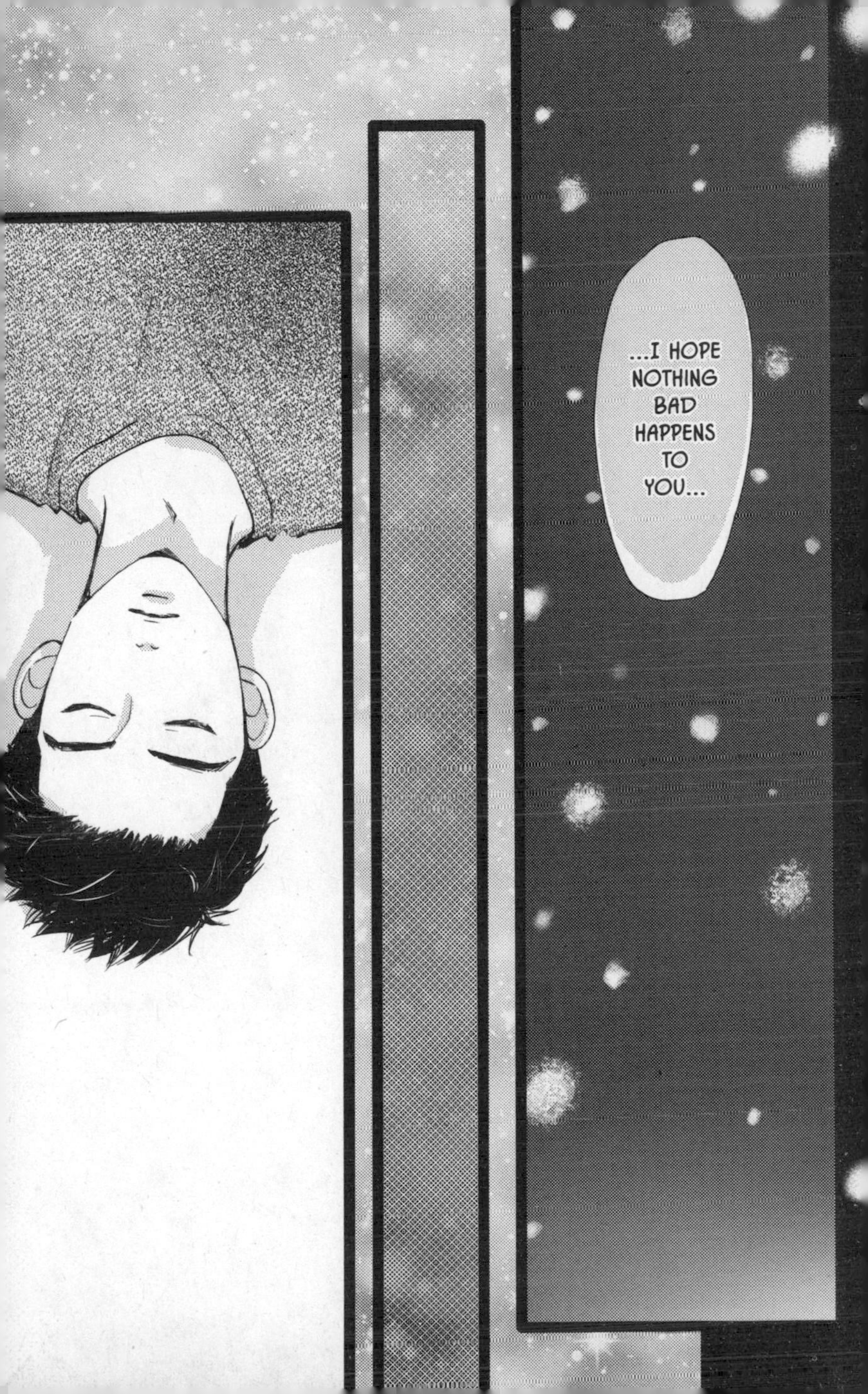
...I HOPE NOTHING BAD HAPPENS TO YOU...

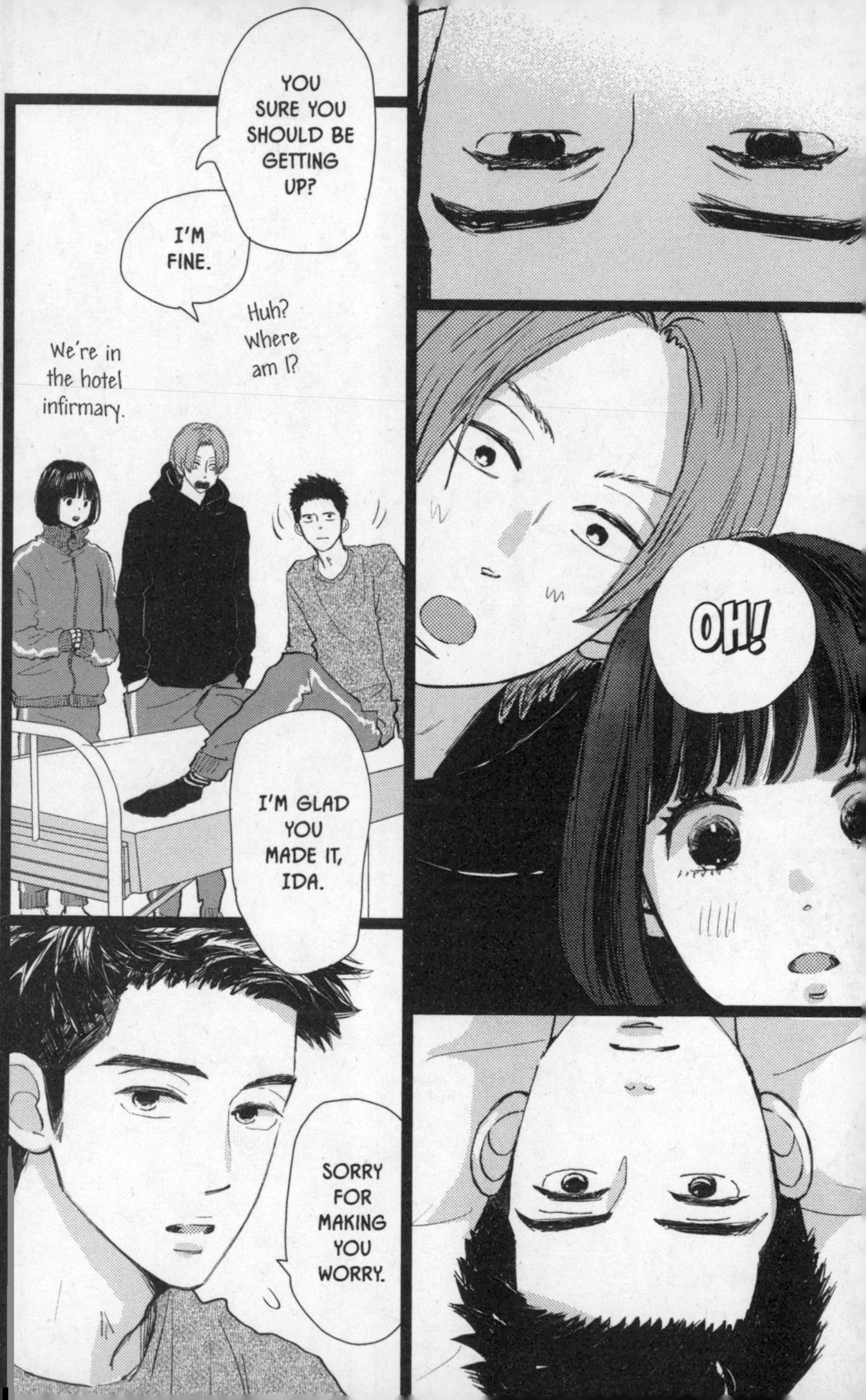
OH!
YOU SURE YOU SHOULD BE GETTING UP?
I'M FINE.
Huh? Where am I?
We're in the hotel infirmary.
I'M GLAD YOU MADE IT, IDA.
SORRY FOR MAKING YOU WORRY.

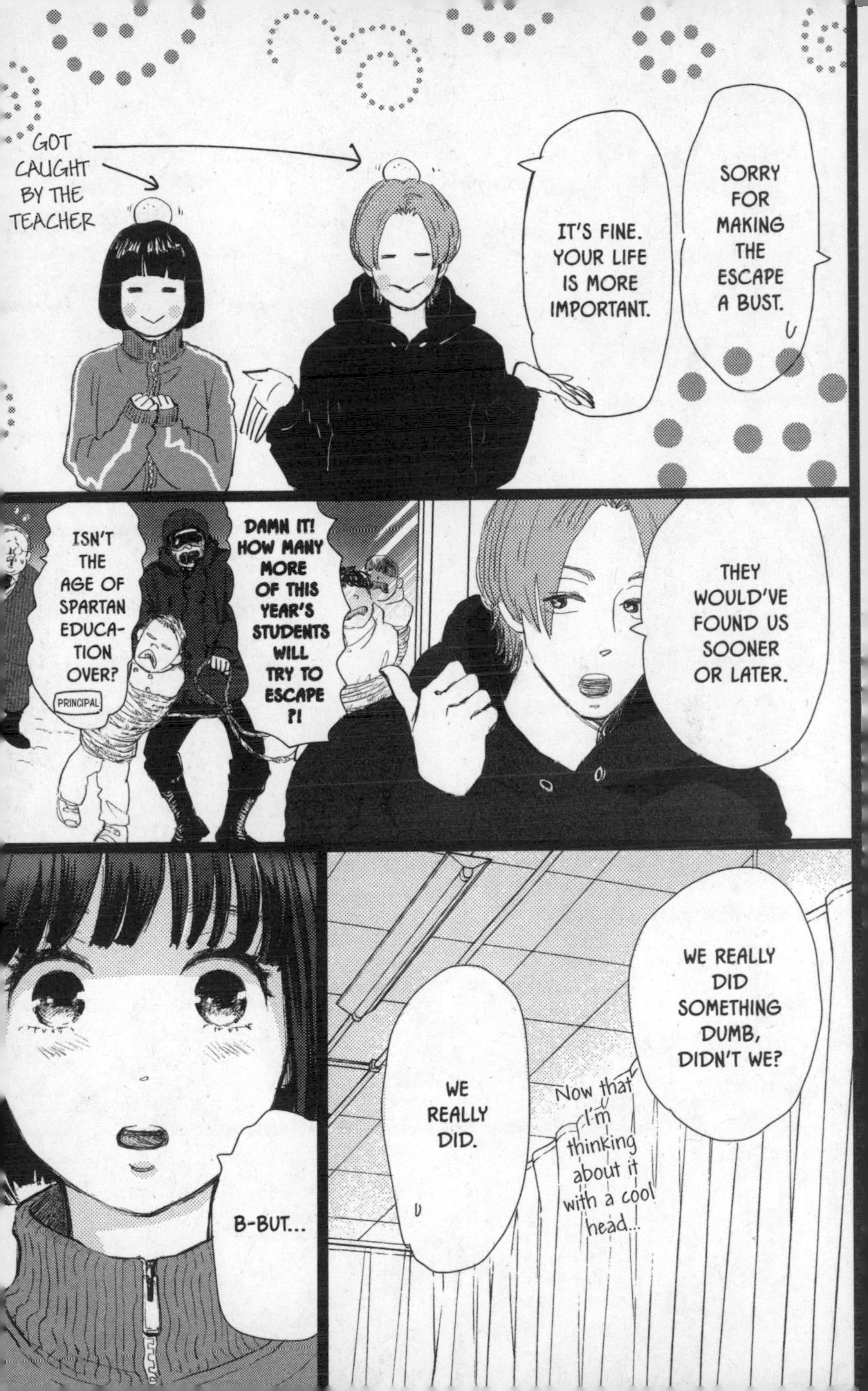
SORRY FOR MAKING THE ESCAPE A BUST.
IT'S FINE. YOUR LIFE IS MORE IMPORTANT.
GOT CAUGHT BY THE TEACHER
THEY WOULD'VE FOUND US SOONER OR LATER.
DAMN IT! HOW MANY MORE OF THIS YEAR'S STUDENTS WILL TRY TO ESCAPE ?!
ISN'T THE AGE OF SPARTAN EDUCATION OVER?
PRINCIPAL
WE REALLY DID SOMETHING DUMB, DIDN'T WE?
Now that I'm thinking about it with a cool head...
WE REALLY DID.
B-BUT...

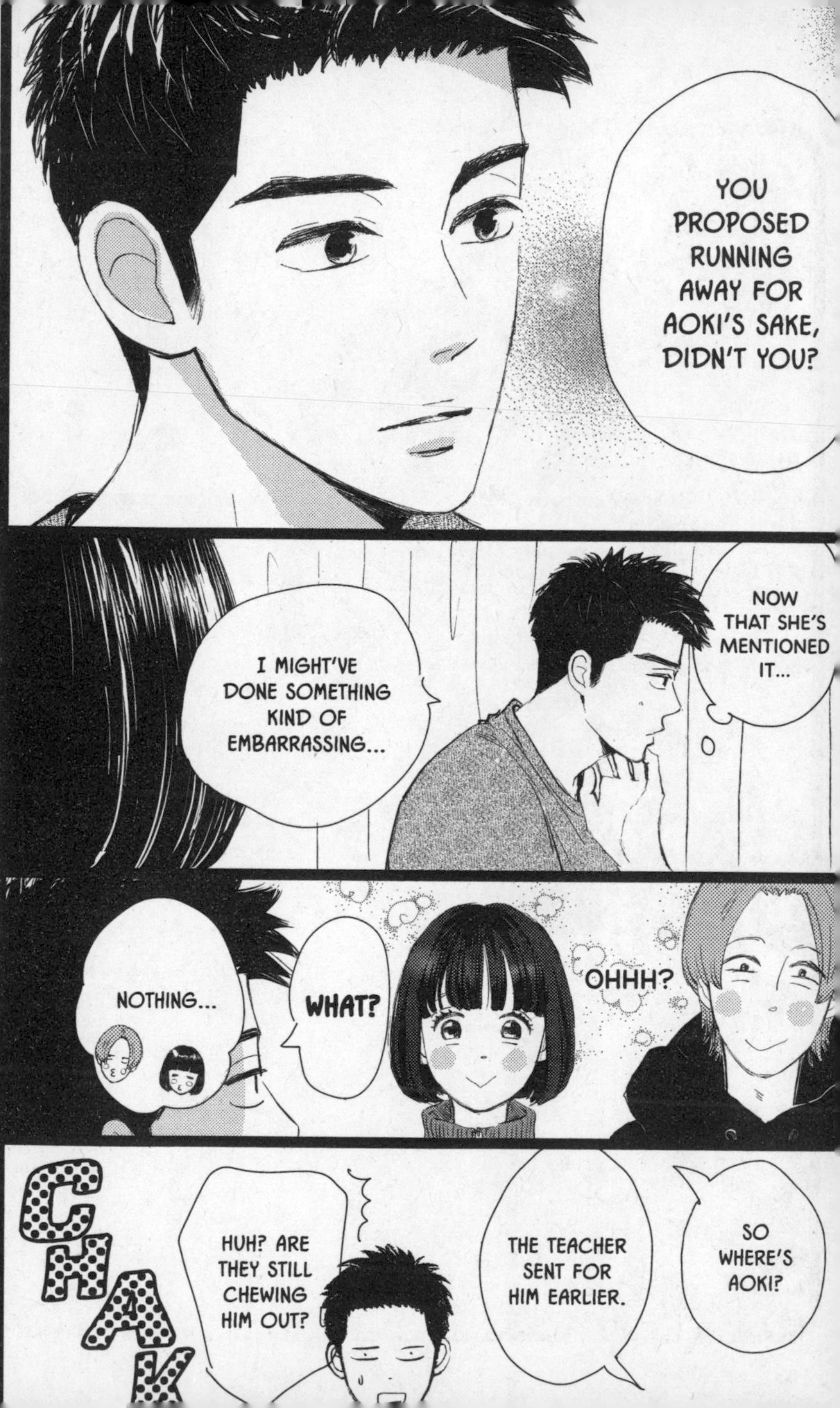
YOU PROPOSED RUNNING AWAY FOR AOKI'S SAKE, DIDN'T YOU?
NOW THAT SHE'S MENTIONED IT...
I MIGHT'VE DONE SOMETHING KIND OF EMBARRASSING...
OHHH?
WHAT?
NOTHING...
SO WHERE'S AOKI?
THE TEACHER SENT FOR HIM EARLIER.
HUH? ARE THEY STILL CHEWING HIM OUT?
CHAK

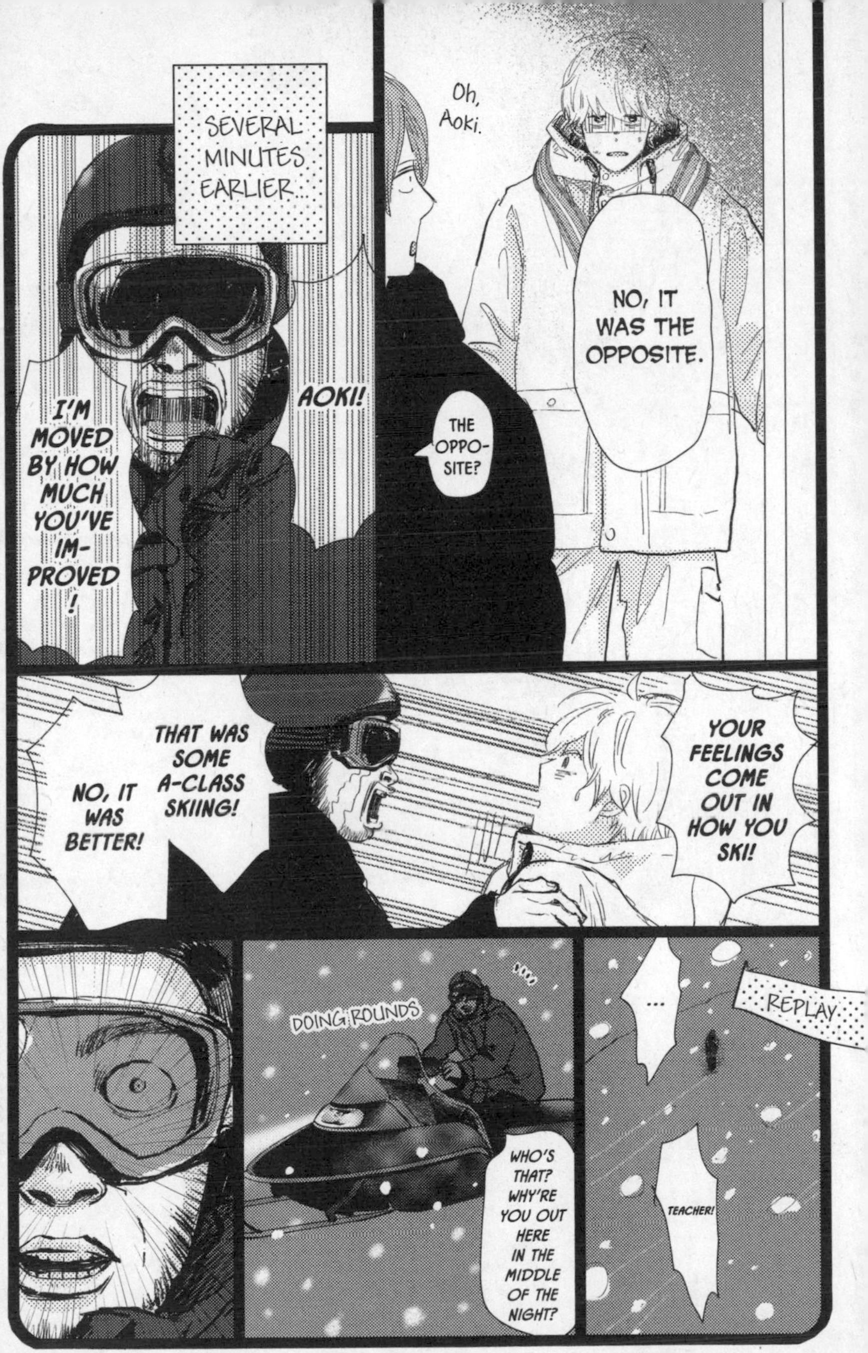
Oh, Aoki.
NO, IT WAS THE OPPOSITE.
THE OPPO-SITE?
SEVERAL MINUTES EARLIER...
AOKI!
I'M MOVED BY HOW MUCH YOU'VE IM-PROVED!
YOUR FEELINGS COME OUT IN HOW YOU SKI!
THAT WAS SOME A-CLASS SKIING!
NO, IT WAS BETTER!
REPLAY
...
TEACHER!
DOING ROUNDS
WHO'S THAT? WHY'RE YOU OUT HERE IN THE MIDDLE OF THE NIGHT?

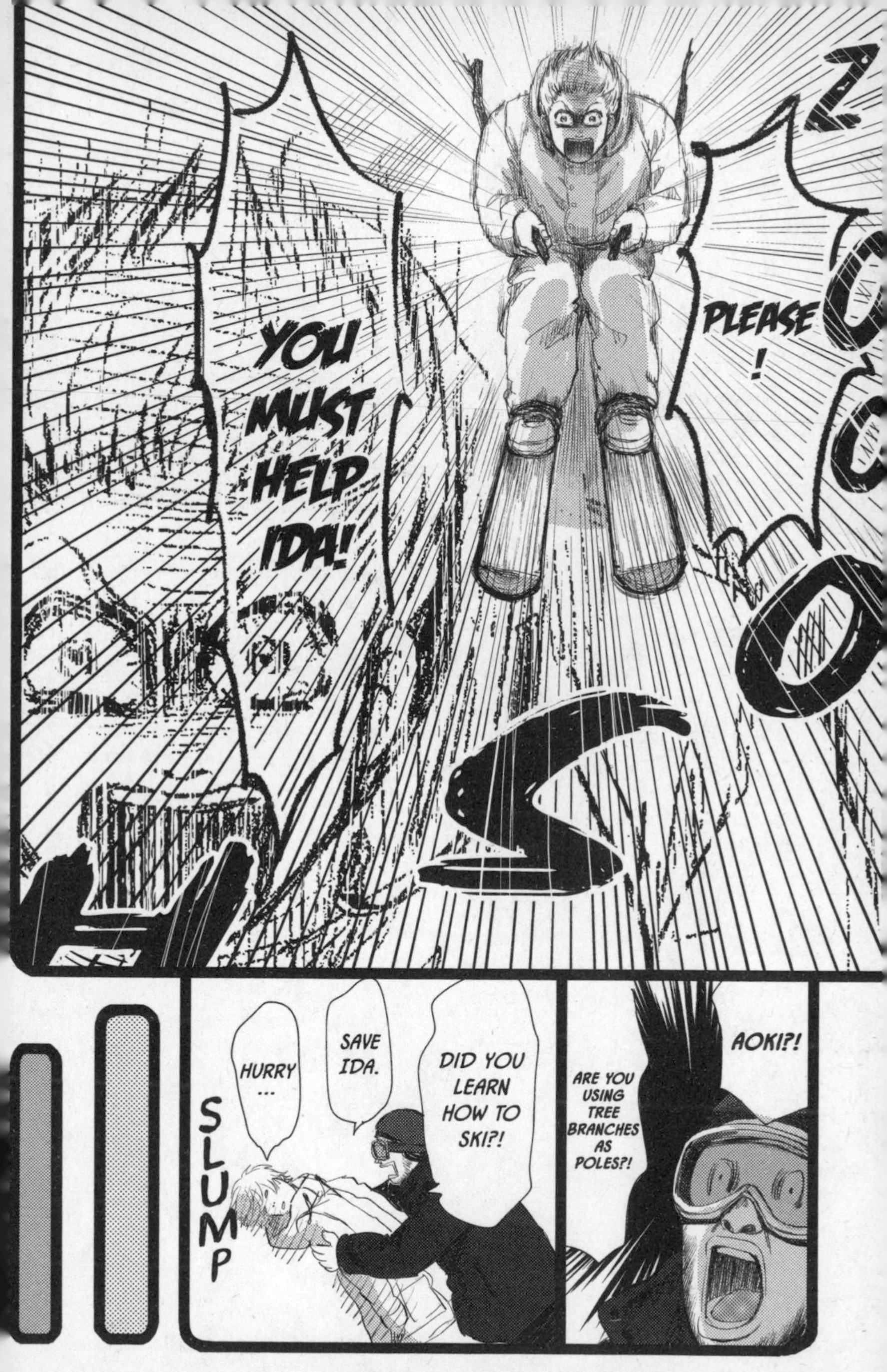
ZOOO
PLEASE!
YOU MUST HELP IDA!
AOKI?!
ARE YOU USING TREE BRANCHES AS POLES?!
DID YOU LEARN HOW TO SKI?!
SAVE IDA.
HURRY...
SLUMP

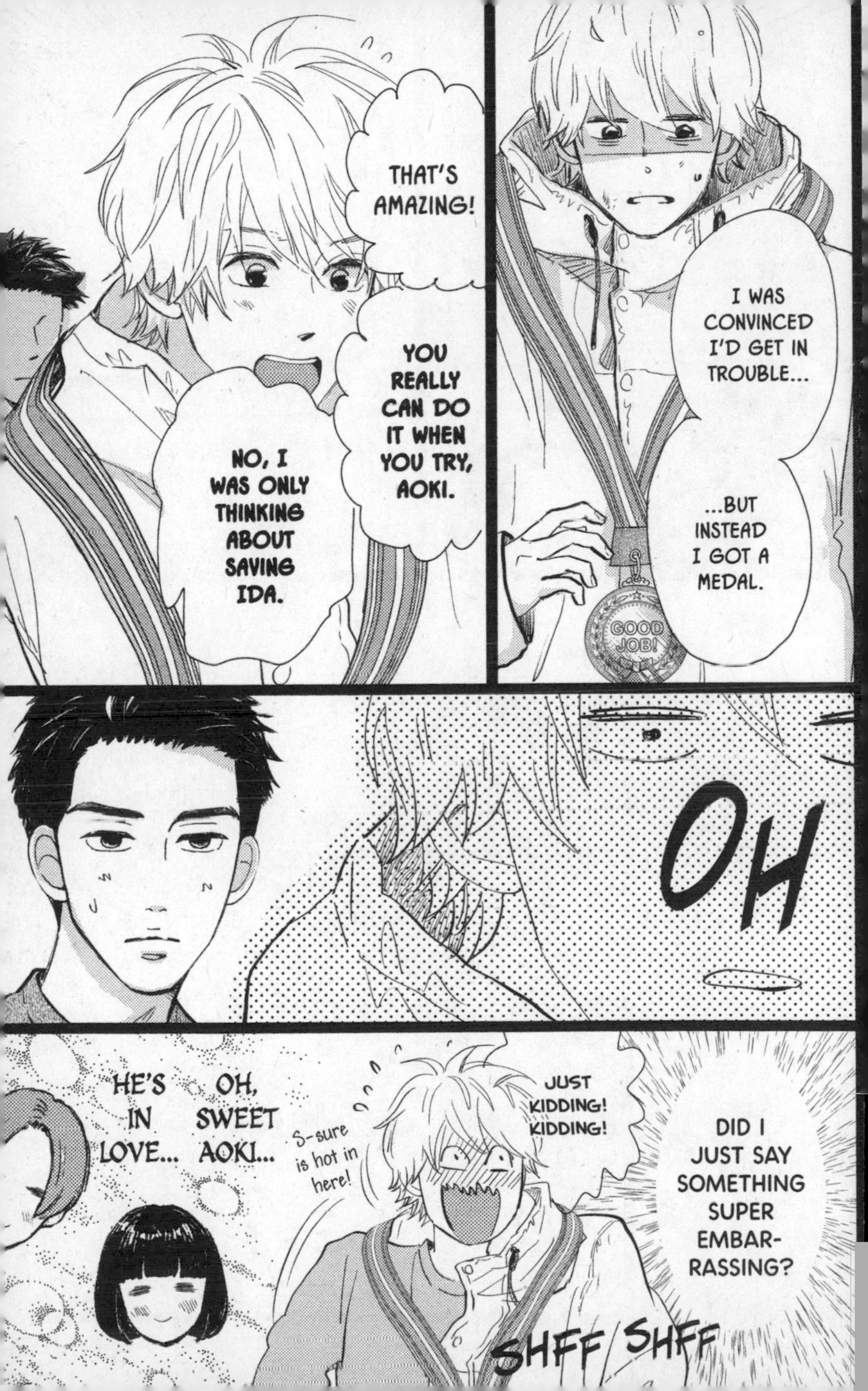
I WAS CONVINCED I'D GET IN TROUBLE...
...BUT INSTEAD I GOT A MEDAL.
GOOD JOB!
THAT'S AMAZING!
YOU REALLY CAN DO IT WHEN YOU TRY, AOKI.
NO, I WAS ONLY THINKING ABOUT SAVING IDA.
OH
DID I JUST SAY SOMETHING SUPER EMBAR-RASSING?
JUST KIDDING! KIDDING!
S-sure is hot in here!
OH, SWEET AOKI...
HE'S IN LOVE...
SHFF SHFF

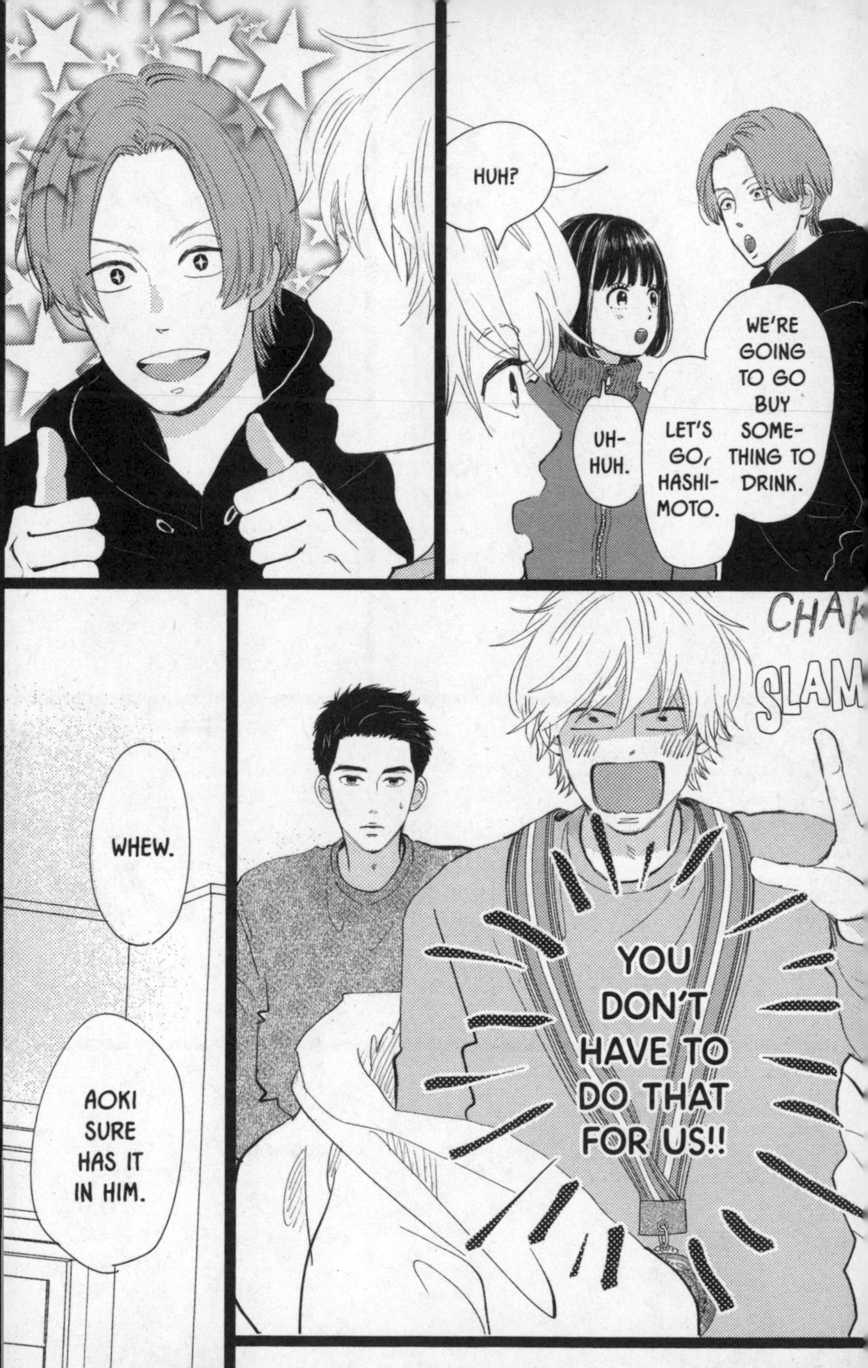
HUH?
WE'RE GOING TO GO BUY SOME-THING TO DRINK.
LET'S GO, HASHI-MOTO.
UH-HUH.
CHA
SLAM
YOU DON'T HAVE TO DO THAT FOR US!!
WHEW.
AOKI SURE HAS IT IN HIM.

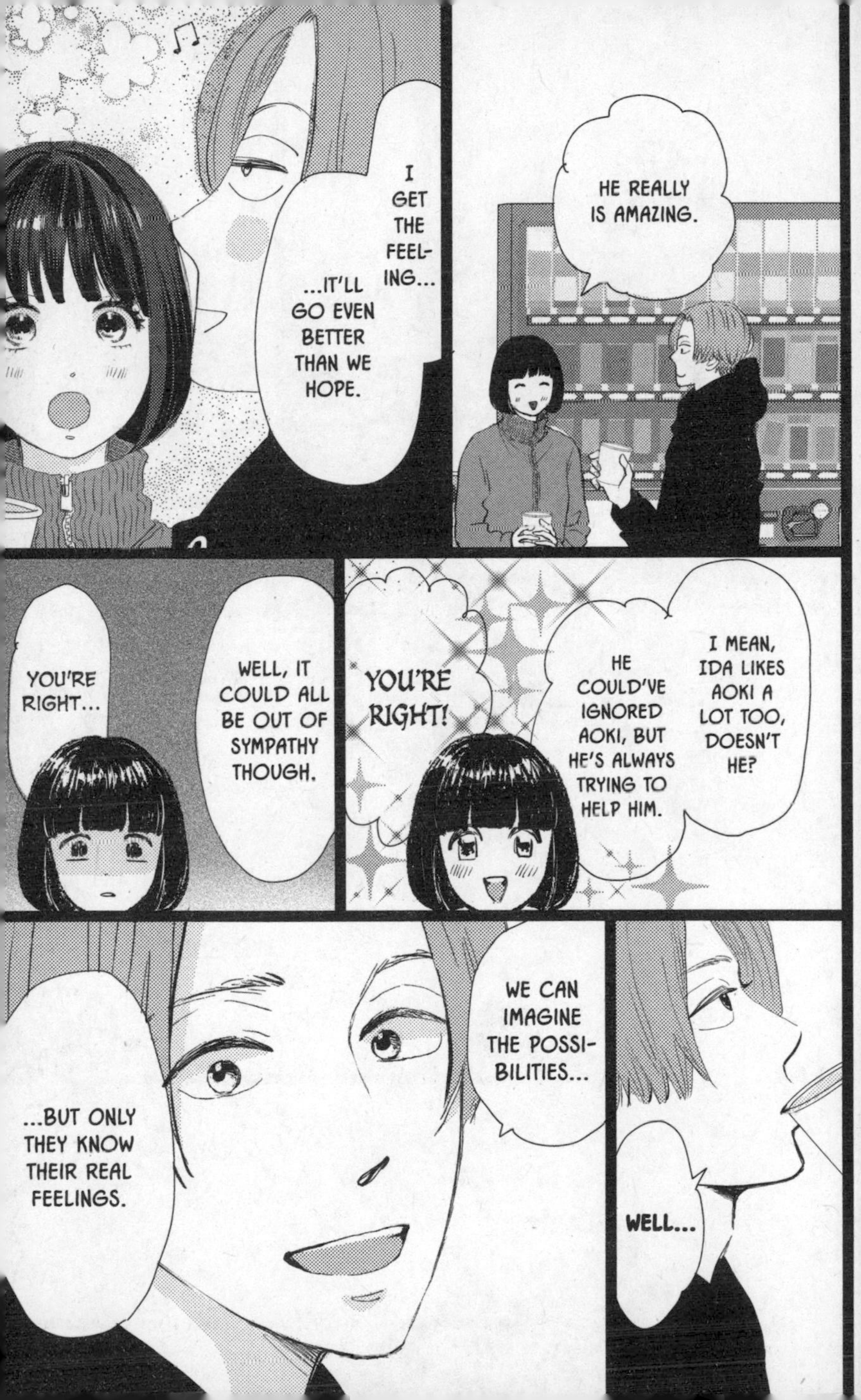
HE REALLY IS AMAZING.
I GET THE FEEL-ING...
...IT'LL GO EVEN BETTER THAN WE HOPE.
I MEAN, IDA LIKES AOKI A LOT TOO, DOESN'T HE?
HE COULD'VE IGNORED AOKI, BUT HE'S ALWAYS TRYING TO HELP HIM.
YOU'RE RIGHT!
WELL, IT COULD ALL BE OUT OF SYMPATHY THOUGH.
YOU'RE RIGHT...
WELL...
WE CAN IMAGINE THE POSSI-BILITIES...
...BUT ONLY THEY KNOW THEIR REAL FEELINGS.

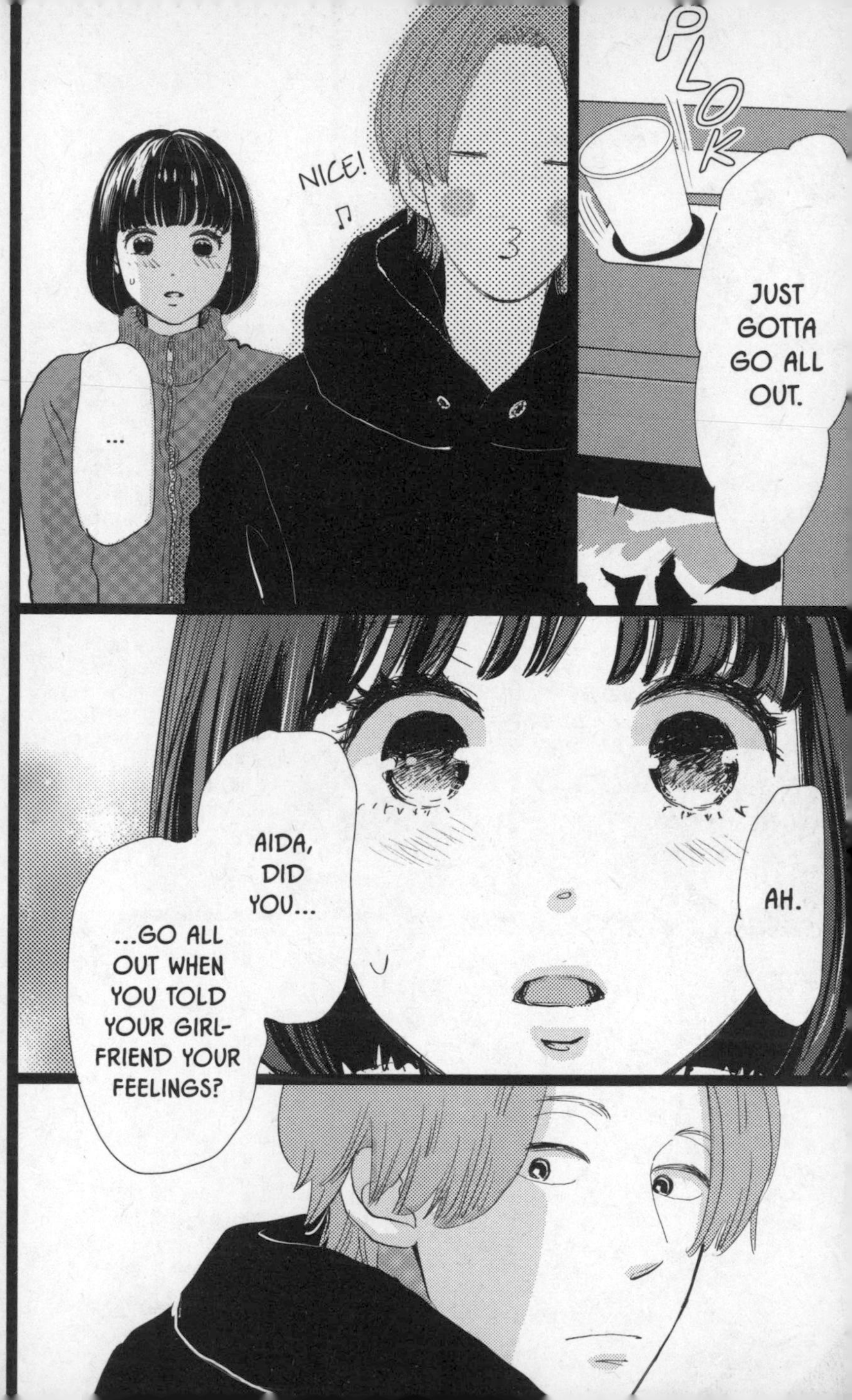
PLOK
JUST GOTTA GO ALL OUT.
NICE! ♫
...
AH.
AIDA, DID YOU...
...GO ALL OUT WHEN YOU TOLD YOUR GIRL-FRIEND YOUR FEELINGS?

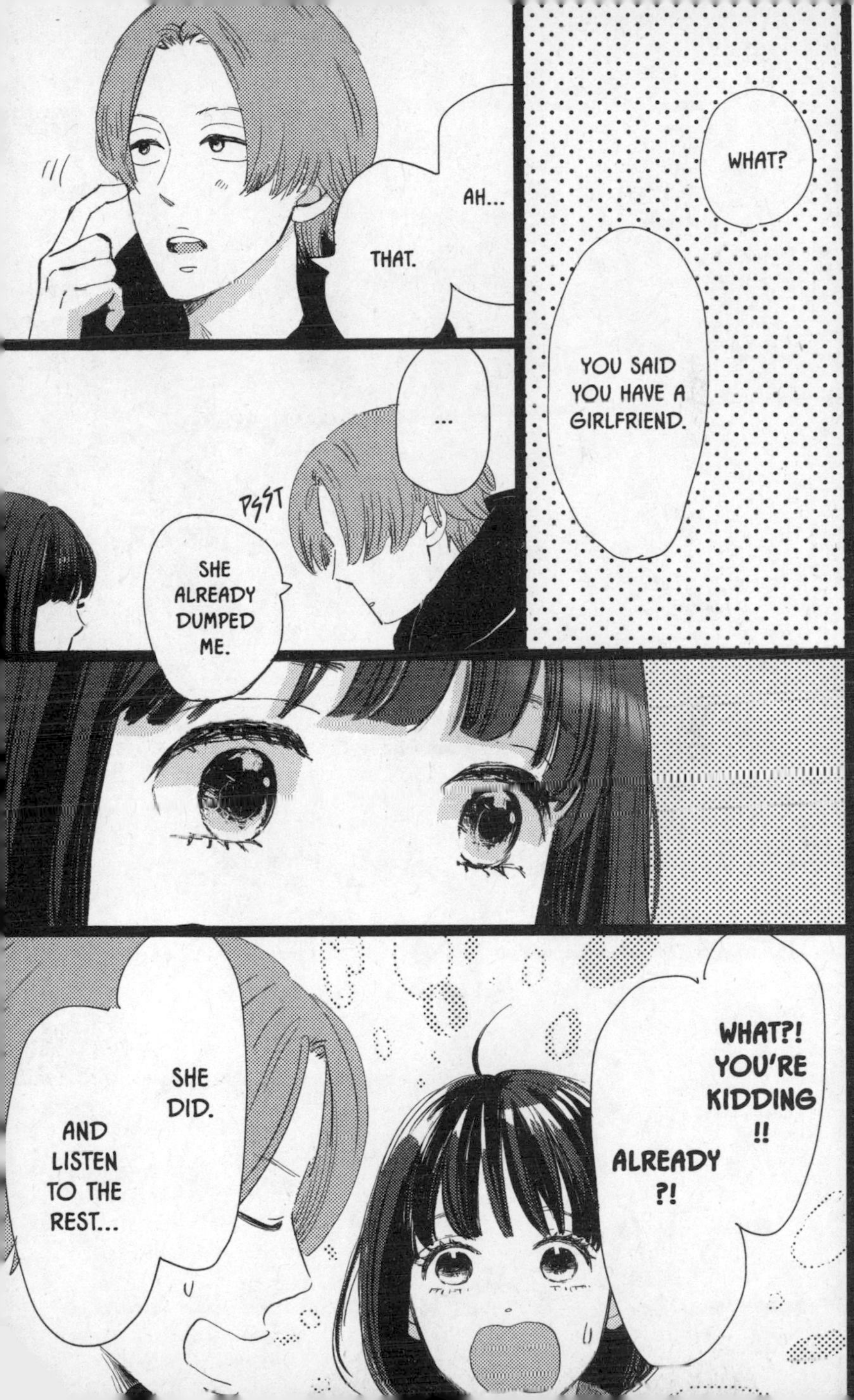
WHAT?
YOU SAID YOU HAVE A GIRLFRIEND.
AH...
THAT.
...
PSST
SHE ALREADY DUMPED ME.
WHAT?! YOU'RE KIDDING!!
ALREADY?!
SHE DID.
AND LISTEN TO THE REST...

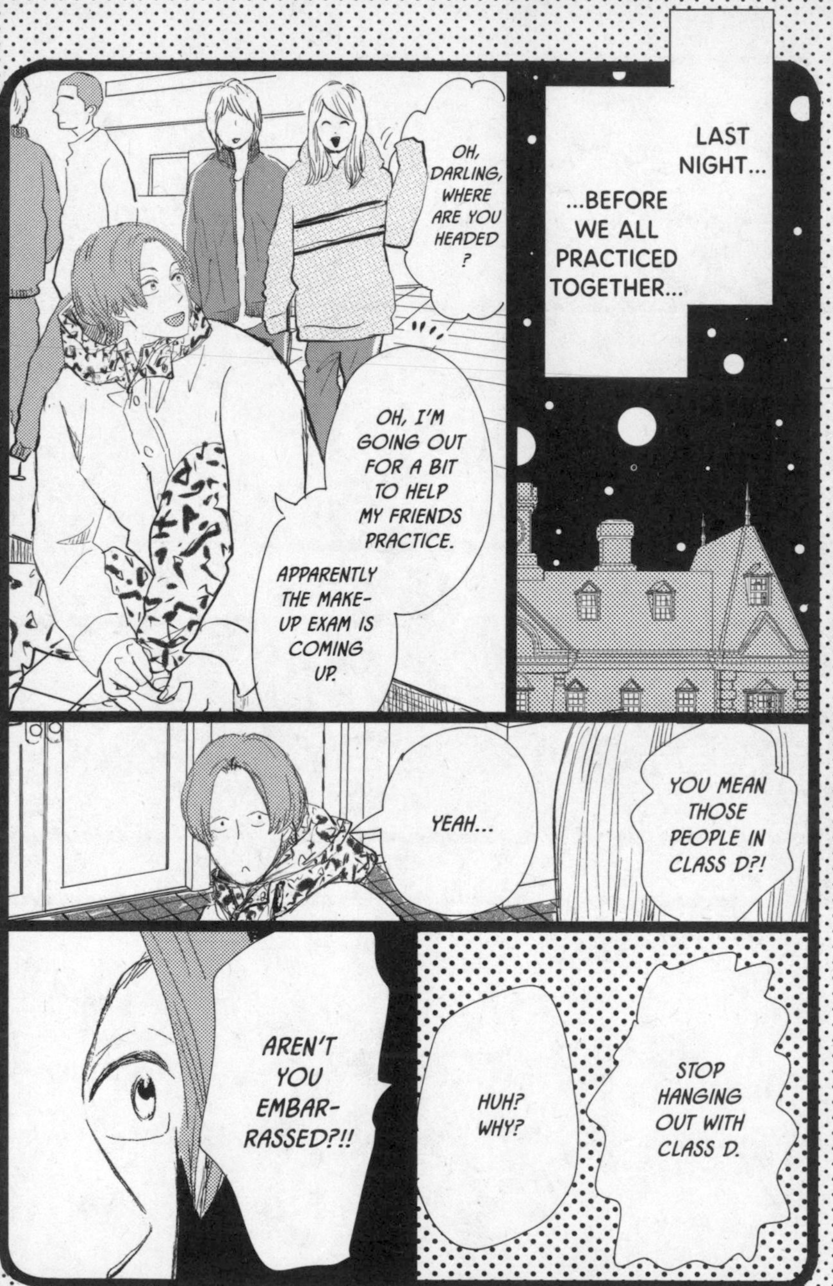
LAST NIGHT...
...BEFORE WE ALL PRACTICED TOGETHER...
OH, DARLING, WHERE ARE YOU HEADED?
OH, I'M GOING OUT FOR A BIT TO HELP MY FRIENDS PRACTICE.
APPARENTLY THE MAKE-UP EXAM IS COMING UP.
YOU MEAN THOSE PEOPLE IN CLASS D?!
YEAH...
STOP HANGING OUT WITH CLASS D.
HUH? WHY?
AREN'T YOU EMBAR-RASSED?!!

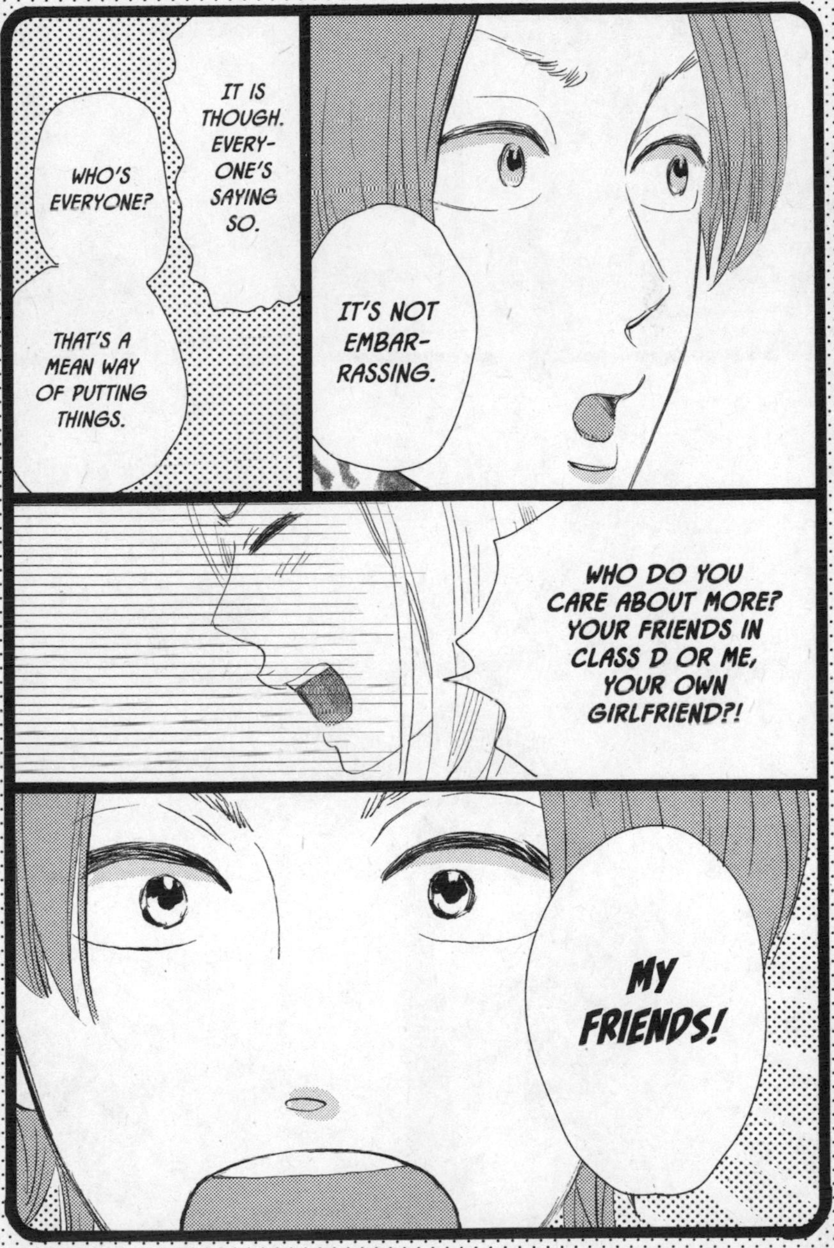
IT'S NOT EMBAR-RASSING.
IT IS THOUGH. EVERY-ONE'S SAYING SO.
WHO'S EVERYONE?
THAT'S A MEAN WAY OF PUTTING THINGS.
WHO DO YOU CARE ABOUT MORE? YOUR FRIENDS IN CLASS D OR ME, YOUR OWN GIRLFRIEND?!
MY FRIENDS!

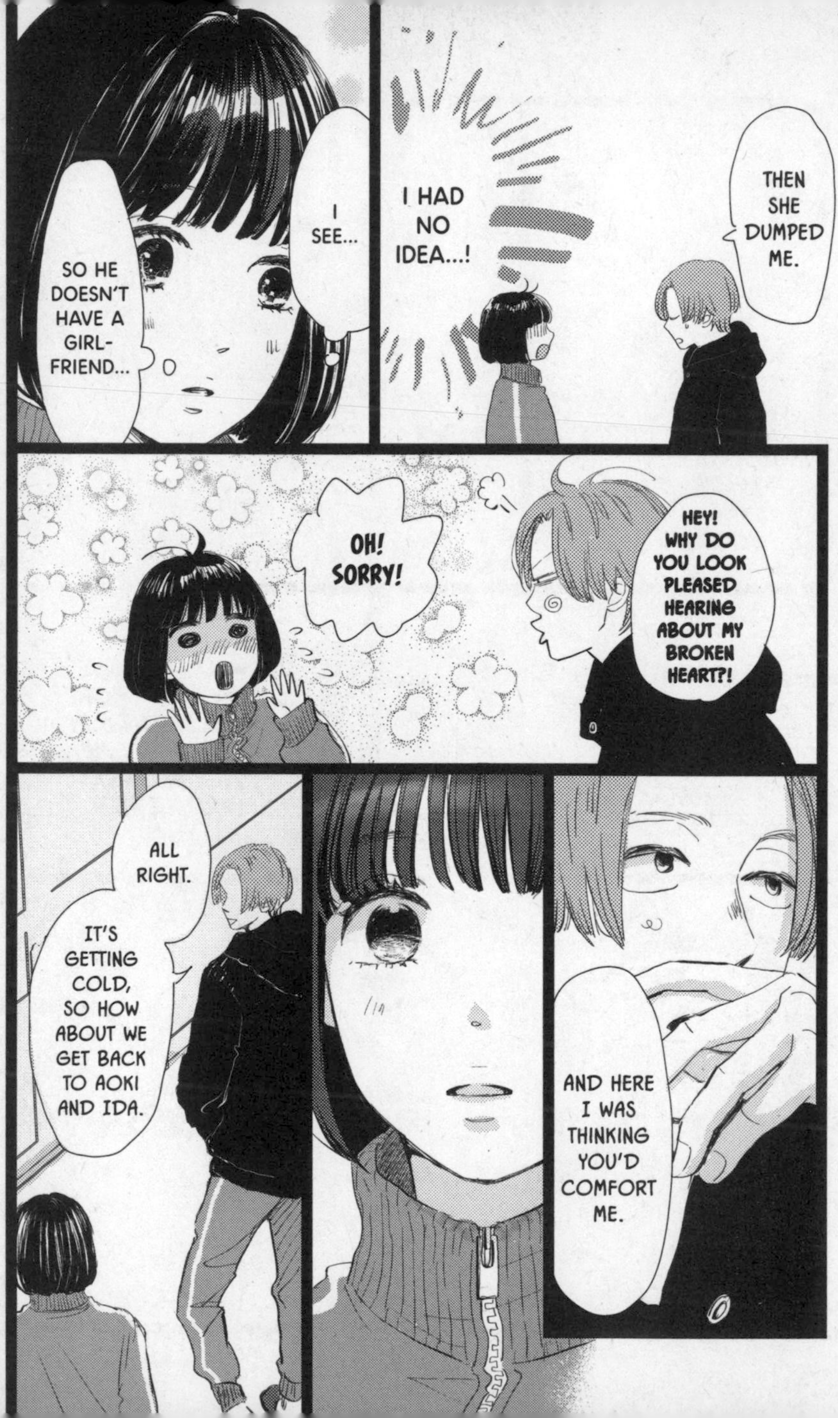
THEN SHE DUMPED ME.
I HAD NO IDEA...!
I SEE...
SO HE DOESN'T HAVE A GIRL-FRIEND...
HEY! WHY DO YOU LOOK PLEASED HEARING ABOUT MY BROKEN HEART?!
OH! SORRY!
AND HERE I WAS THINKING YOU'D COMFORT ME.
ALL RIGHT.
IT'S GETTING COLD, SO HOW ABOUT WE GET BACK TO AOKI AND IDA.

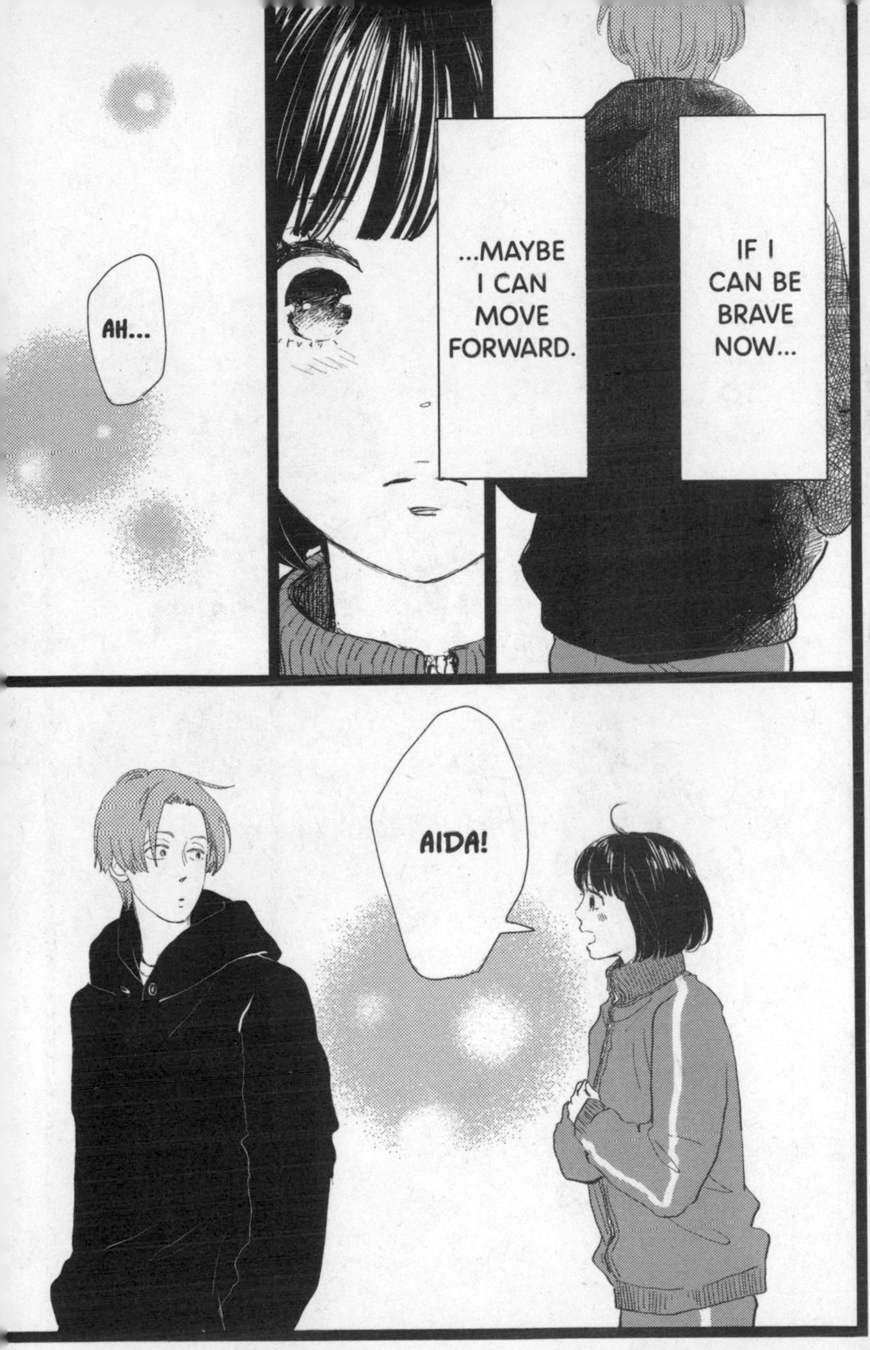
IF I CAN BE BRAVE NOW...
...MAYBE I CAN MOVE FORWARD.
AH...
AIDA!

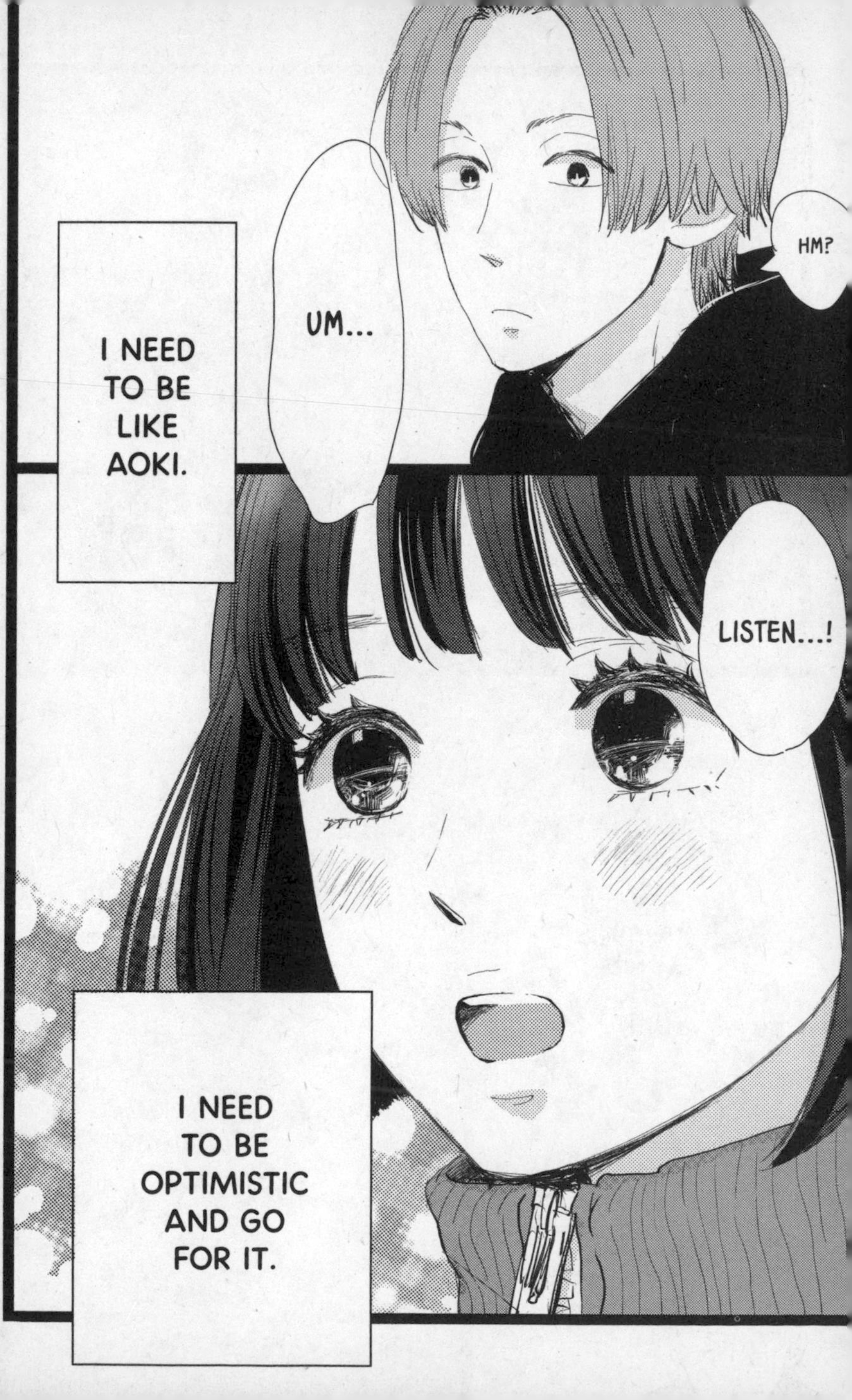
HM?
UM...
I NEED TO BE LIKE AOKI.
LISTEN...!
I NEED TO BE OPTIMISTIC AND GO FOR IT.

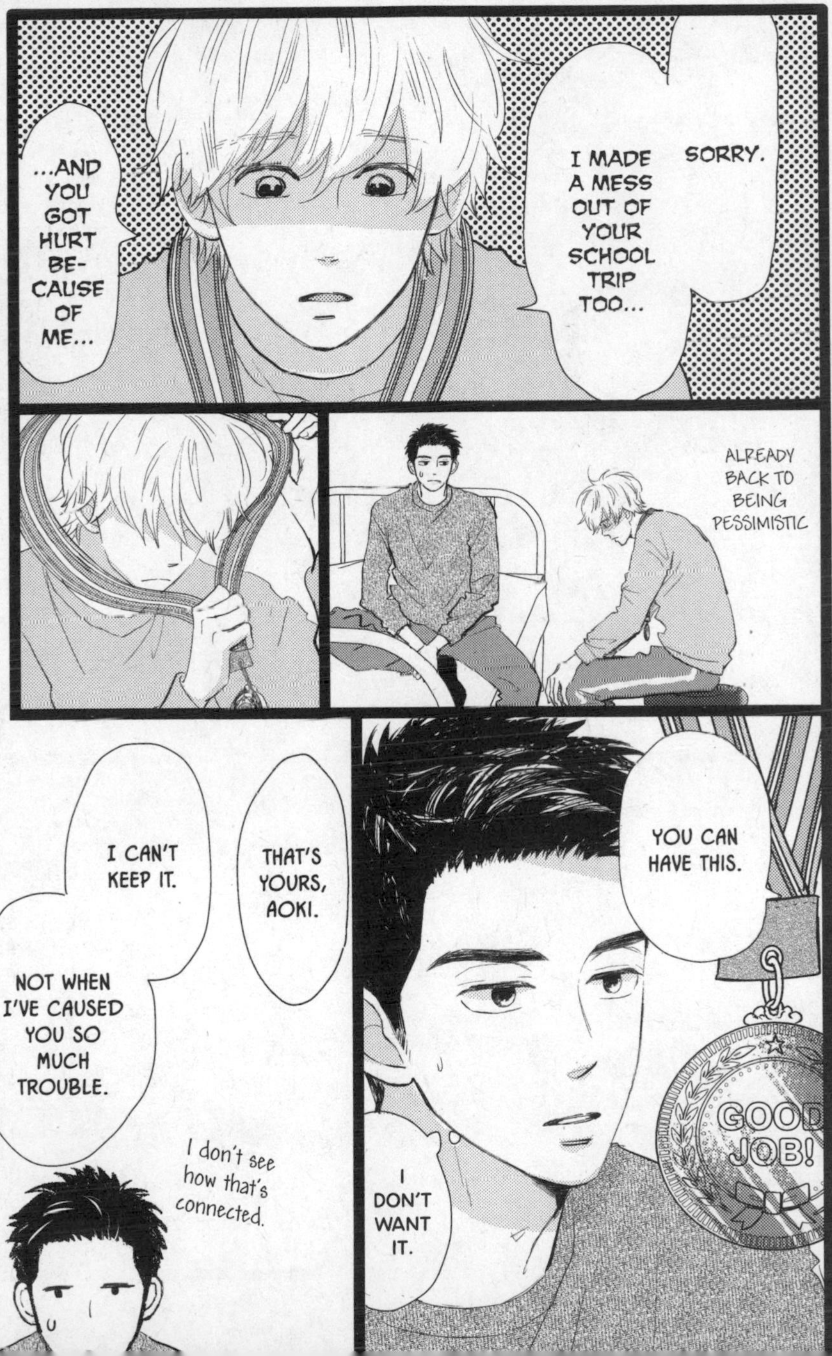
SORRY.
I MADE A MESS OUT OF YOUR SCHOOL TRIP TOO...
...AND YOU GOT HURT BE-CAUSE OF ME...
ALREADY BACK TO BEING PESSIMISTIC
YOU CAN HAVE THIS.
GOOD JOB!
I DON'T WANT IT.
THAT'S YOURS, AOKI.
I CAN'T KEEP IT.
NOT WHEN I'VE CAUSED YOU SO MUCH TROUBLE.
I don't see how that's connected.

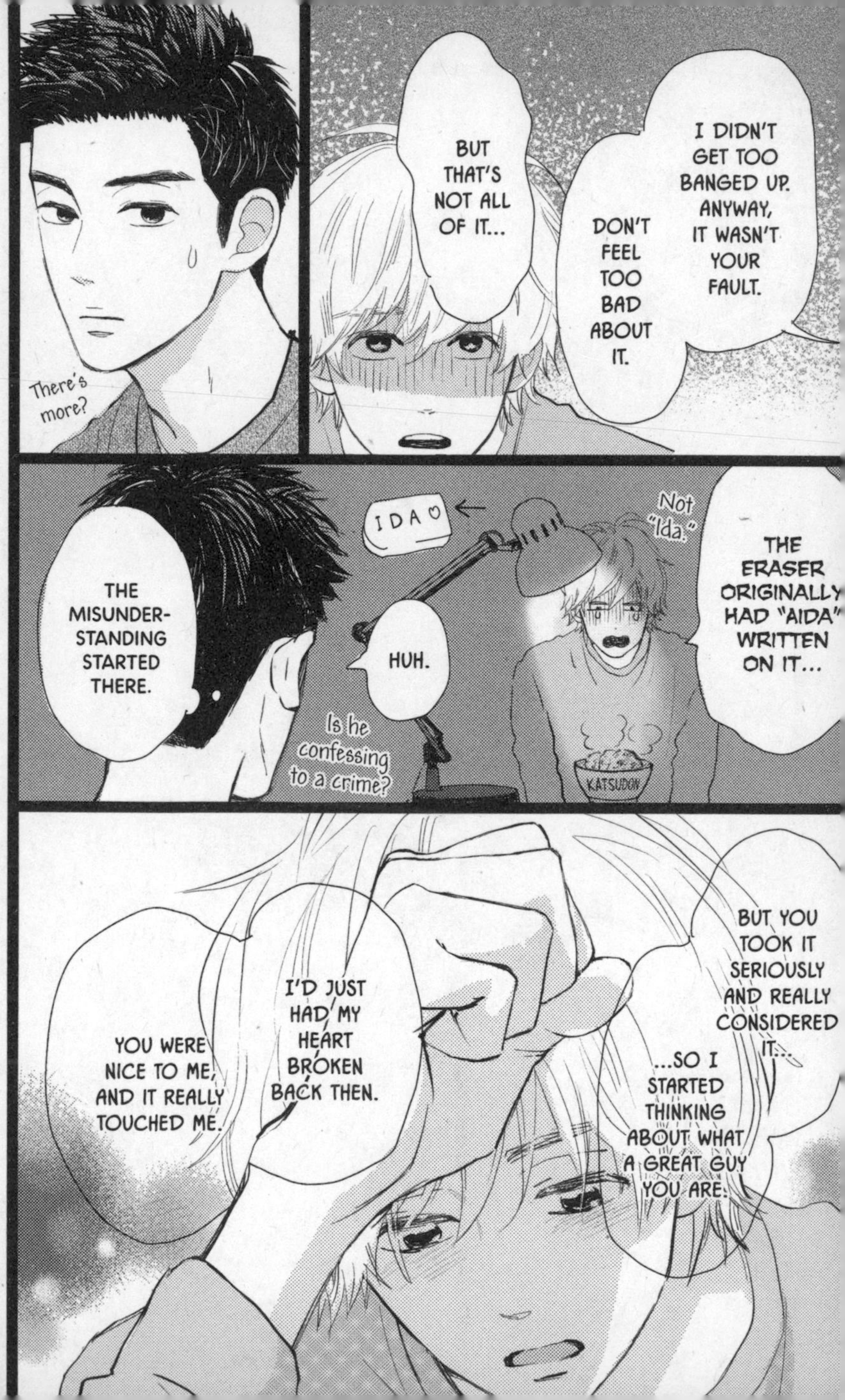
I DIDN'T GET TOO BANGED UP. ANYWAY, IT WASN'T YOUR FAULT.
DON'T FEEL TOO BAD ABOUT IT.
BUT THAT'S NOT ALL OF IT...
There's more?
THE ERASER ORIGINALLY HAD "AIDA" WRITTEN ON IT...
Not "Ida."
IDA
KATSUDON
HUH.
Is he confessing to a crime?
THE MISUNDER-STANDING STARTED THERE.
BUT YOU TOOK IT SERIOUSLY AND REALLY CONSIDERED IT...
...SO I STARTED THINKING ABOUT WHAT A GREAT GUY YOU ARE.
I'D JUST HAD MY HEART BROKEN BACK THEN.
YOU WERE NICE TO ME, AND IT REALLY TOUCHED ME.

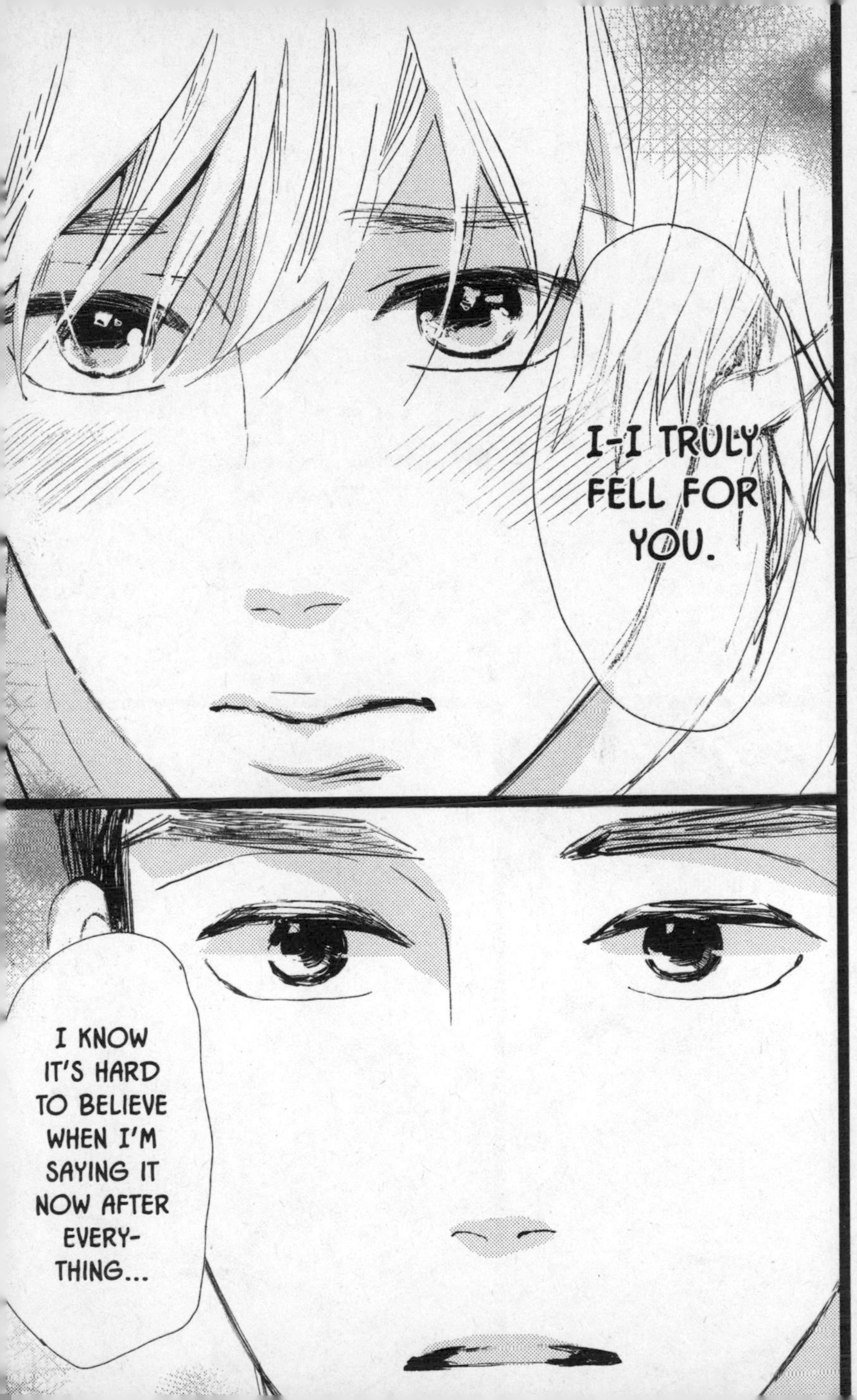
I-I TRULY FELL FOR YOU.
I KNOW IT'S HARD TO BELIEVE WHEN I'M SAYING IT NOW AFTER EVERY-THING...

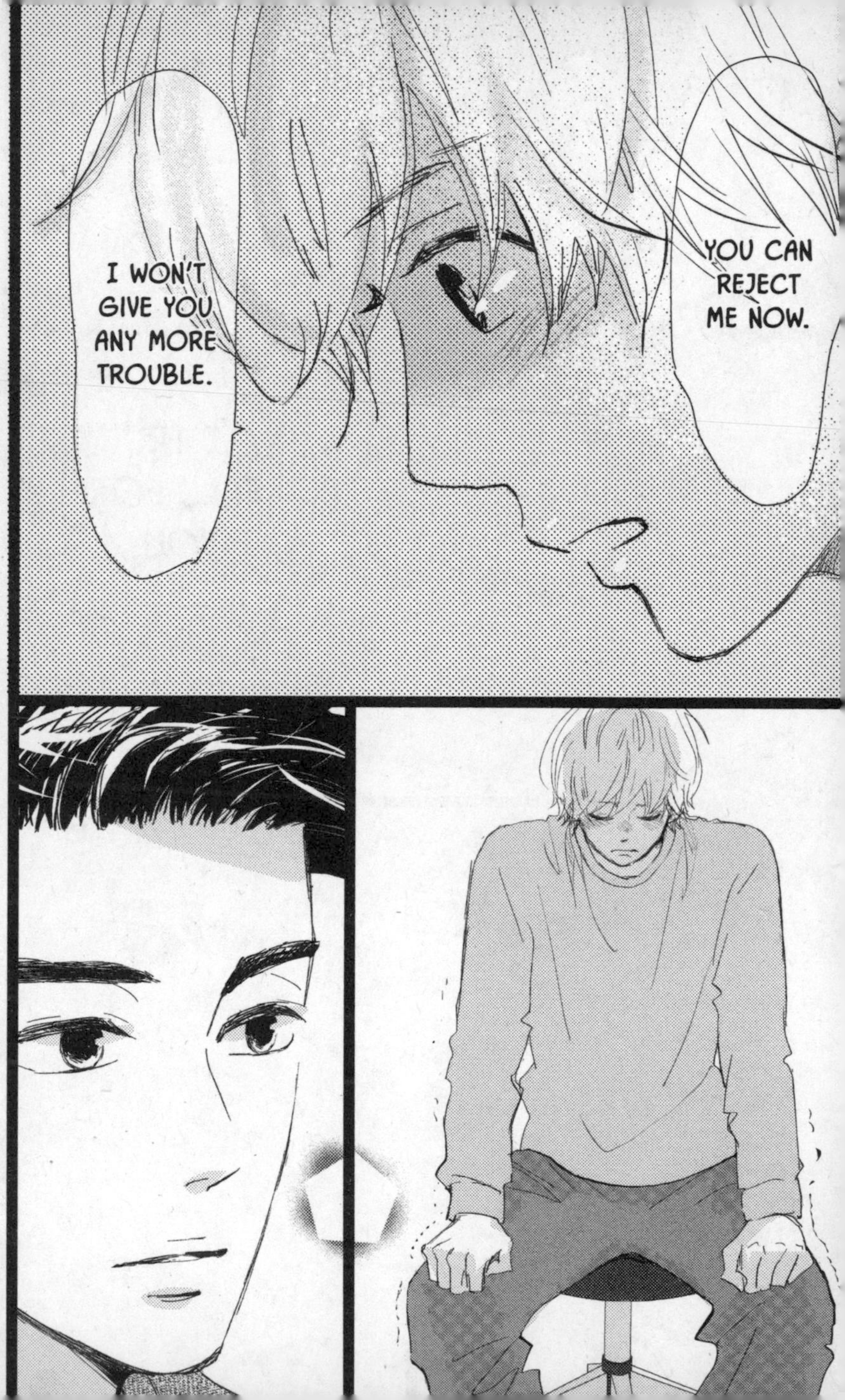
YOU CAN REJECT ME NOW.
I WON'T GIVE YOU ANY MORE TROUBLE.

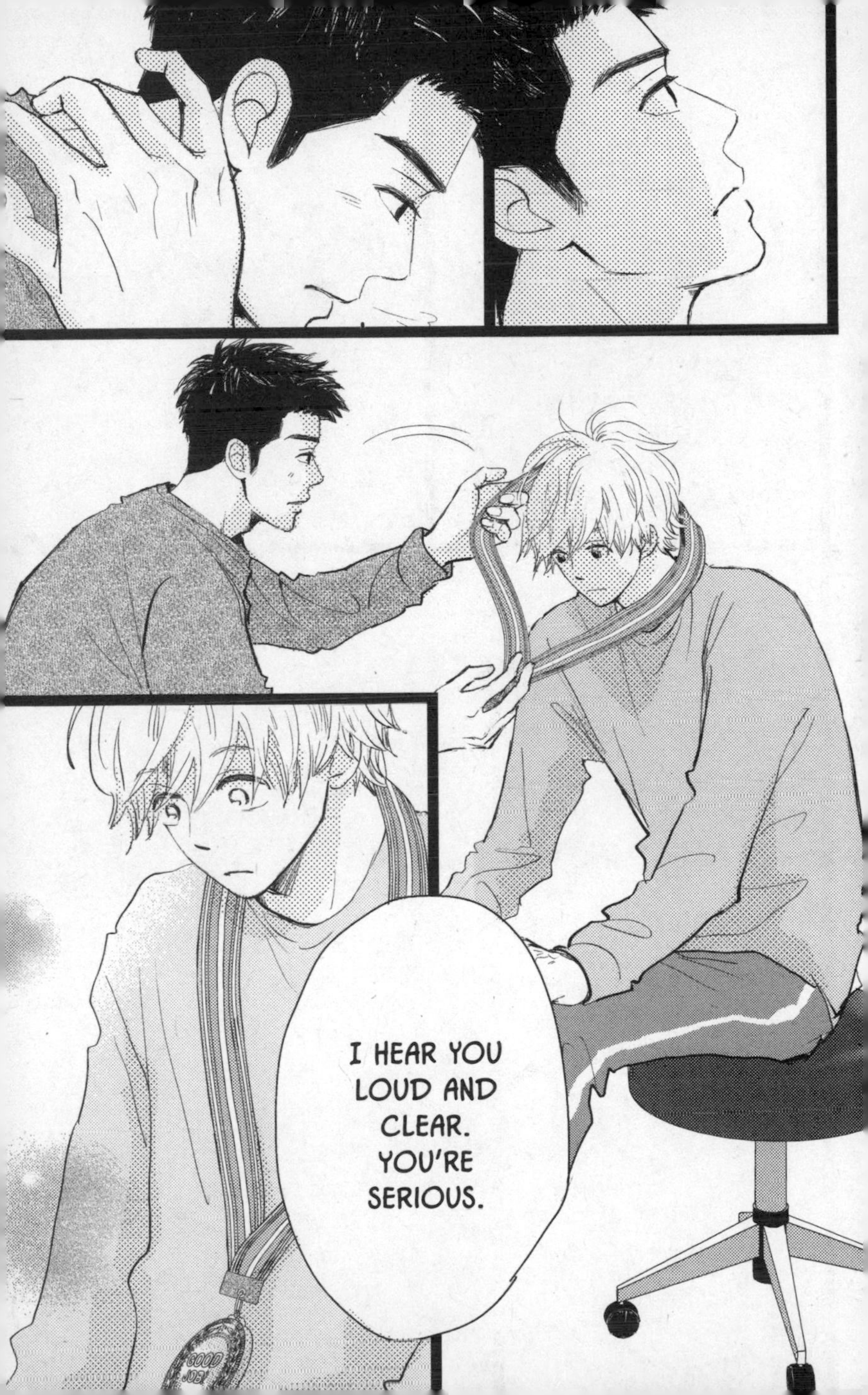
I HEAR YOU LOUD AND CLEAR. YOU'RE SERIOUS.
GOOD JOB!

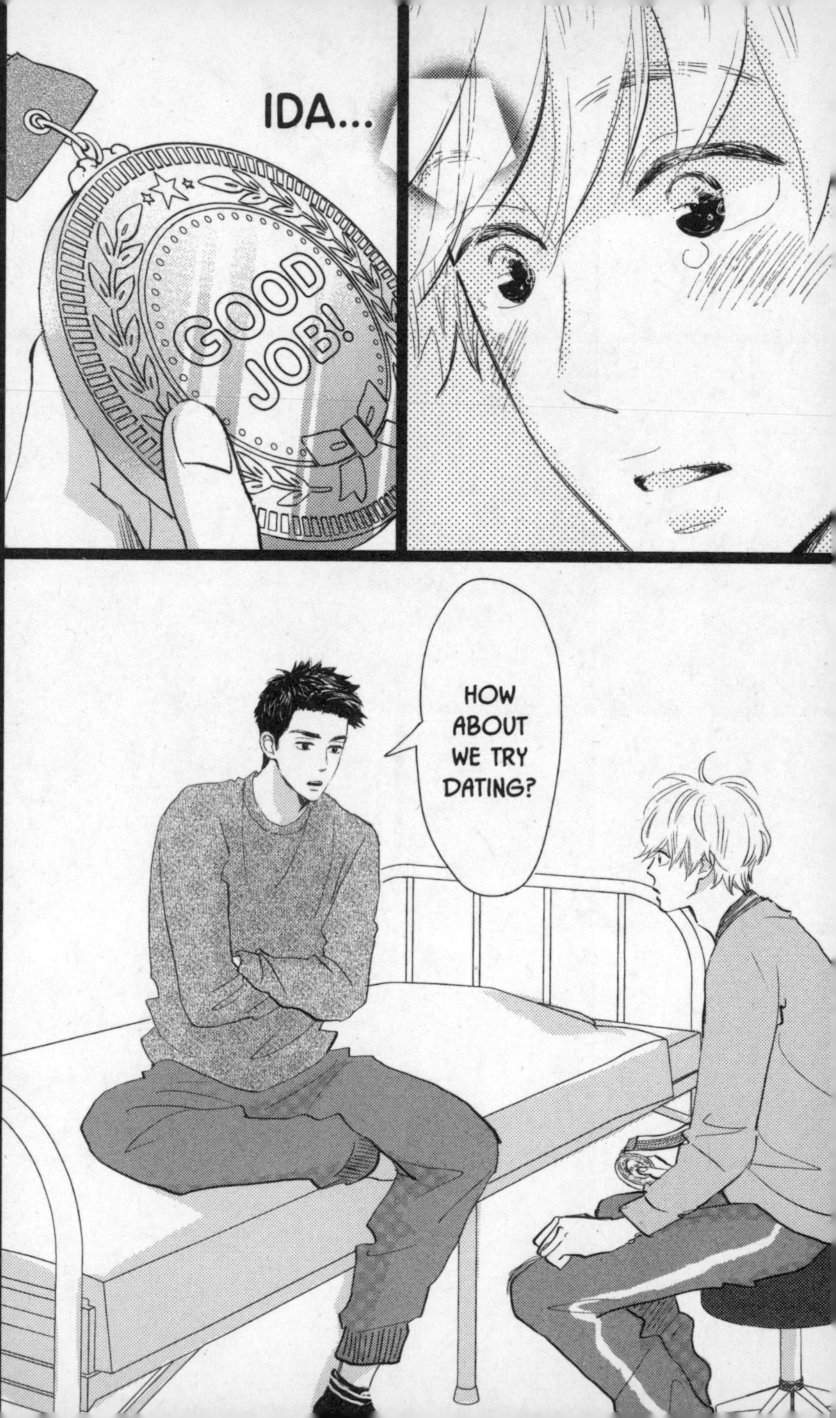
IDA...
GOOD JOB!
HOW ABOUT WE TRY DATING?

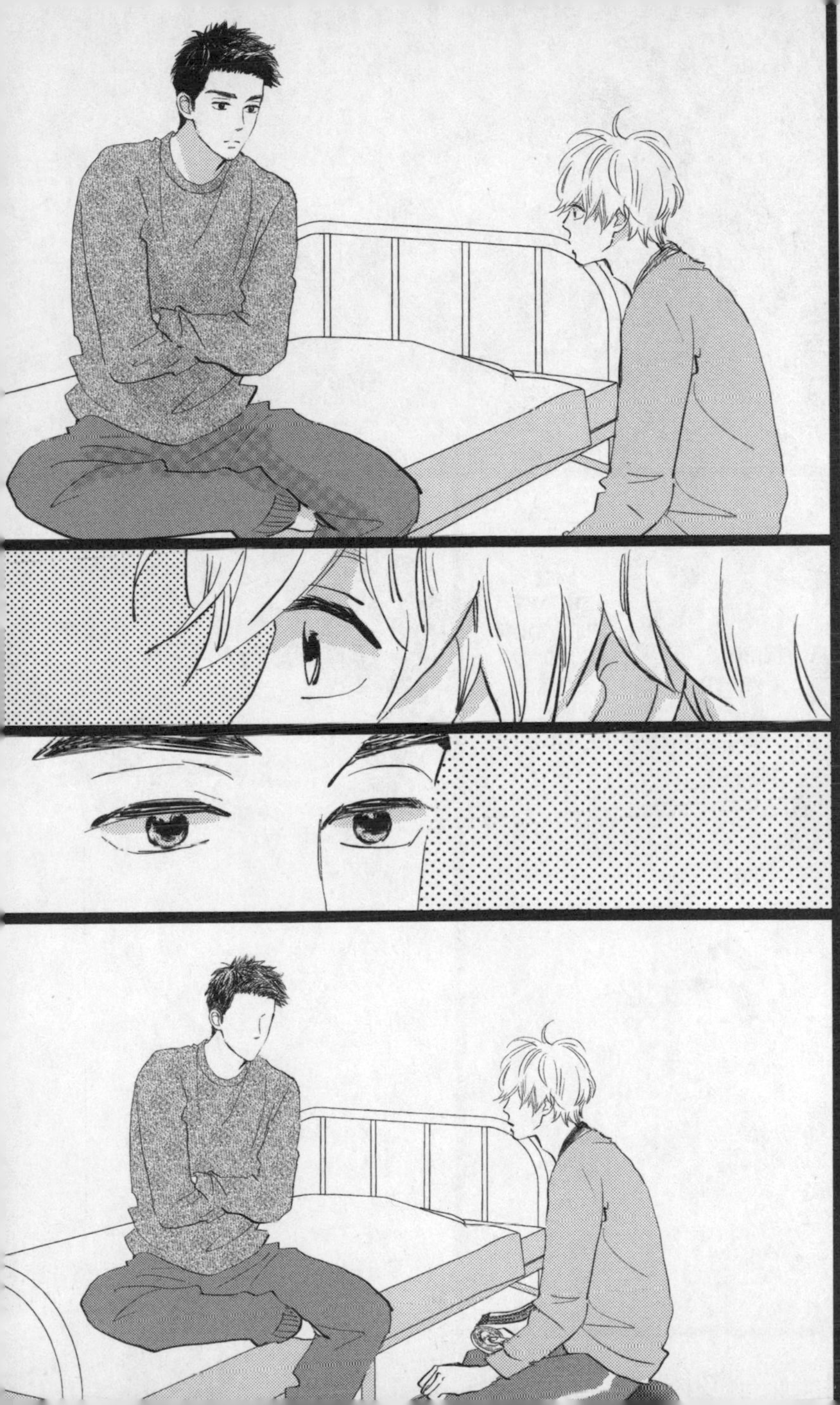

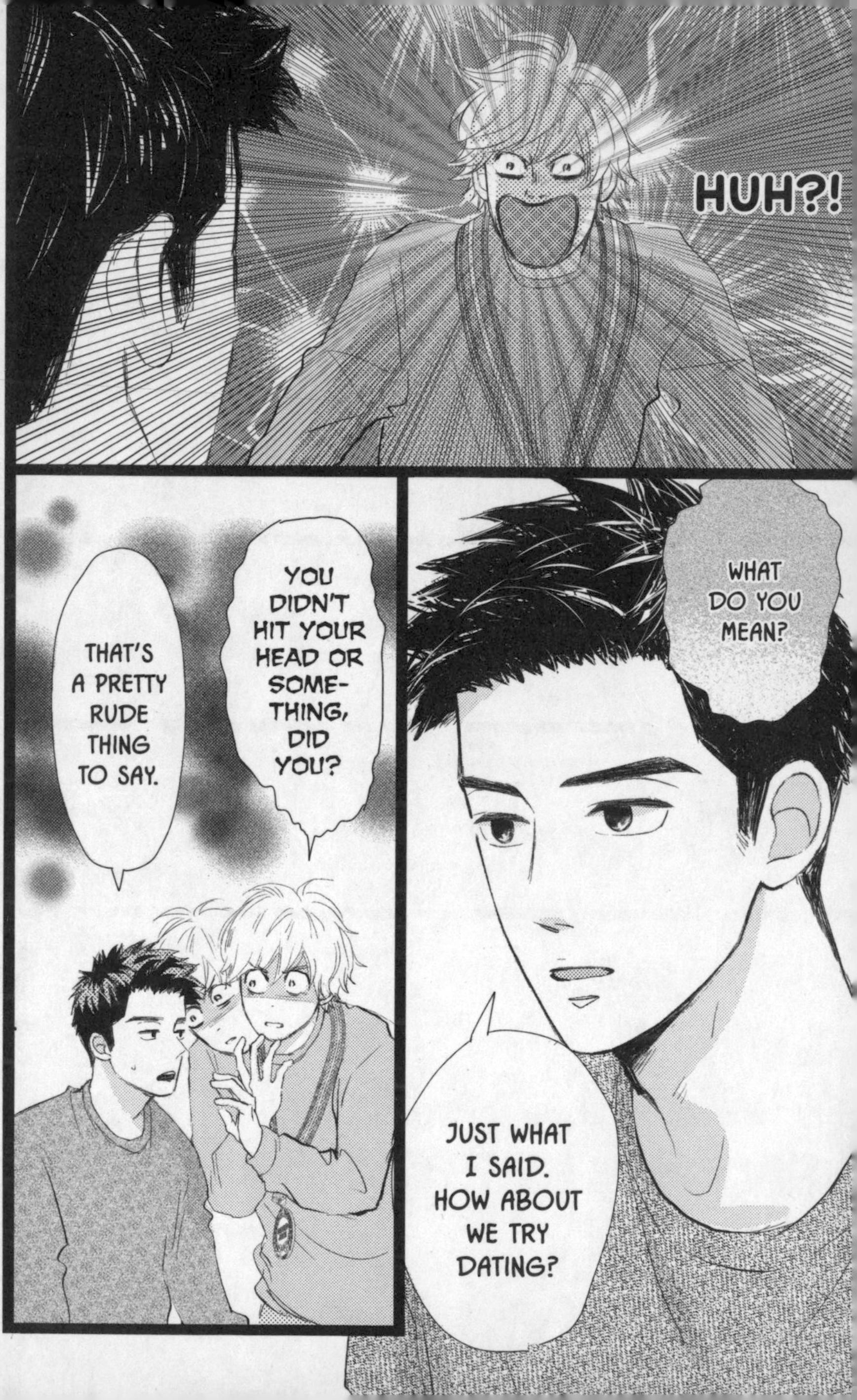
HUH?!
WHAT DO YOU MEAN?
JUST WHAT I SAID. HOW ABOUT WE TRY DATING?
YOU DIDN'T HIT YOUR HEAD OR SOME-THING, DID YOU?
THAT'S A PRETTY RUDE THING TO SAY.

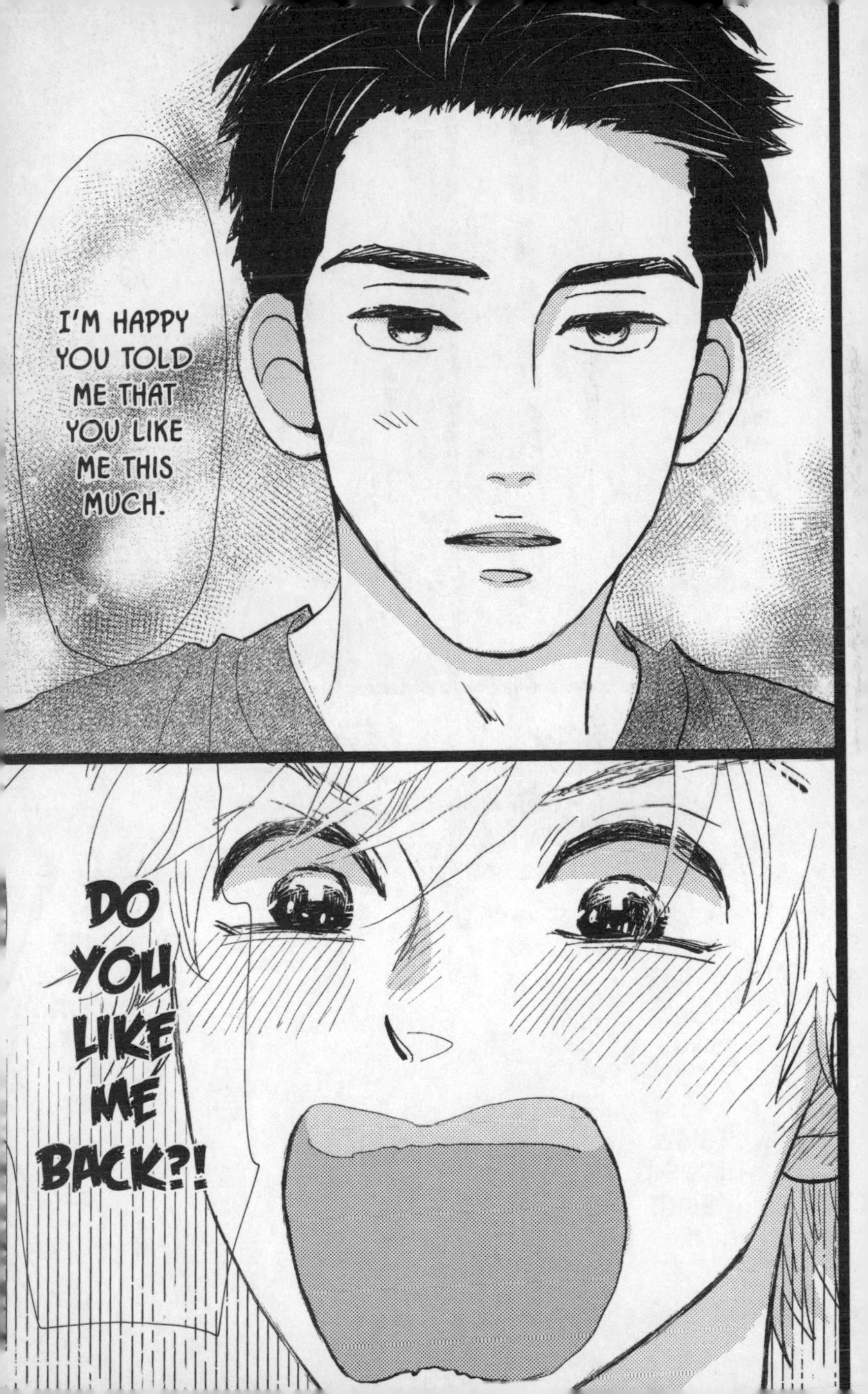
I'M HAPPY YOU TOLD ME THAT YOU LIKE ME THIS MUCH.
DO YOU LIKE ME BACK?!

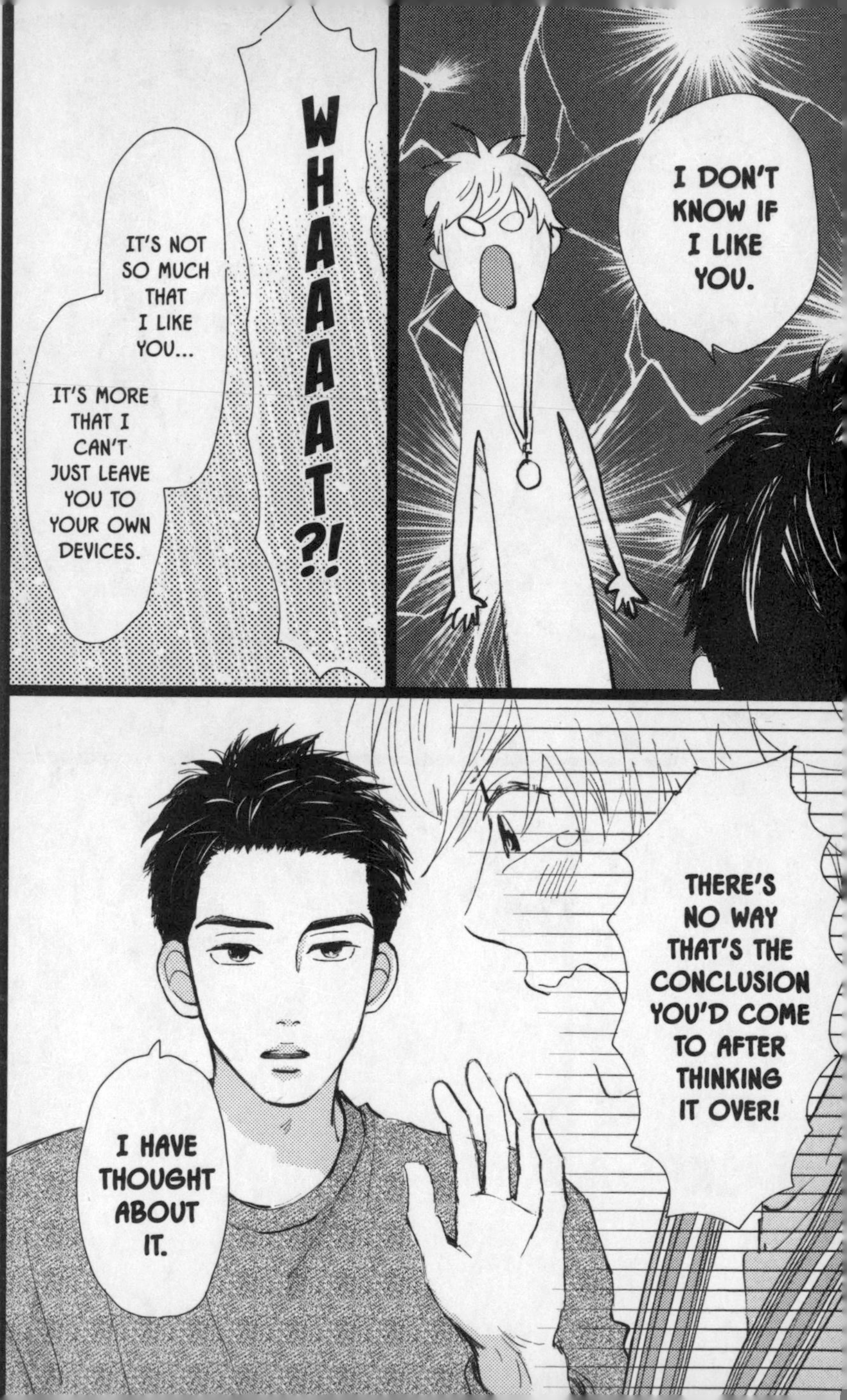
I DON'T KNOW IF I LIKE YOU.
WHAAAAAT?!
IT'S NOT SO MUCH THAT I LIKE YOU...
IT'S MORE THAT I CAN'T JUST LEAVE YOU TO YOUR OWN DEVICES.
THERE'S NO WAY THAT'S THE CONCLUSION YOU'D COME TO AFTER THINKING IT OVER!
I HAVE THOUGHT ABOUT IT.

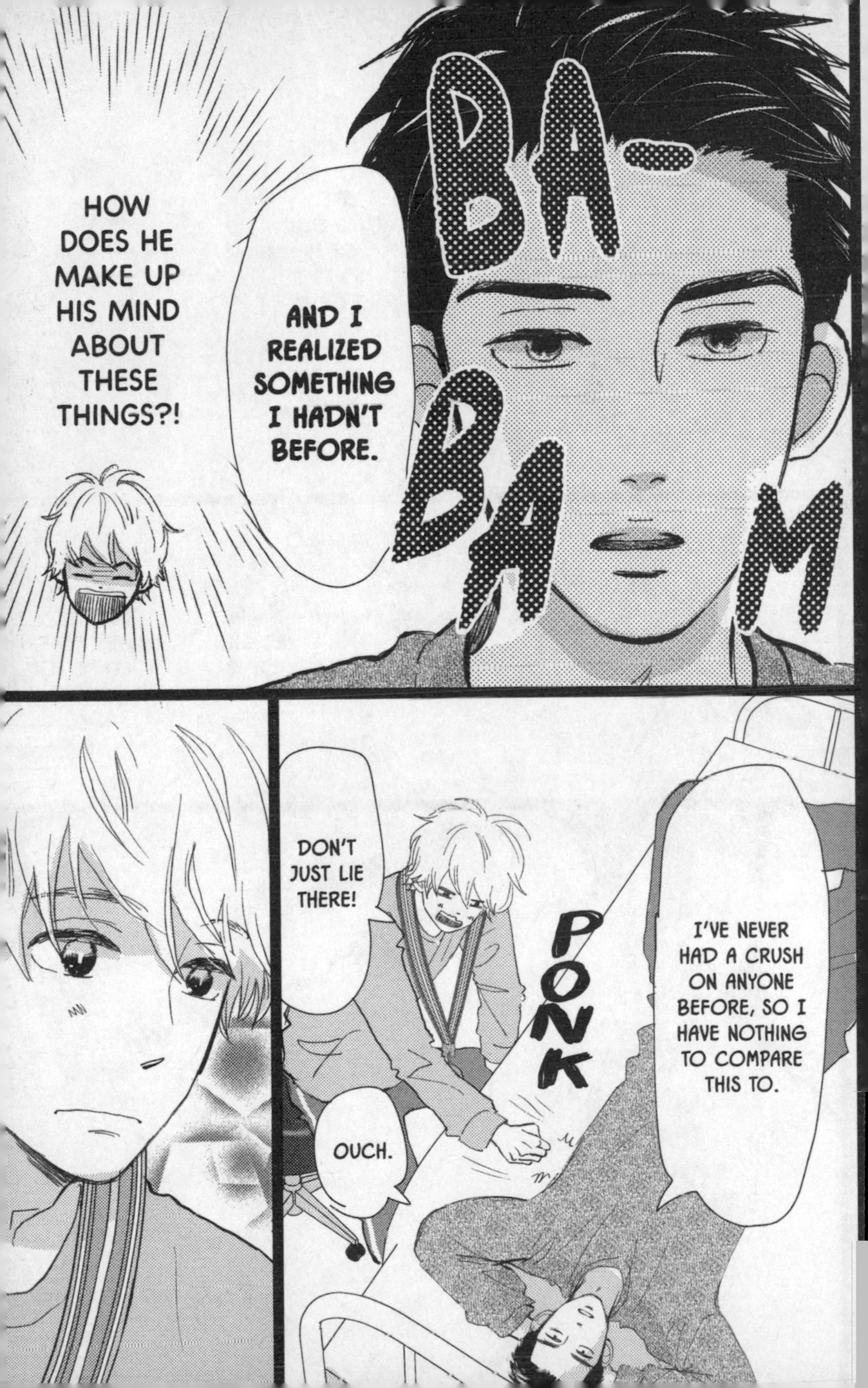
BA-BA-M
AND I REALIZED SOMETHING I HADN'T BEFORE.
HOW DOES HE MAKE UP HIS MIND ABOUT THESE THINGS?!
I'VE NEVER HAD A CRUSH ON ANYONE BEFORE, SO I HAVE NOTHING TO COMPARE THIS TO.
PONK
DON'T JUST LIE THERE!
OUCH.

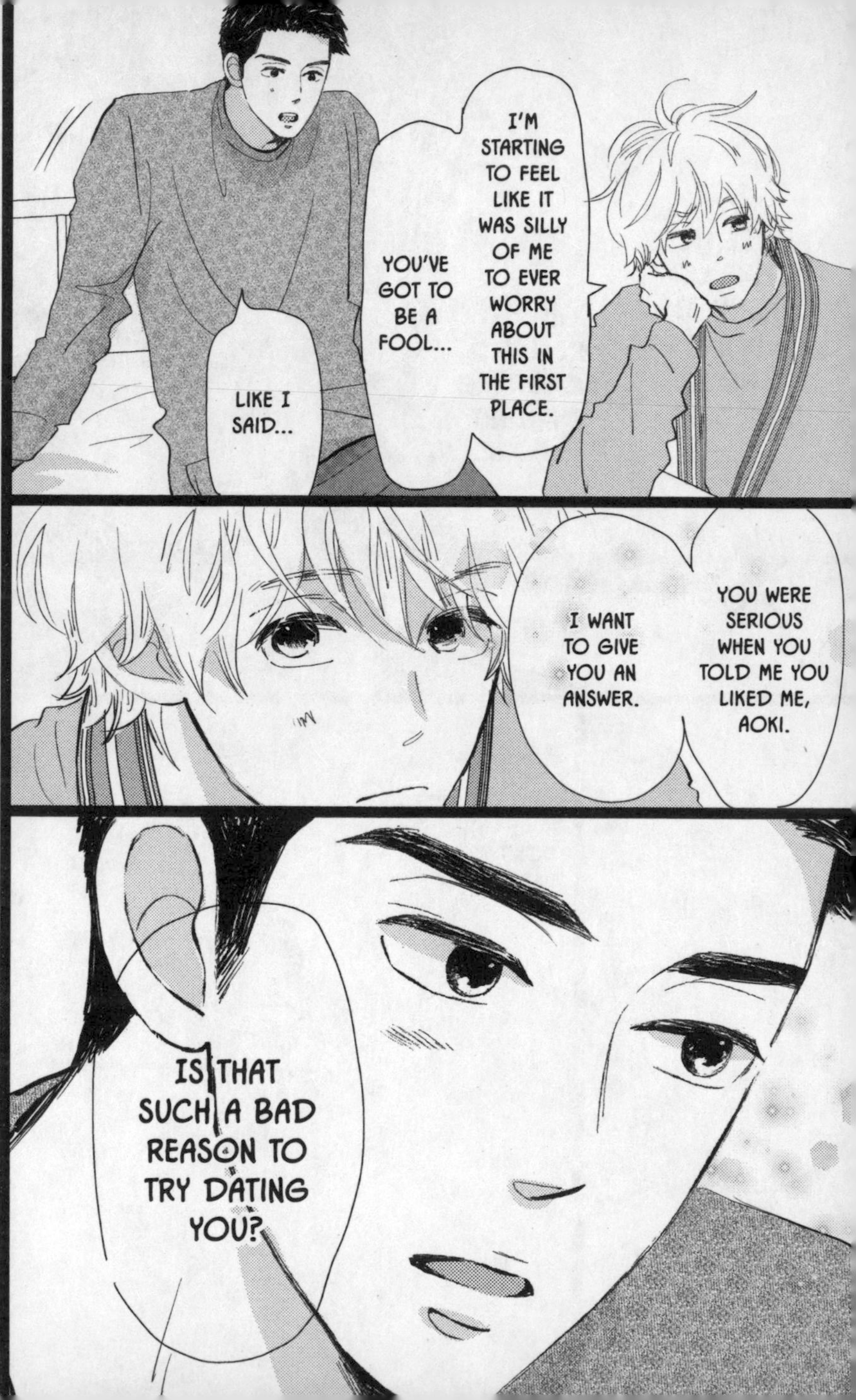
I'M STARTING TO FEEL LIKE IT WAS SILLY OF ME TO EVER WORRY ABOUT THIS IN THE FIRST PLACE.
YOU'VE GOT TO BE A FOOL...
LIKE I SAID...
YOU WERE SERIOUS WHEN YOU TOLD ME YOU LIKED ME, AOKI.
I WANT TO GIVE YOU AN ANSWER.
IS THAT SUCH A BAD REASON TO TRY DATING YOU?

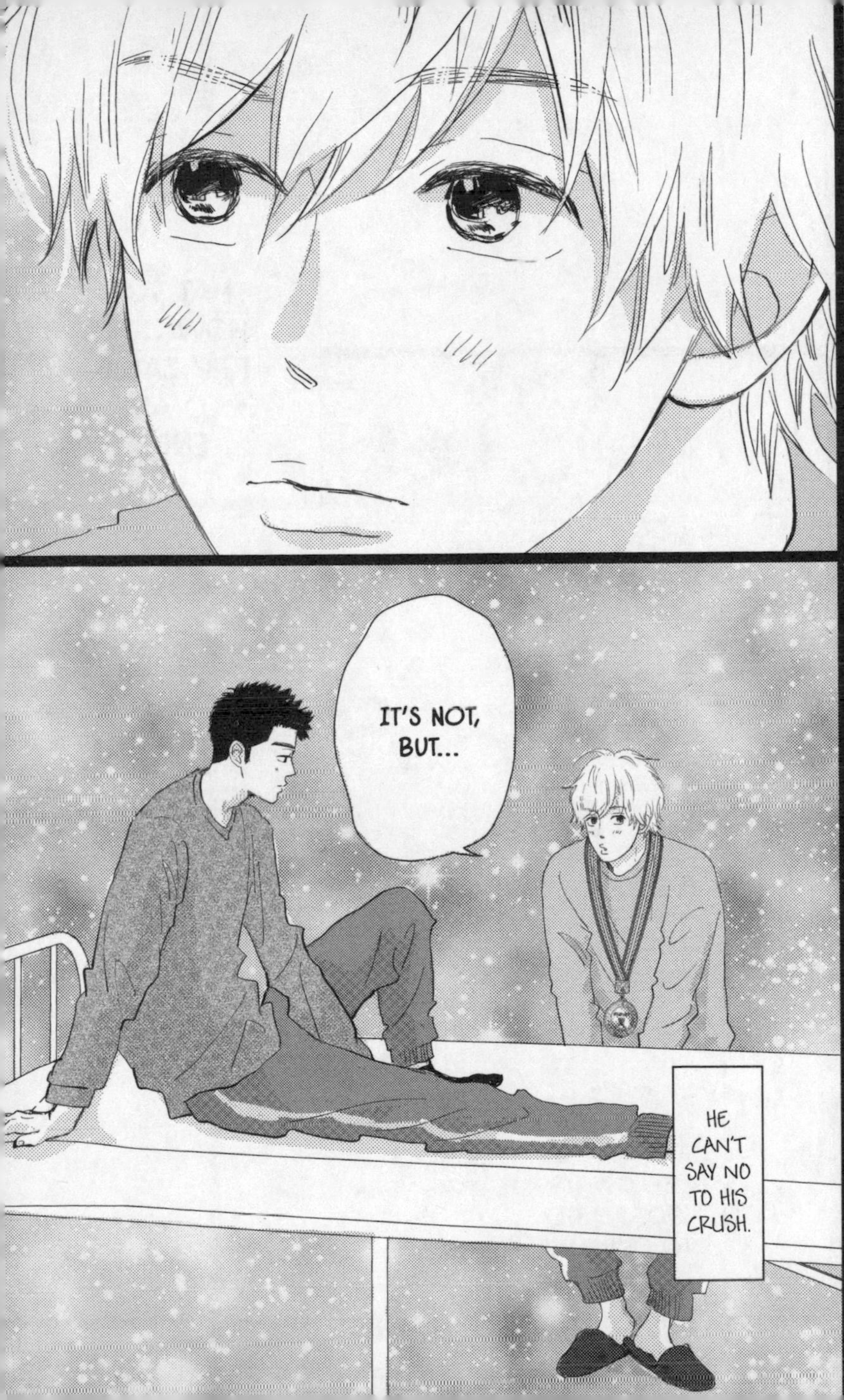
IT'S NOT, BUT...
HE CAN'T SAY NO TO HIS CRUSH.

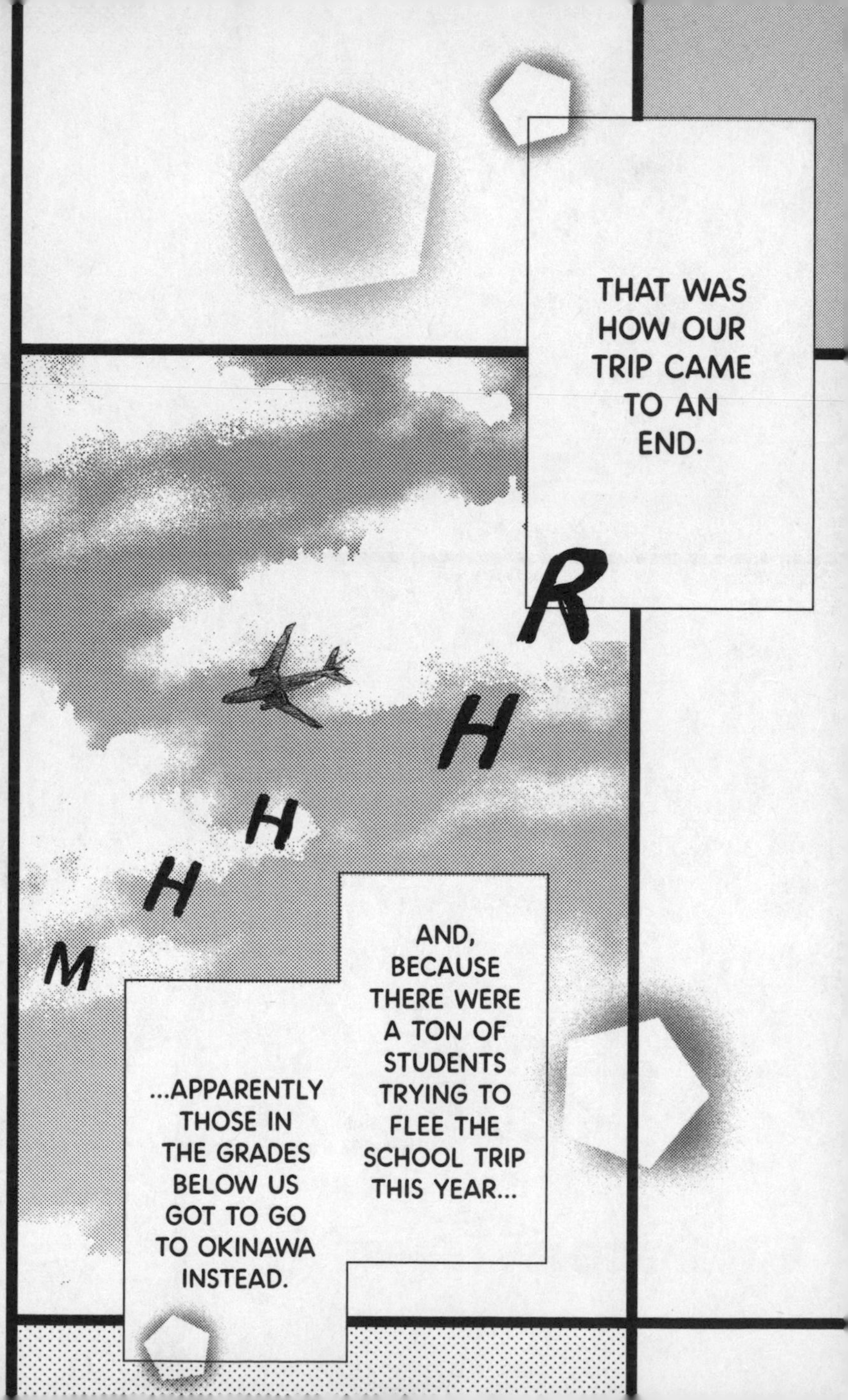
THAT WAS HOW OUR TRIP CAME TO AN END.
MHHHR
AND, BECAUSE THERE WERE A TON OF STUDENTS TRYING TO FLEE THE SCHOOL TRIP THIS YEAR...
...APPARENTLY THOSE IN THE GRADES BELOW US GOT TO GO TO OKINAWA INSTEAD.

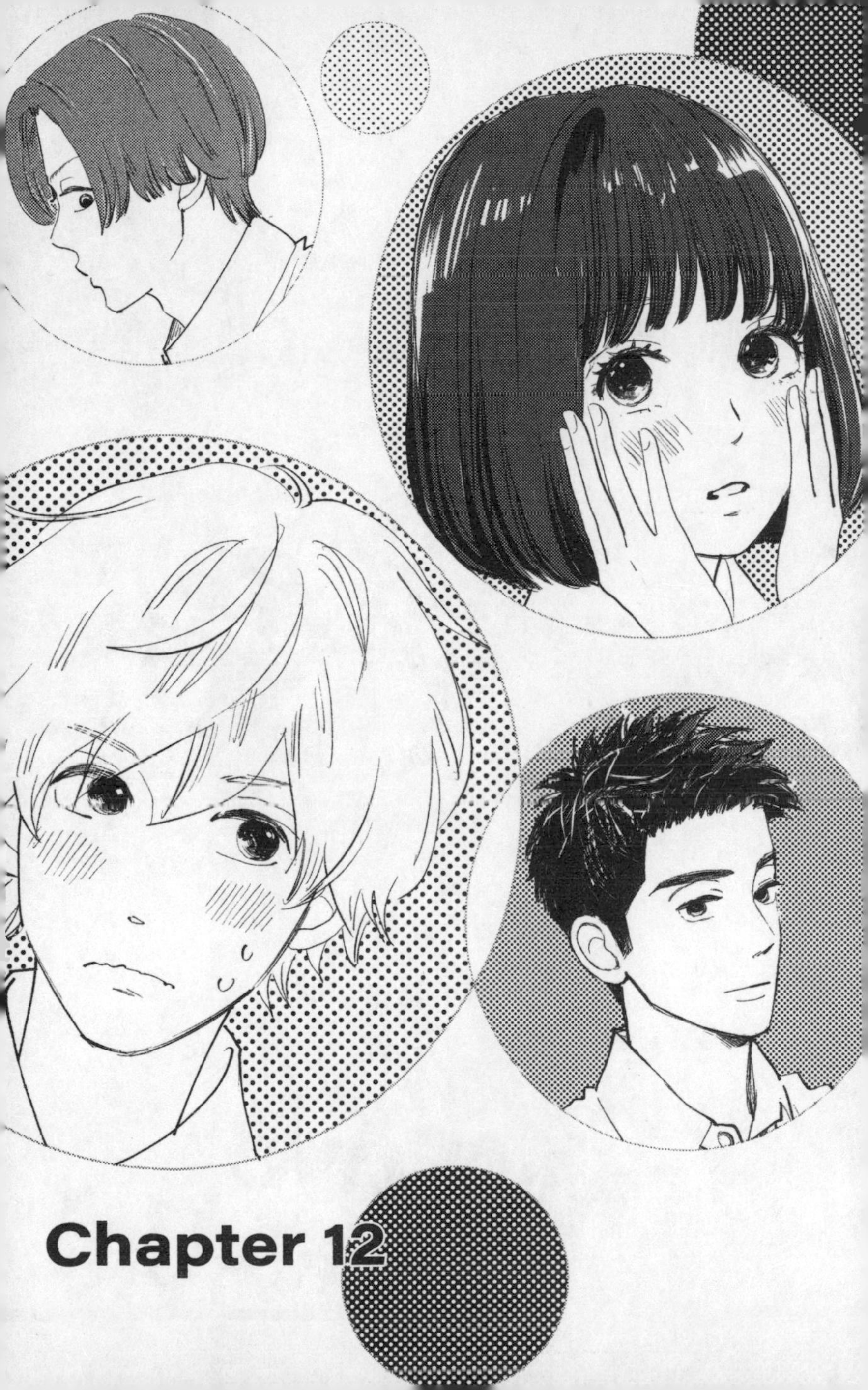

Chapter 12

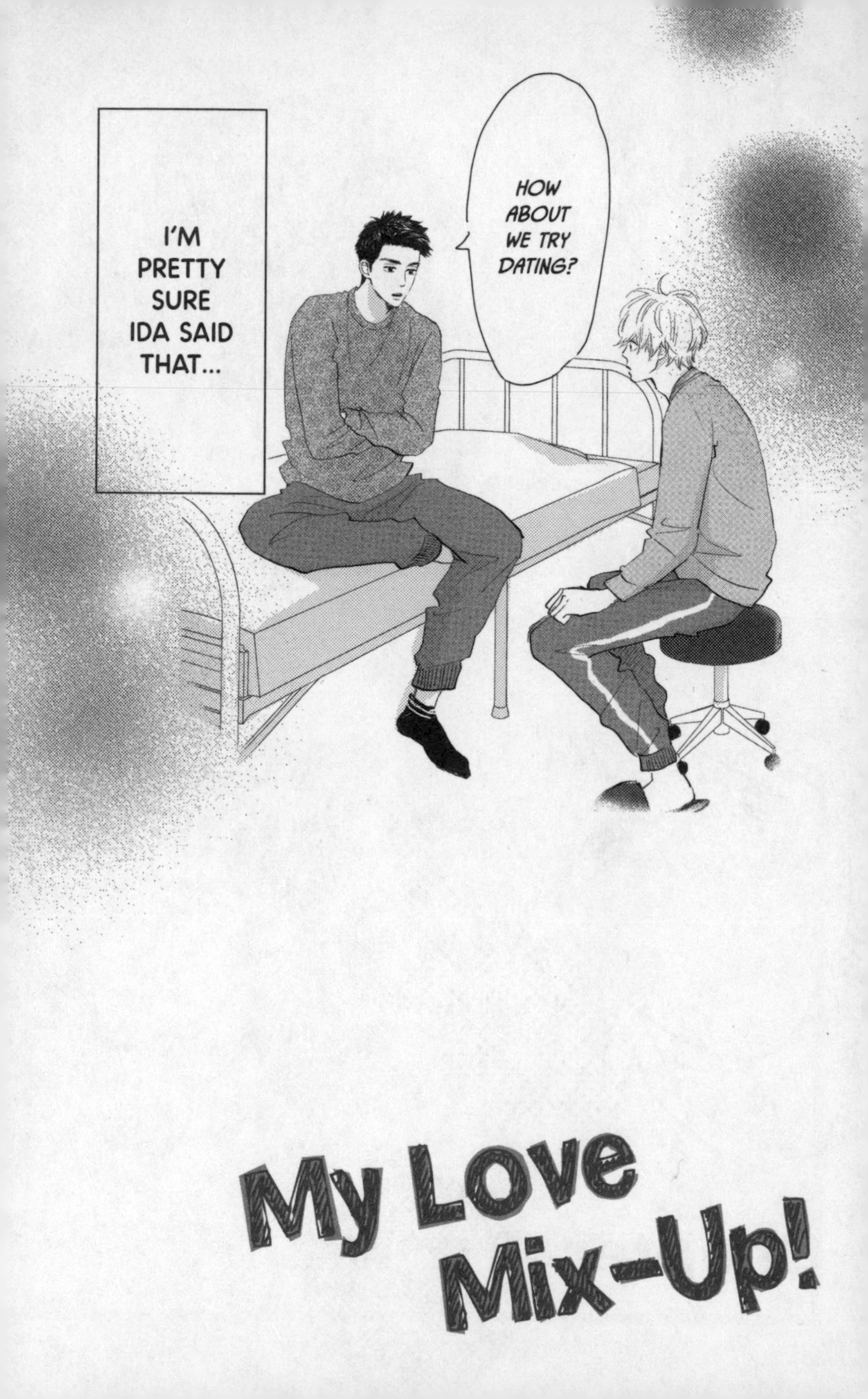
HOW ABOUT WE TRY DATING?
I'M PRETTY SURE IDA SAID THAT...
My Love Mix-Up!

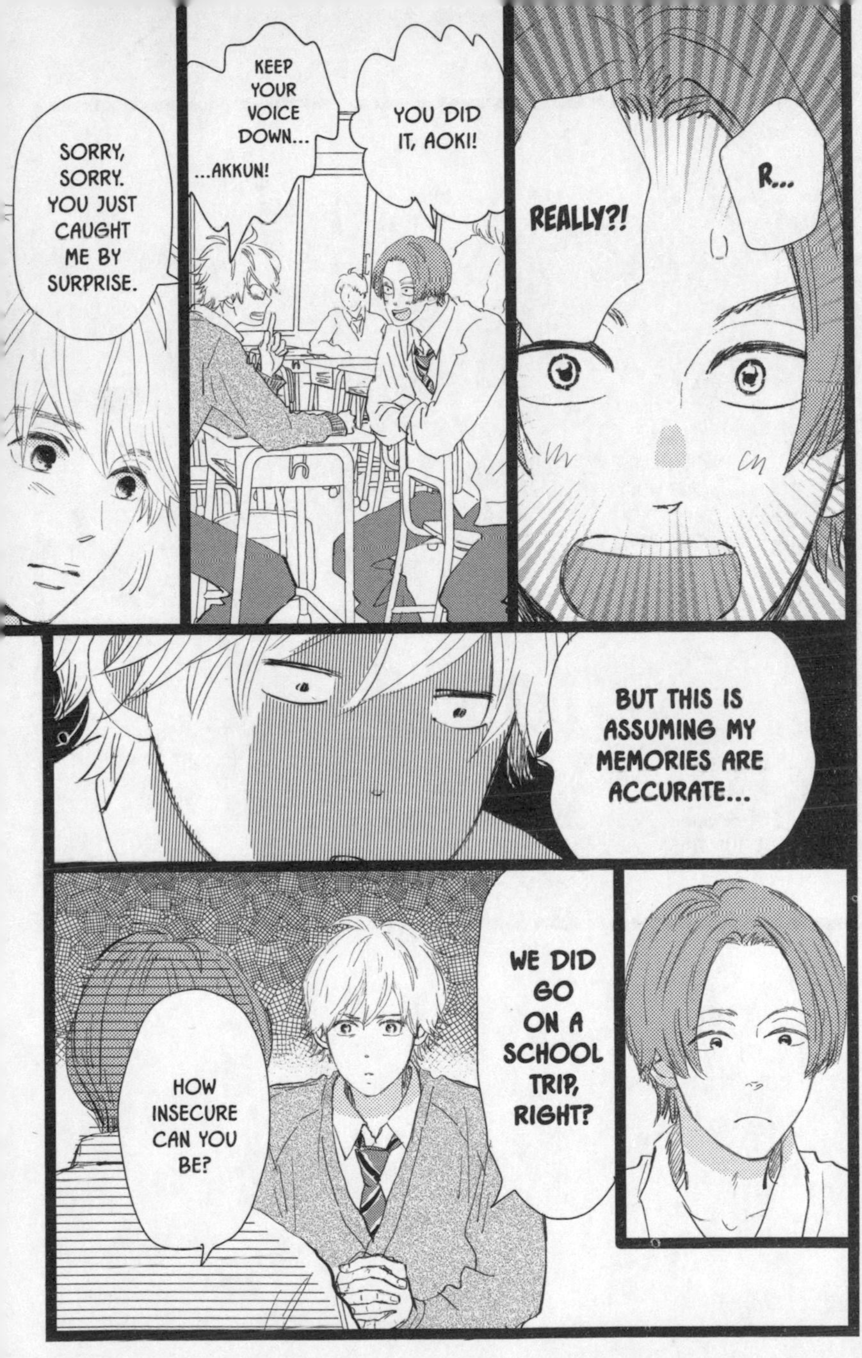
R...
REALLY?!
YOU DID IT, AOKI!
KEEP YOUR VOICE DOWN... ...AKKUN!
SORRY, SORRY. YOU JUST CAUGHT ME BY SURPRISE.
BUT THIS IS ASSUMING MY MEMORIES ARE ACCURATE...
WE DID GO ON A SCHOOL TRIP, RIGHT?
HOW INSECURE CAN YOU BE?

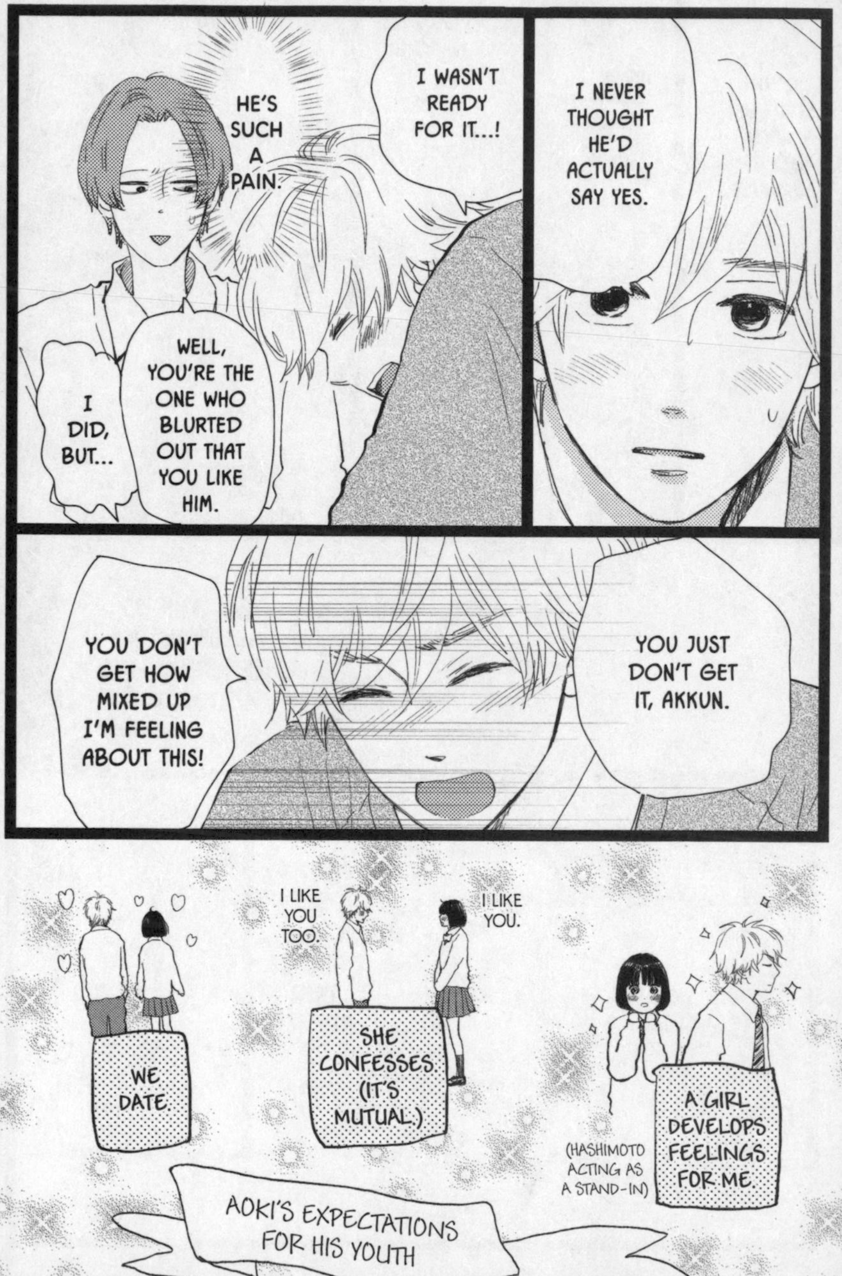
I NEVER THOUGHT HE'D ACTUALLY SAY YES.
I WASN'T READY FOR IT...!
HE'S SUCH A PAIN.
WELL, YOU'RE THE ONE WHO BLURTED OUT THAT YOU LIKE HIM.
I DID, BUT...
YOU JUST DON'T GET IT, AKKUN.
YOU DON'T GET HOW MIXED UP I'M FEELING ABOUT THIS!
A GIRL DEVELOPS FEELINGS FOR ME.
(HASHIMOTO ACTING AS A STAND-IN)
I LIKE YOU.
I LIKE YOU TOO.
SHE CONFESSES. (IT'S MUTUAL.)
WE DATE.
AOKI'S EXPECTATIONS FOR HIS YOUTH

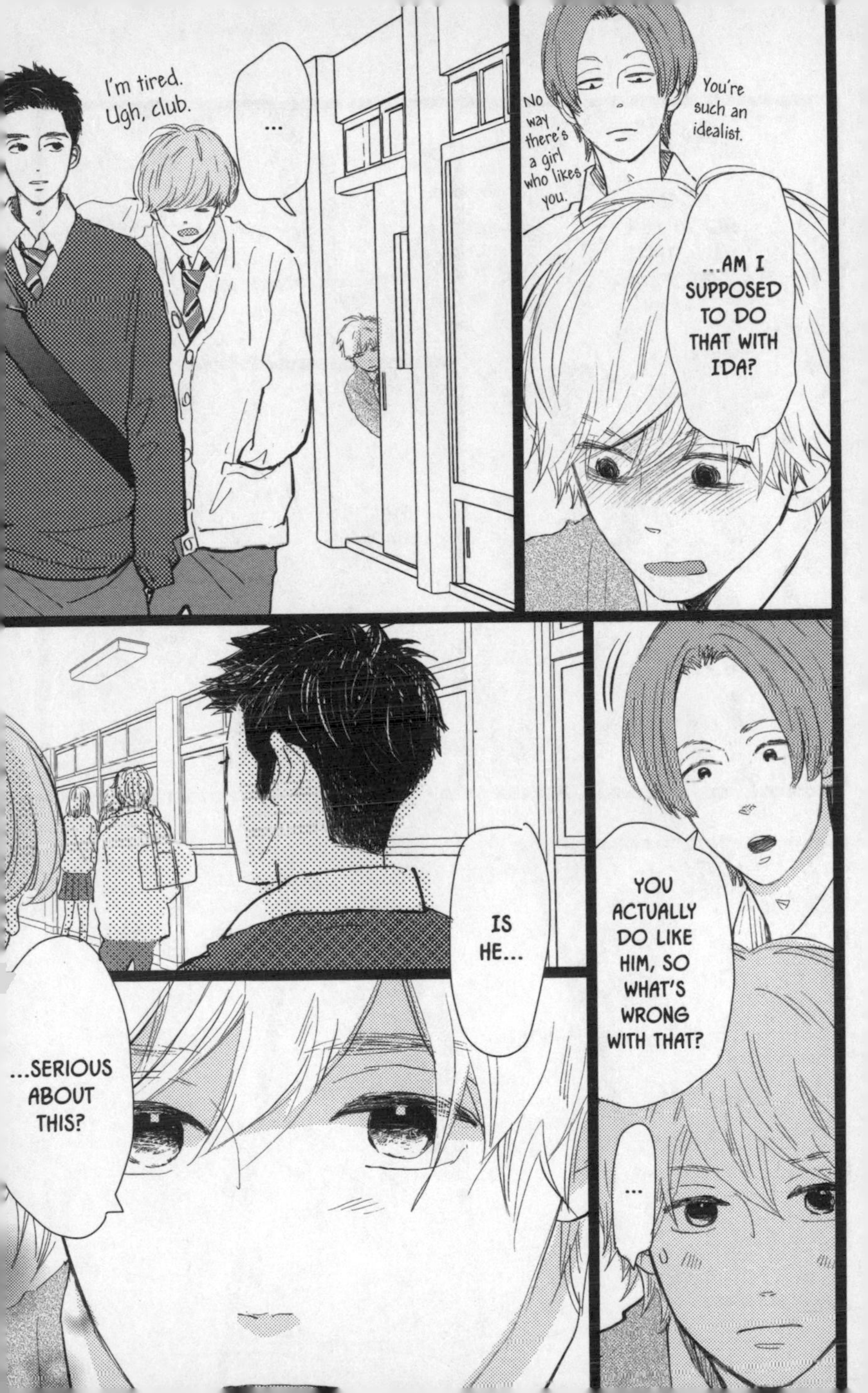
You're such an idealist.
No way there's a girl who likes you.
...AM I SUPPOSED TO DO THAT WITH IDA?
...
I'm tired. Ugh, club.
YOU ACTUALLY DO LIKE HIM, SO WHAT'S WRONG WITH THAT?
...
IS HE...
...SERIOUS ABOUT THIS?

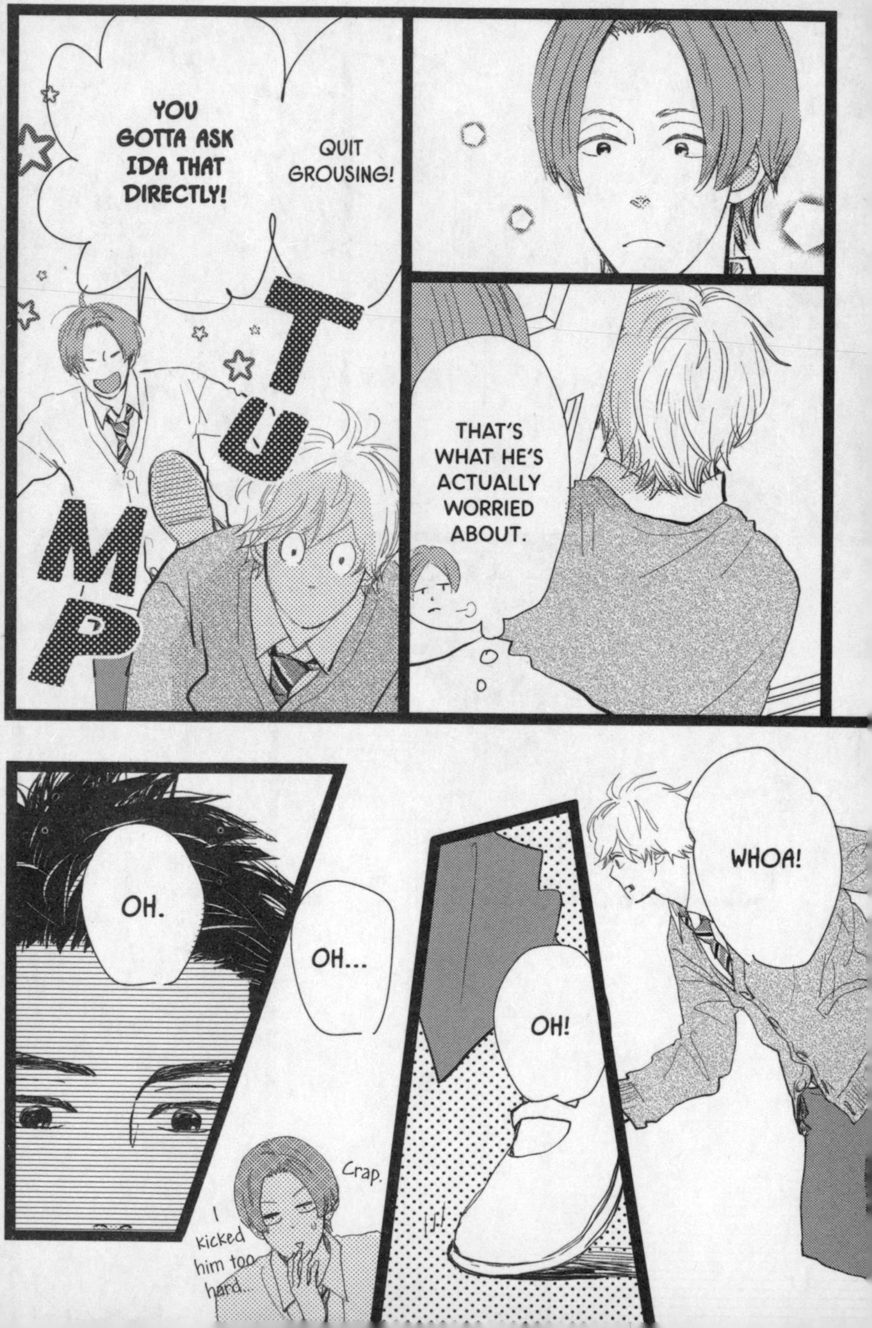
THAT'S WHAT HE'S ACTUALLY WORRIED ABOUT.
QUIT GROUSING!
YOU GOTTA ASK IDA THAT DIRECTLY!
TUMP
WHOA!
OH!
OH...
OH.
Crap.
I kicked him too hard.

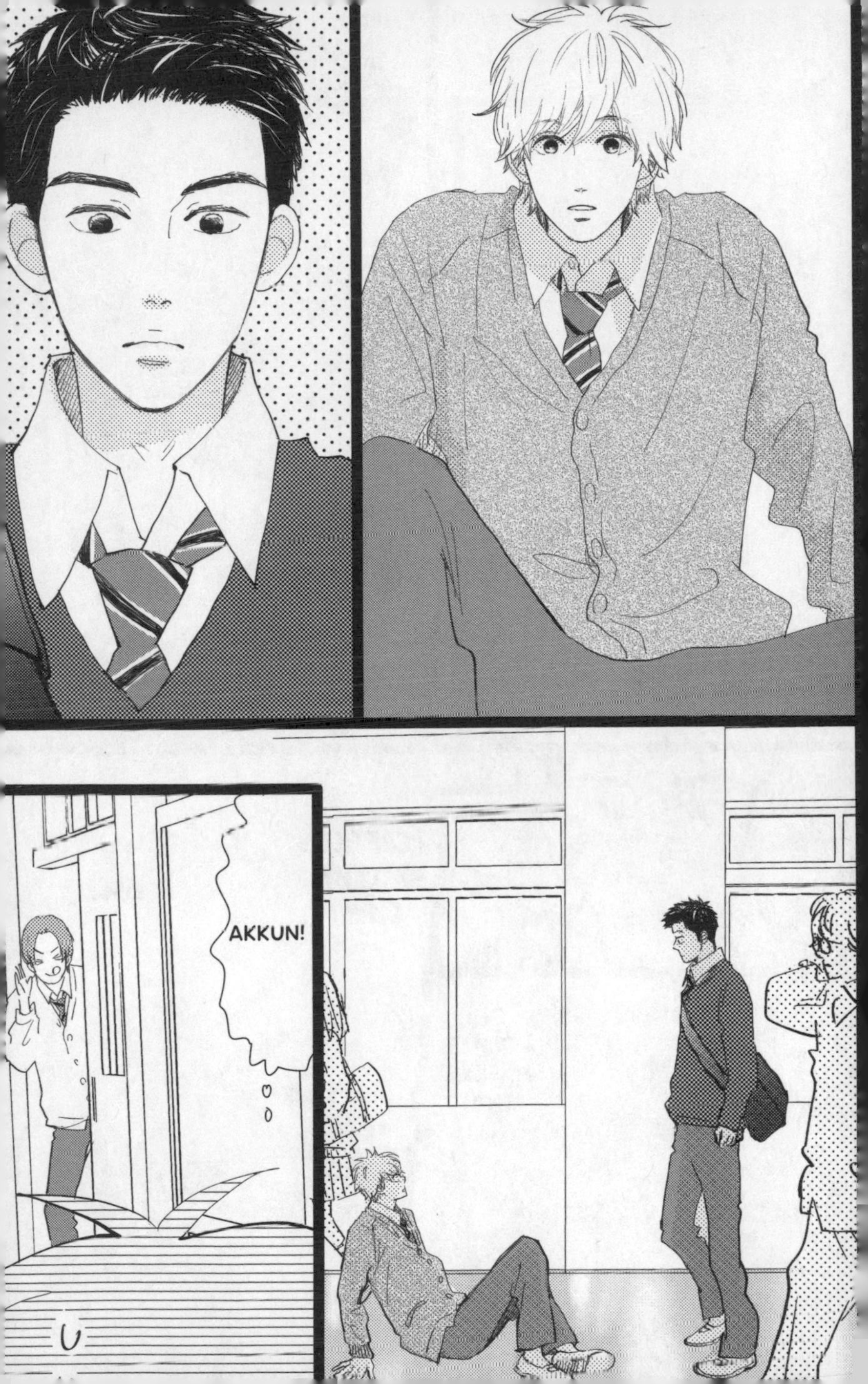
AKKUN!

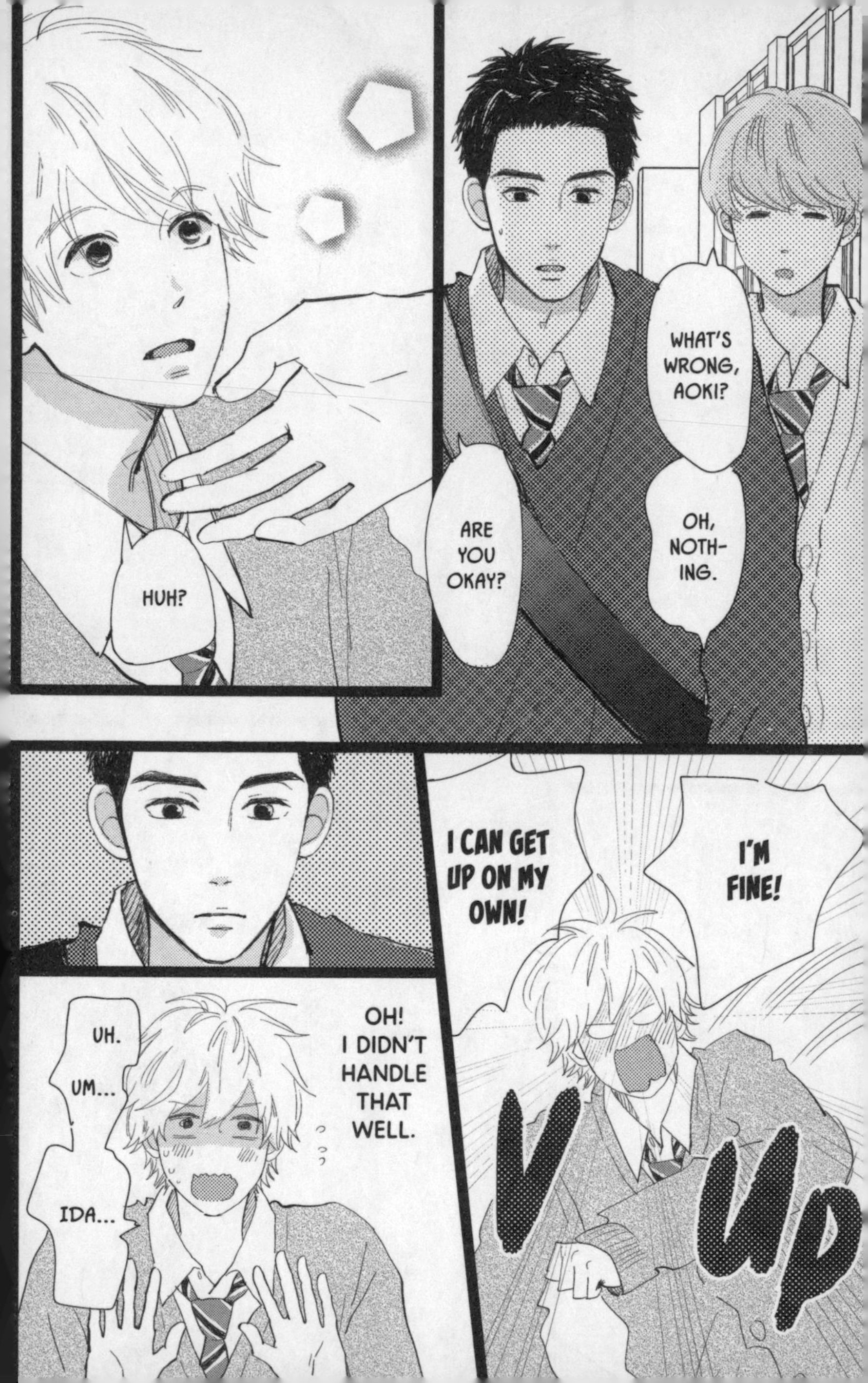
WHAT'S WRONG, AOKI?
OH, NOTHING.
ARE YOU OKAY?
HUH?
I'M FINE!
I CAN GET UP ON MY OWN!
VUP
OH! I DIDN'T HANDLE THAT WELL.
UH.
UM...
IDA...

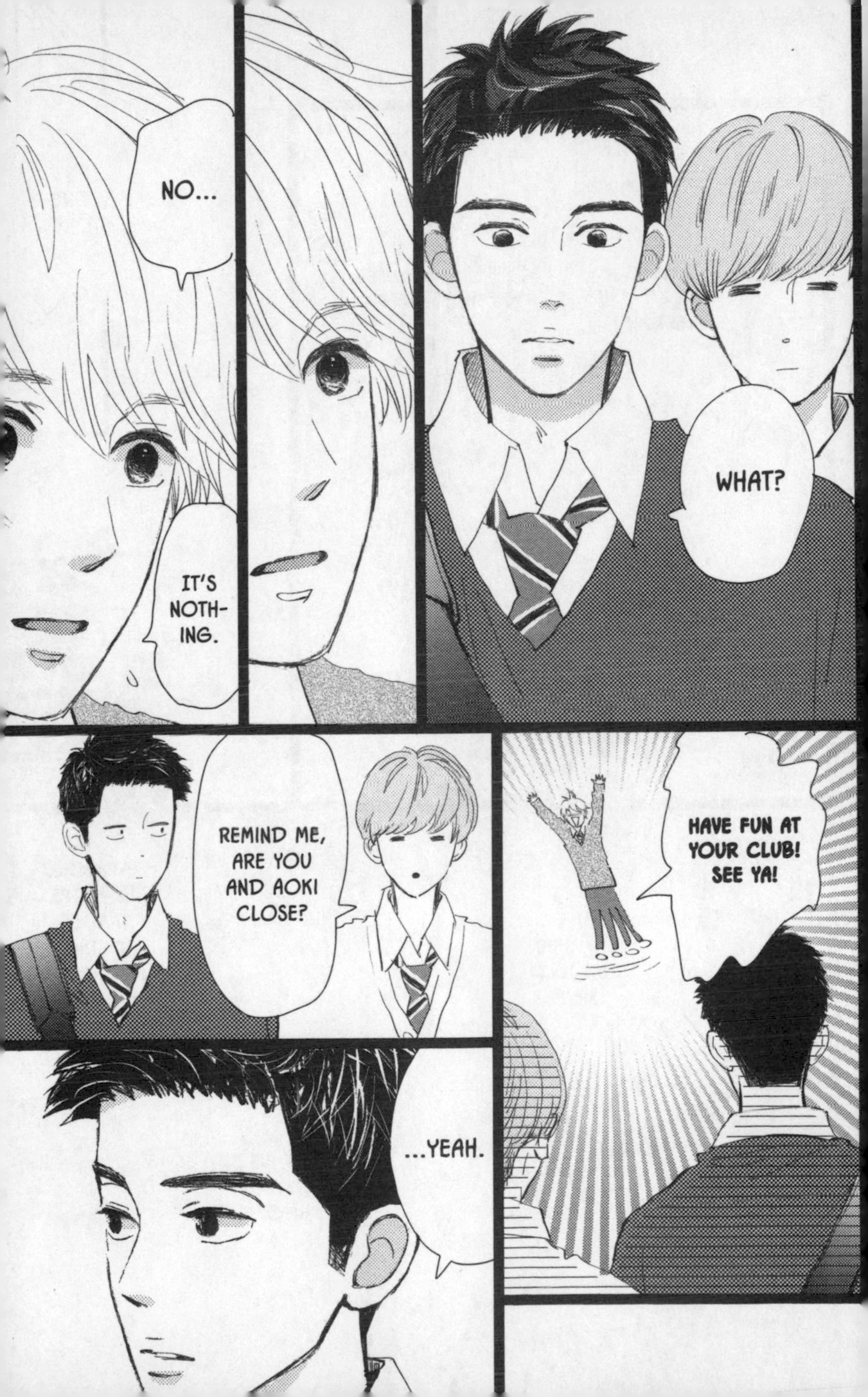
WHAT?
NO...
IT'S NOTHING.
HAVE FUN AT YOUR CLUB! SEE YA!
REMIND ME, ARE YOU AND AOKI CLOSE?
...YEAH.

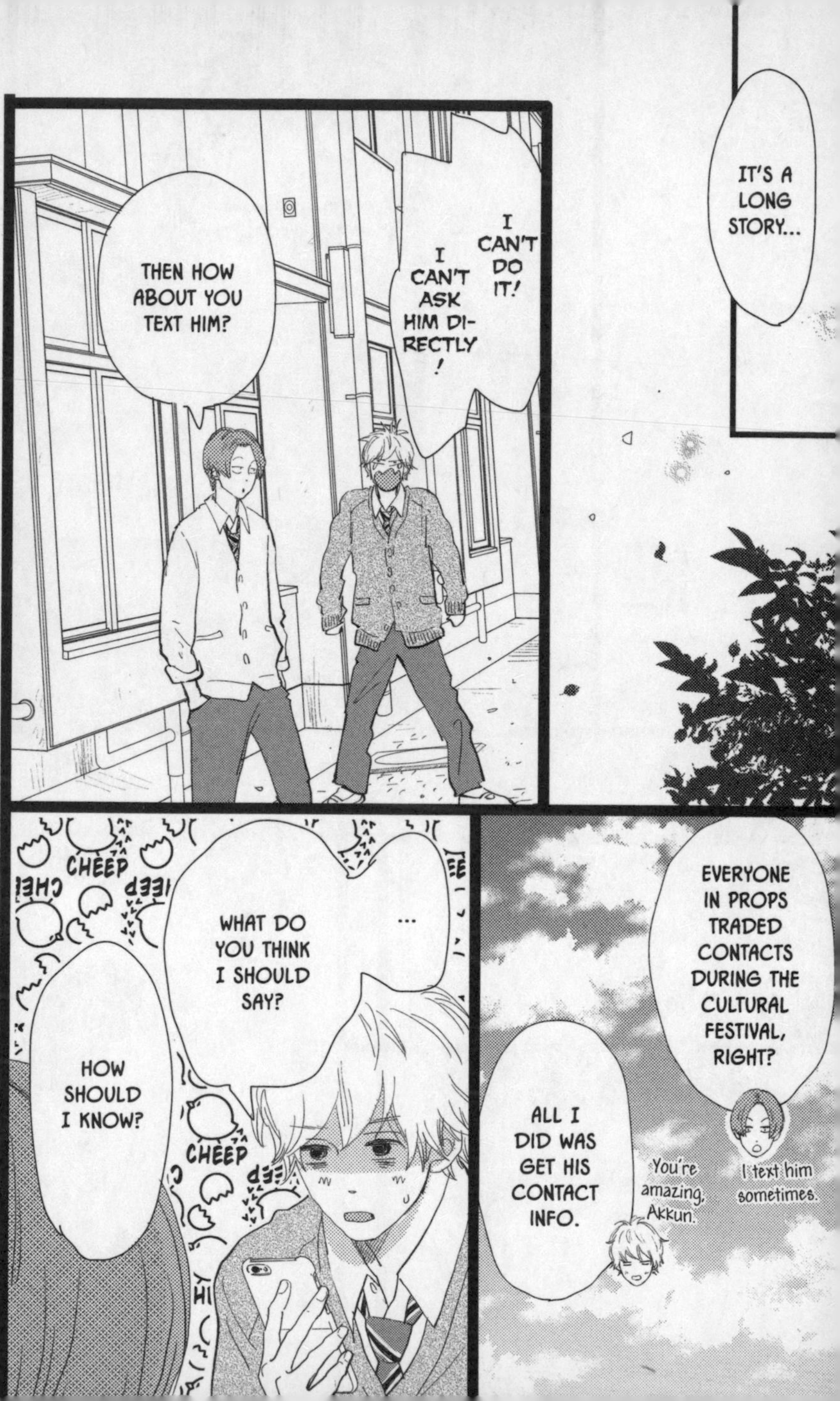
IT'S A LONG STORY...
I CAN'T DO IT!
I CAN'T ASK HIM DIRECTLY!
THEN HOW ABOUT YOU TEXT HIM?
EVERYONE IN PROPS TRADED CONTACTS DURING THE CULTURAL FESTIVAL, RIGHT?
I text him sometimes.
ALL I DID WAS GET HIS CONTACT INFO.
You're amazing, Akkun.
...
WHAT DO YOU THINK I SHOULD SAY?
CHEEP
CHEEP
HOW SHOULD I KNOW?

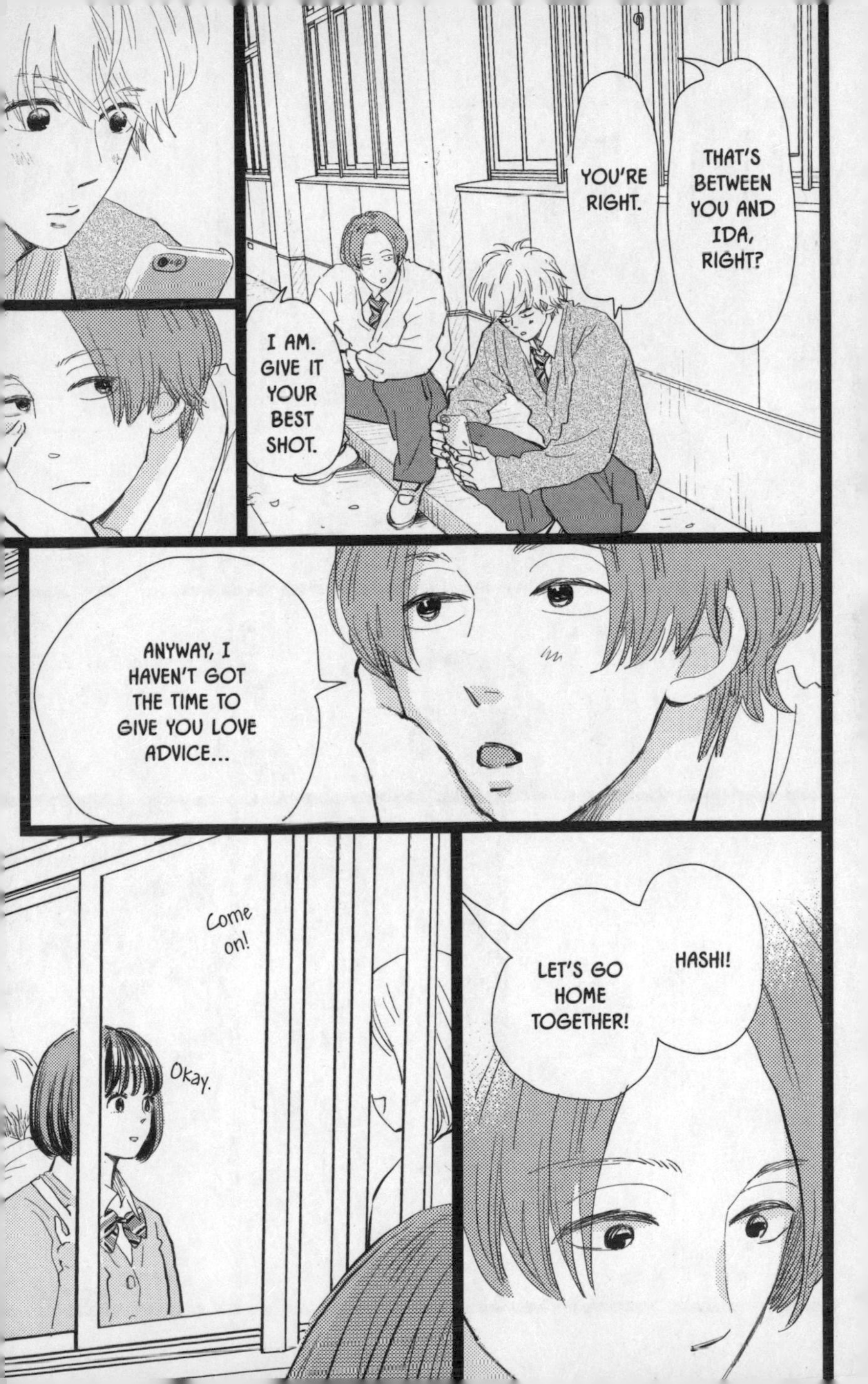
THAT'S BETWEEN YOU AND IDA, RIGHT?
YOU'RE RIGHT.
I AM. GIVE IT YOUR BEST SHOT.
ANYWAY, I HAVEN'T GOT THE TIME TO GIVE YOU LOVE ADVICE...
HASHI!
LET'S GO HOME TOGETHER!
Come on!
Okay.

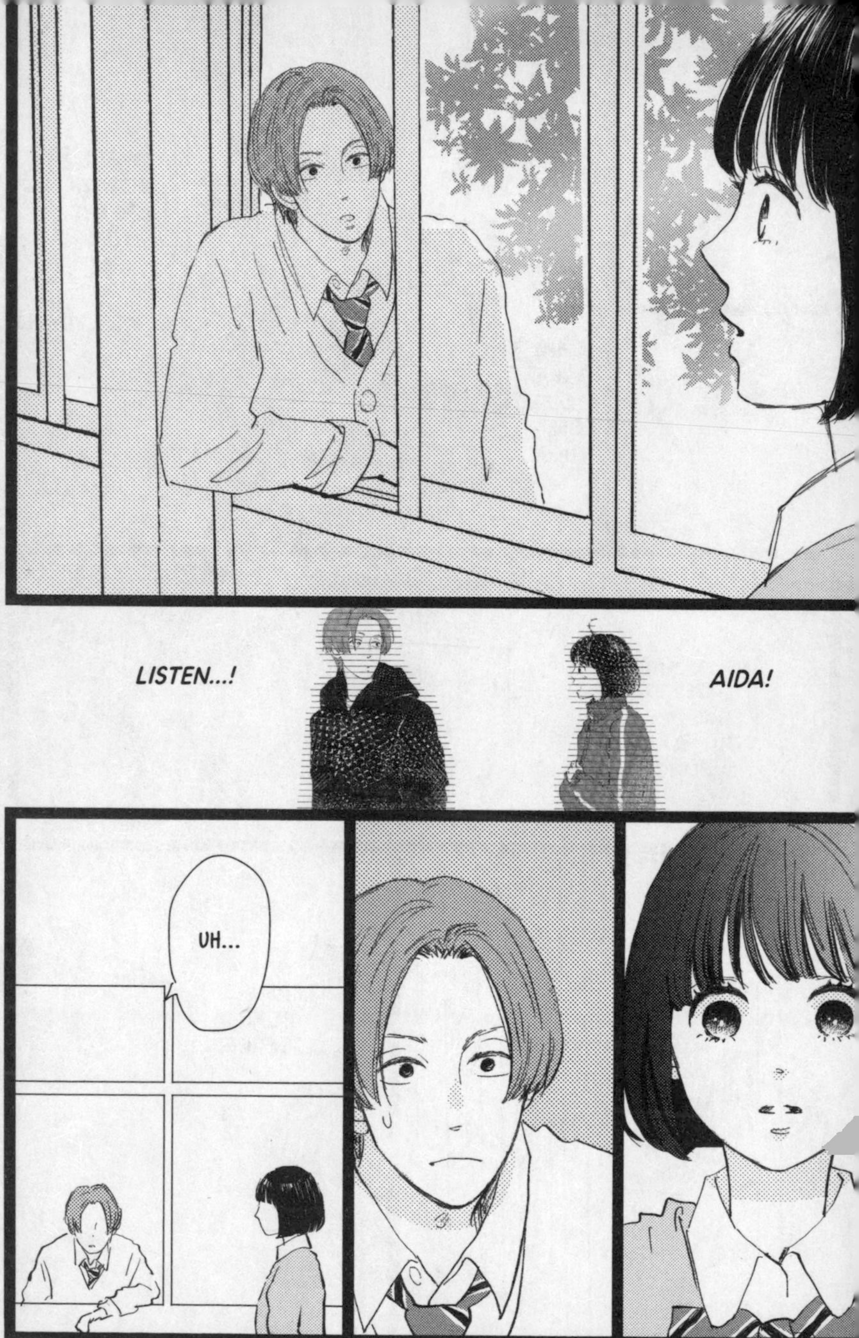
AIDA!
LISTEN...!
UH...

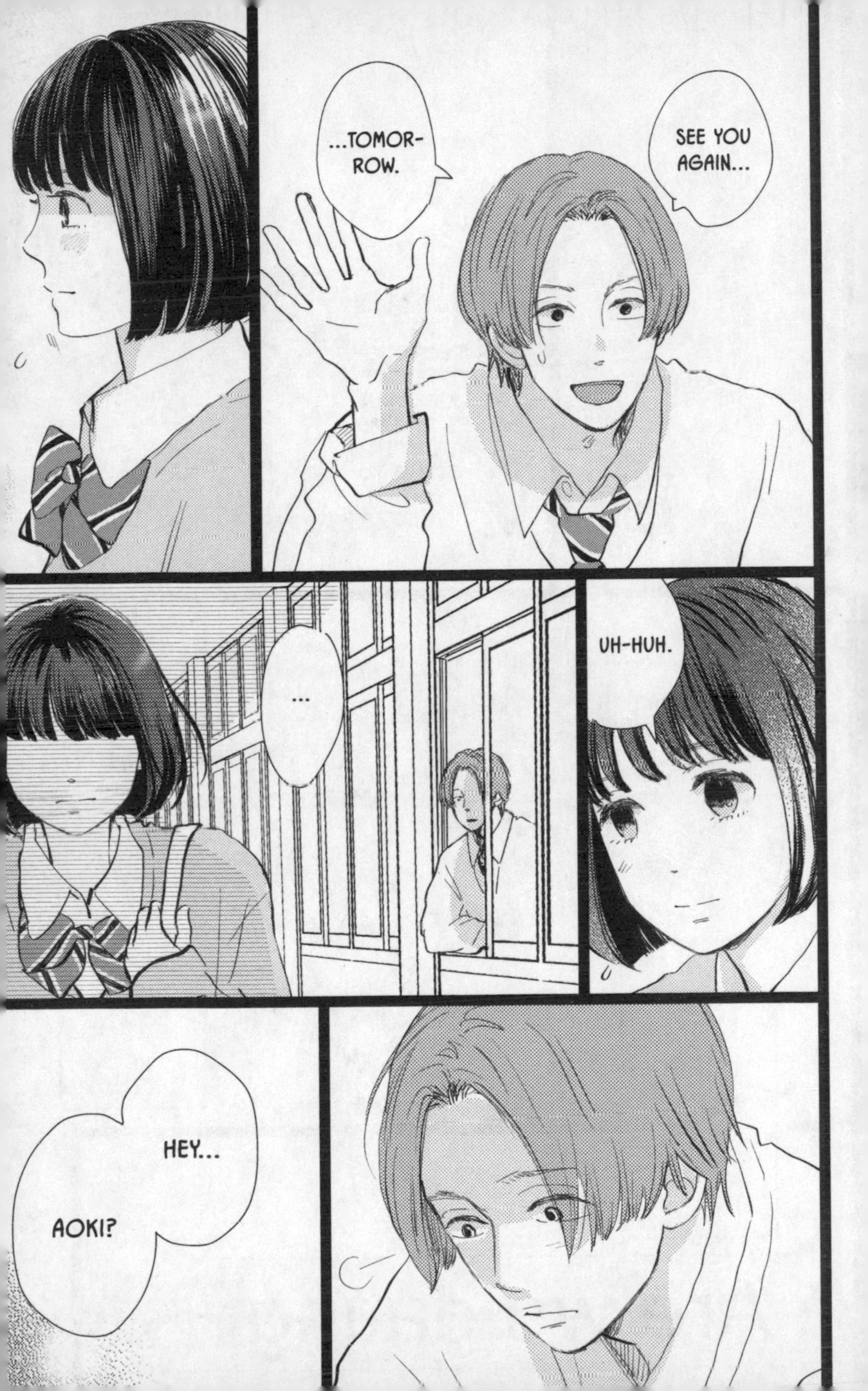
SEE YOU AGAIN...
...TOMOR-ROW.
UH-HUH.
...
HEY...
AOKI?

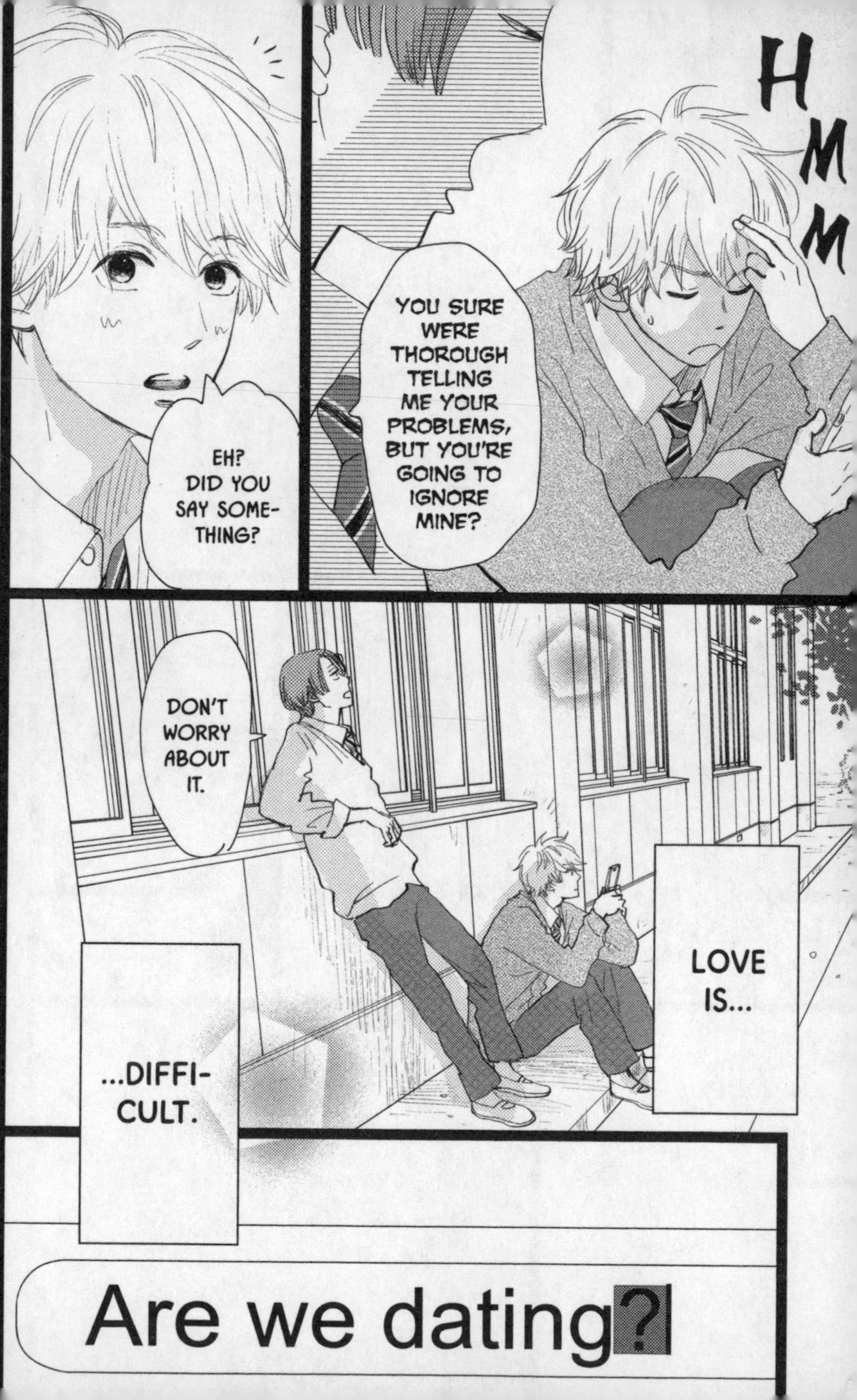
HMM
YOU SURE WERE THOROUGH TELLING ME YOUR PROBLEMS, BUT YOU'RE GOING TO IGNORE MINE?
EH? DID YOU SAY SOME-THING?
DON'T WORRY ABOUT IT.
LOVE IS...
...DIFFI-CULT.
Are we dating?

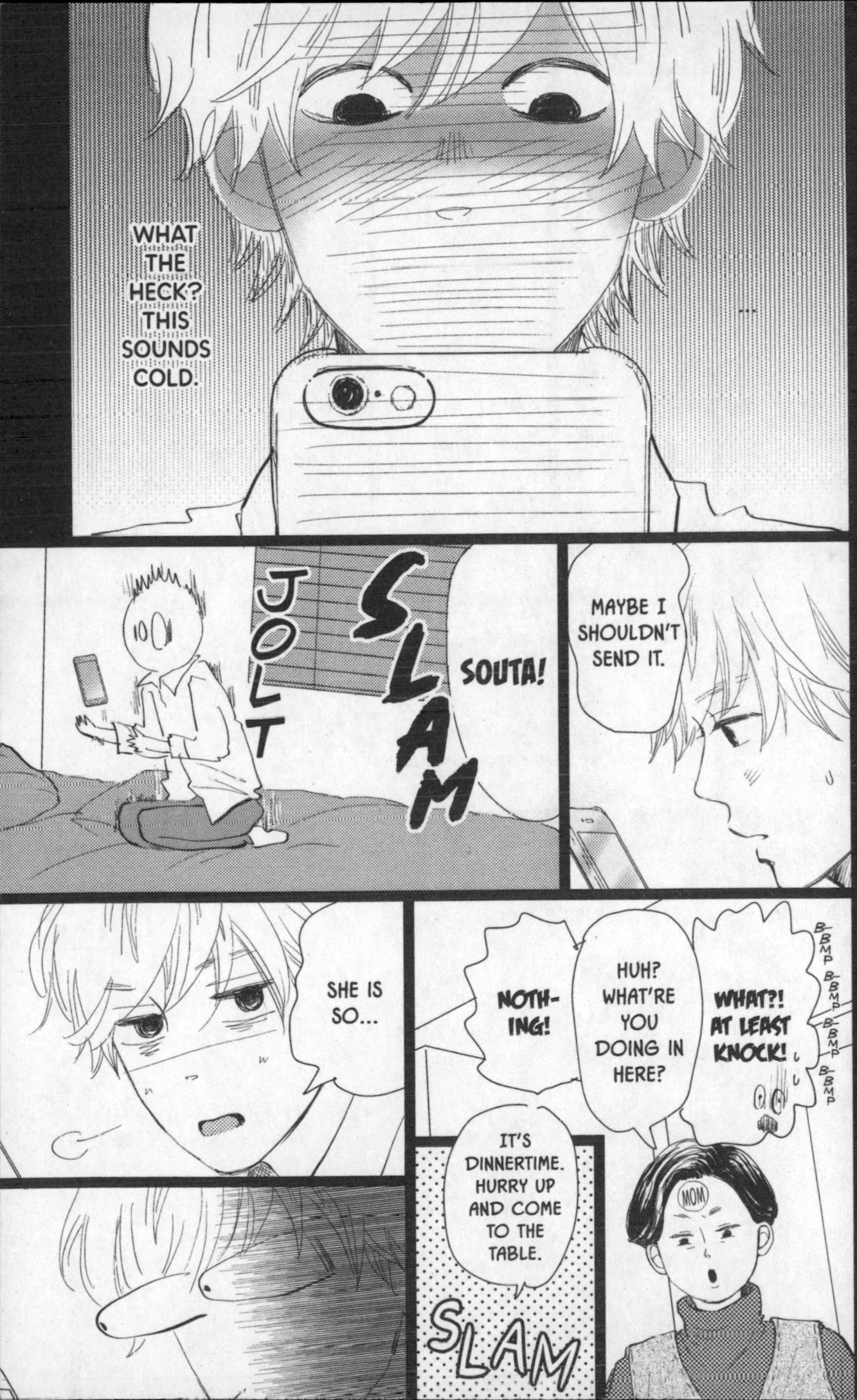
WHAT THE HECK? THIS SOUNDS COLD.
...
MAYBE I SHOULDN'T SEND IT.
SOUTA!
SLAM
JOLT
B-BMP B-BMP B-BMP B-BMP
WHAT?! AT LEAST KNOCK!
HUH? WHAT'RE YOU DOING IN HERE?
NOTH-ING!
IT'S DINNERTIME. HURRY UP AND COME TO THE TABLE.
MOM
SLAM
SHE IS SO...

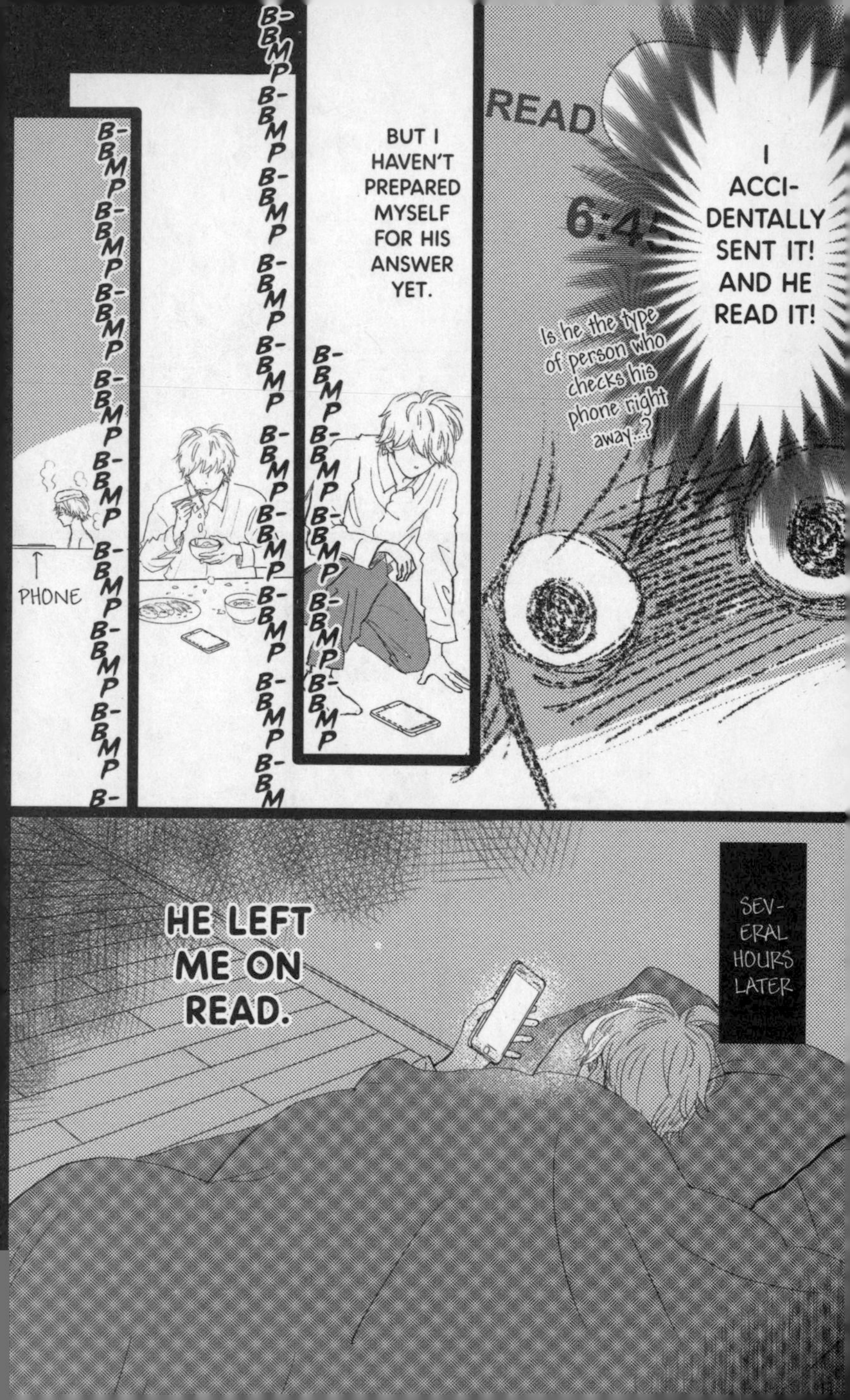
READ
6:4
I ACCI-DENTALLY SENT IT! AND HE READ IT!
Is he the type of person who checks his phone right away...?
BUT I HAVEN'T PREPARED MYSELF FOR HIS ANSWER YET.
B-BMP B-BMP B-BMP B-BMP B-BMP B-BMP
B-BMP B-BMP B-BMP B-BMP B-BMP B-BMP B-BMP B-BMP B-BM
PHONE
B-BMP B-BMP B-BMP B-BMP B-BMP B-BMP B-BMP B-BMP B-BMP B-BMP B-
SEV-ERAL HOURS LATER
HE LEFT ME ON READ.

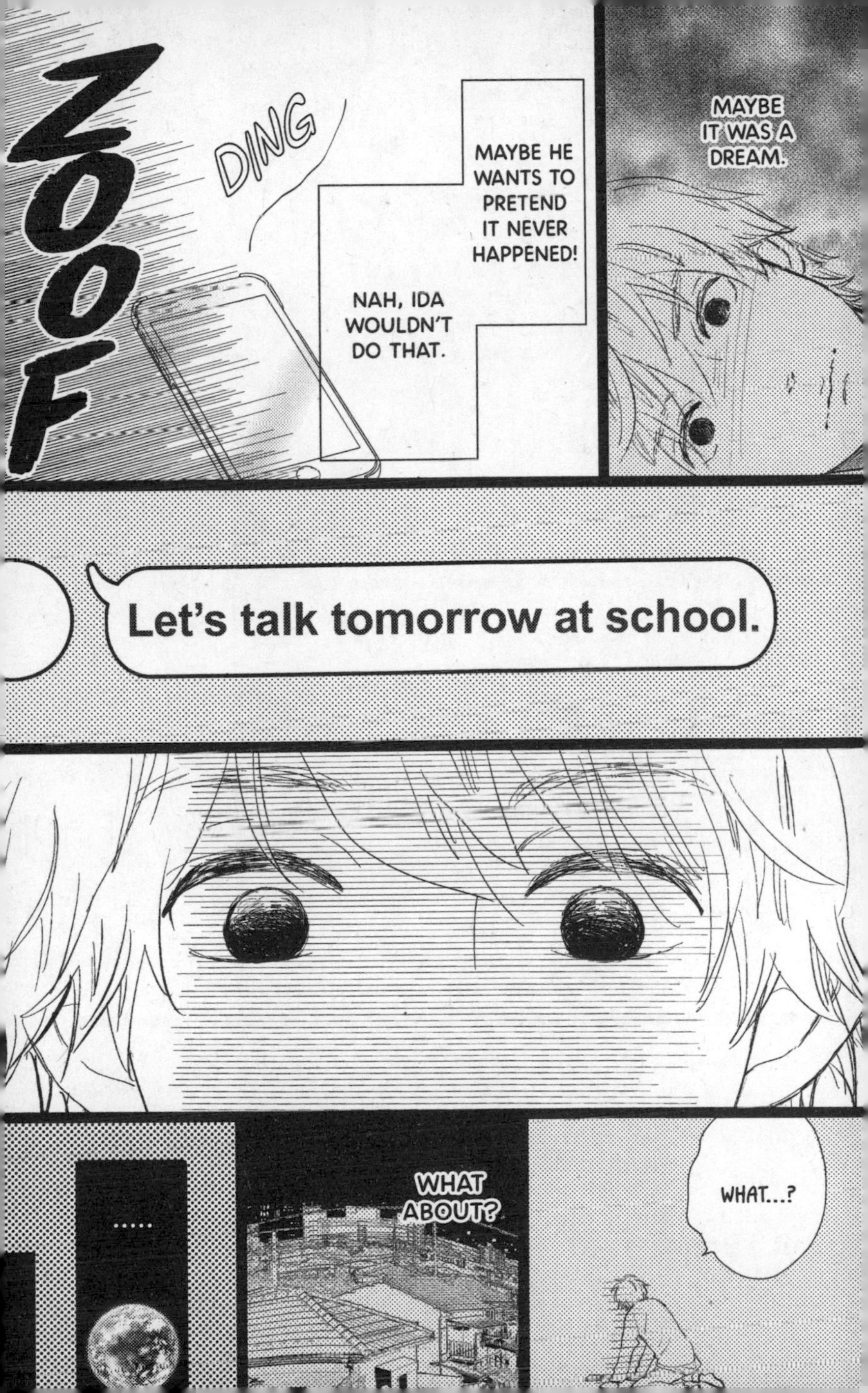
MAYBE IT WAS A DREAM.
MAYBE HE WANTS TO PRETEND IT NEVER HAPPENED!
NAH, IDA WOULDN'T DO THAT.
DING
ZOOF
Let's talk tomorrow at school.
WHAT...?
WHAT ABOUT?
......

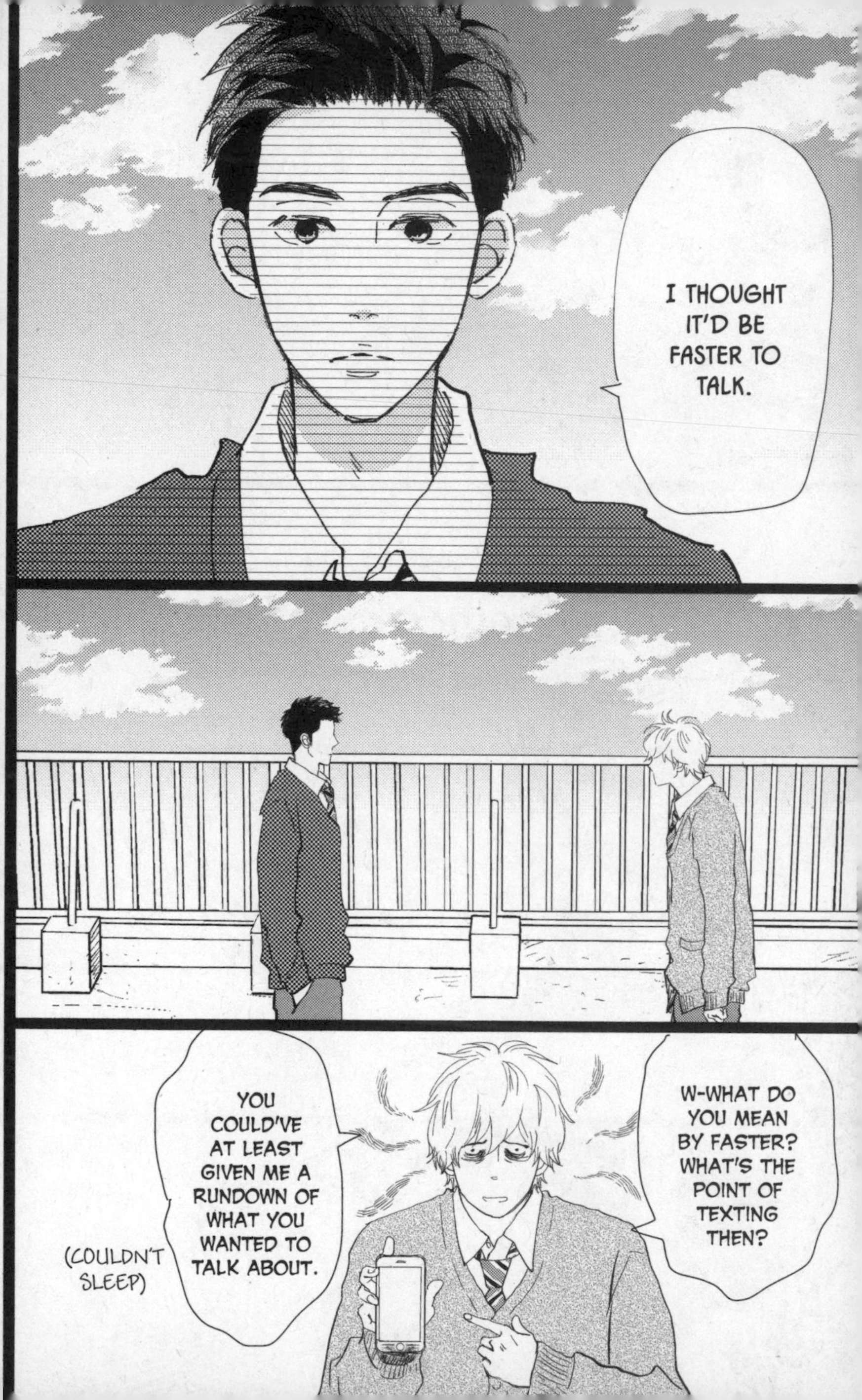
I THOUGHT IT'D BE FASTER TO TALK.
W-WHAT DO YOU MEAN BY FASTER? WHAT'S THE POINT OF TEXTING THEN?
YOU COULD'VE AT LEAST GIVEN ME A RUNDOWN OF WHAT YOU WANTED TO TALK ABOUT.
(COULDN'T SLEEP)

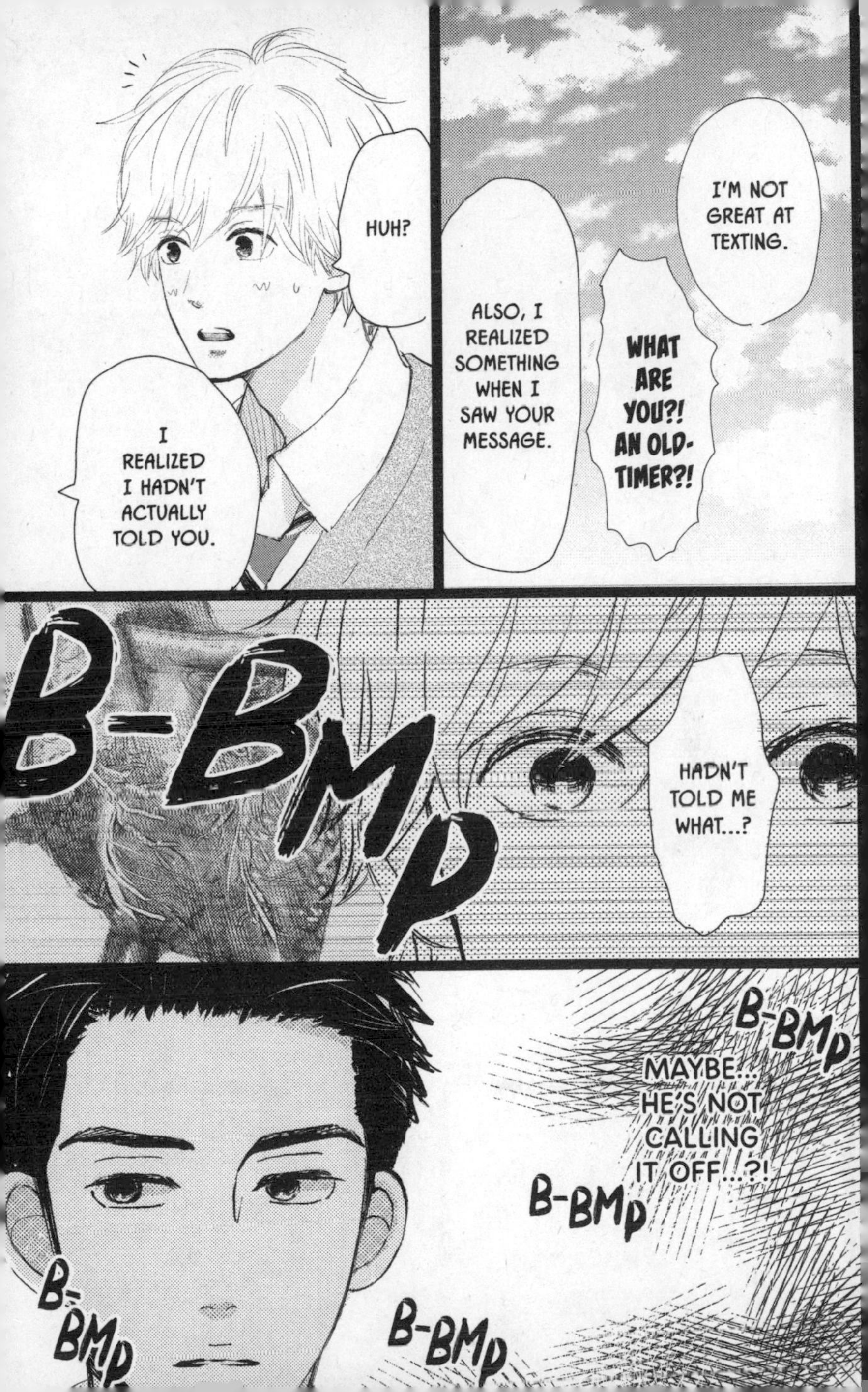
I'M NOT GREAT AT TEXTING.
WHAT ARE YOU?! AN OLD-TIMER?!
ALSO, I REALIZED SOMETHING WHEN I SAW YOUR MESSAGE.
HUH?
I REALIZED I HADN'T ACTUALLY TOLD YOU.
HADN'T TOLD ME WHAT...?
B-BMP
B-BMP
MAYBE... HE'S NOT CALLING IT OFF...?!
B-BMP
B-BMP
B-BMP

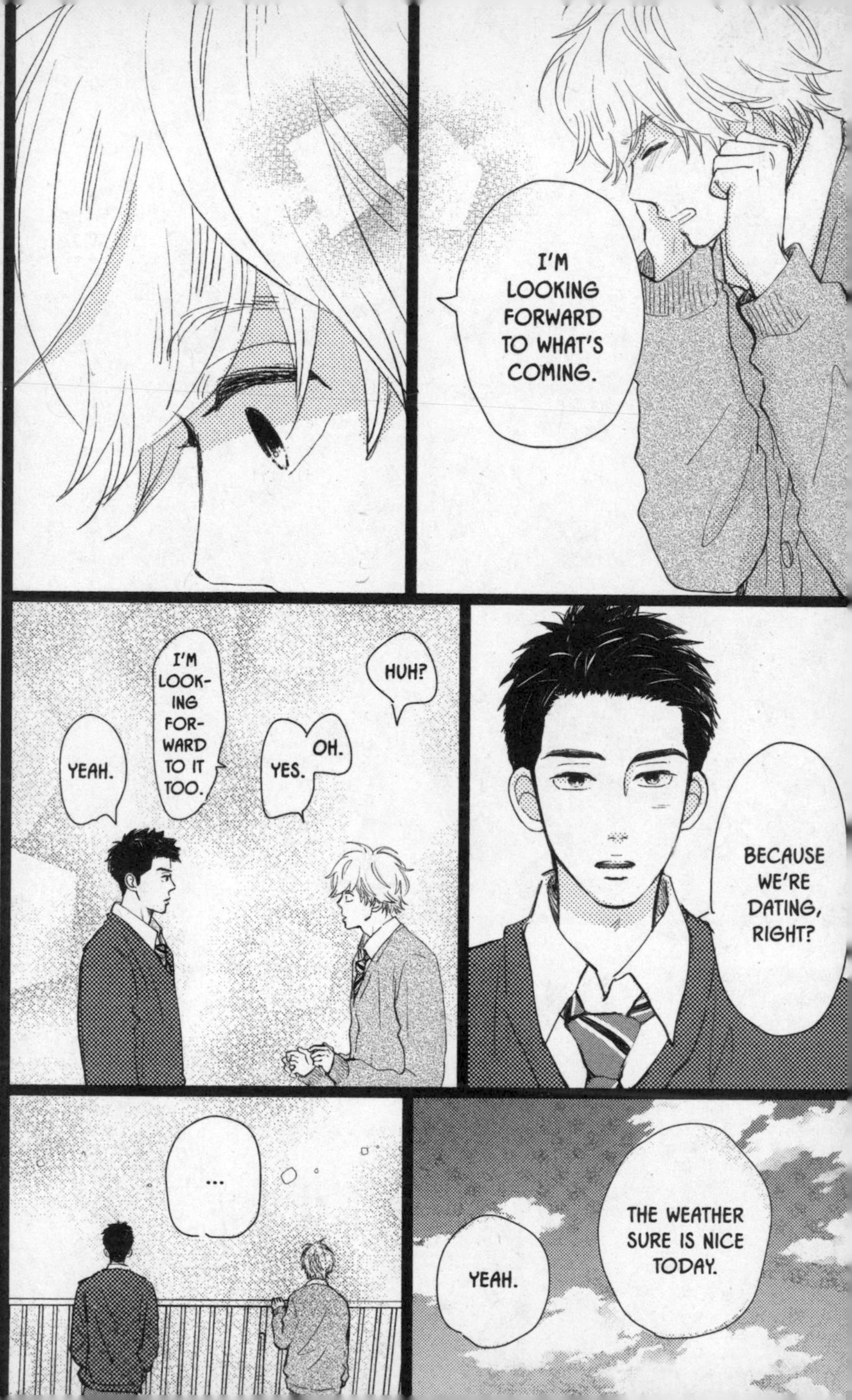
I'M LOOKING FORWARD TO WHAT'S COMING.
BECAUSE WE'RE DATING, RIGHT?
HUH?
OH. YES.
I'M LOOKING-FORWARD TO IT TOO.
YEAH.
THE WEATHER SURE IS NICE TODAY.
YEAH.
...

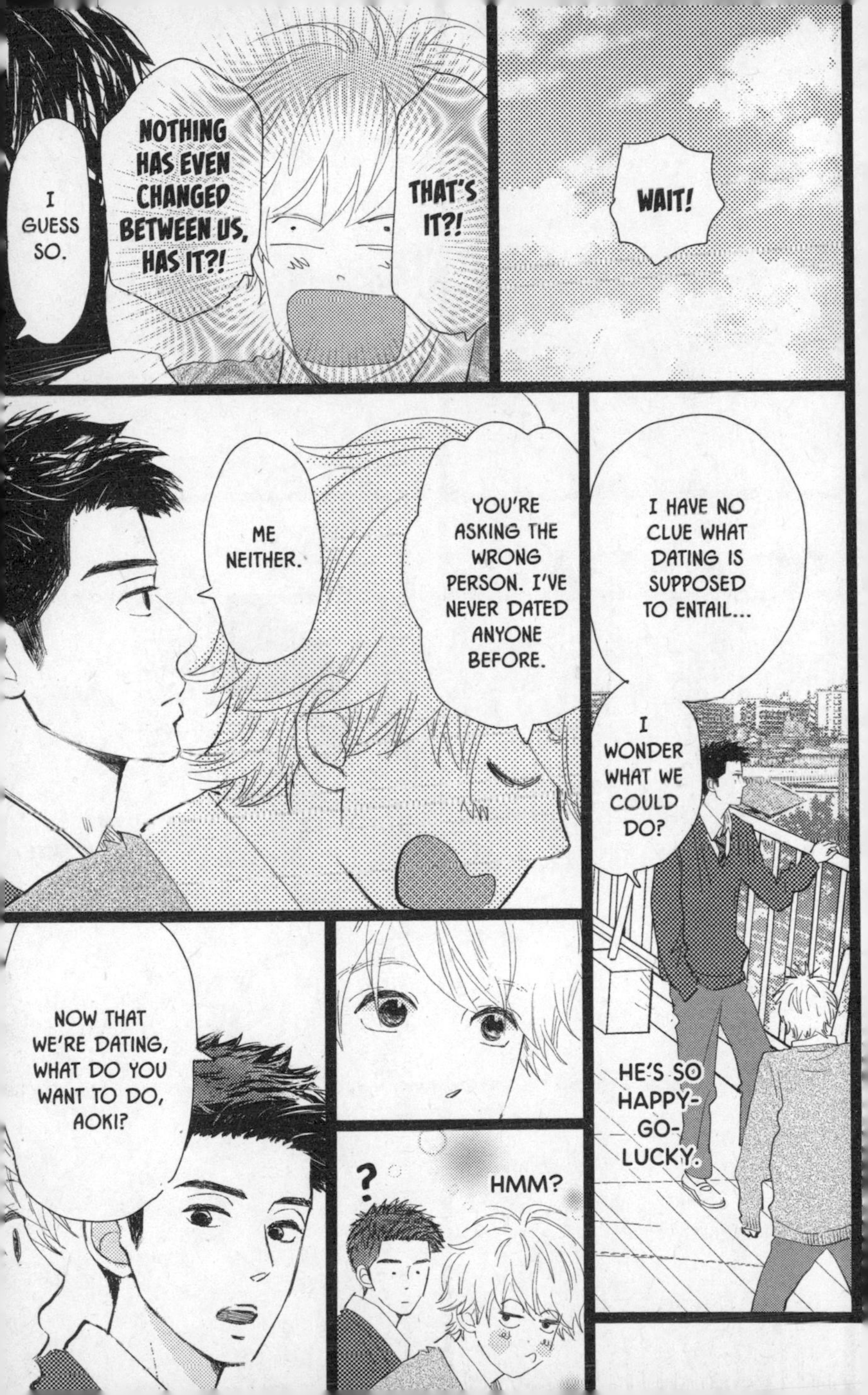
WAIT!
THAT'S IT?!
NOTHING HAS EVEN CHANGED BETWEEN US, HAS IT?!
I GUESS SO.
I HAVE NO CLUE WHAT DATING IS SUPPOSED TO ENTAIL...
I WONDER WHAT WE COULD DO?
HE'S SO HAPPY-GO-LUCKY.
YOU'RE ASKING THE WRONG PERSON. I'VE NEVER DATED ANYONE BEFORE.
ME NEITHER.
?
HMM?
NOW THAT WE'RE DATING, WHAT DO YOU WANT TO DO, AOKI?

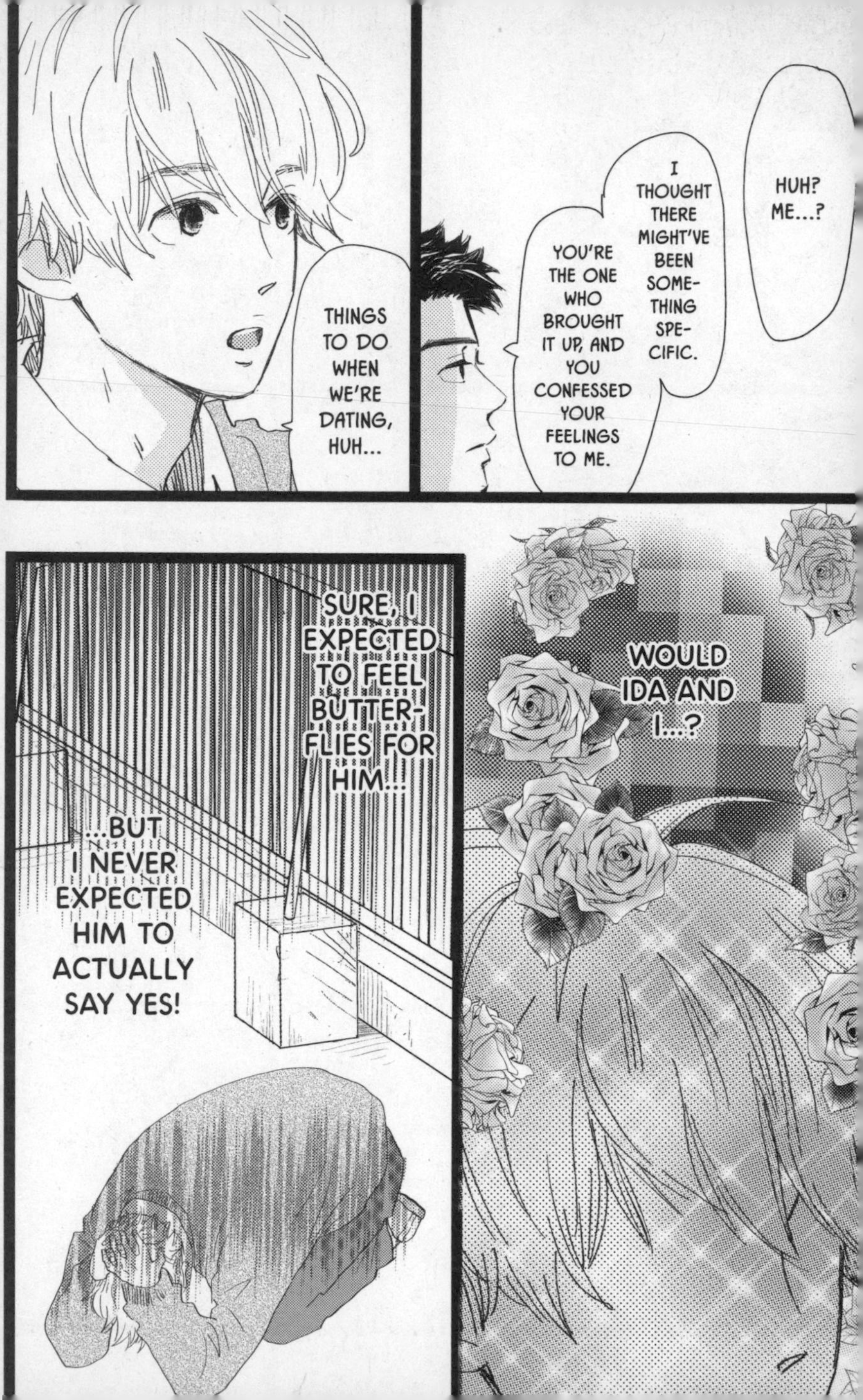
HUH? ME...?
I THOUGHT THERE MIGHT'VE BEEN SOME-THING SPE-CIFIC.
YOU'RE THE ONE WHO BROUGHT IT UP, AND YOU CONFESSED YOUR FEELINGS TO ME.
THINGS TO DO WHEN WE'RE DATING, HUH...
WOULD IDA AND I...?
SURE, I EXPECTED TO FEEL BUTTER-FLIES FOR HIM...
...BUT I NEVER EXPECTED HIM TO ACTUALLY SAY YES!

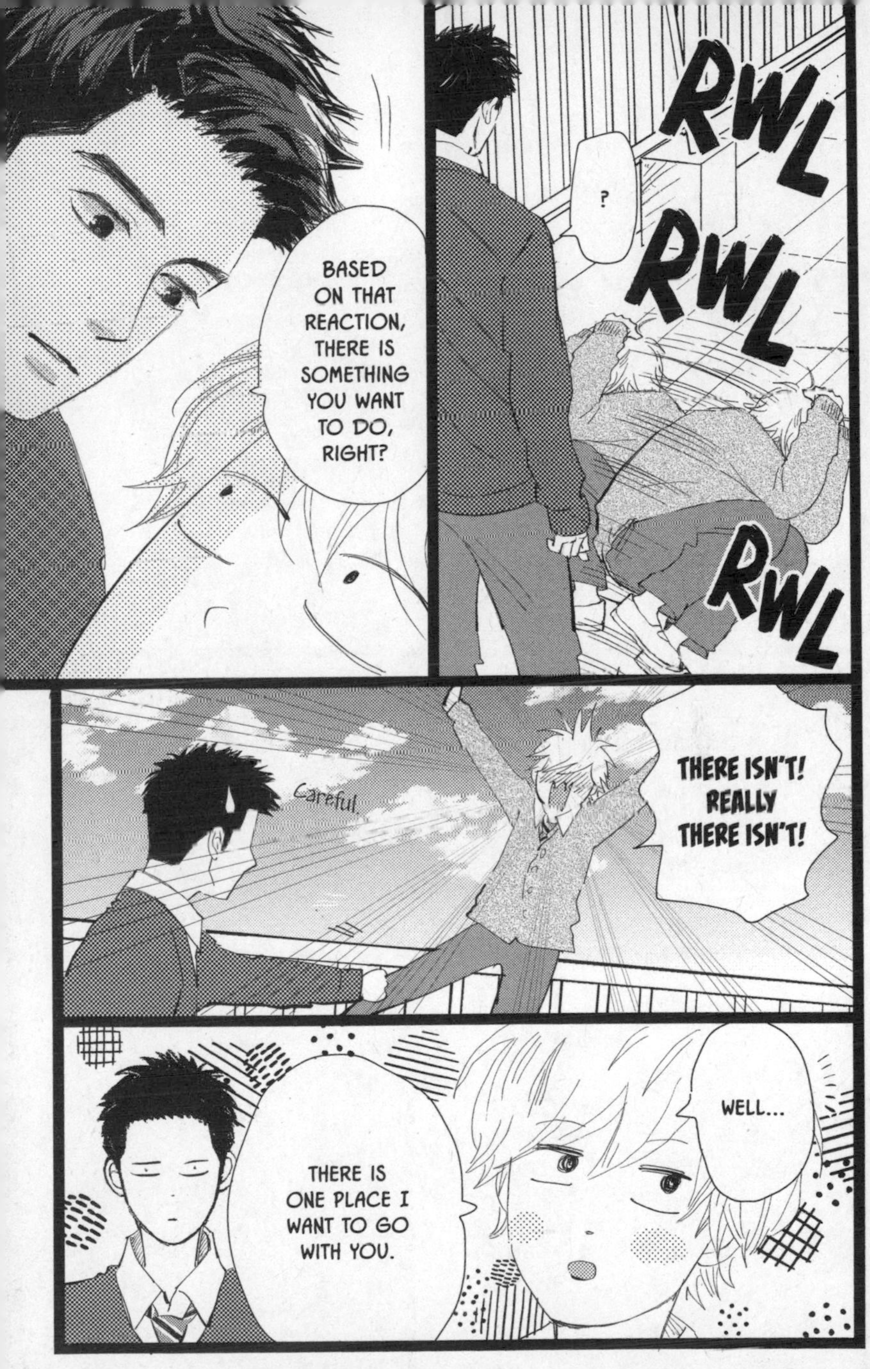
RWL
RWL
?
RWL
BASED ON THAT REACTION, THERE IS SOMETHING YOU WANT TO DO, RIGHT?
THERE ISN'T! REALLY THERE ISN'T!
Careful.
WELL...
THERE IS ONE PLACE I WANT TO GO WITH YOU.

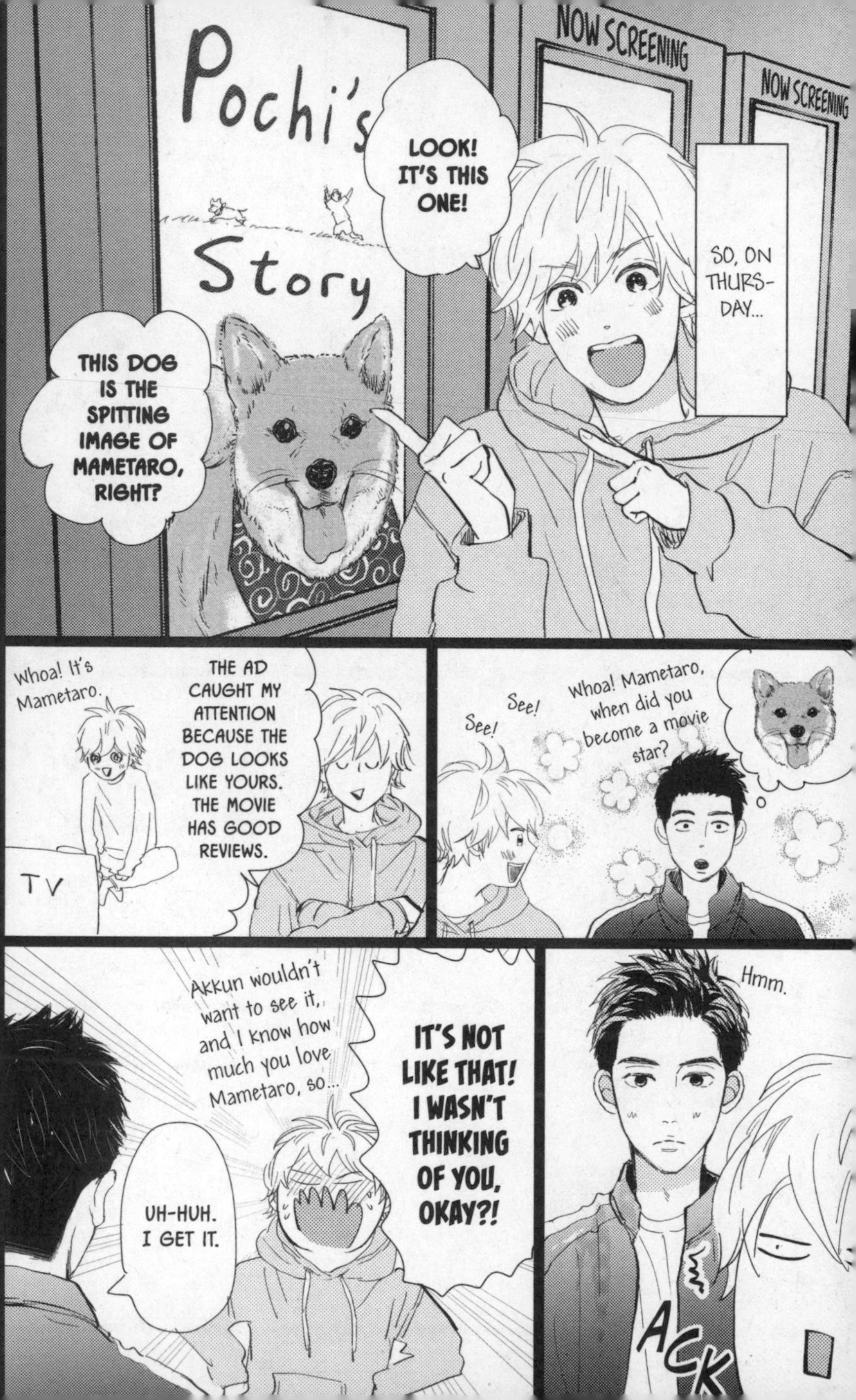
NOW SCREENING
NOW SCREENING
Pochi's Story
SO, ON THURSDAY...
LOOK! IT'S THIS ONE!
THIS DOG IS THE SPITTING IMAGE OF MAMETARO, RIGHT?
Whoa! Mametaro, when did you become a movie star?
See!
See!
THE AD CAUGHT MY ATTENTION BECAUSE THE DOG LOOKS LIKE YOURS. THE MOVIE HAS GOOD REVIEWS.
Whoa! It's Mametaro.
TV
Hmm.
ACK
Akkun wouldn't want to see it, and I know how much you love Mametaro, so...
IT'S NOT LIKE THAT! I WASN'T THINKING OF YOU, OKAY?!
UH-HUH. I GET IT.

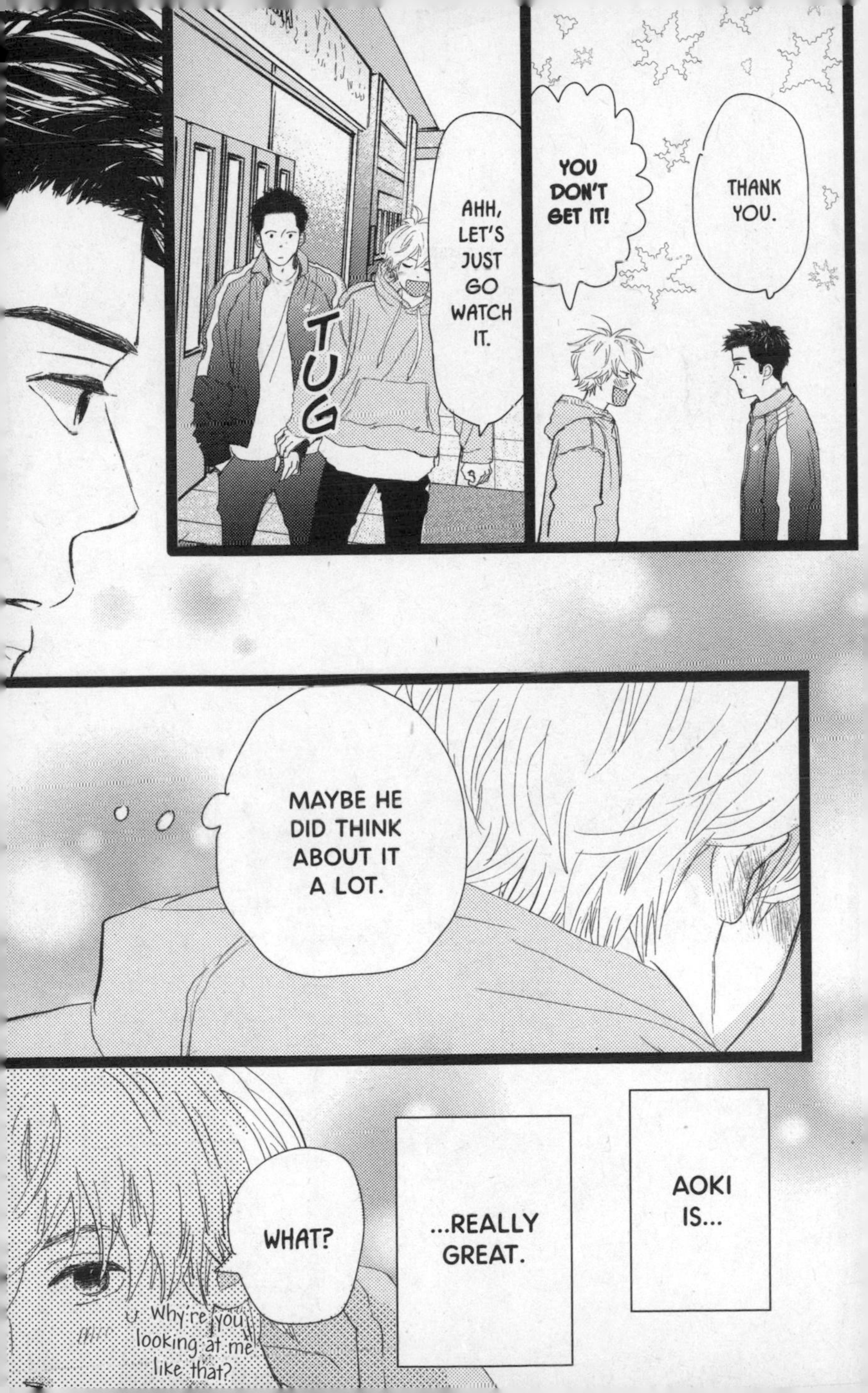
THANK YOU.
YOU DON'T GET IT!
AHH, LET'S JUST GO WATCH IT.
TUG
MAYBE HE DID THINK ABOUT IT A LOT.
AOKI IS...
...REALLY GREAT.
WHAT?
Why're you looking at me like that?

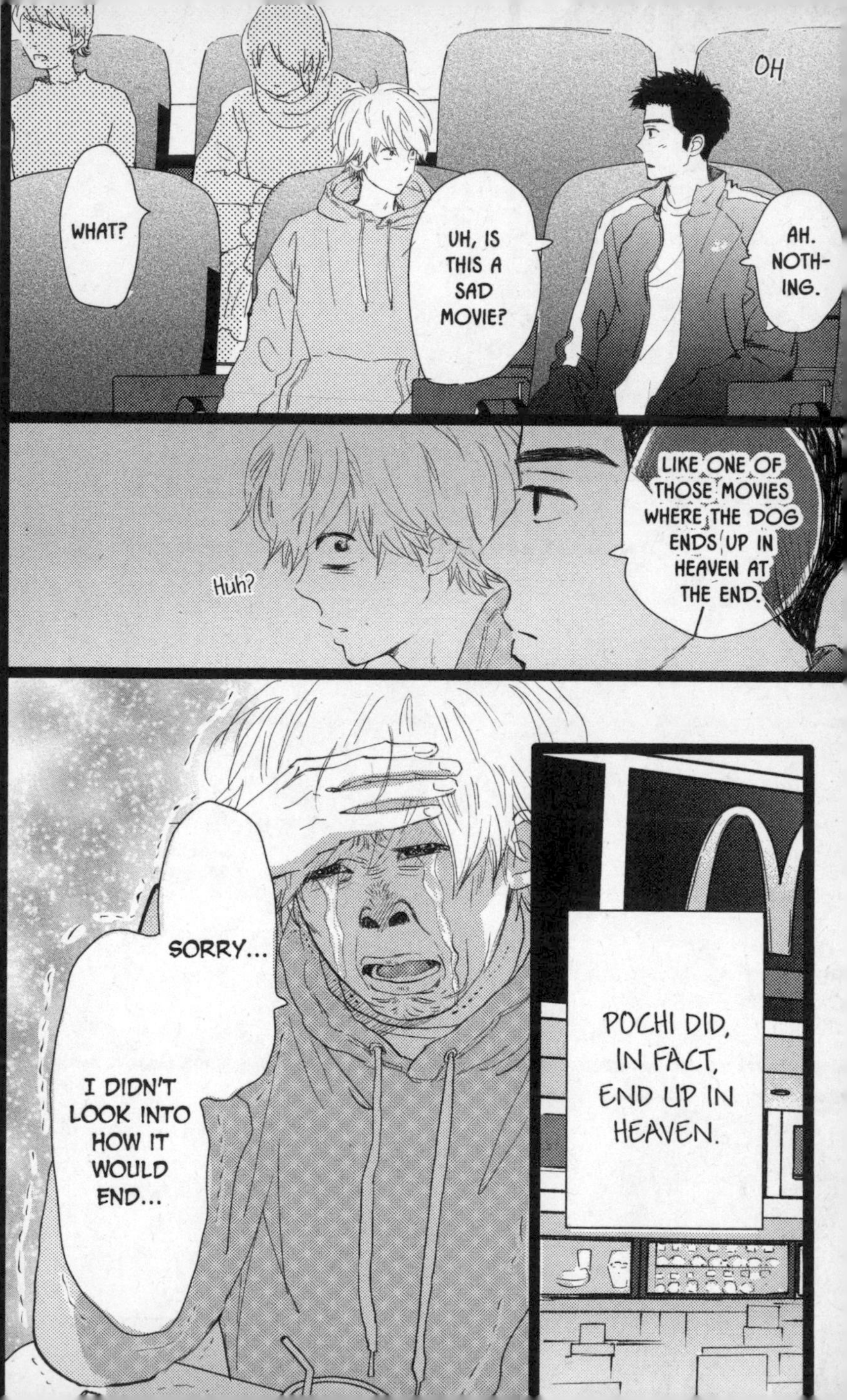
OH
AH. NOTH-ING.
UH, IS THIS A SAD MOVIE?
WHAT?
LIKE ONE OF THOSE MOVIES WHERE THE DOG ENDS UP IN HEAVEN AT THE END.
Huh?
SORRY...
I DIDN'T LOOK INTO HOW IT WOULD END...
POCHI DID, IN FACT, END UP IN HEAVEN.

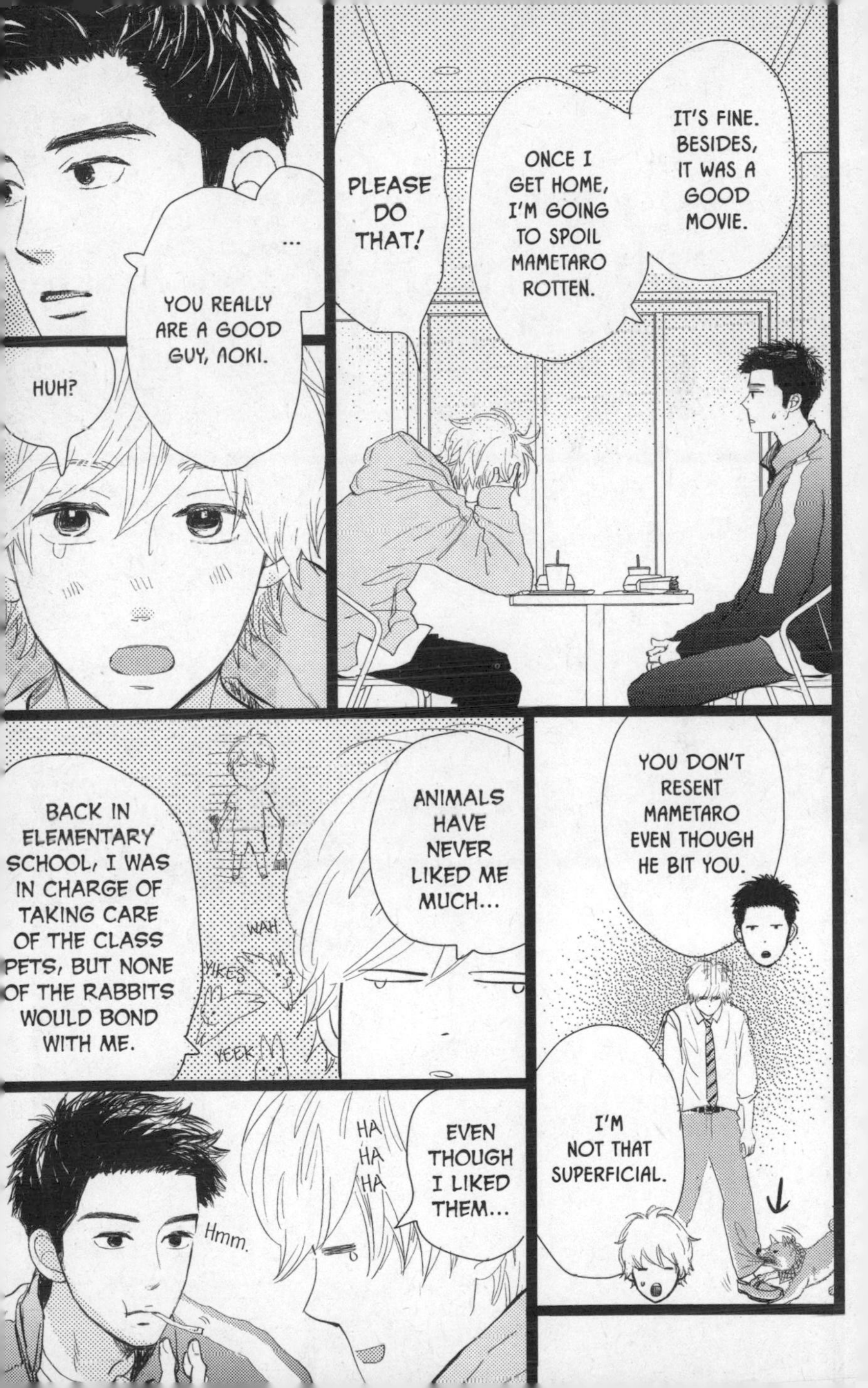
IT'S FINE. BESIDES, IT WAS A GOOD MOVIE.
ONCE I GET HOME, I'M GOING TO SPOIL MAMETARO ROTTEN.
PLEASE DO THAT!
...
YOU REALLY ARE A GOOD GUY, AOKI.
HUH?
YOU DON'T RESENT MAMETARO EVEN THOUGH HE BIT YOU.
I'M NOT THAT SUPERFICIAL.
ANIMALS HAVE NEVER LIKED ME MUCH...
BACK IN ELEMENTARY SCHOOL, I WAS IN CHARGE OF TAKING CARE OF THE CLASS PETS, BUT NONE OF THE RABBITS WOULD BOND WITH ME.
WAH
YIKES
YEEK
EVEN THOUGH I LIKED THEM...
HA HA HA
Hmm.

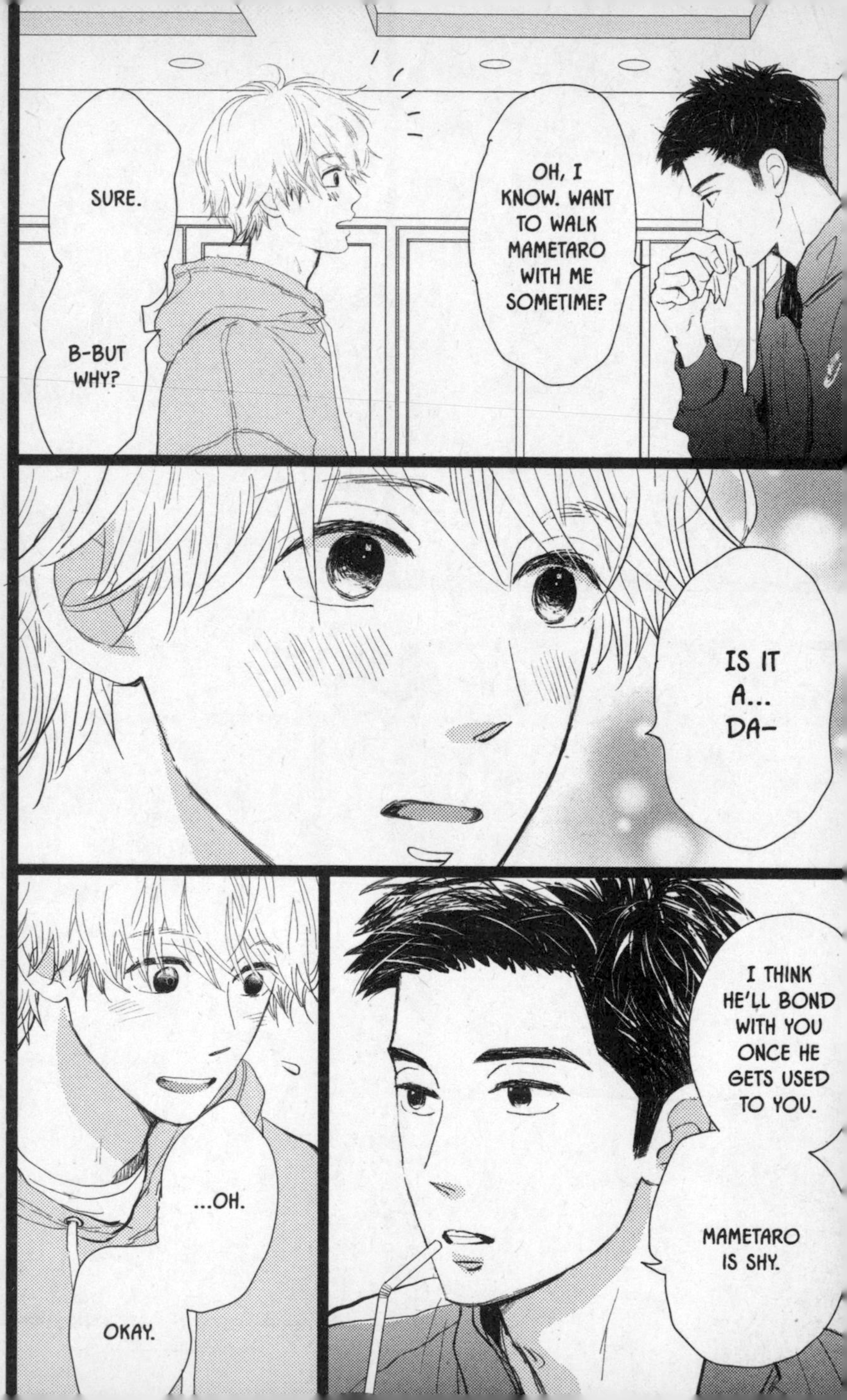

OH, I KNOW. WANT TO WALK MAMETARO WITH ME SOMETIME?
SURE.
B-BUT WHY?
IS IT A... DA-
I THINK HE'LL BOND WITH YOU ONCE HE GETS USED TO YOU.
MAMETARO IS SHY.
...OH.
OKAY.

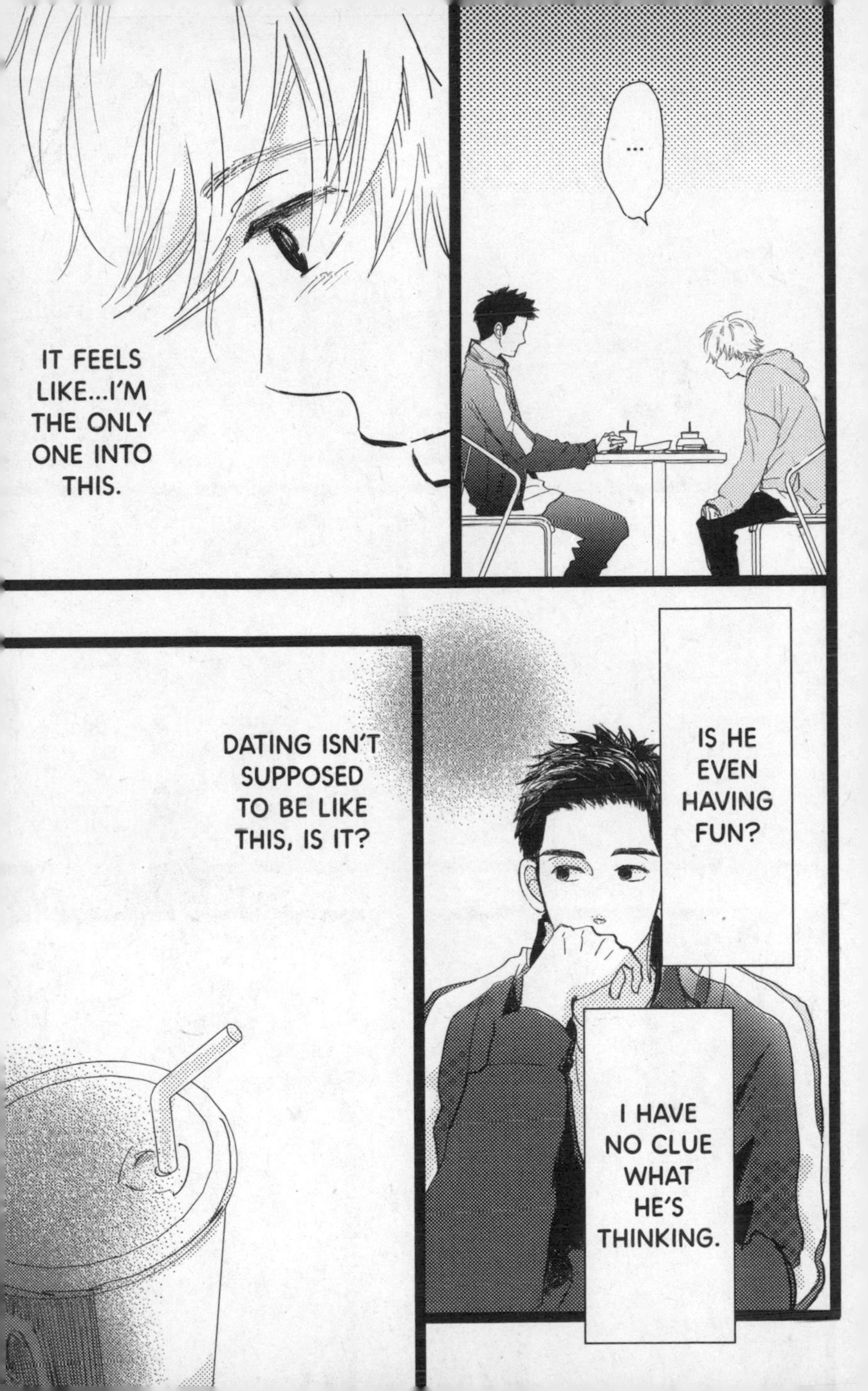
...
IT FEELS LIKE...I'M THE ONLY ONE INTO THIS.
IS HE EVEN HAVING FUN?
I HAVE NO CLUE WHAT HE'S THINKING.
DATING ISN'T SUPPOSED TO BE LIKE THIS, IS IT?

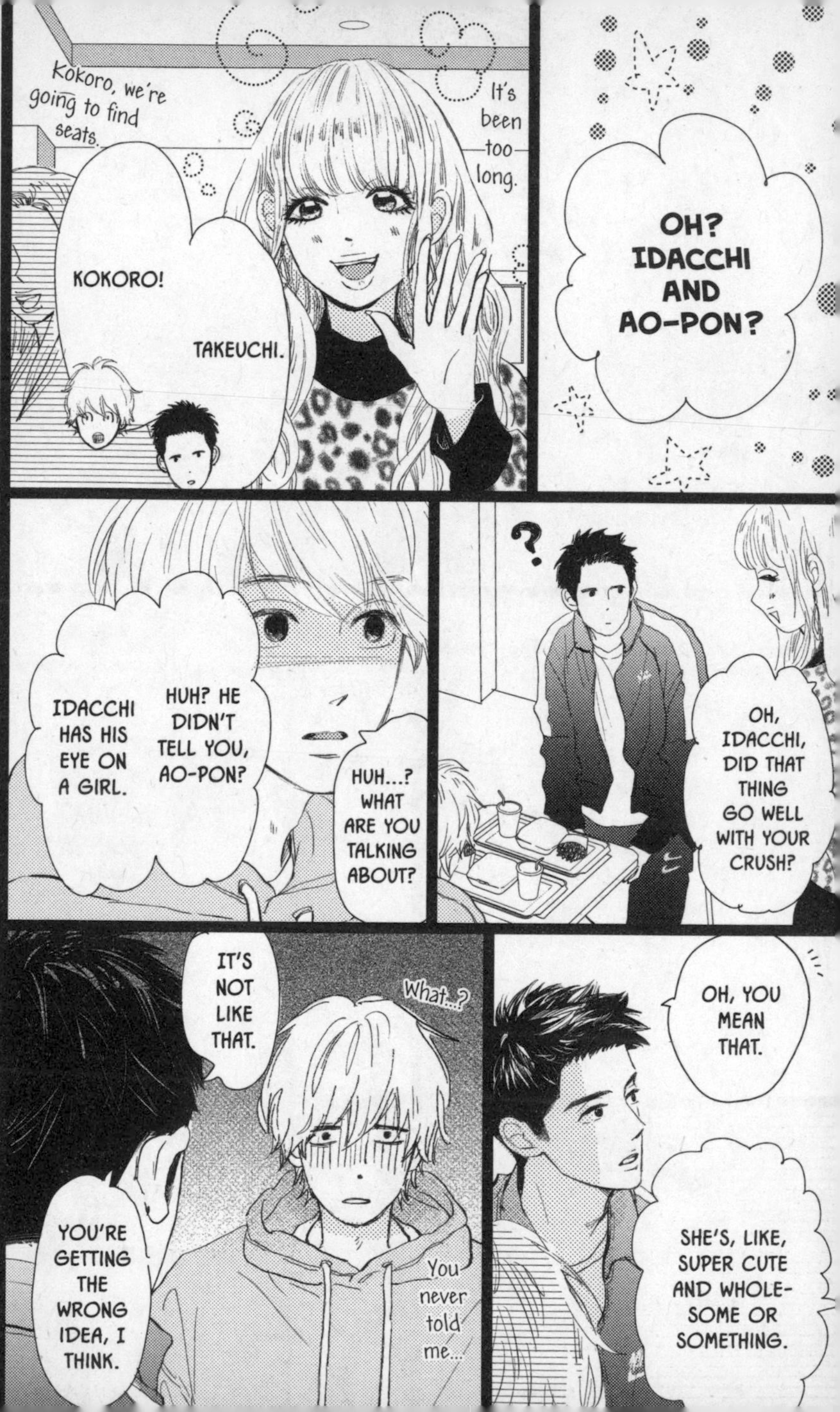
OH? IDACCHI AND AO-PON?
It's been too long.
Kokoro, we're going to find seats.
KOKORO!
TAKEUCHI.
OH, IDACCHI, DID THAT THING GO WELL WITH YOUR CRUSH?
HUH...? WHAT ARE YOU TALKING ABOUT?
HUH? HE DIDN'T TELL YOU, AO-PON?
IDACCHI HAS HIS EYE ON A GIRL.
OH, YOU MEAN THAT.
SHE'S, LIKE, SUPER CUTE AND WHOLE-SOME OR SOMETHING.
What...?
IT'S NOT LIKE THAT.
You never told me...
YOU'RE GETTING THE WRONG IDEA, I THINK.

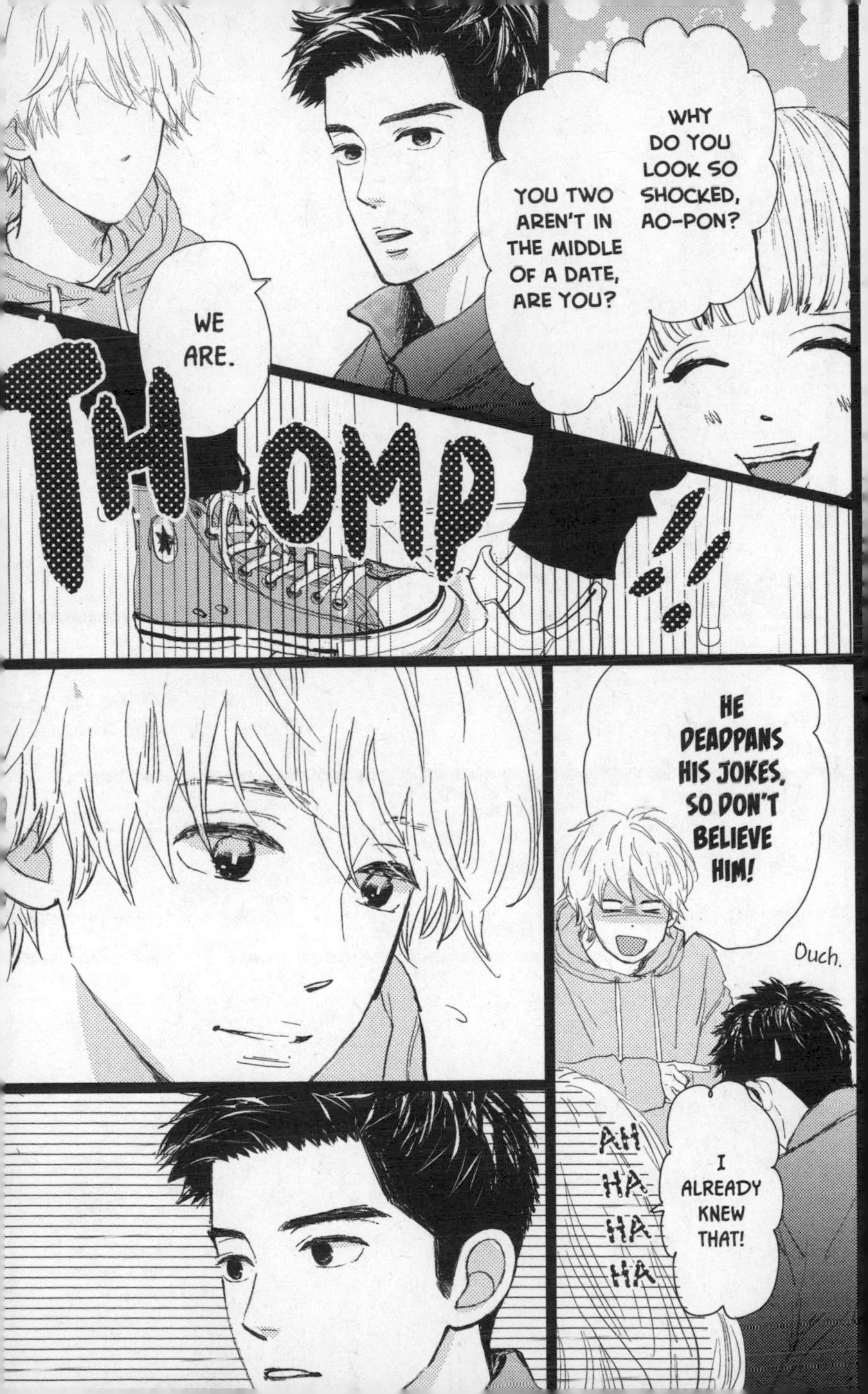
WHY DO YOU LOOK SO SHOCKED, AO-PON?
YOU TWO AREN'T IN THE MIDDLE OF A DATE, ARE YOU?
WE ARE.
THOMP!!
HE DEADPANS HIS JOKES, SO DON'T BELIEVE HIM!
Ouch.
I ALREADY KNEW THAT!
AH HA HA HA

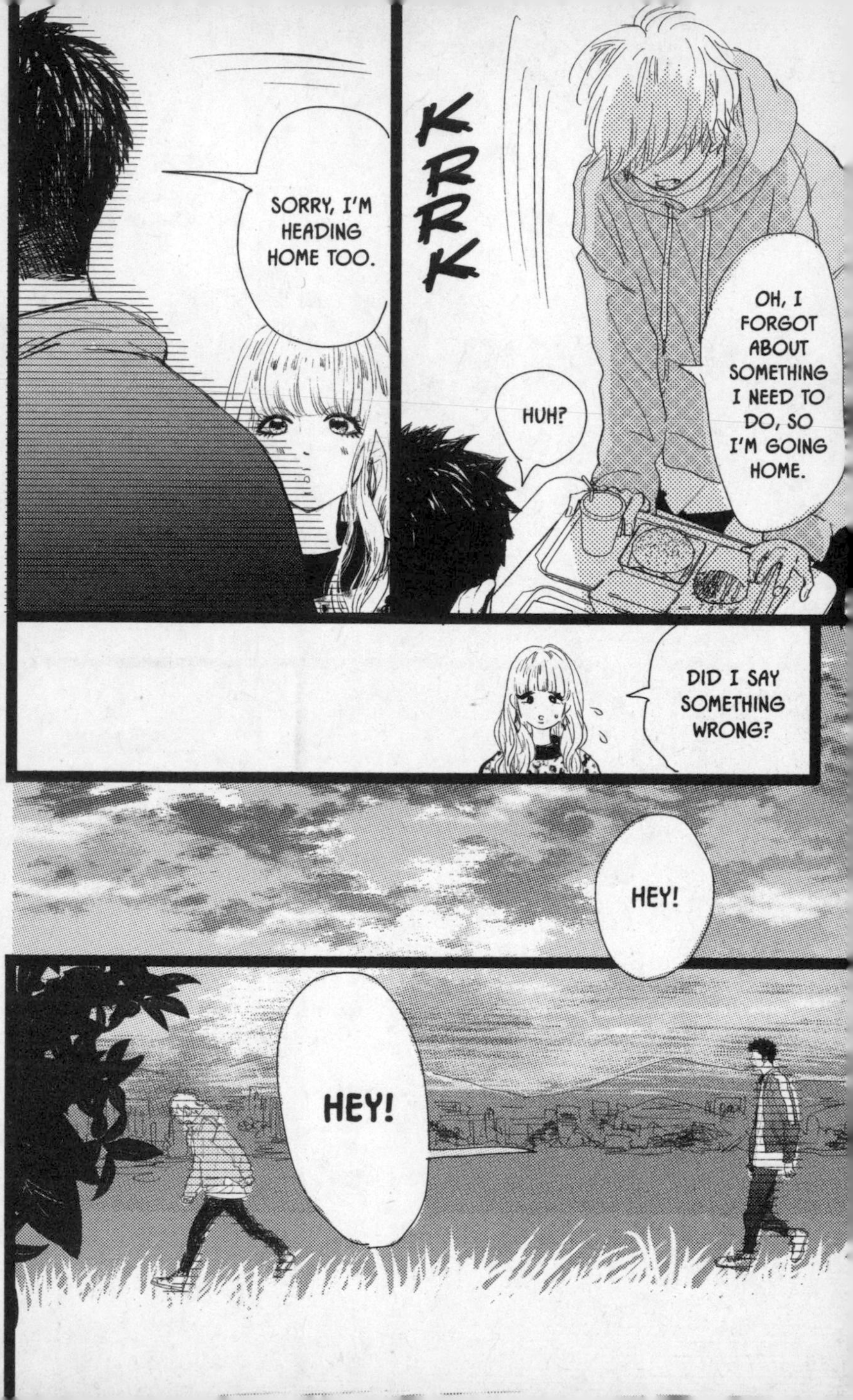
KRRK
OH, I FORGOT ABOUT SOMETHING I NEED TO DO, SO I'M GOING HOME.
HUH?
SORRY, I'M HEADING HOME TOO.
DID I SAY SOMETHING WRONG?
HEY!
HEY!

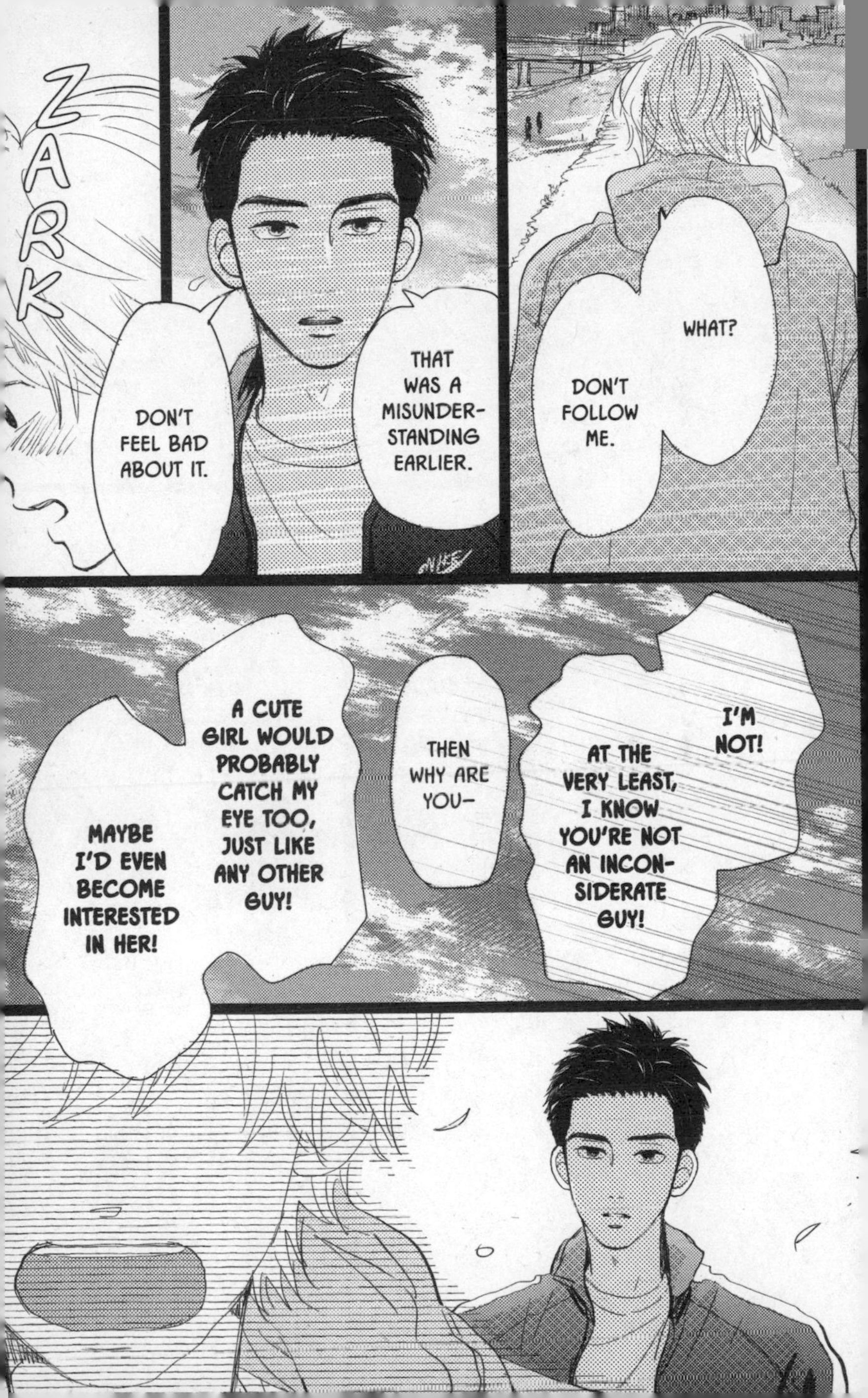
WHAT?
DON'T FOLLOW ME.
THAT WAS A MISUNDERSTANDING EARLIER.
ZARK
DON'T FEEL BAD ABOUT IT.
I'M NOT!
AT THE VERY LEAST, I KNOW YOU'RE NOT AN INCONSIDERATE GUY!
THEN WHY ARE YOU—
A CUTE GIRL WOULD PROBABLY CATCH MY EYE TOO, JUST LIKE ANY OTHER GUY!
MAYBE I'D EVEN BECOME INTERESTED IN HER!

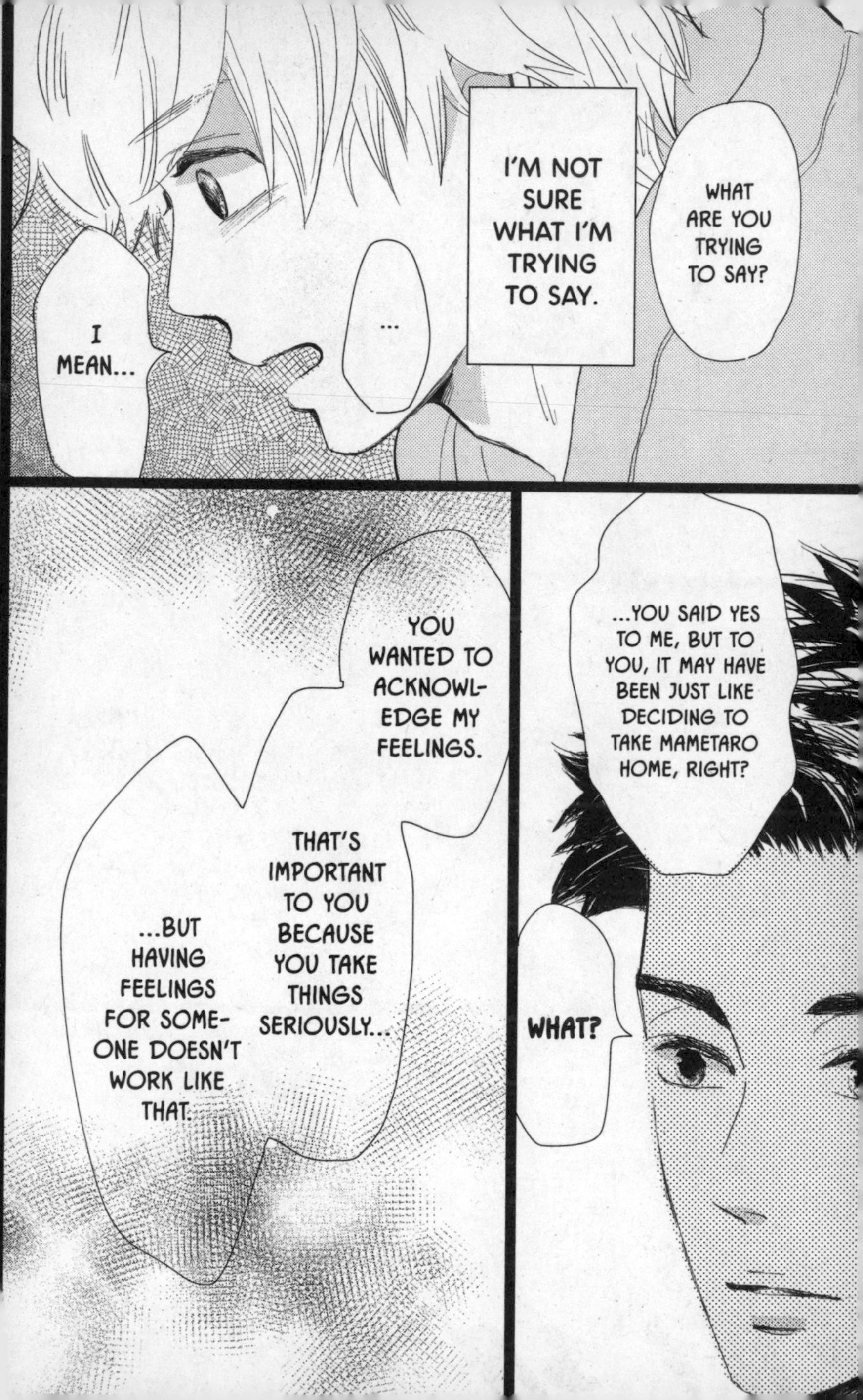
WHAT ARE YOU TRYING TO SAY?
I'M NOT SURE WHAT I'M TRYING TO SAY.
...
I MEAN...
...YOU SAID YES TO ME, BUT TO YOU, IT MAY HAVE BEEN JUST LIKE DECIDING TO TAKE MAMETARO HOME, RIGHT?
WHAT?
YOU WANTED TO ACKNOWL-EDGE MY FEELINGS.
THAT'S IMPORTANT TO YOU BECAUSE YOU TAKE THINGS SERIOUSLY...
...BUT HAVING FEELINGS FOR SOME-ONE DOESN'T WORK LIKE THAT.

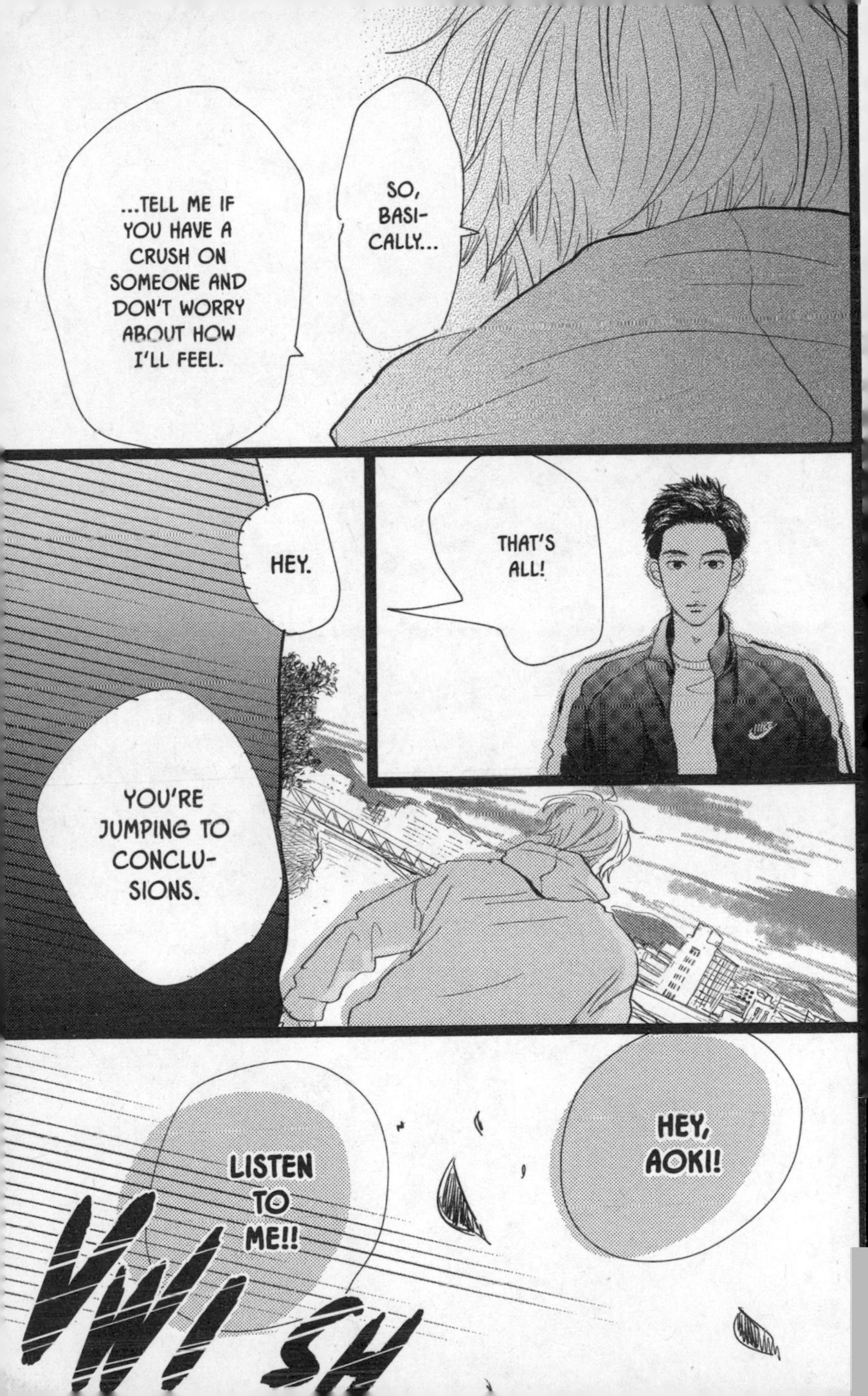
SO, BASI-CALLY...
...TELL ME IF YOU HAVE A CRUSH ON SOMEONE AND DON'T WORRY ABOUT HOW I'LL FEEL.
THAT'S ALL!
HEY.
YOU'RE JUMPING TO CONCLU-SIONS.
HEY, AOKI!
LISTEN TO ME!!
WHISH

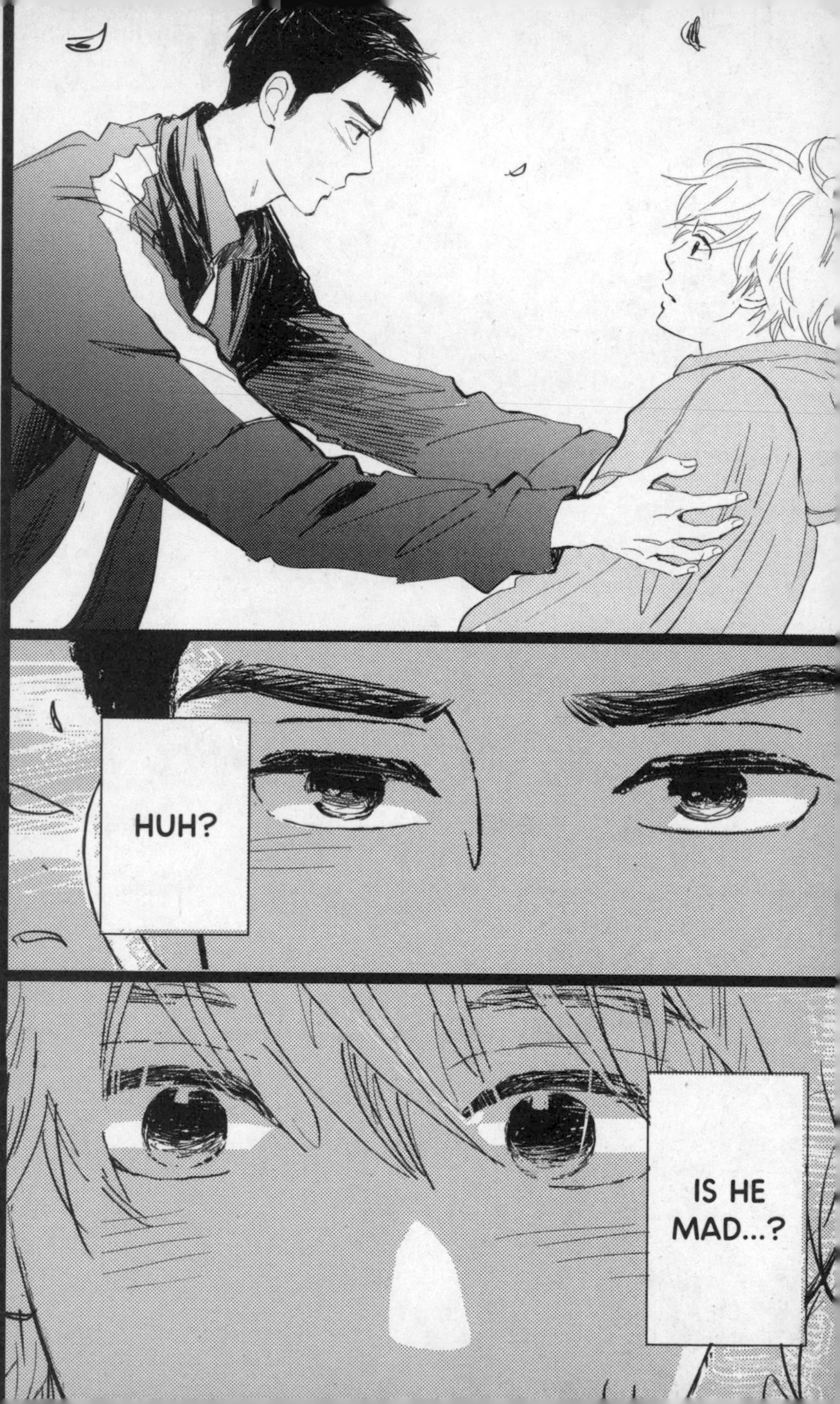
HUH?
IS HE MAD...?

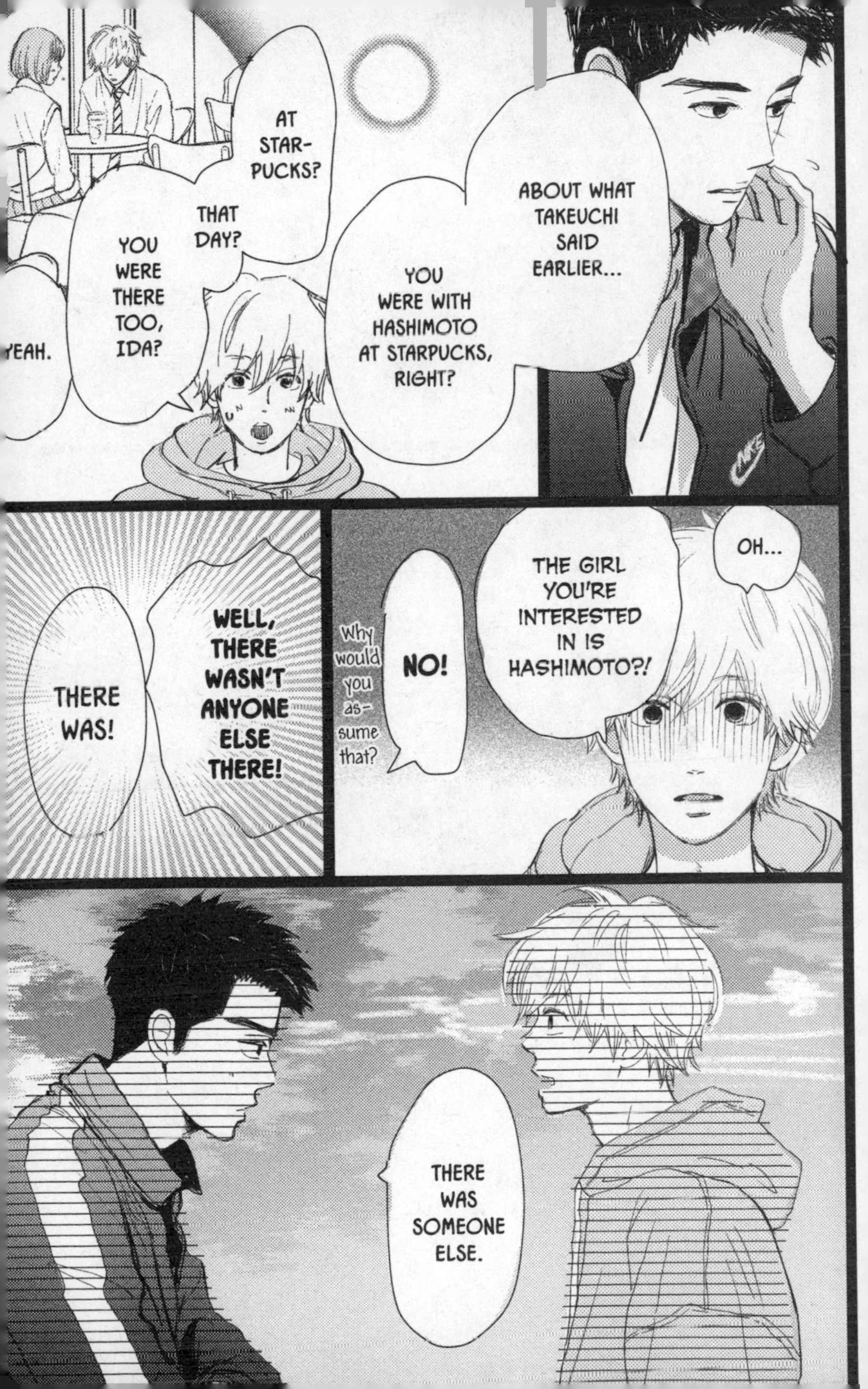
ABOUT WHAT TAKEUCHI SAID EARLIER...
YOU WERE WITH HASHIMOTO AT STARPUCKS, RIGHT?
AT STARPUCKS?
THAT DAY?
YOU WERE THERE TOO, IDA?
YEAH.
OH...
THE GIRL YOU'RE INTERESTED IN IS HASHIMOTO?!
NO!
Why would you assume that?
WELL, THERE WASN'T ANYONE ELSE THERE!
THERE WAS!
THERE WAS SOMEONE ELSE.

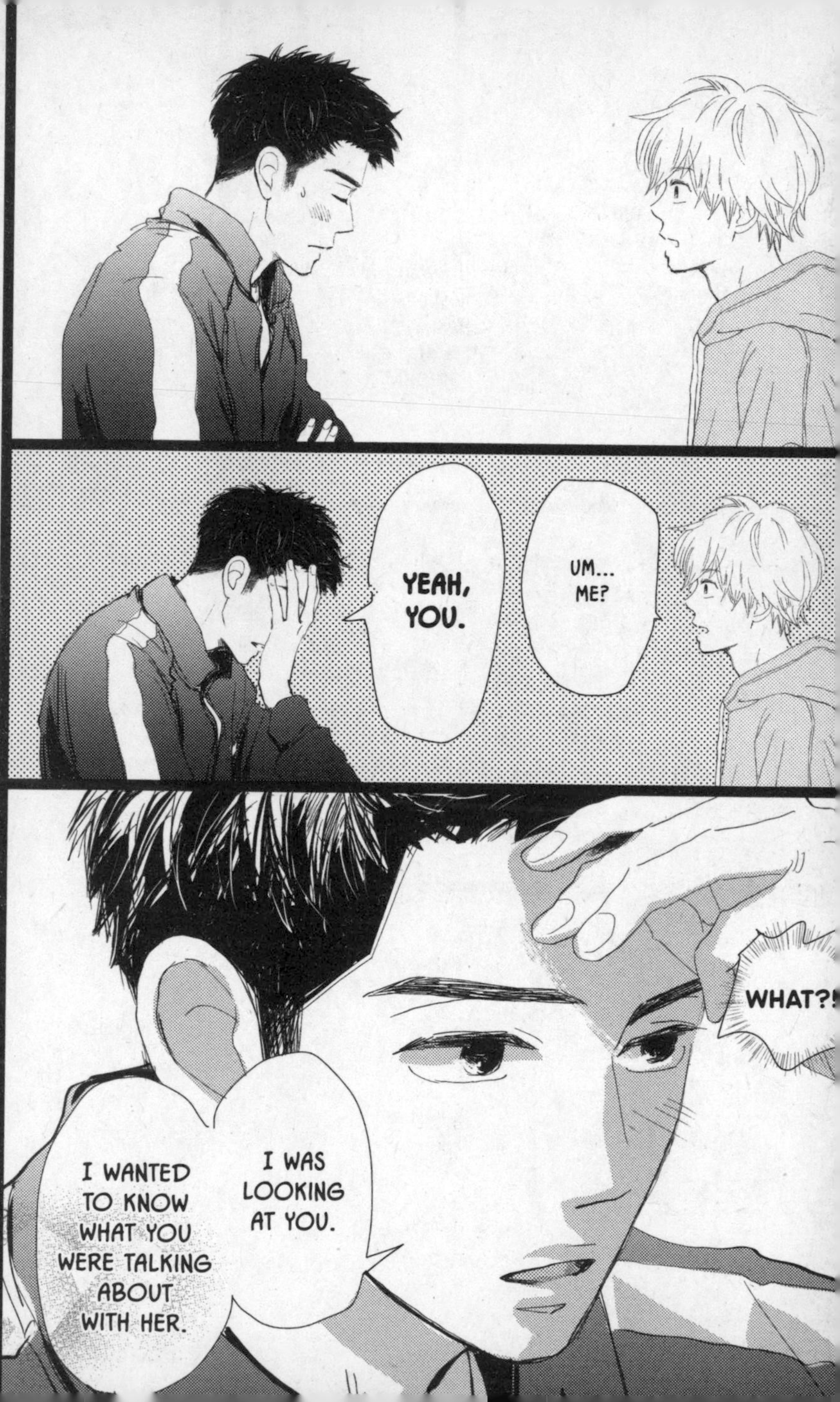
UM... ME?
YEAH, YOU.
WHAT?!
I WAS LOOKING AT YOU.
I WANTED TO KNOW WHAT YOU WERE TALKING ABOUT WITH HER.

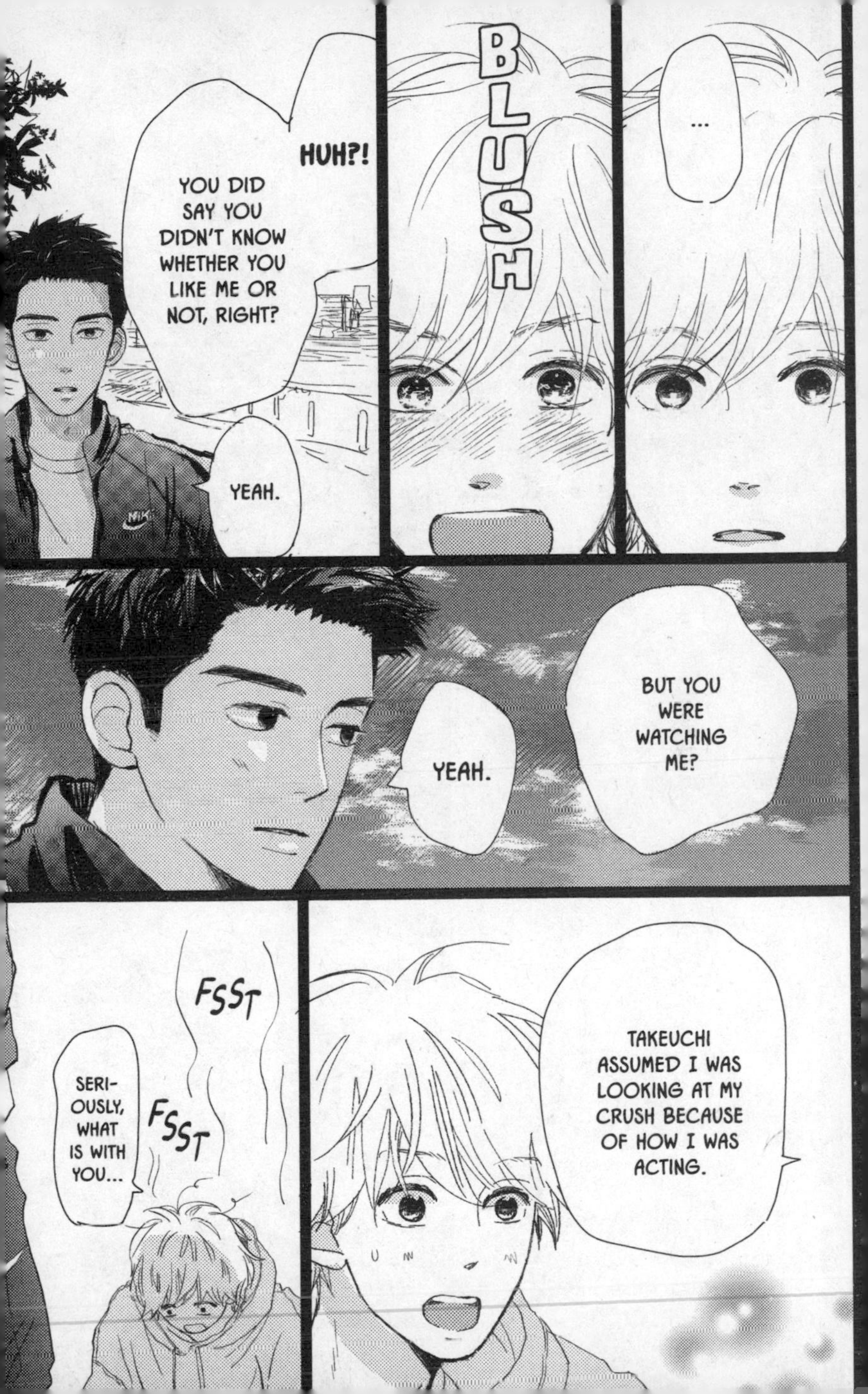
...
BLUSH
HUH?!
YOU DID SAY YOU DIDN'T KNOW WHETHER YOU LIKE ME OR NOT, RIGHT?
YEAH.
BUT YOU WERE WATCHING ME?
YEAH.
TAKEUCHI ASSUMED I WAS LOOKING AT MY CRUSH BECAUSE OF HOW I WAS ACTING.
FSST
FSST
SERI-OUSLY, WHAT IS WITH YOU...

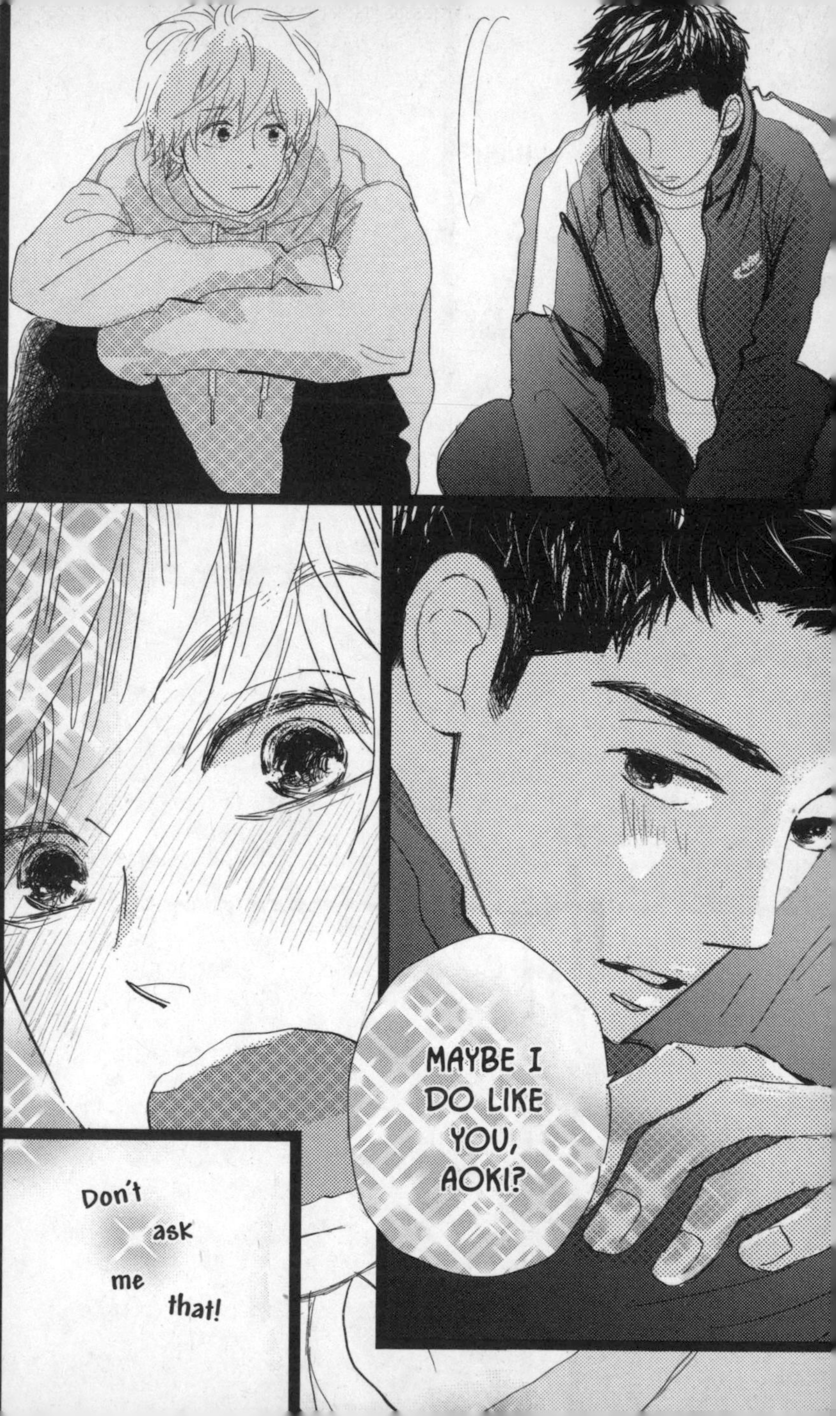
MAYBE I DO LIKE YOU, AOKI?
Don't ask me that!

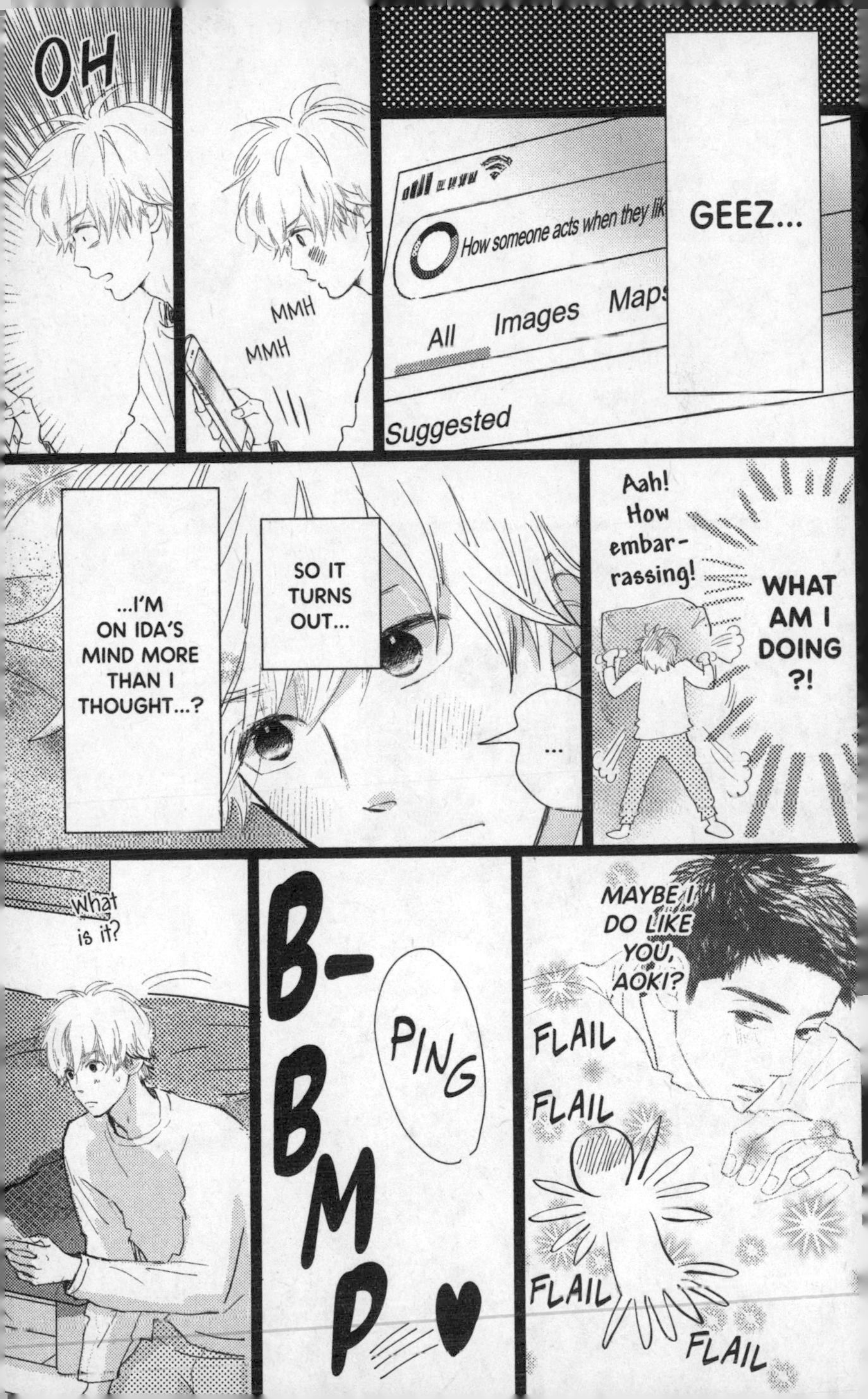
GEEZ...
How someone acts when they lik
All
Images
Maps
Suggested
MMH
MMH
OH
Aah! How embarrassing!
WHAT AM I DOING ?!
...
SO IT TURNS OUT...
...I'M ON IDA'S MIND MORE THAN I THOUGHT...?
MAYBE I DO LIKE YOU, AOKI?
FLAIL
FLAIL
FLAIL
FLAIL
B-BMP
PING
What is it?

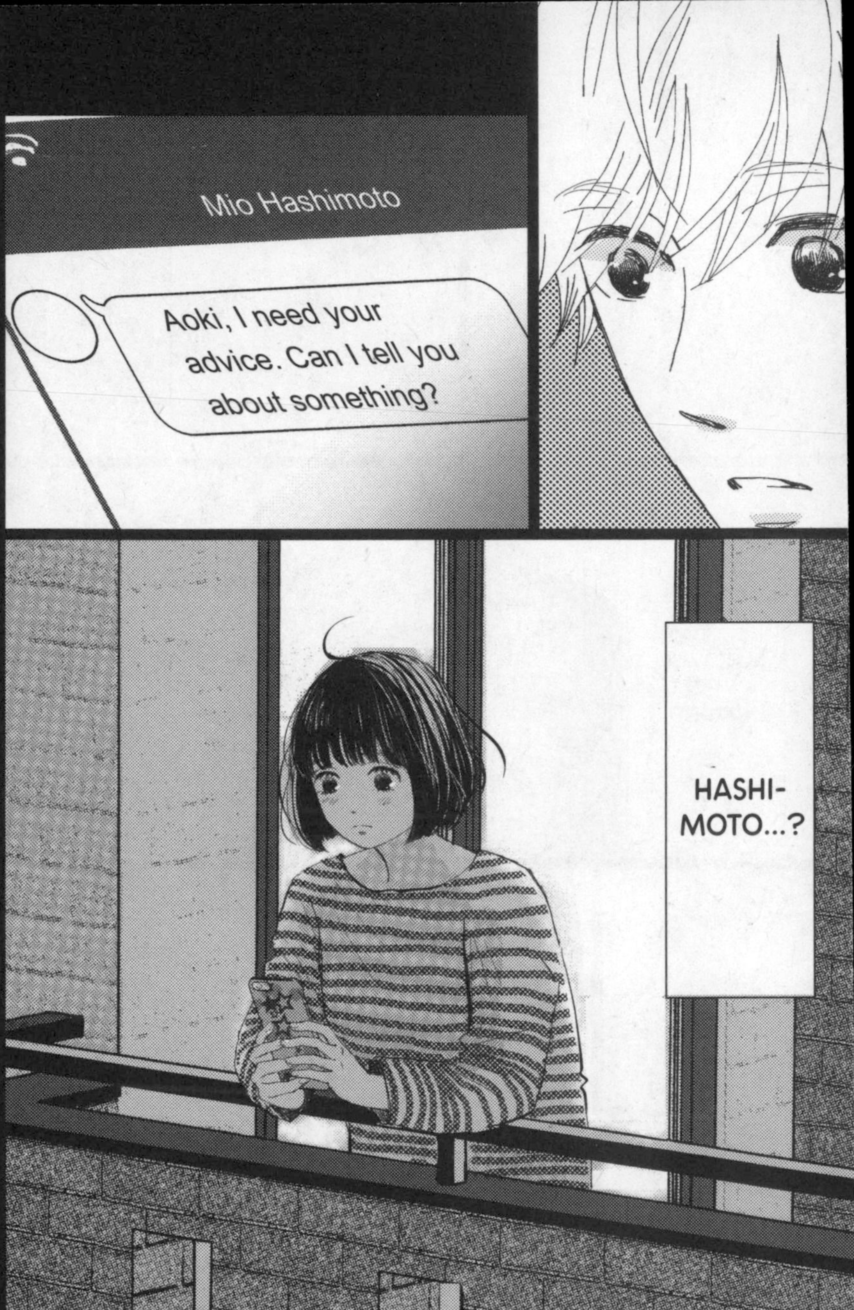
Mio Hashimoto
Aoki, I need your advice. Can I tell you about something?
HASHI-MOTO...?

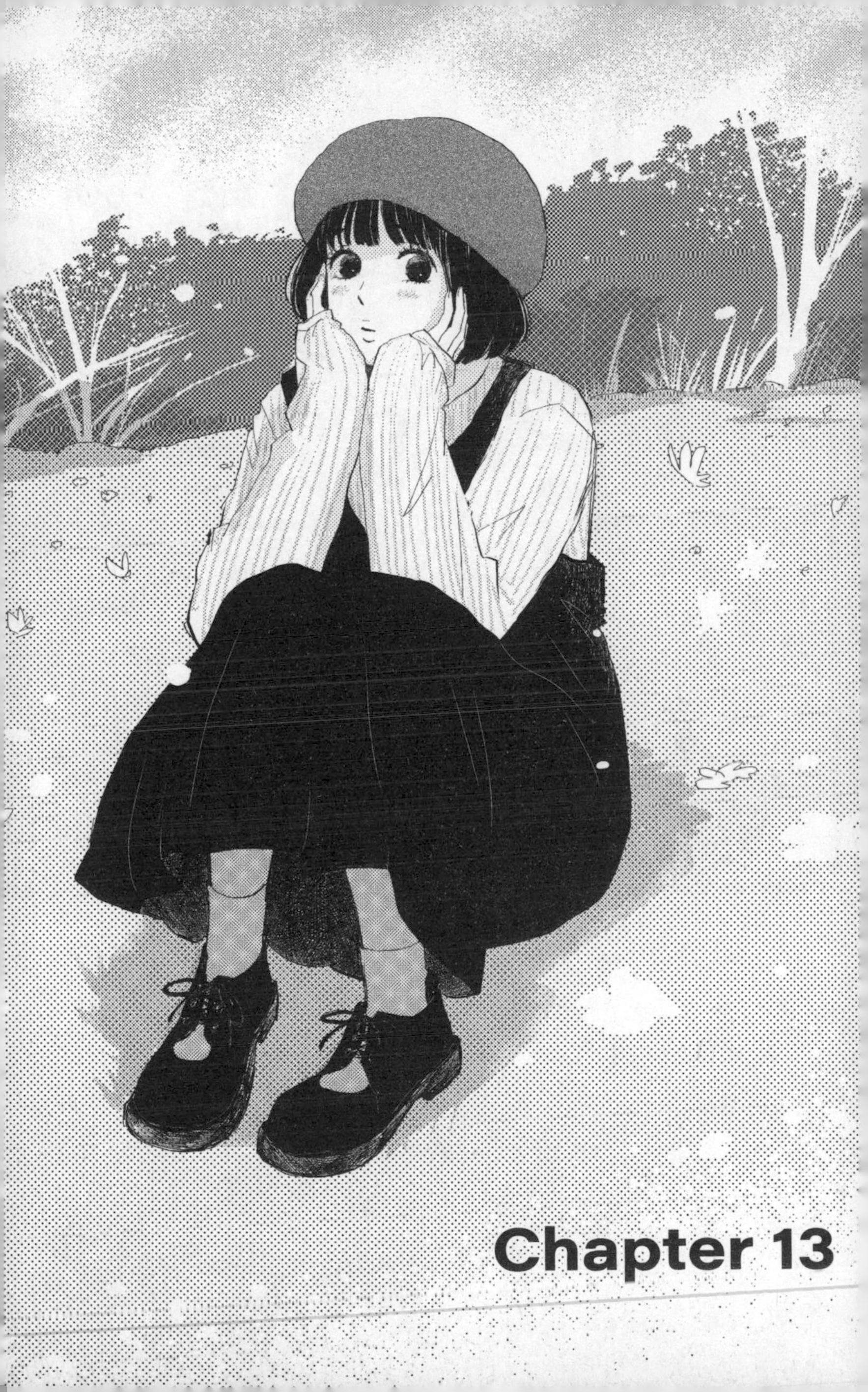

Chapter 13

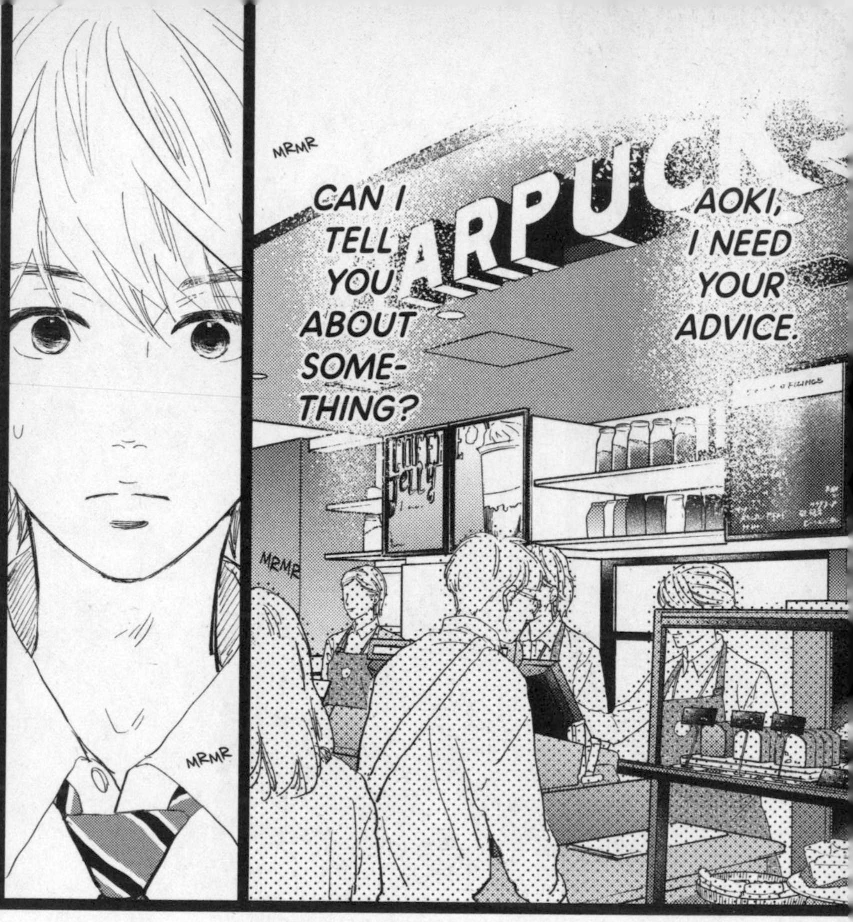
AOKI, I NEED YOUR ADVICE.
CAN I TELL YOU ABOUT SOME-THING?
MRMR
ARPUC
MRMR
MRMR

My Love Mix-Up!

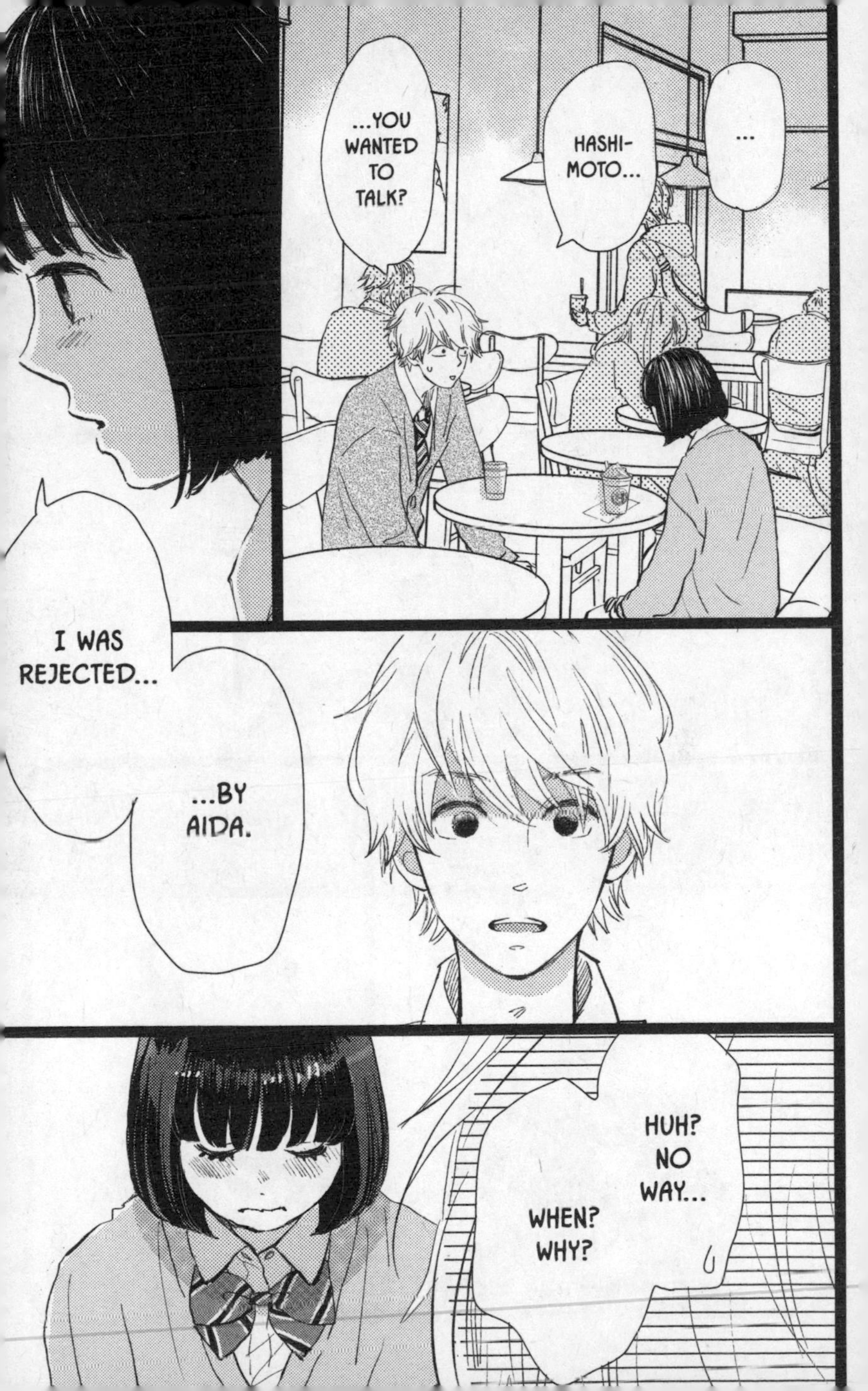
...
HASHIMOTO...
...YOU WANTED TO TALK?
I WAS REJECTED...
...BY AIDA.
HUH? NO WAY...
WHEN? WHY?

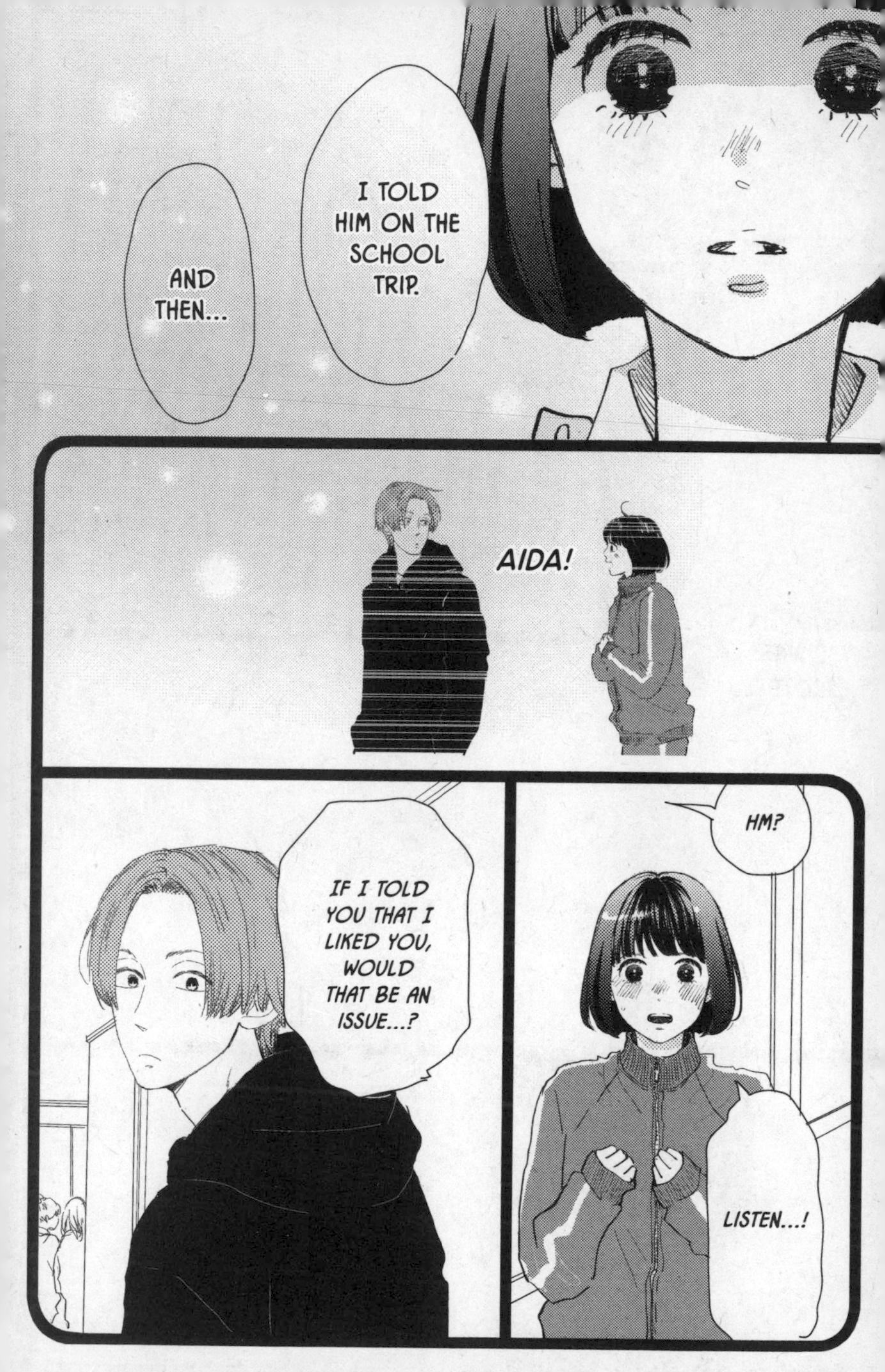
I TOLD HIM ON THE SCHOOL TRIP.
AND THEN...
AIDA!
HM?
LISTEN...!
IF I TOLD YOU THAT I LIKED YOU, WOULD THAT BE AN ISSUE...?

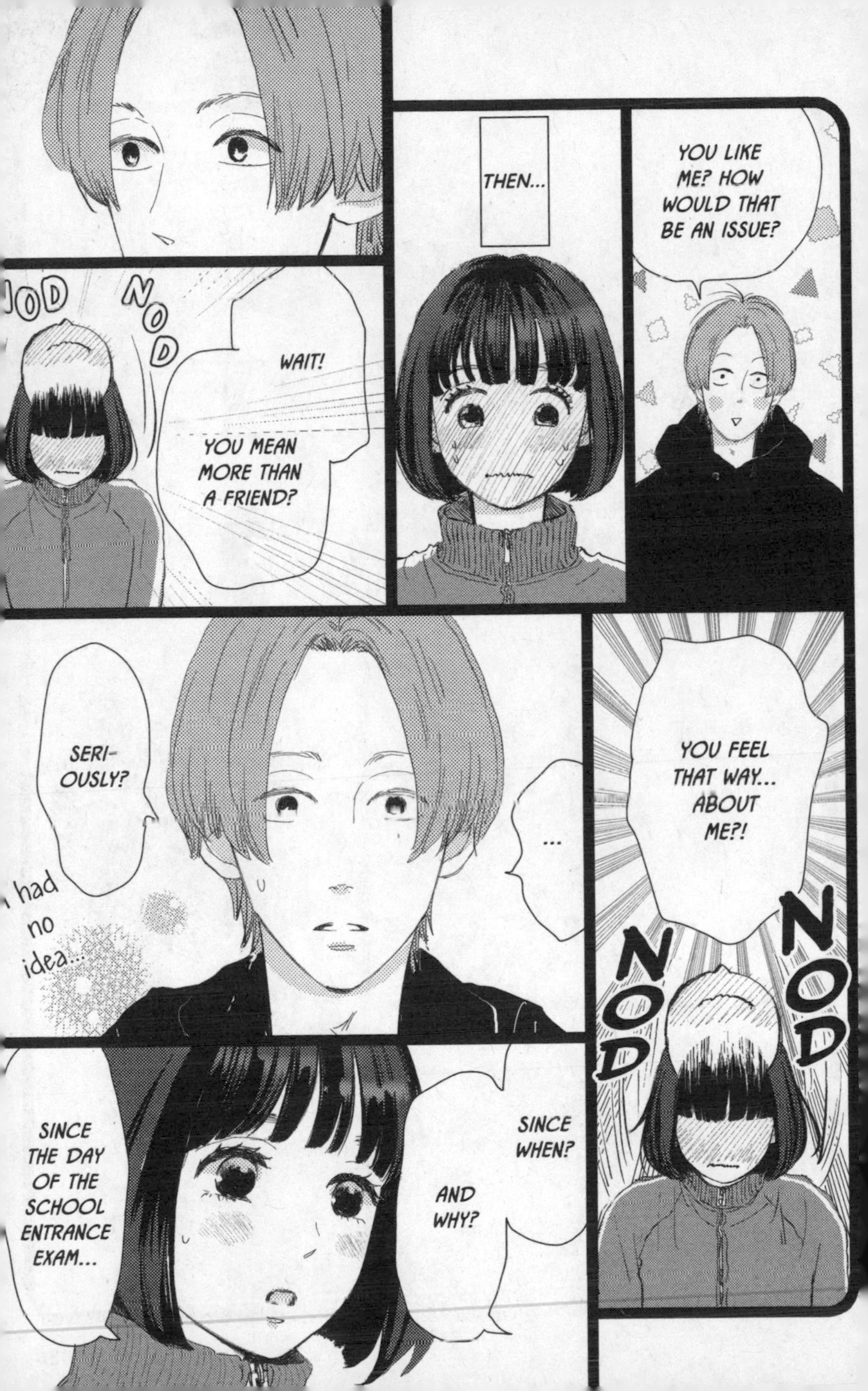
YOU LIKE ME? HOW WOULD THAT BE AN ISSUE?
THEN...
NOD
WAIT!
YOU MEAN MORE THAN A FRIEND?
YOU FEEL THAT WAY... ABOUT ME?!
NOD NOD
...
SERI-OUSLY?
had no idea...
SINCE WHEN?
AND WHY?
SINCE THE DAY OF THE SCHOOL ENTRANCE EXAM...

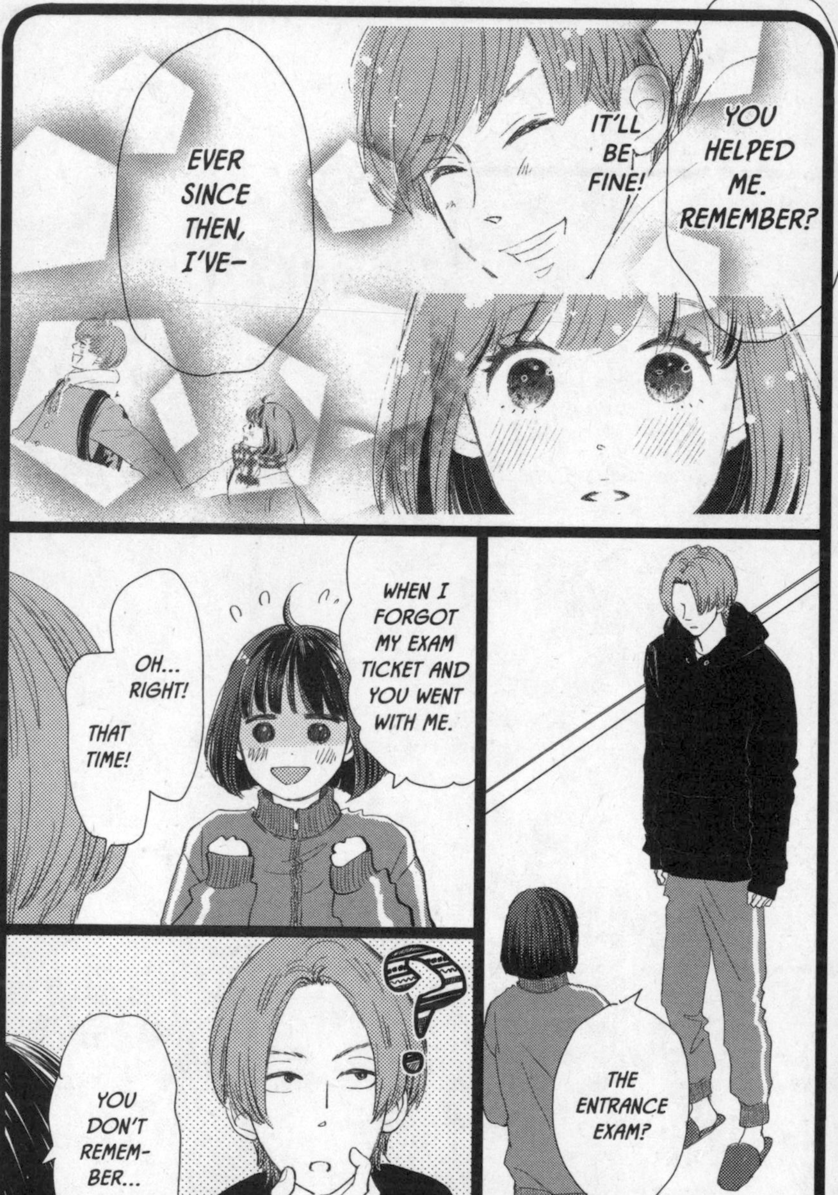
YOU HELPED ME. REMEMBER?
IT'LL BE FINE!
EVER SINCE THEN, I'VE—
THE ENTRANCE EXAM?
WHEN I FORGOT MY EXAM TICKET AND YOU WENT WITH ME.
OH... RIGHT!
THAT TIME!
YOU DON'T REMEM-BER...

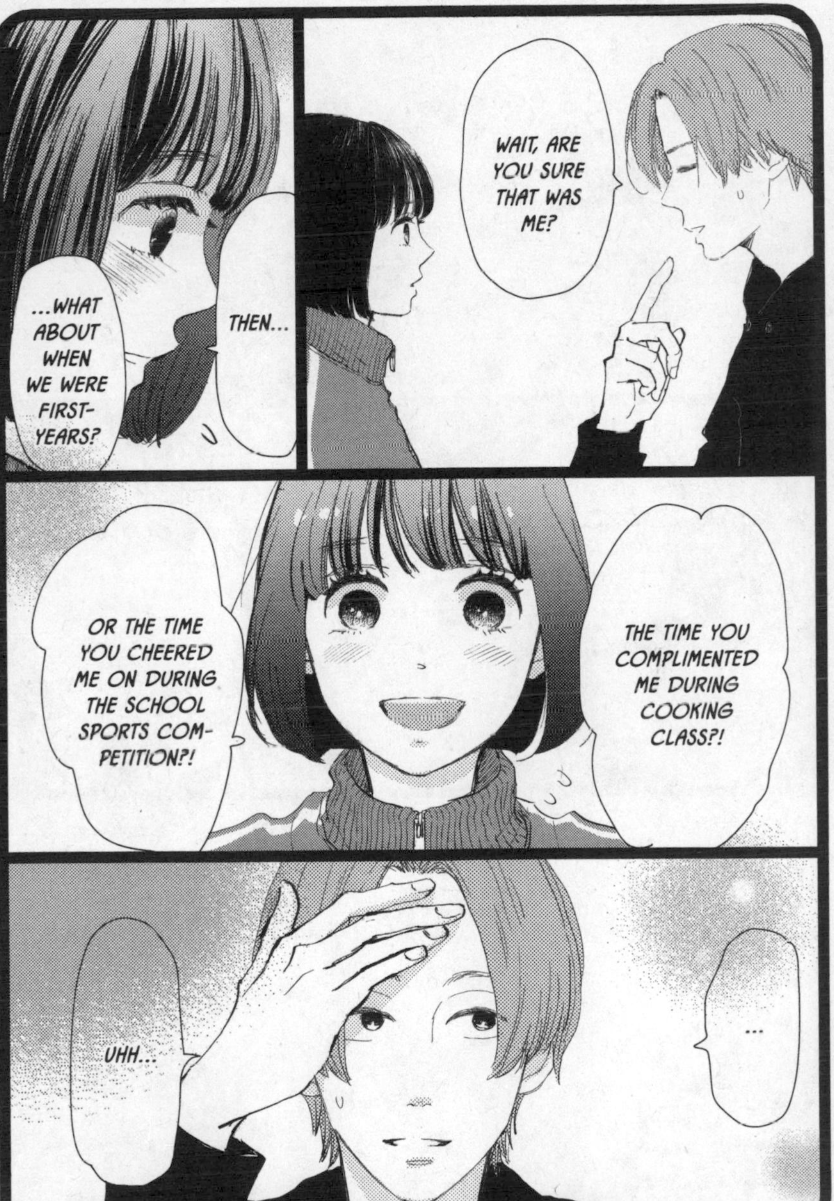
WAIT, ARE YOU SURE THAT WAS ME?
THEN...
...WHAT ABOUT WHEN WE WERE FIRST-YEARS?
THE TIME YOU COMPLIMENTED ME DURING COOKING CLASS?!
OR THE TIME YOU CHEERED ME ON DURING THE SCHOOL SPORTS COMPETITION?!
...
UHH...

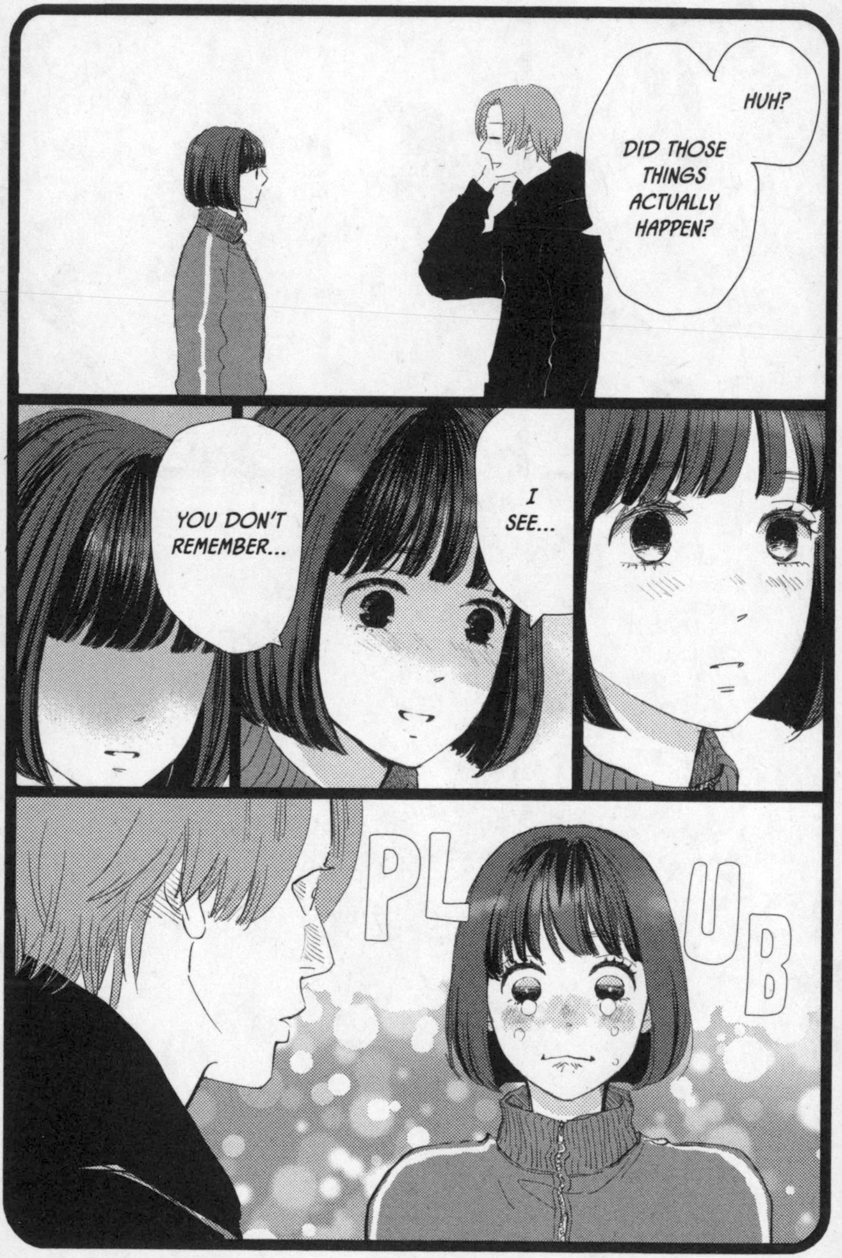
HUH?
DID THOSE THINGS ACTUALLY HAPPEN?
I SEE...
YOU DON'T REMEMBER...
PLUB

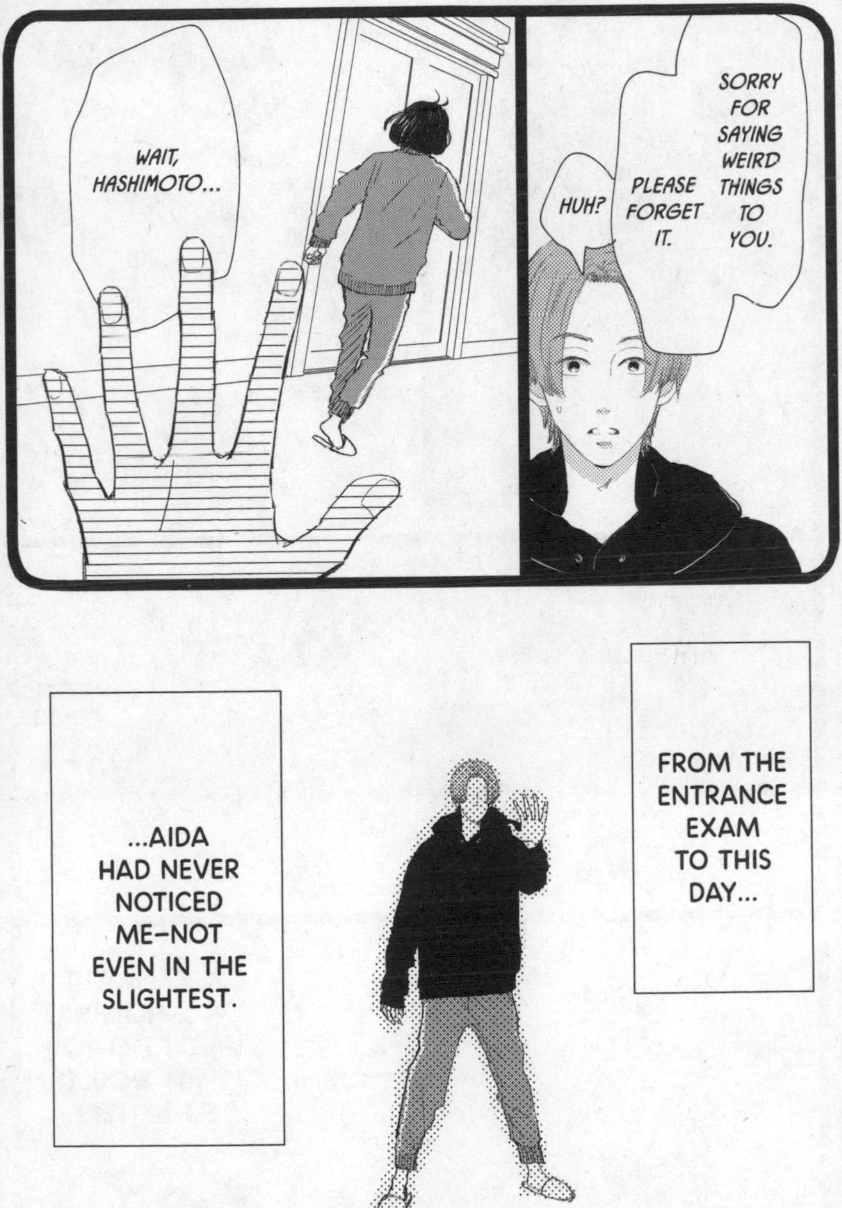
SORRY FOR SAYING WEIRD THINGS TO YOU.
PLEASE FORGET IT.
HUH?
WAIT, HASHIMOTO...
FROM THE ENTRANCE EXAM TO THIS DAY...
...AIDA HAD NEVER NOTICED ME—NOT EVEN IN THE SLIGHTEST.

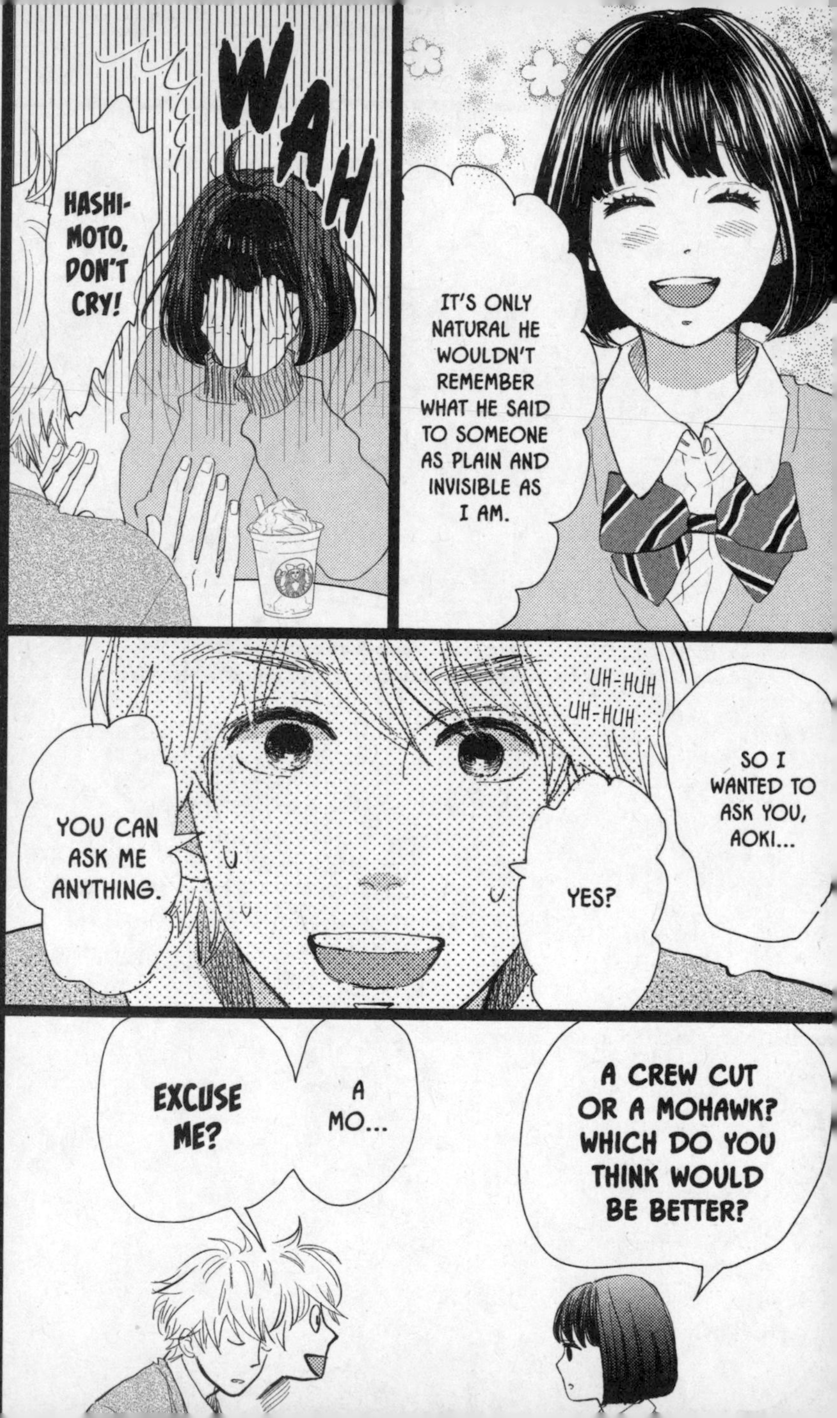
IT'S ONLY NATURAL HE WOULDN'T REMEMBER WHAT HE SAID TO SOMEONE AS PLAIN AND INVISIBLE AS I AM.
WAH
HASHI-MOTO, DON'T CRY!
SO I WANTED TO ASK YOU, AOKI...
UH-HUH UH-HUH
YES?
YOU CAN ASK ME ANYTHING.
A CREW CUT OR A MOHAWK? WHICH DO YOU THINK WOULD BE BETTER?
A MO...
EXCUSE ME?

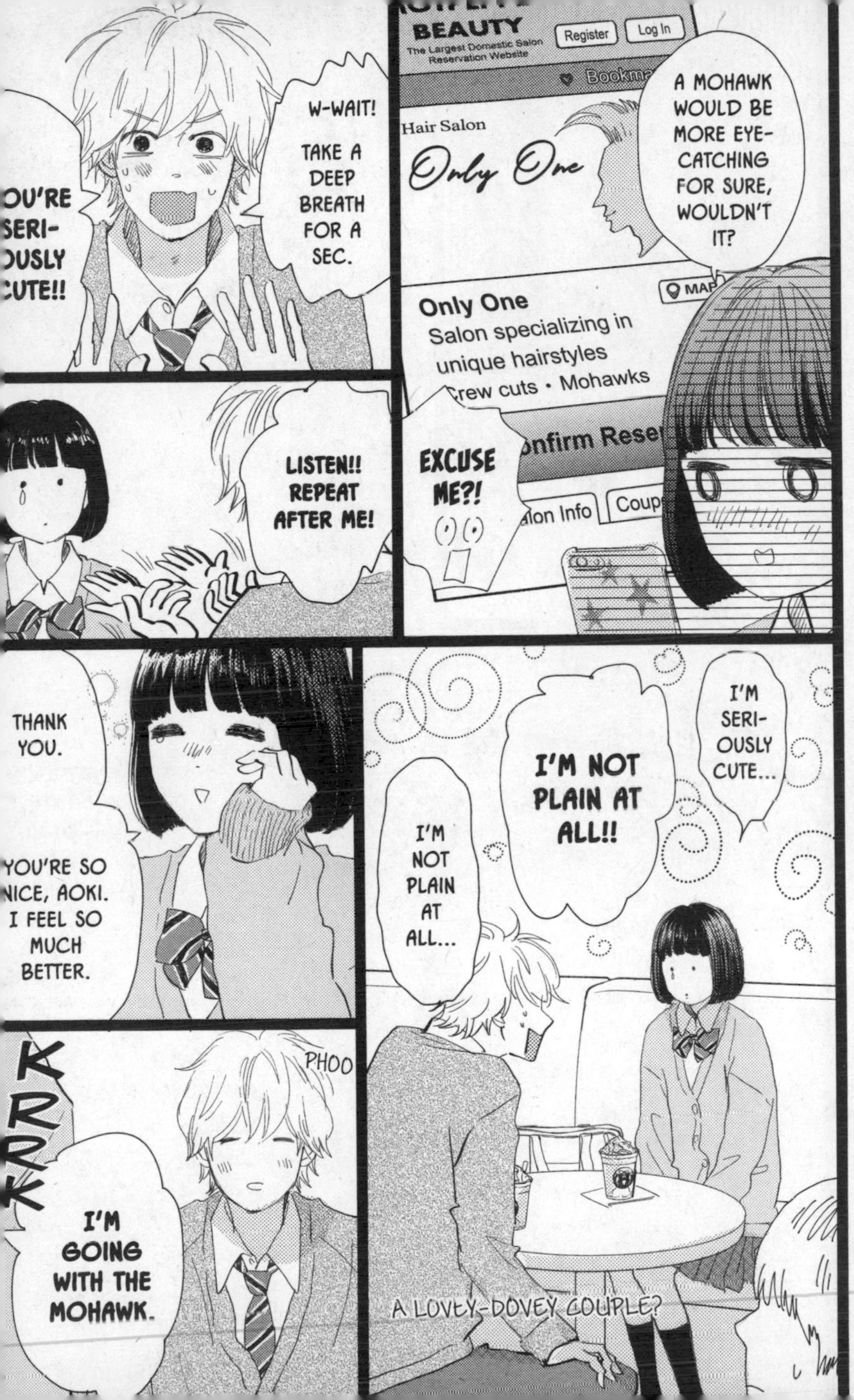
BEAUTY
The Largest Domestic Salon Reservation Website
Register
Log In
Hair Salon
Only One
A MOHAWK WOULD BE MORE EYE-CATCHING FOR SURE, WOULDN'T IT?
Only One
Salon specializing in unique hairstyles
Crew cuts • Mohawks
EXCUSE ME?!
W-WAIT! TAKE A DEEP BREATH FOR A SEC.
OU'RE SERI-OUSLY CUTE!!
LISTEN!! REPEAT AFTER ME!
I'M SERI-OUSLY CUTE...
I'M NOT PLAIN AT ALL!!
I'M NOT PLAIN AT ALL...
A LOVEY-DOVEY COUPLE?
THANK YOU.
YOU'RE SO NICE, AOKI. I FEEL SO MUCH BETTER.
PHOO
KRRR
I'M GOING WITH THE MOHAWK.

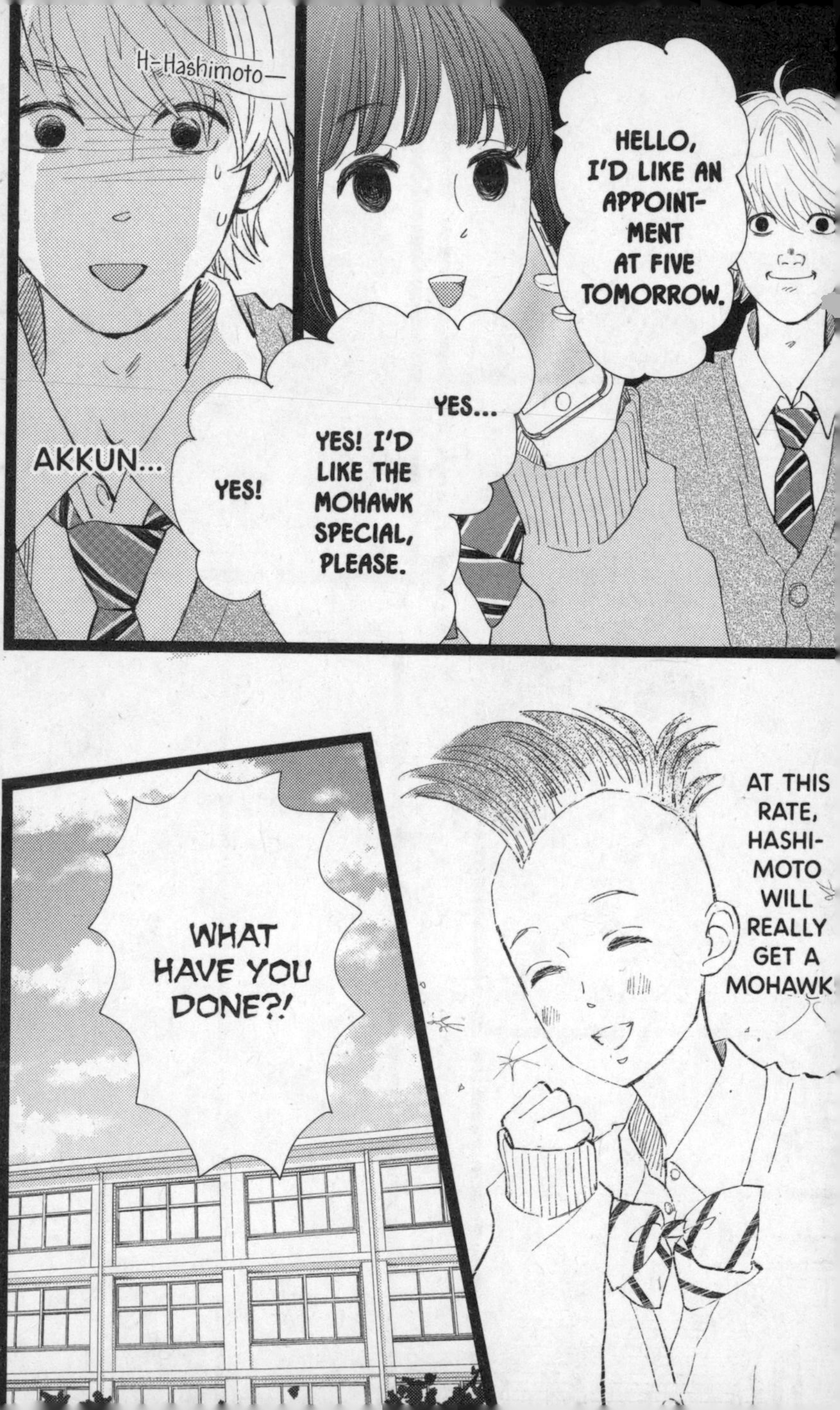
HELLO, I'D LIKE AN APPOINTMENT AT FIVE TOMORROW.
YES...
YES! I'D LIKE THE MOHAWK SPECIAL, PLEASE.
YES!
H-Hashimoto—
AKKUN...
AT THIS RATE, HASHIMOTO WILL REALLY GET A MOHAWK
WHAT HAVE YOU DONE?!

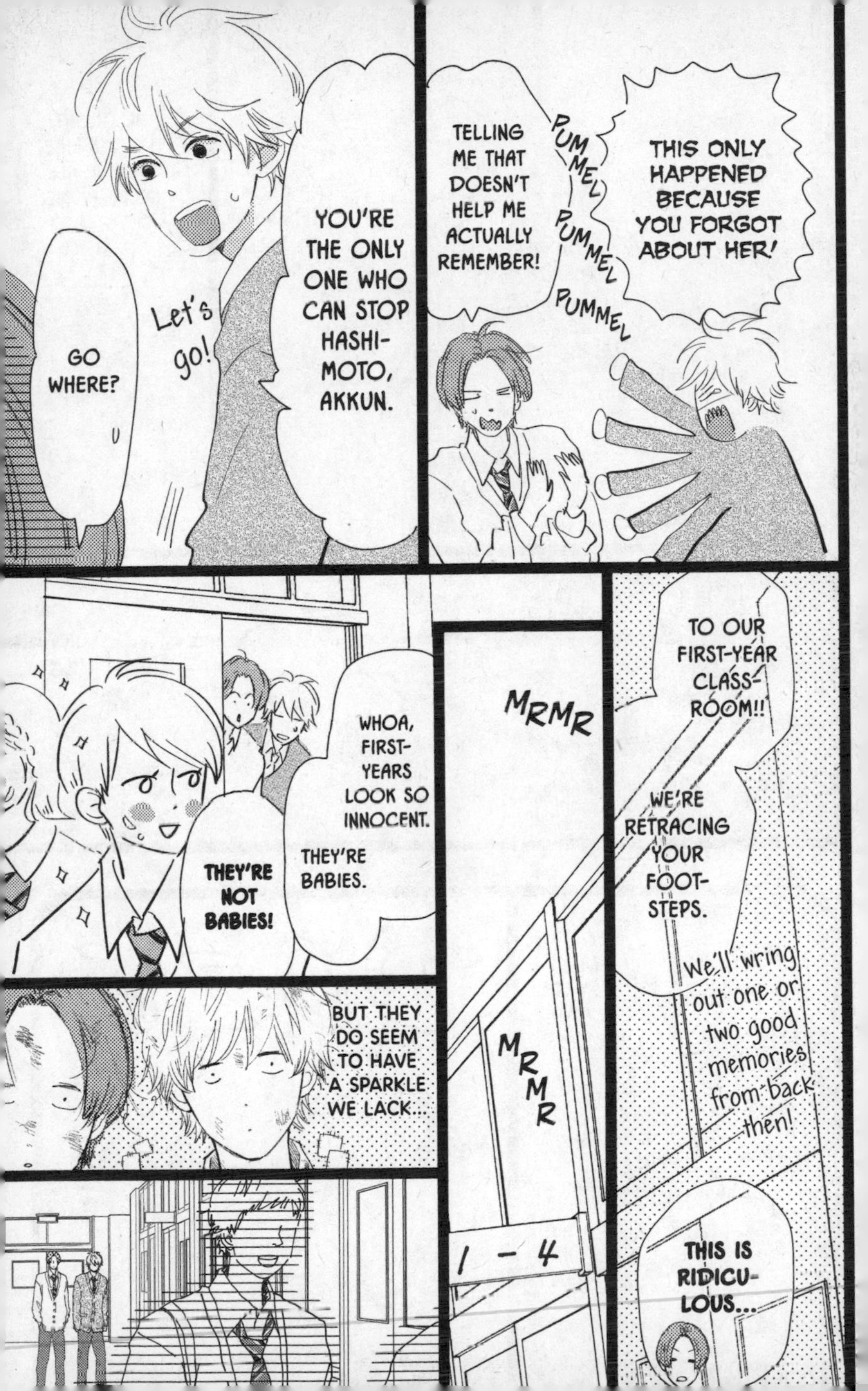
THIS ONLY HAPPENED BECAUSE YOU FORGOT ABOUT HER!
PUMMEL PUMMEL PUMMEL
TELLING ME THAT DOESN'T HELP ME ACTUALLY REMEMBER!
YOU'RE THE ONLY ONE WHO CAN STOP HASHIMOTO, AKKUN.
Let's go!
GO WHERE?
TO OUR FIRST-YEAR CLASSROOM!!
WE'RE RETRACING YOUR FOOTSTEPS.
We'll wring out one or two good memories from back then!
THIS IS RIDICULOUS...
MRMR
MRMR
1 - 4
WHOA, FIRST-YEARS LOOK SO INNOCENT.
THEY'RE BABIES.
THEY'RE NOT BABIES!
BUT THEY DO SEEM TO HAVE A SPARKLE WE LACK...

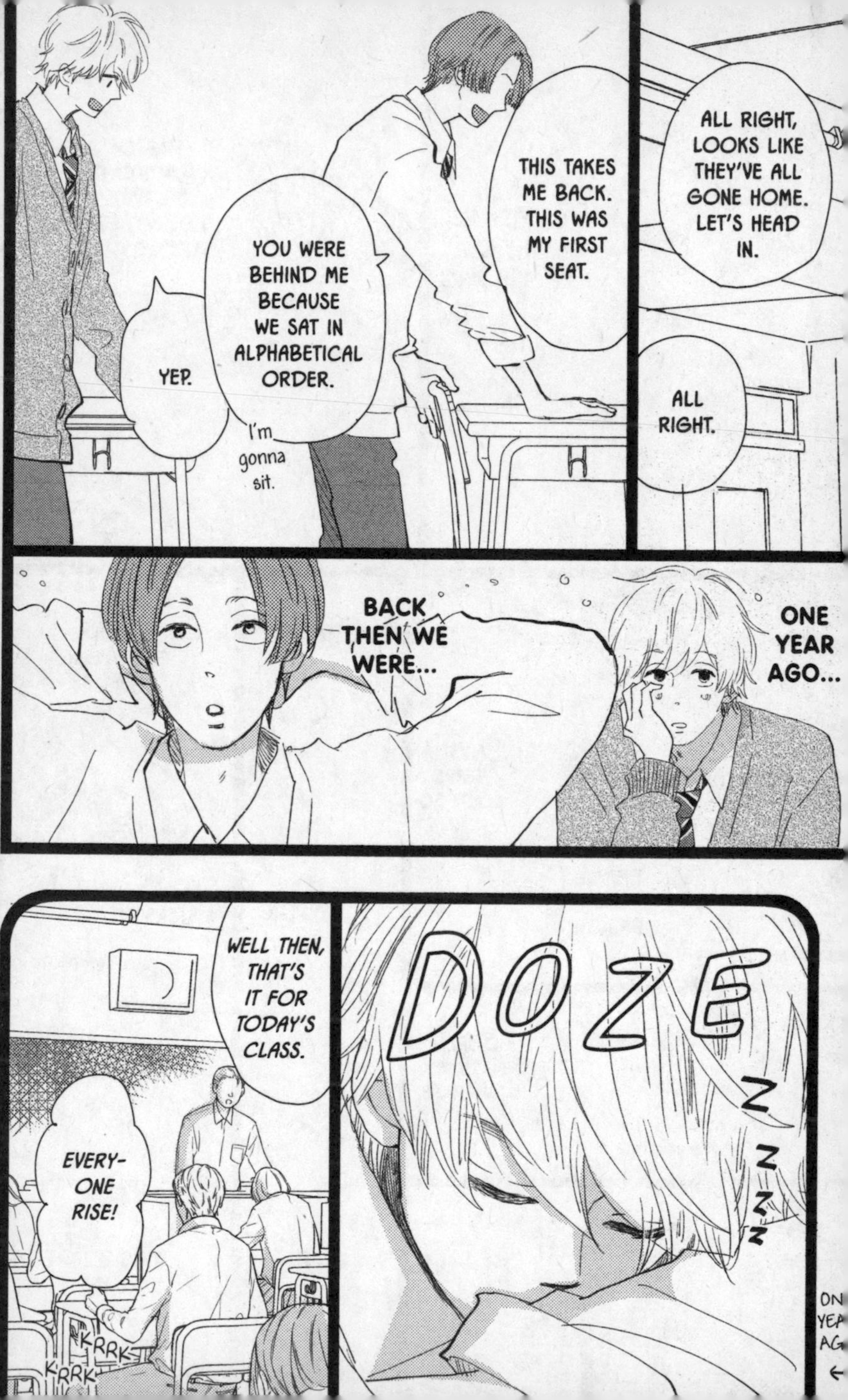
ALL RIGHT, LOOKS LIKE THEY'VE ALL GONE HOME. LET'S HEAD IN.
ALL RIGHT.
THIS TAKES ME BACK. THIS WAS MY FIRST SEAT.
YOU WERE BEHIND ME BECAUSE WE SAT IN ALPHABETICAL ORDER.
YEP.
I'm gonna sit.
ONE YEAR AGO...
BACK THEN WE WERE...
DOZE
Z Z Z Z
WELL THEN, THAT'S IT FOR TODAY'S CLASS.
EVERY-ONE RISE!
KRRK
KRRK

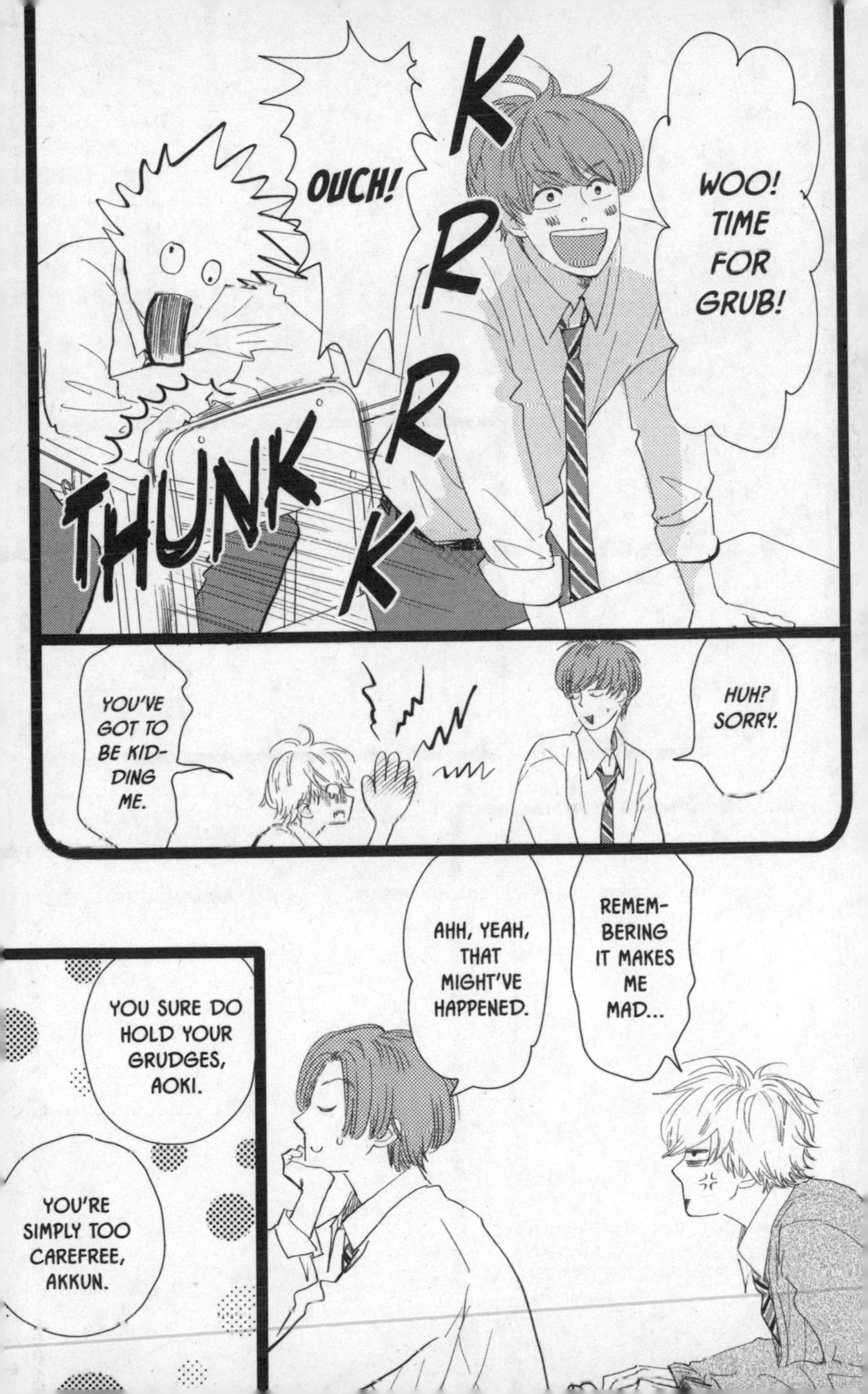
WOO! TIME FOR GRUB!
KRRK
OUCH!
THUNK
HUH? SORRY.
YOU'VE GOT TO BE KID-DING ME.
REMEM-BERING IT MAKES ME MAD...
AHH, YEAH, THAT MIGHT'VE HAPPENED.
YOU SURE DO HOLD YOUR GRUDGES, AOKI.
YOU'RE SIMPLY TOO CAREFREE, AKKUN.

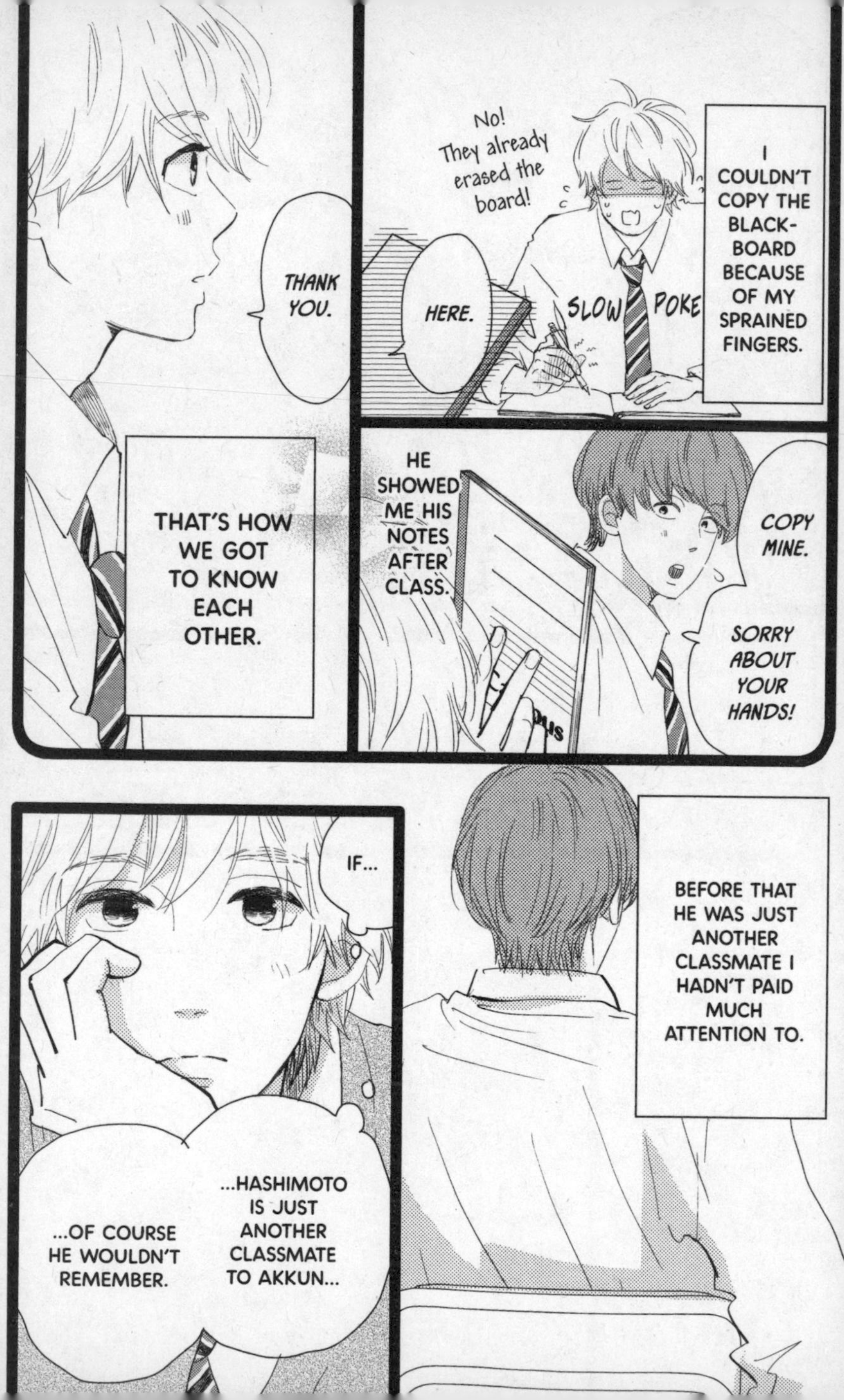
I COULDN'T COPY THE BLACK-BOARD BECAUSE OF MY SPRAINED FINGERS.
No! They already erased the board!
SLOW POKE
HERE.
COPY MINE.
SORRY ABOUT YOUR HANDS!
HE SHOWED ME HIS NOTES AFTER CLASS.
THANK YOU.
THAT'S HOW WE GOT TO KNOW EACH OTHER.
BEFORE THAT HE WAS JUST ANOTHER CLASSMATE I HADN'T PAID MUCH ATTENTION TO.
IF...
...HASHIMOTO IS JUST ANOTHER CLASSMATE TO AKKUN...
...OF COURSE HE WOULDN'T REMEMBER.

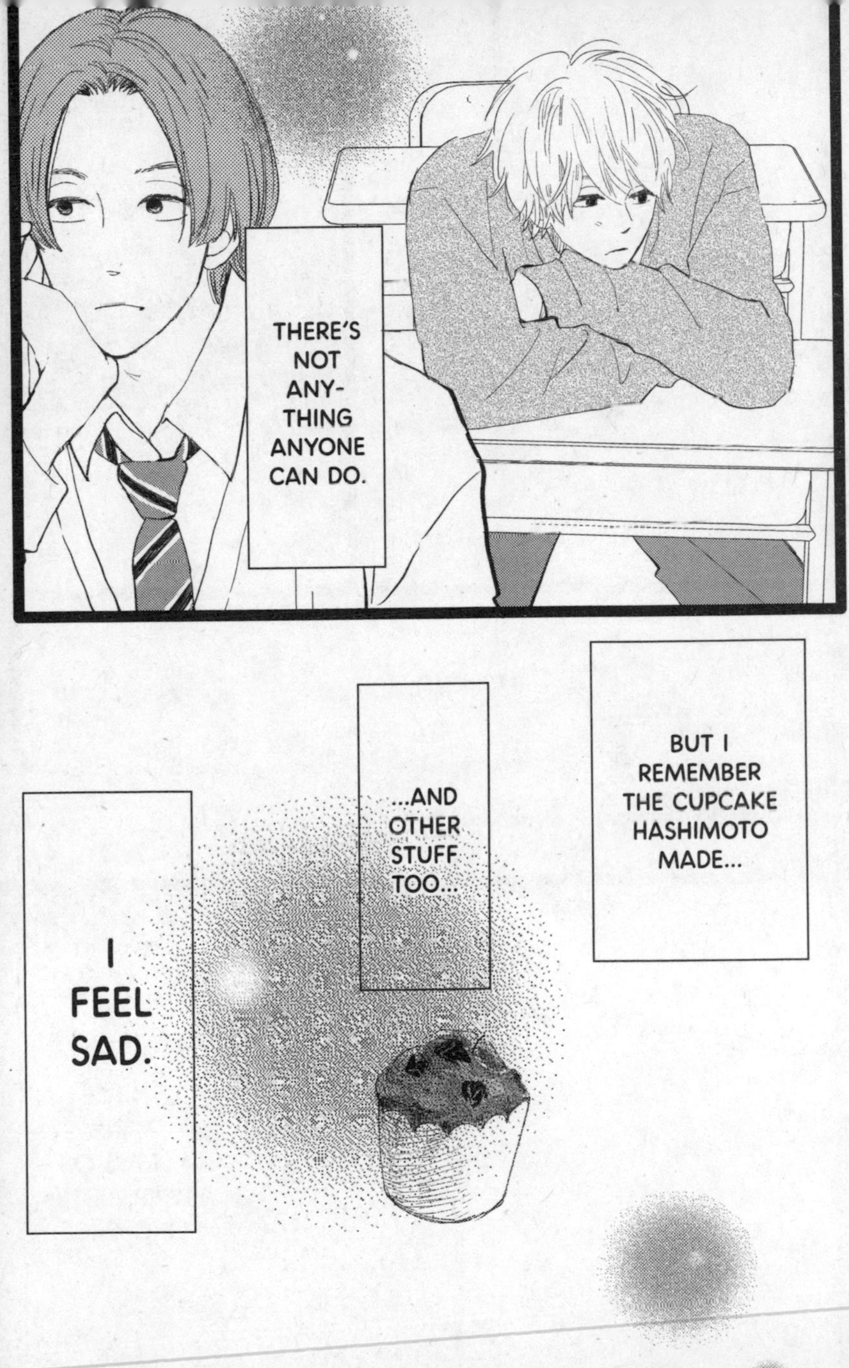
THERE'S NOT ANY-THING ANYONE CAN DO.
BUT I REMEMBER THE CUPCAKE HASHIMOTO MADE...
...AND OTHER STUFF TOO...
I FEEL SAD.

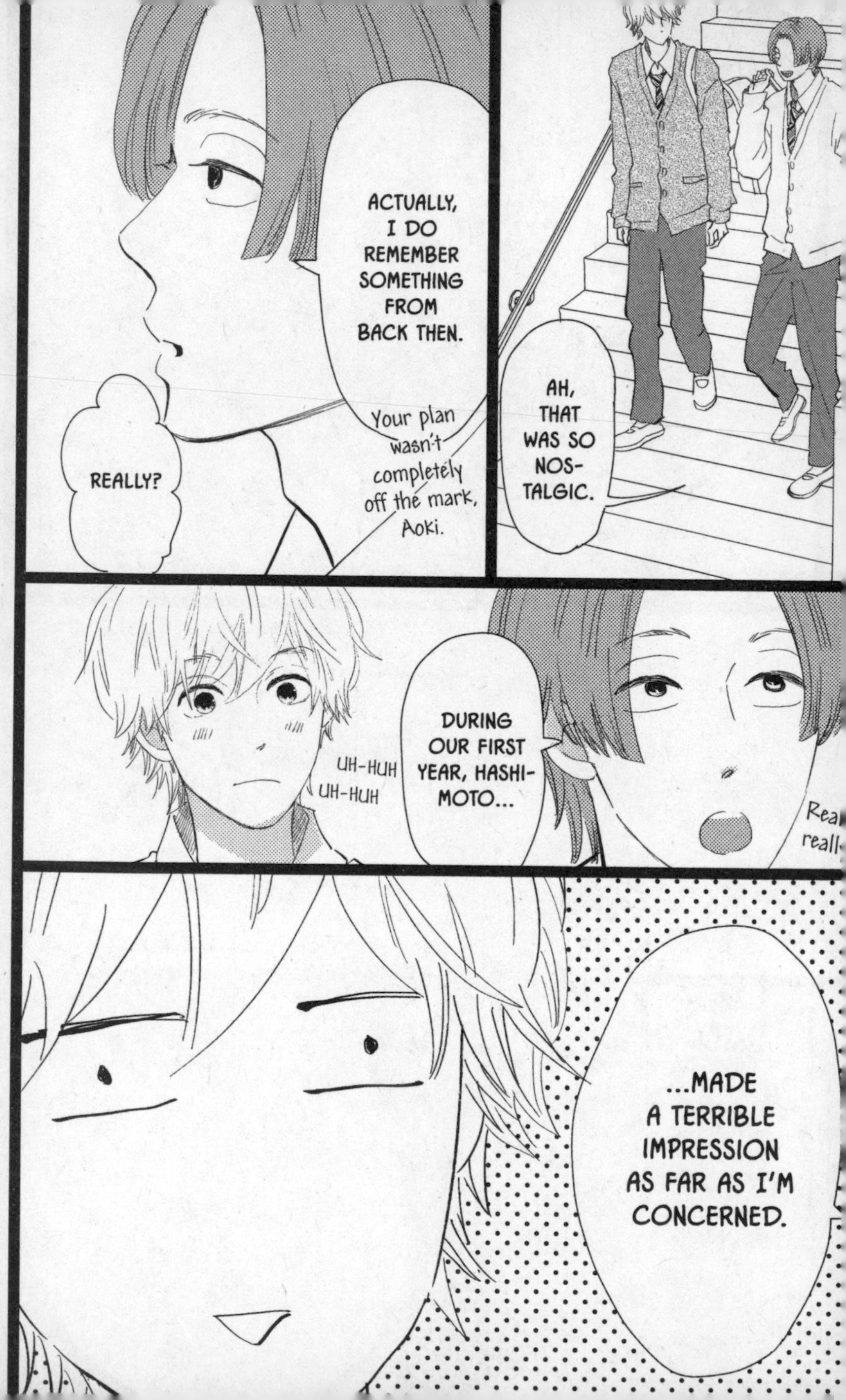
AH, THAT WAS SO NOS-TALGIC.
ACTUALLY, I DO REMEMBER SOMETHING FROM BACK THEN.
Your plan wasn't completely off the mark, Aoki.
REALLY?
DURING OUR FIRST YEAR, HASHIMOTO...
UH-HUH UH-HUH
...MADE A TERRIBLE IMPRESSION AS FAR AS I'M CONCERNED.

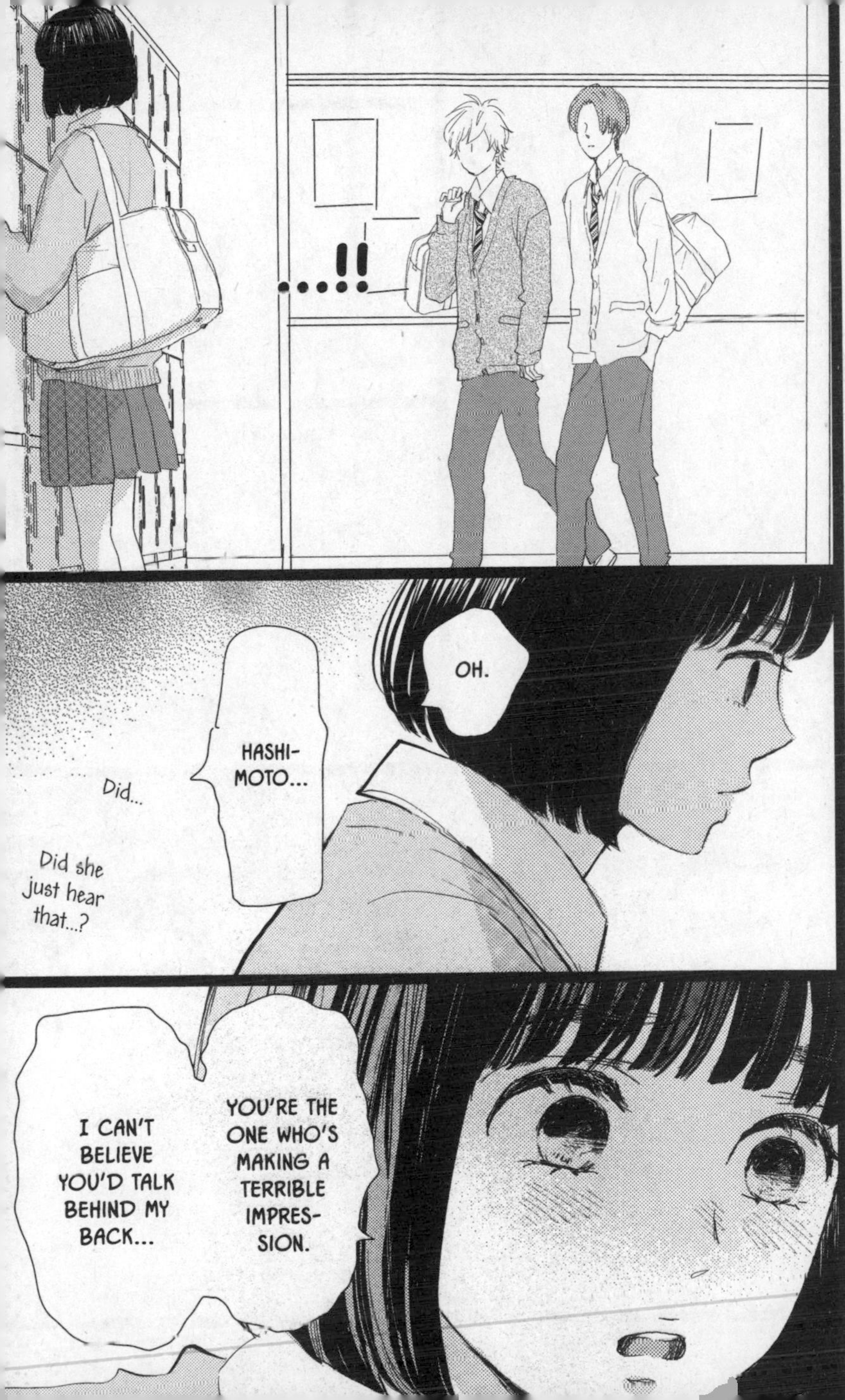
...!!
OH.
HASHI-MOTO...
Did...
Did she just hear that...?
YOU'RE THE ONE WHO'S MAKING A TERRIBLE IMPRES-SION.
I CAN'T BELIEVE YOU'D TALK BEHIND MY BACK...

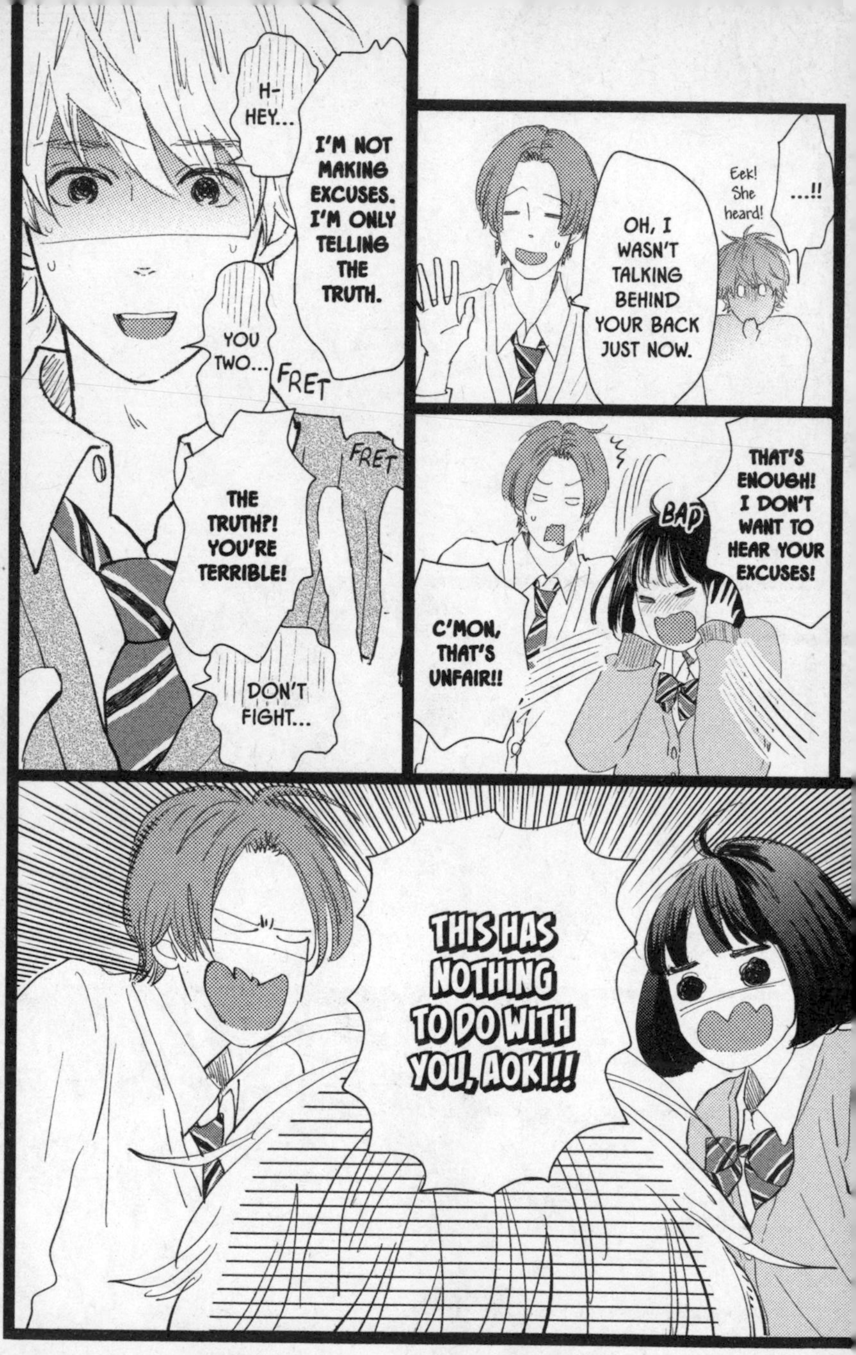
...!!
Eek! She heard!
OH, I WASN'T TALKING BEHIND YOUR BACK JUST NOW.
THAT'S ENOUGH! I DON'T WANT TO HEAR YOUR EXCUSES!
BAP
C'MON, THAT'S UNFAIR!!
H-HEY...
I'M NOT MAKING EXCUSES. I'M ONLY TELLING THE TRUTH.
YOU TWO...
FRET
FRET
THE TRUTH?! YOU'RE TERRIBLE!
DON'T FIGHT...
THIS HAS NOTHING TO DO WITH YOU, AOKI!!

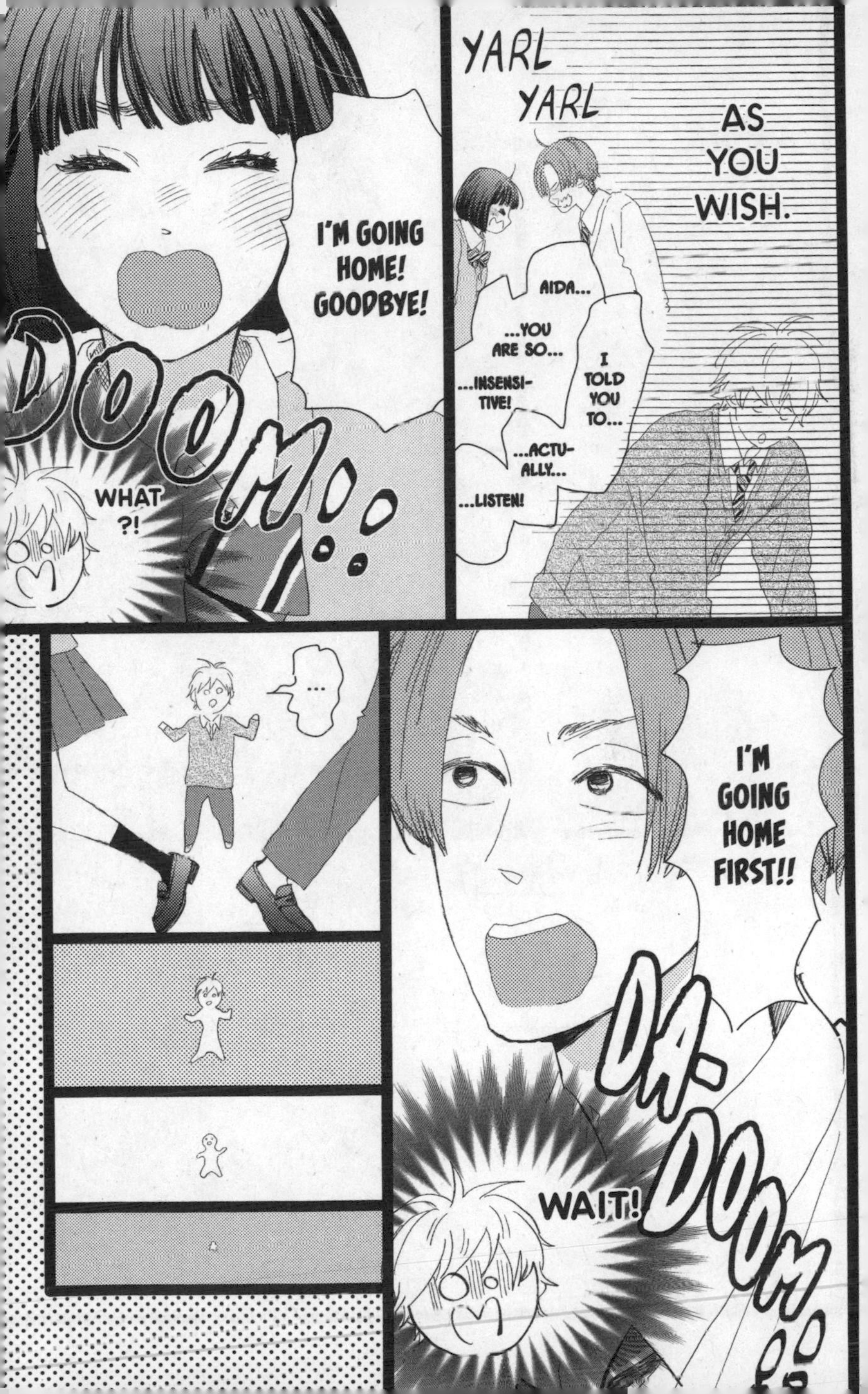
AS YOU WISH.
YARL YARL
AIDA...
...YOU ARE SO...
...INSENSI-TIVE!
I TOLD YOU TO...
...ACTU-ALLY...
...LISTEN!
I'M GOING HOME! GOODBYE!
DOOM
WHAT?!
I'M GOING HOME FIRST!!
DA-DOOM
WAIT!
...

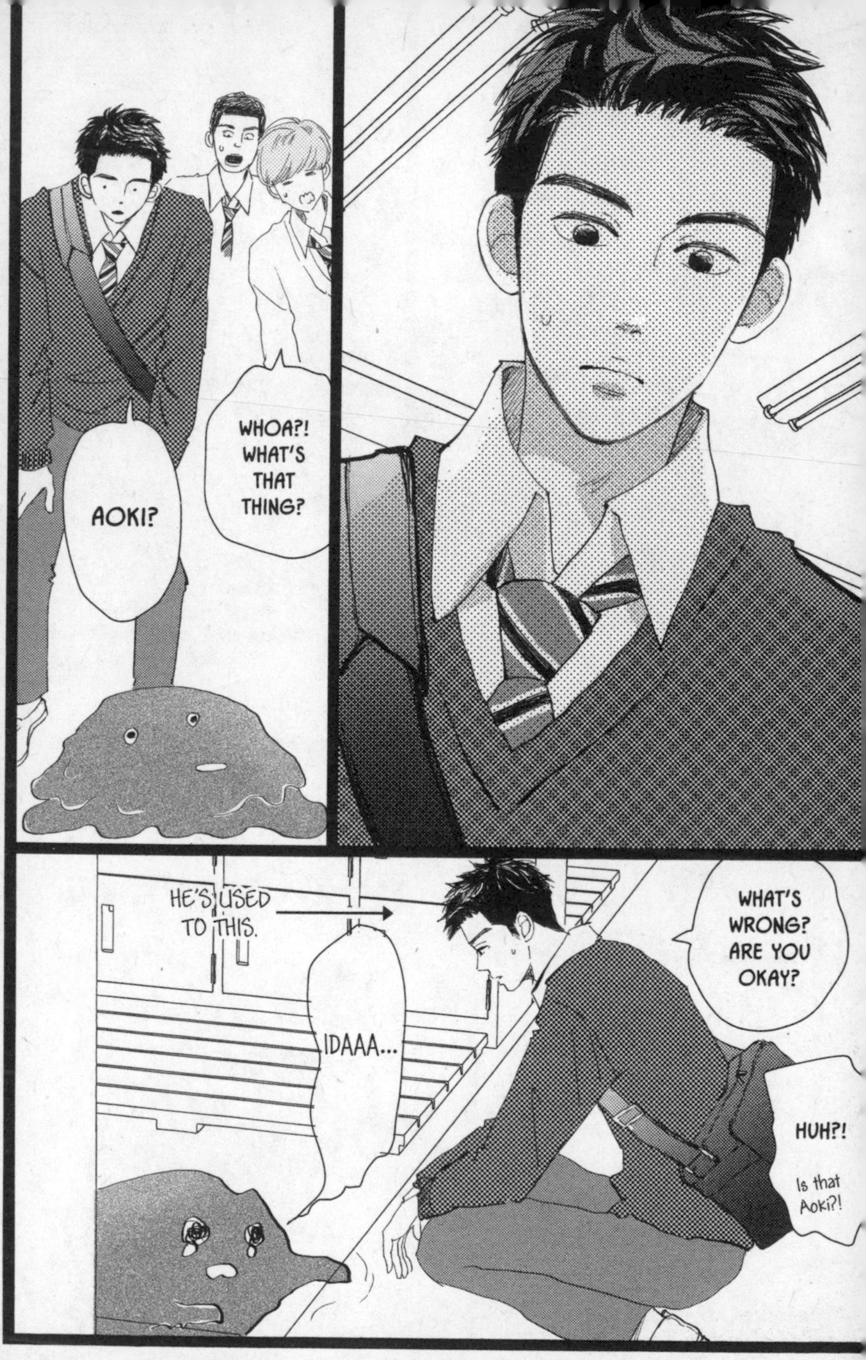
WHOA?! WHAT'S THAT THING?
AOKI?
WHAT'S WRONG? ARE YOU OKAY?
HUH?!
Is that Aoki?!
IDAAA...
HE'S USED TO THIS.

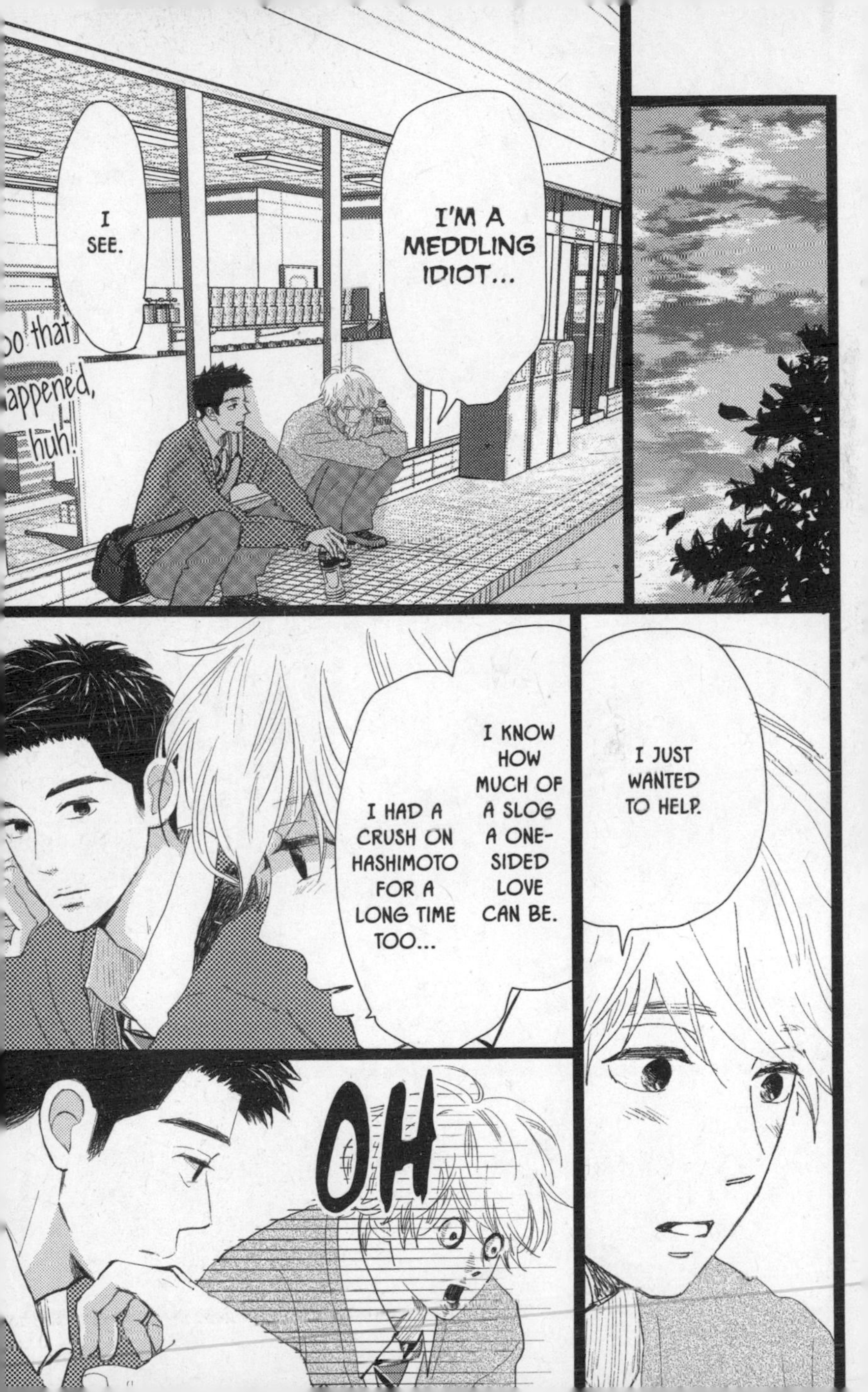
I'M A MEDDLING IDIOT...
I SEE.
o that appened, huh!
I JUST WANTED TO HELP.
I KNOW HOW MUCH OF A SLOG A ONE-SIDED LOVE CAN BE.
I HAD A CRUSH ON HASHIMOTO FOR A LONG TIME TOO...
OH

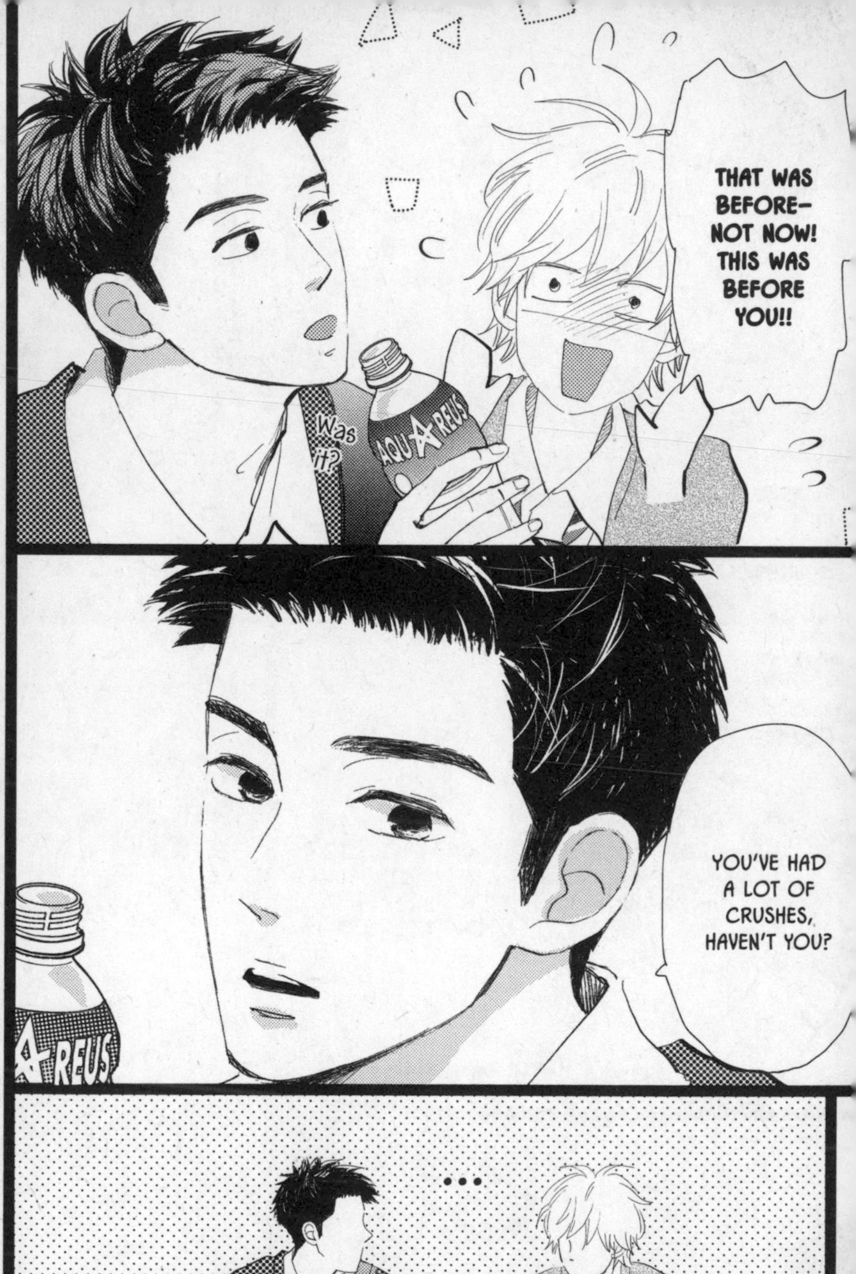
THAT WAS BEFORE—NOT NOW! THIS WAS BEFORE YOU!!
Was it?
YOU'VE HAD A LOT OF CRUSHES, HAVEN'T YOU?
...

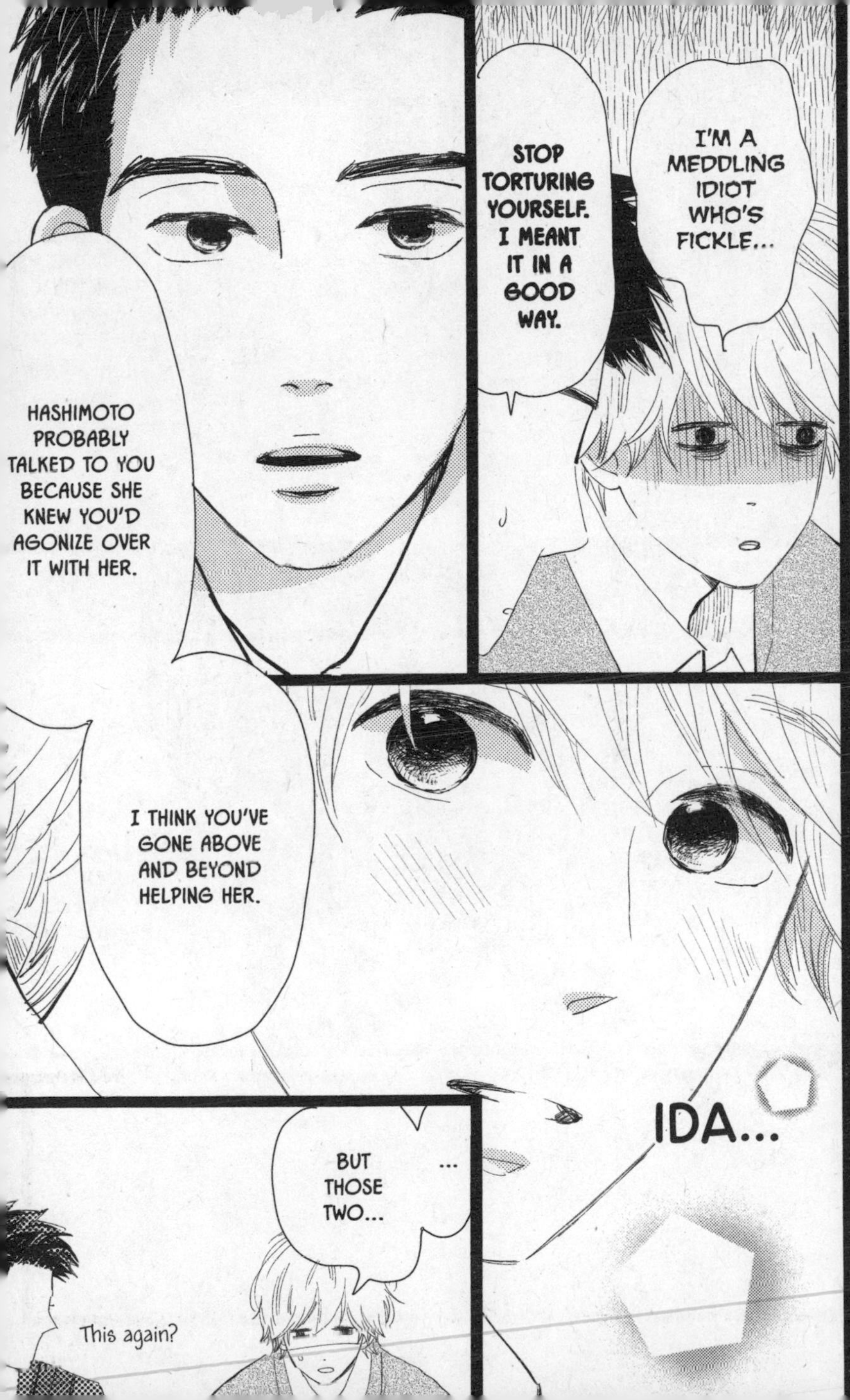
I'M A MEDDLING IDIOT WHO'S FICKLE...
STOP TORTURING YOURSELF. I MEANT IT IN A GOOD WAY.
HASHIMOTO PROBABLY TALKED TO YOU BECAUSE SHE KNEW YOU'D AGONIZE OVER IT WITH HER.
I THINK YOU'VE GONE ABOVE AND BEYOND HELPING HER.
IDA...
...
BUT THOSE TWO...
This again?

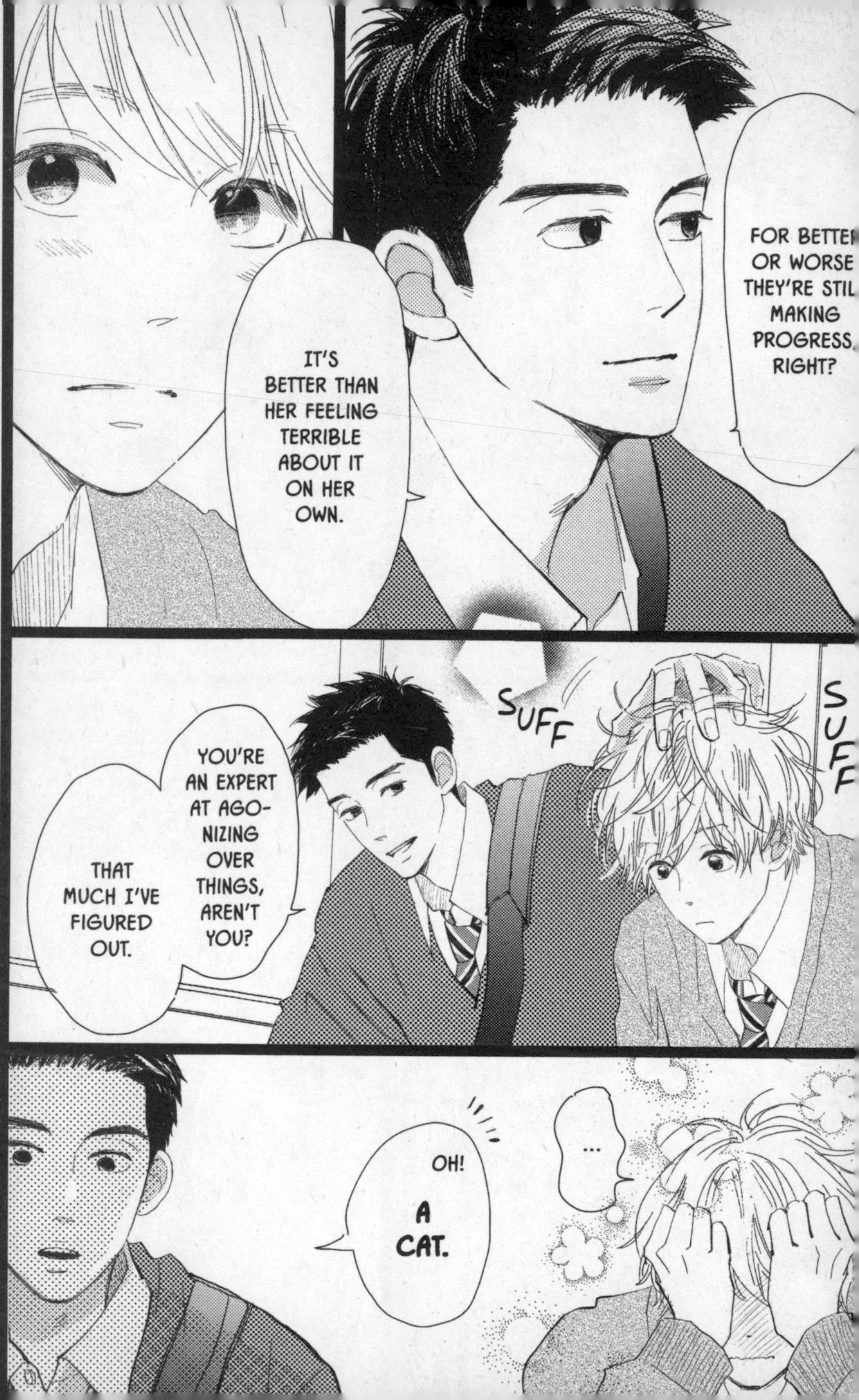
FOR BETTE OR WORSE THEY'RE STIL MAKING PROGRESS, RIGHT?
IT'S BETTER THAN HER FEELING TERRIBLE ABOUT IT ON HER OWN.
SUFF
SUFF
YOU'RE AN EXPERT AT AGO-NIZING OVER THINGS, AREN'T YOU?
THAT MUCH I'VE FIGURED OUT.
...
OH!
A CAT.

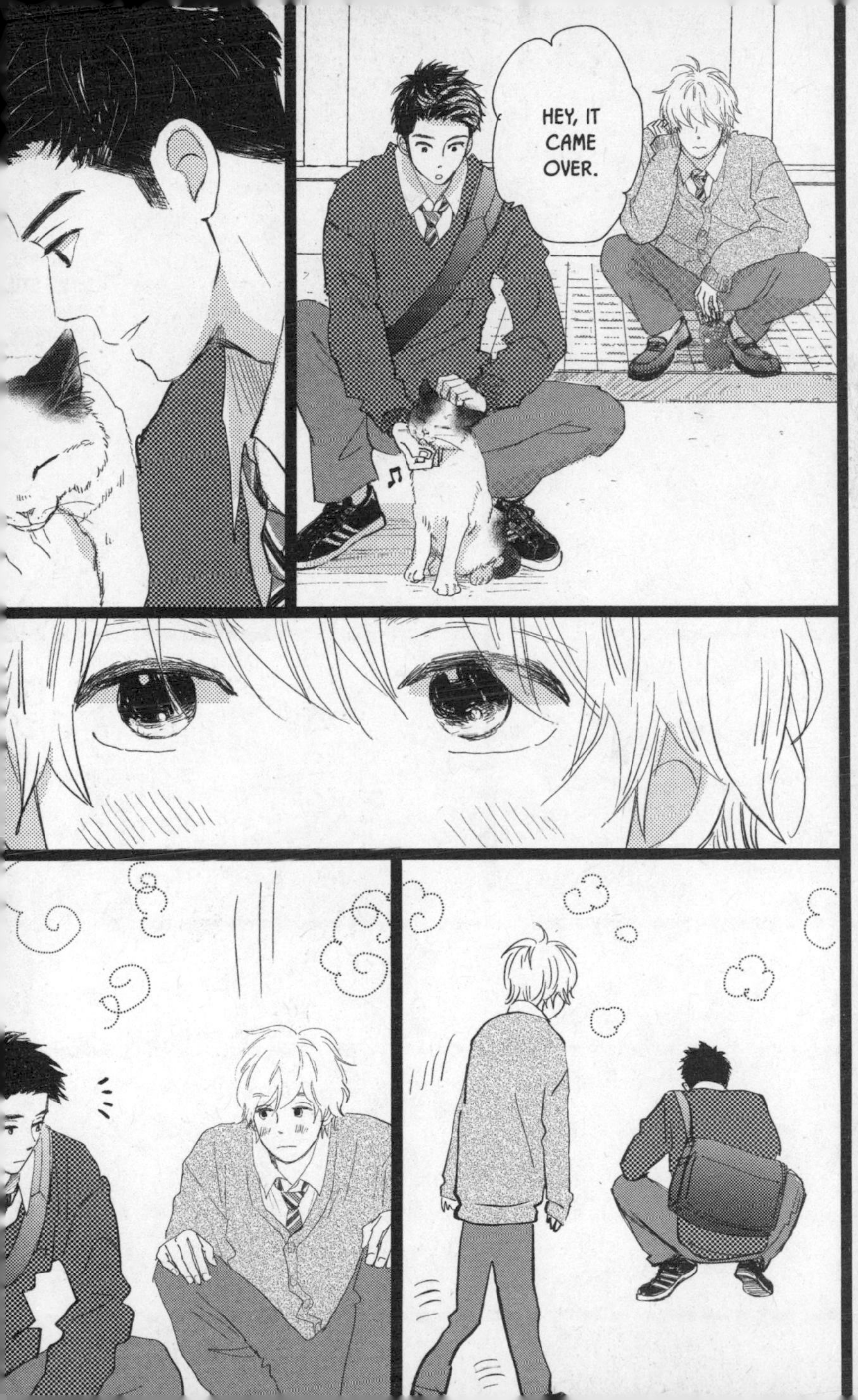
HEY, IT CAME OVER.

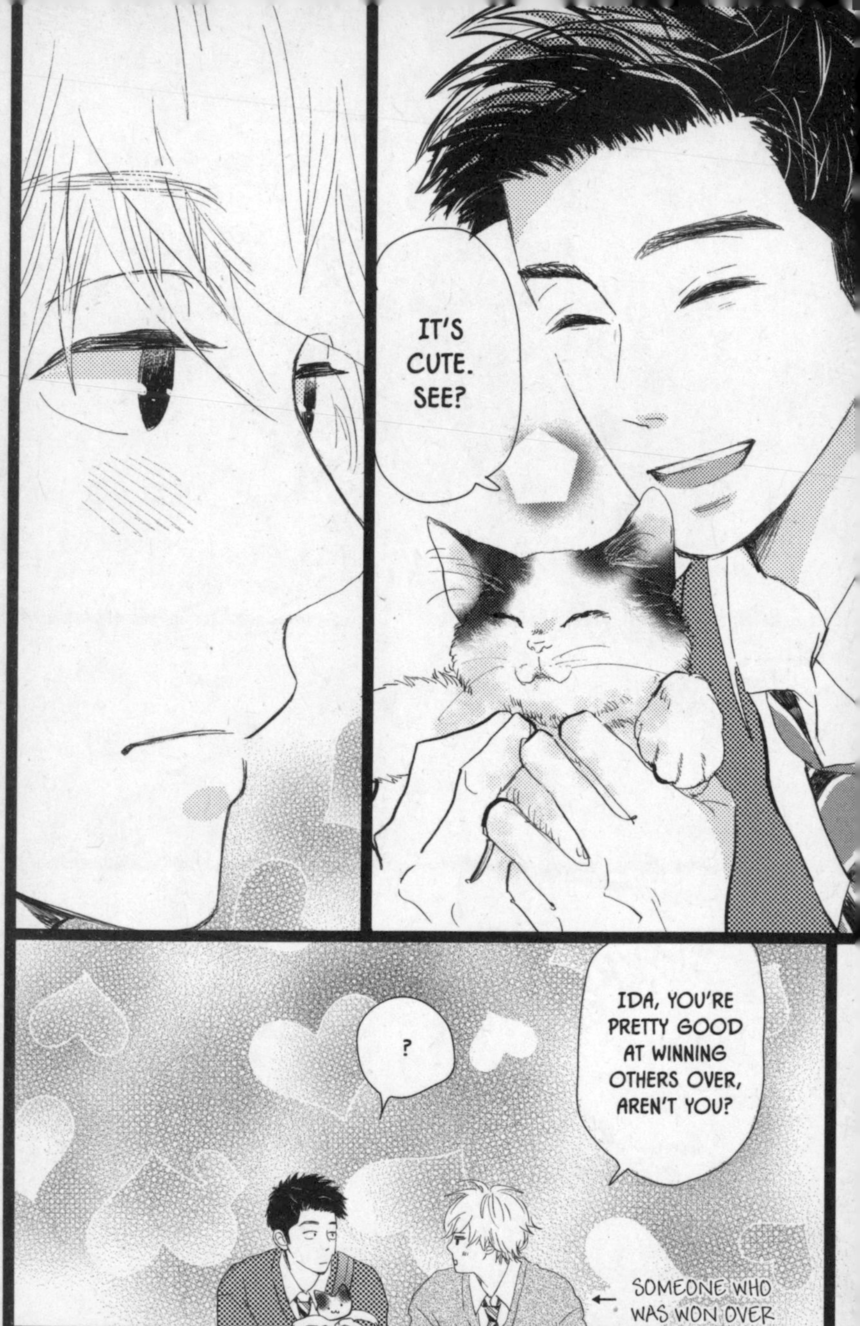
IT'S CUTE. SEE?
IDA, YOU'RE PRETTY GOOD AT WINNING OTHERS OVER, AREN'T YOU?
?
← SOMEONE WHO WAS WON OVER

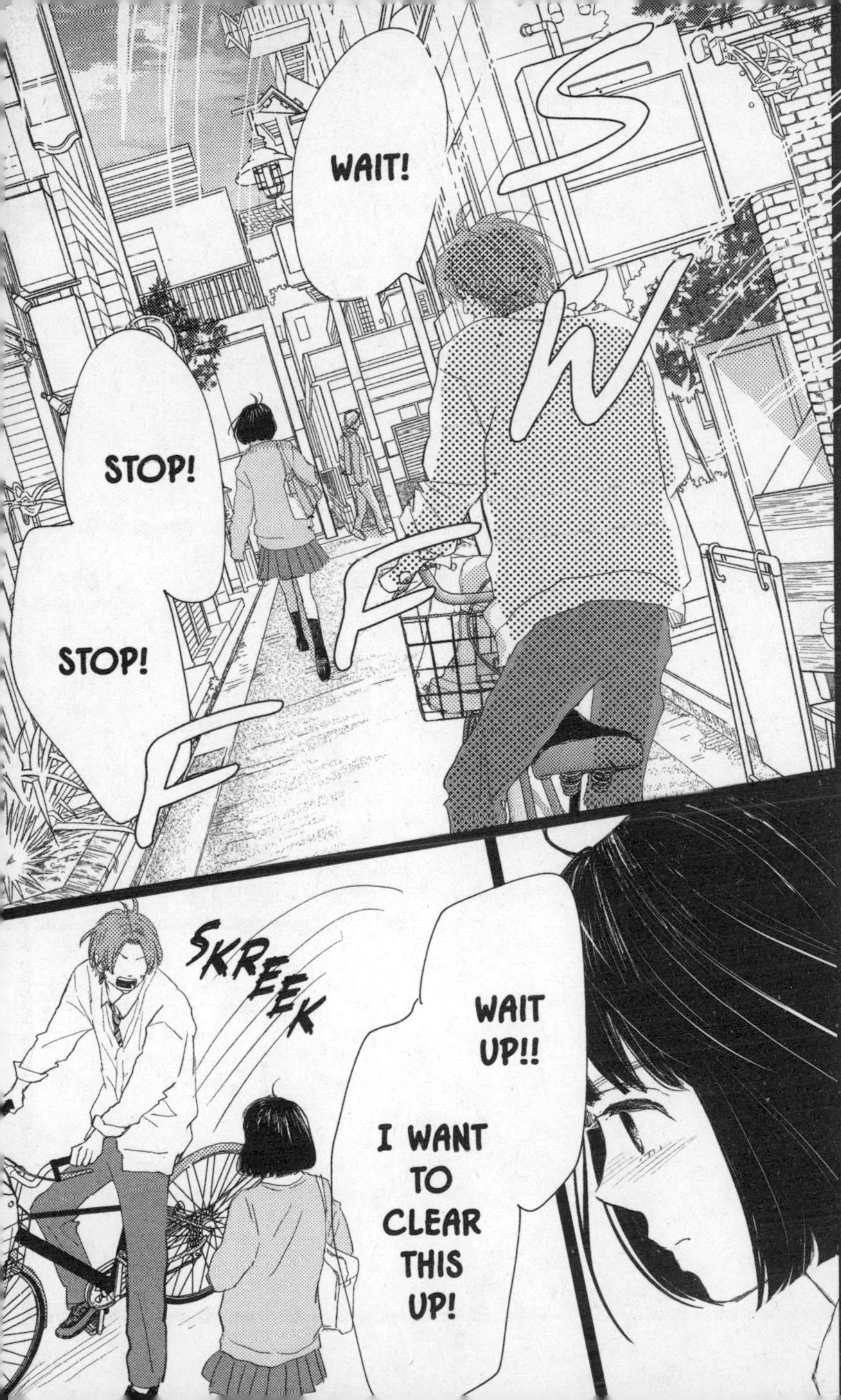
WAIT!
SWFF
STOP! STOP!
WAIT UP!! I WANT TO CLEAR THIS UP!
SKREEK

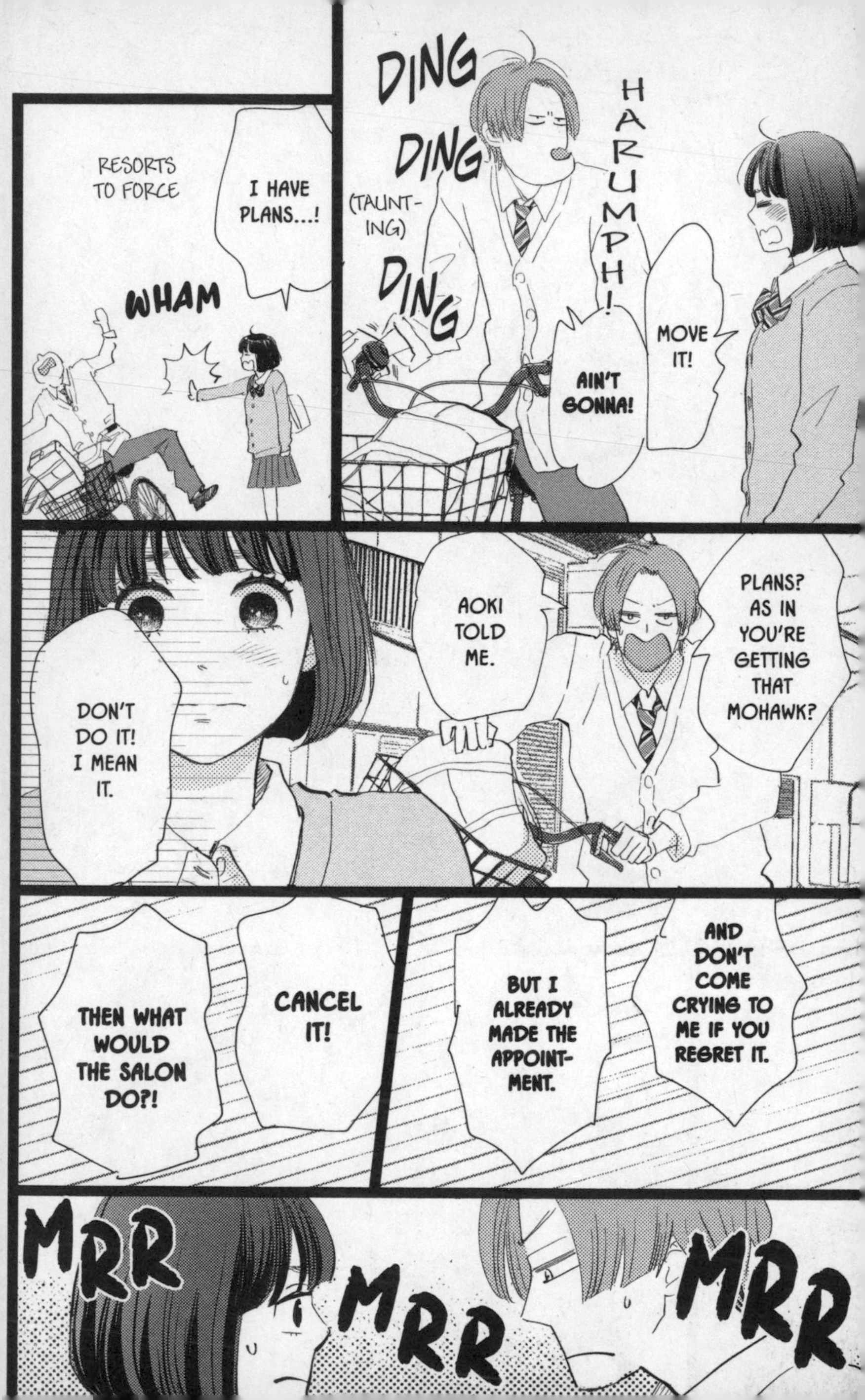
HARUMPH!
MOVE IT!
DING
DING
(TAUNT-ING)
AIN'T GONNA!
DING
I HAVE PLANS...!
RESORTS TO FORCE
WHAM
PLANS? AS IN YOU'RE GETTING THAT MOHAWK?
AOKI TOLD ME.
DON'T DO IT! I MEAN IT.
AND DON'T COME CRYING TO ME IF YOU REGRET IT.
BUT I ALREADY MADE THE APPOINT-MENT.
CANCEL IT!
THEN WHAT WOULD THE SALON DO?!
MRR
MRR
MRR
MRR

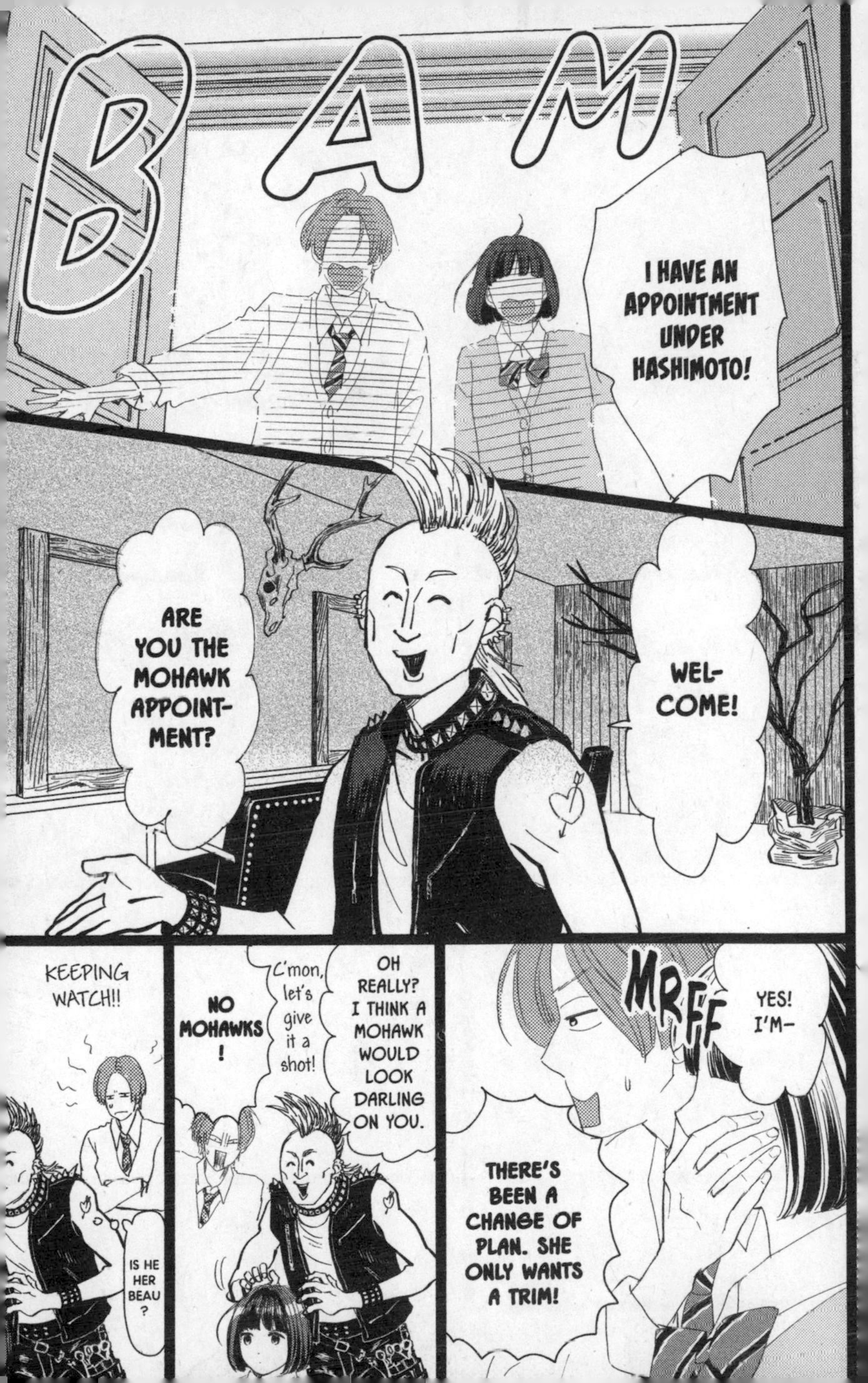
BAM
I HAVE AN APPOINTMENT UNDER HASHIMOTO!
WEL-COME!
ARE YOU THE MOHAWK APPOINT-MENT?
YES! I'M-
MRFF
THERE'S BEEN A CHANGE OF PLAN. SHE ONLY WANTS A TRIM!
OH REALLY? I THINK A MOHAWK WOULD LOOK DARLING ON YOU.
C'mon, let's give it a shot!
NO MOHAWKS!
KEEPING WATCH!!
IS HE HER BEAU?

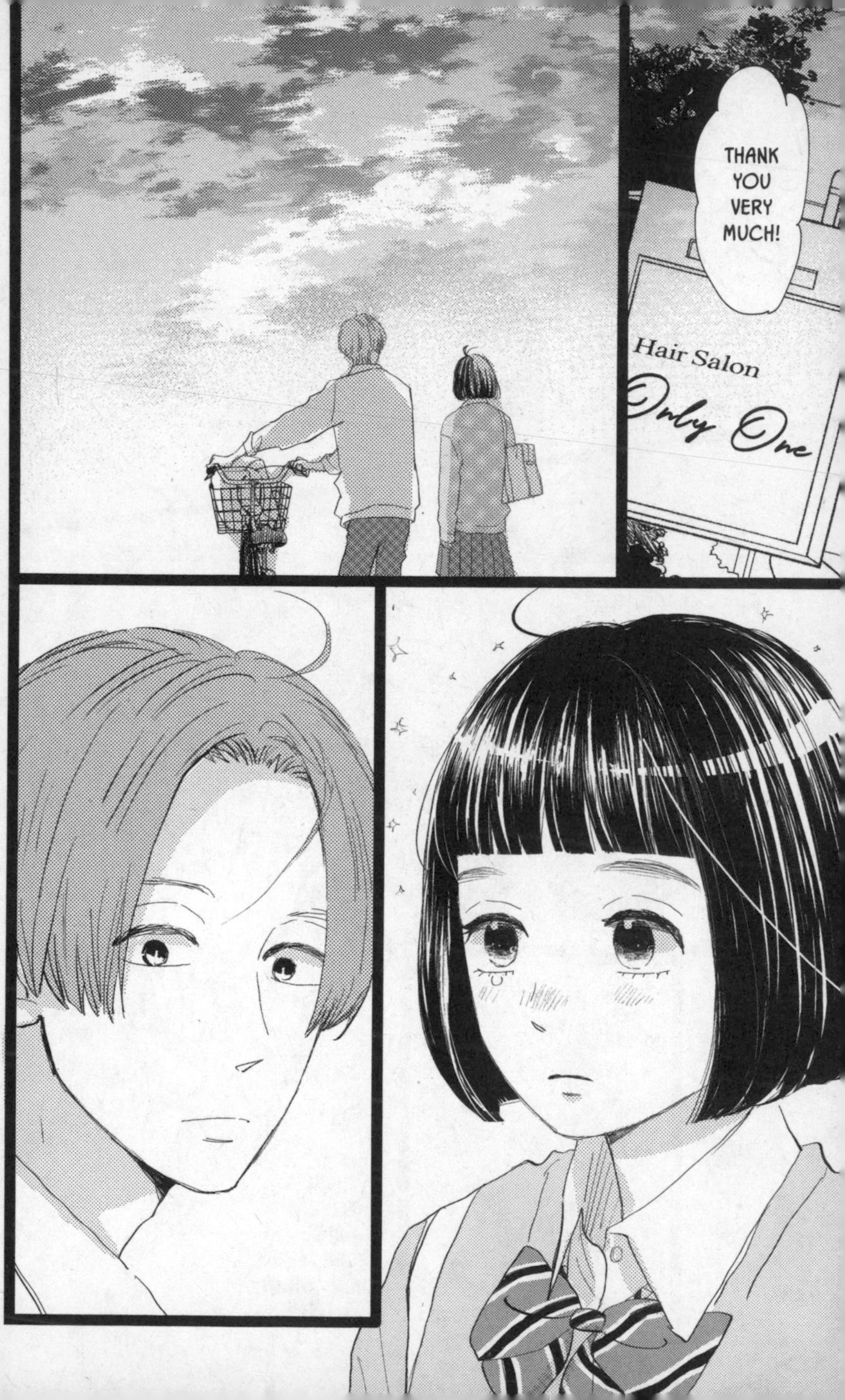
THANK YOU VERY MUCH!
Hair Salon
Only One

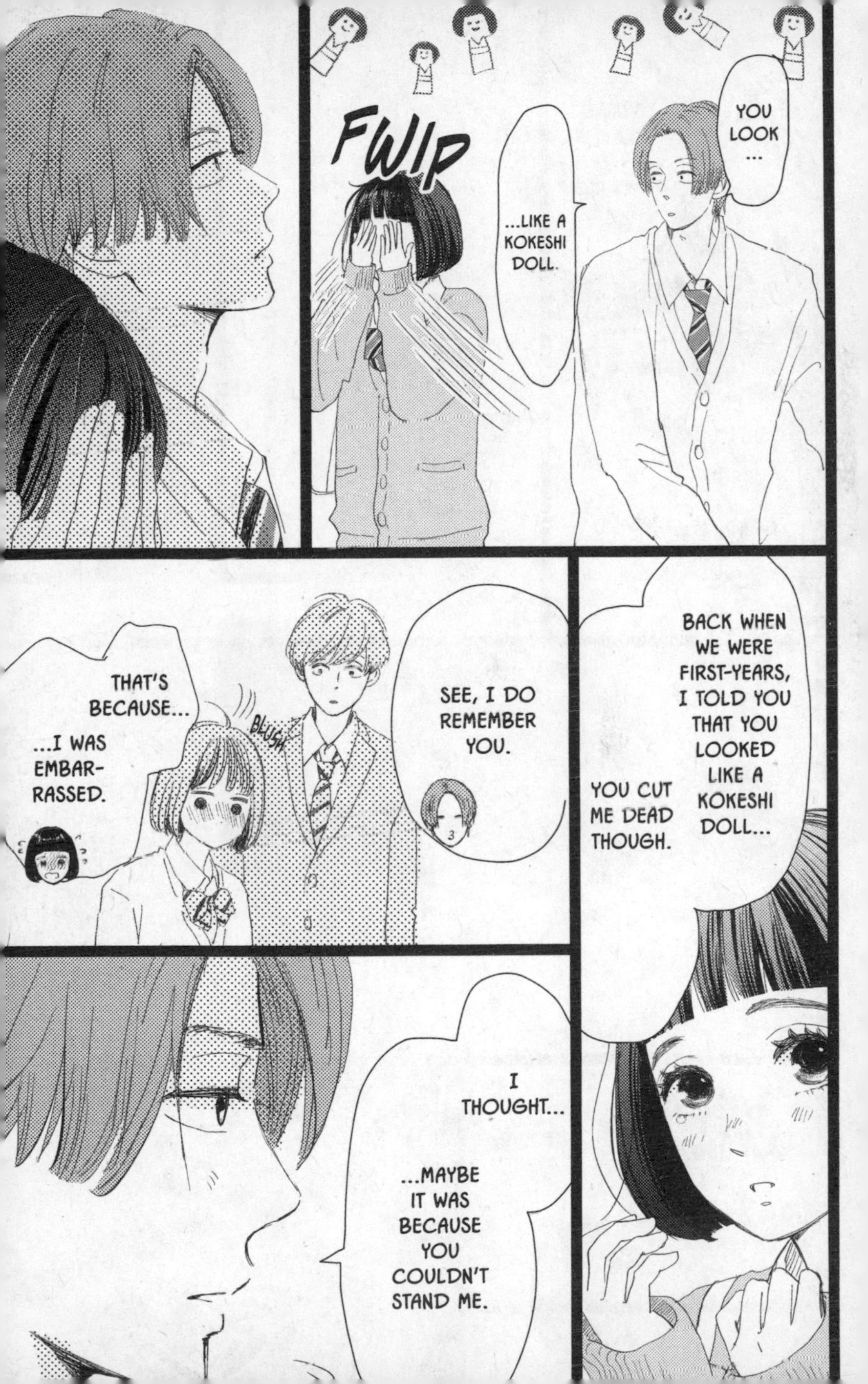
YOU LOOK ...
...LIKE A KOKESHI DOLL.
FWIP
BACK WHEN WE WERE FIRST-YEARS, I TOLD YOU THAT YOU LOOKED LIKE A KOKESHI DOLL...
YOU CUT ME DEAD THOUGH.
SEE, I DO REMEMBER YOU.
BLUSH
THAT'S BECAUSE...
...I WAS EMBARRASSED.
I THOUGHT...
...MAYBE IT WAS BECAUSE YOU COULDN'T STAND ME.

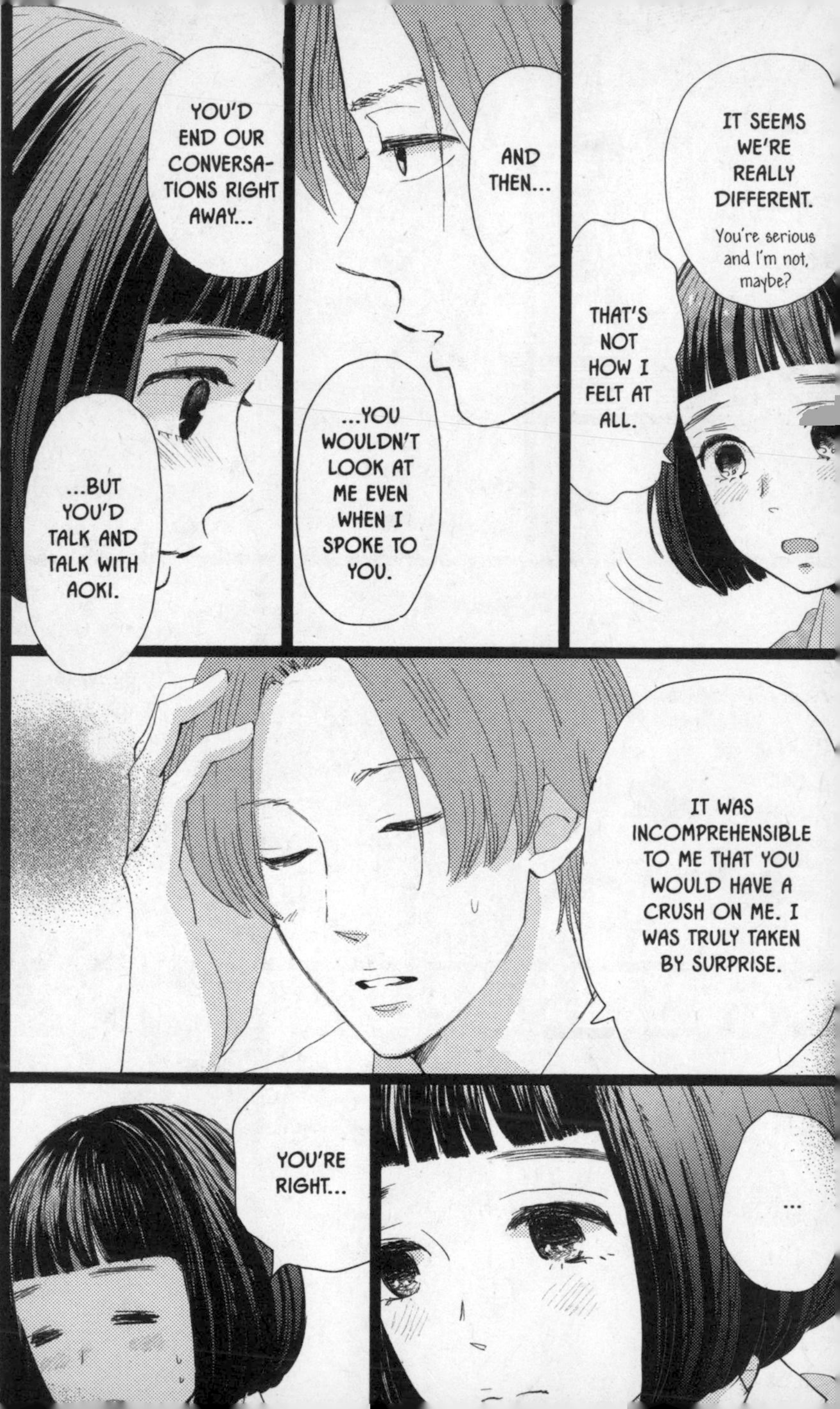
IT SEEMS WE'RE REALLY DIFFERENT.
You're serious and I'm not, maybe?
THAT'S NOT HOW I FELT AT ALL.
AND THEN...
...YOU WOULDN'T LOOK AT ME EVEN WHEN I SPOKE TO YOU.
YOU'D END OUR CONVERSATIONS RIGHT AWAY...
...BUT YOU'D TALK AND TALK WITH AOKI.
IT WAS INCOMPREHENSIBLE TO ME THAT YOU WOULD HAVE A CRUSH ON ME. I WAS TRULY TAKEN BY SURPRISE.
...
YOU'RE RIGHT...

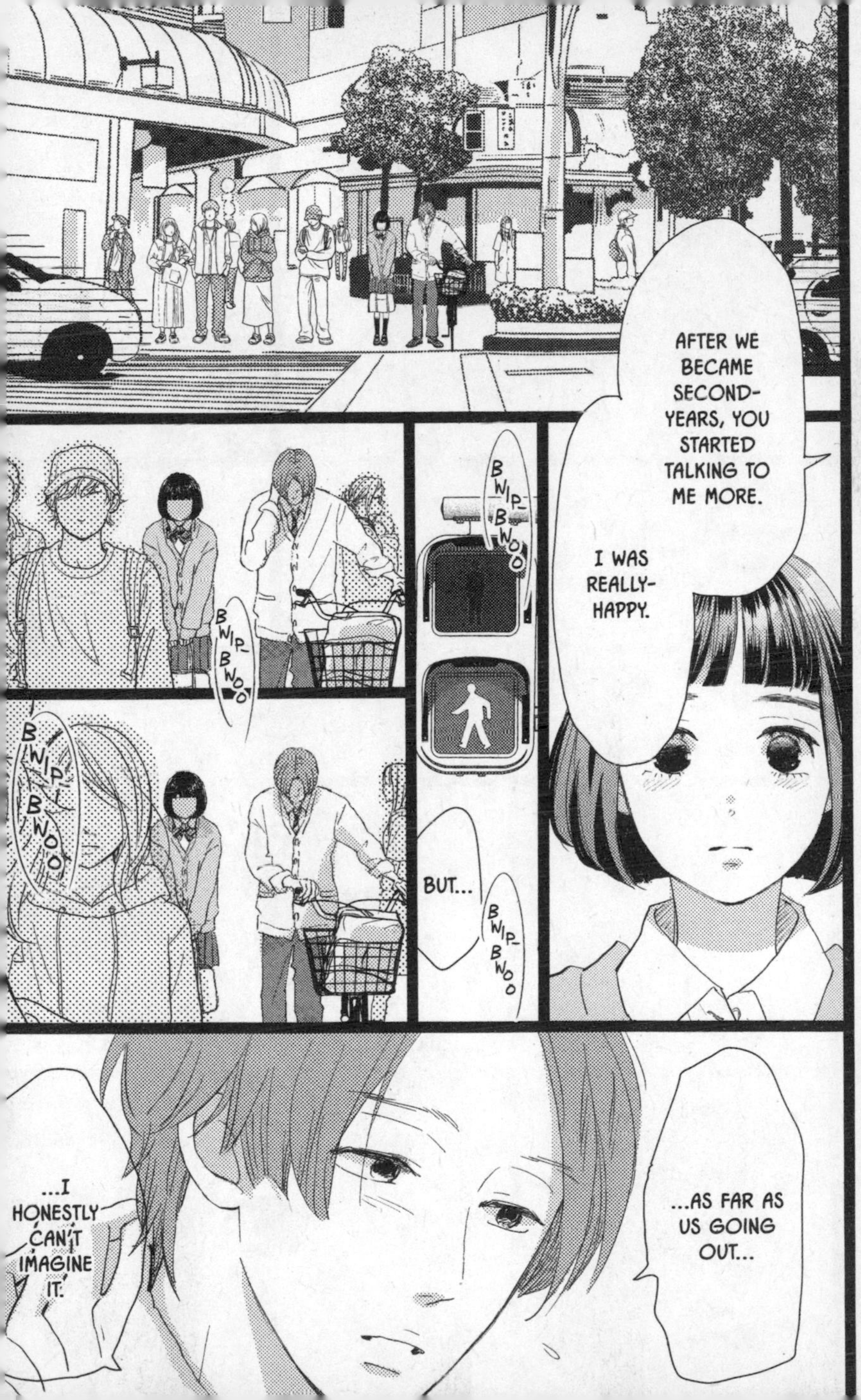
AFTER WE BECAME SECOND-YEARS, YOU STARTED TALKING TO ME MORE.
I WAS REALLY-HAPPY.
BWIP-BWOO
BUT...
BWIP-BWOO
BWIP-BWOO
BWIP-BWOO
...AS FAR AS US GOING OUT...
...I HONESTLY CAN'T IMAGINE IT.

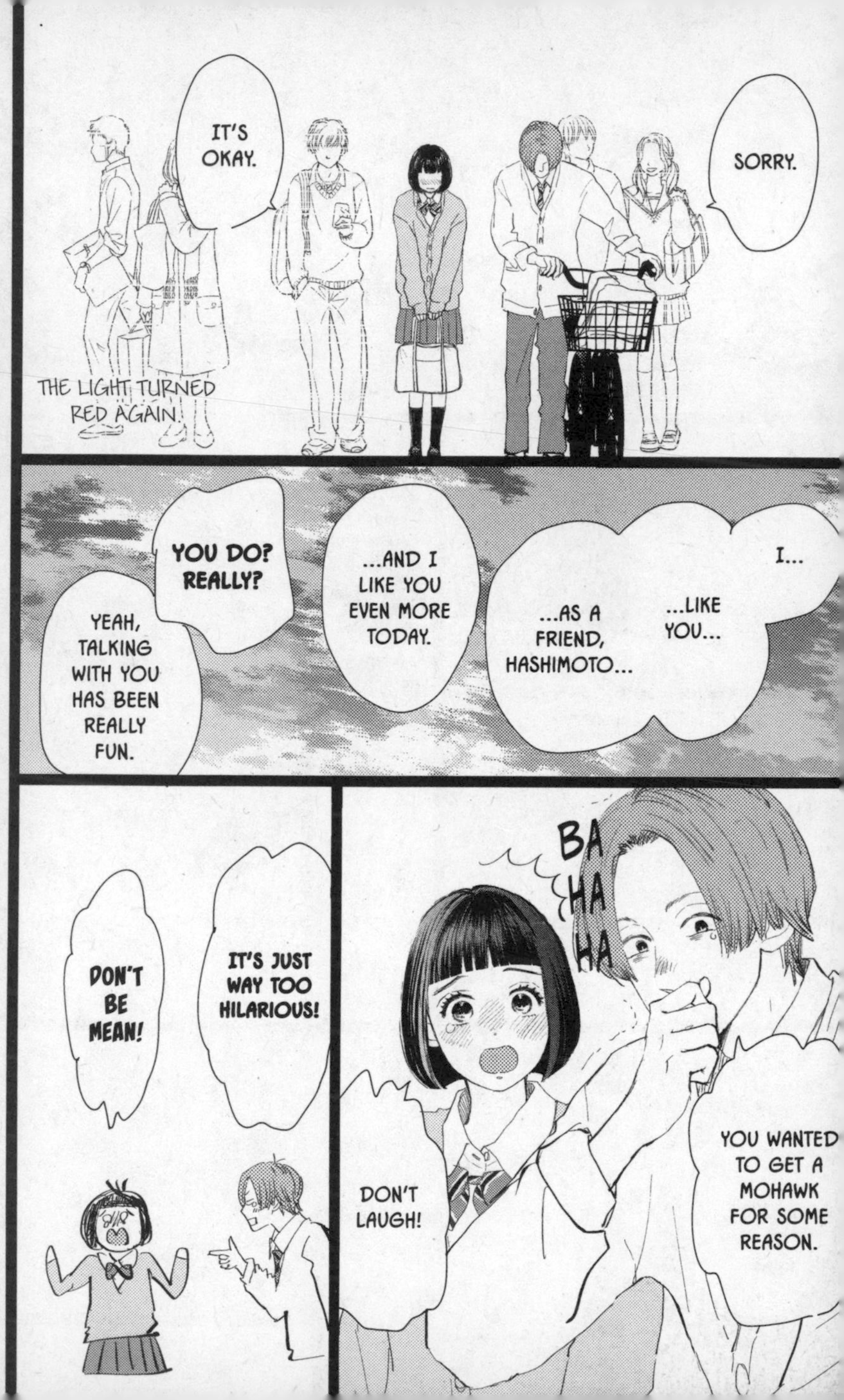
SORRY.
IT'S OKAY.
THE LIGHT TURNED RED AGAIN.
I...
...LIKE YOU...
...AS A FRIEND, HASHIMOTO...
...AND I LIKE YOU EVEN MORE TODAY.
YOU DO? REALLY?
YEAH, TALKING WITH YOU HAS BEEN REALLY FUN.
BA HA HA HA
YOU WANTED TO GET A MOHAWK FOR SOME REASON.
DON'T LAUGH!
IT'S JUST WAY TOO HILARIOUS!
DON'T BE MEAN!

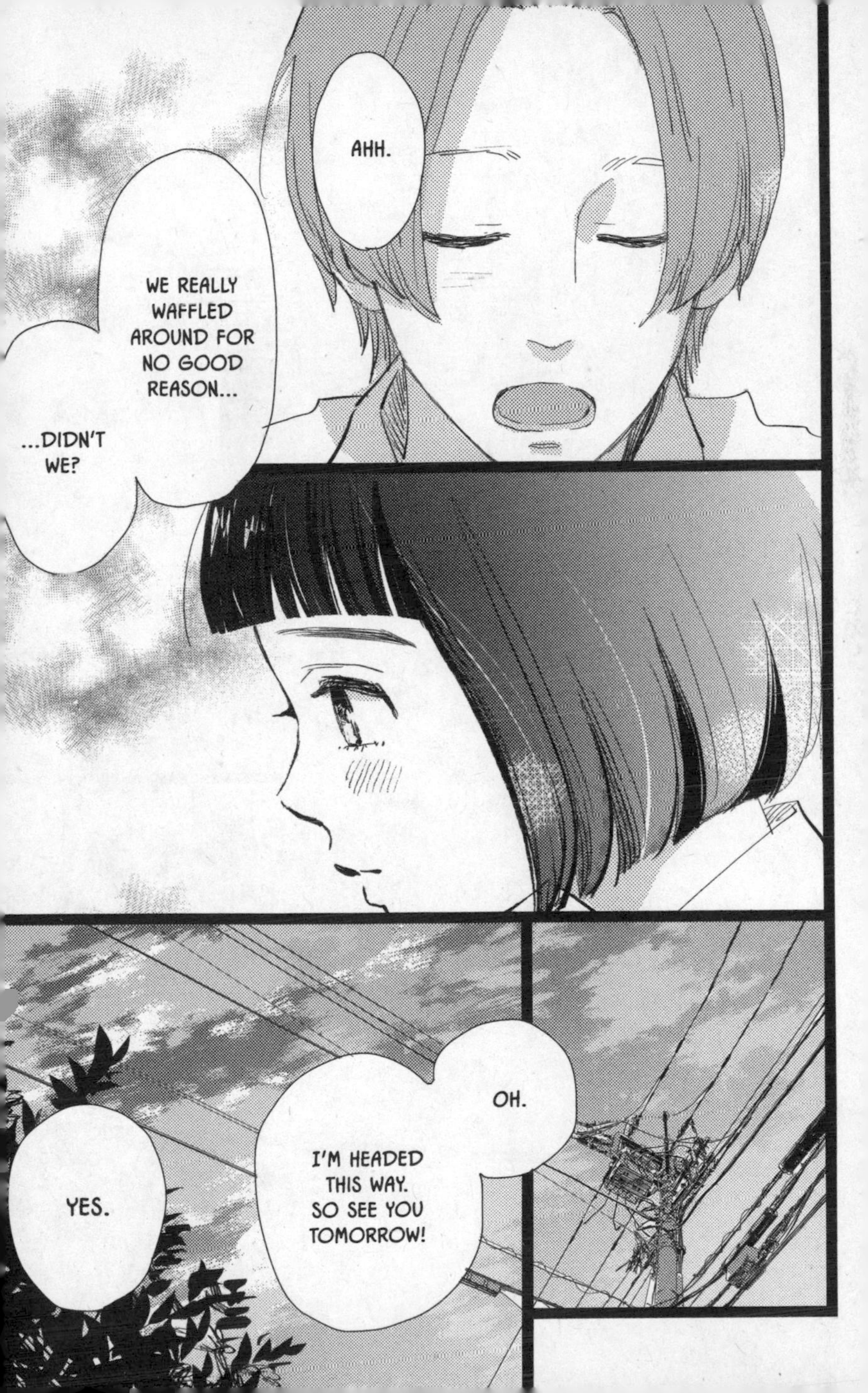
AHH.
WE REALLY WAFFLED AROUND FOR NO GOOD REASON...
...DIDN'T WE?
OH.
I'M HEADED THIS WAY. SO SEE YOU TOMORROW!
YES.

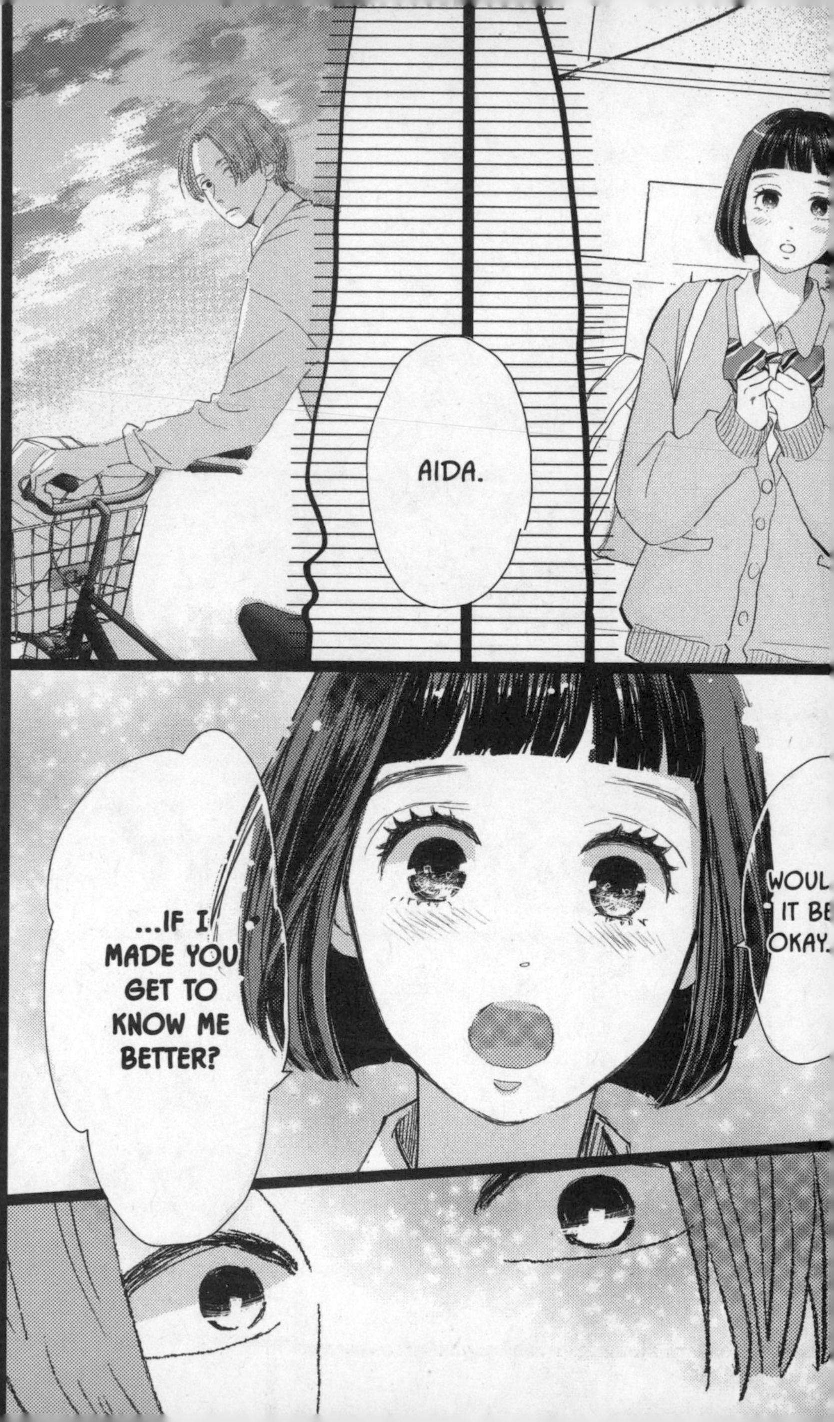
AIDA.
WOUL IT BE OKAY.
...IF I MADE YOU GET TO KNOW ME BETTER?

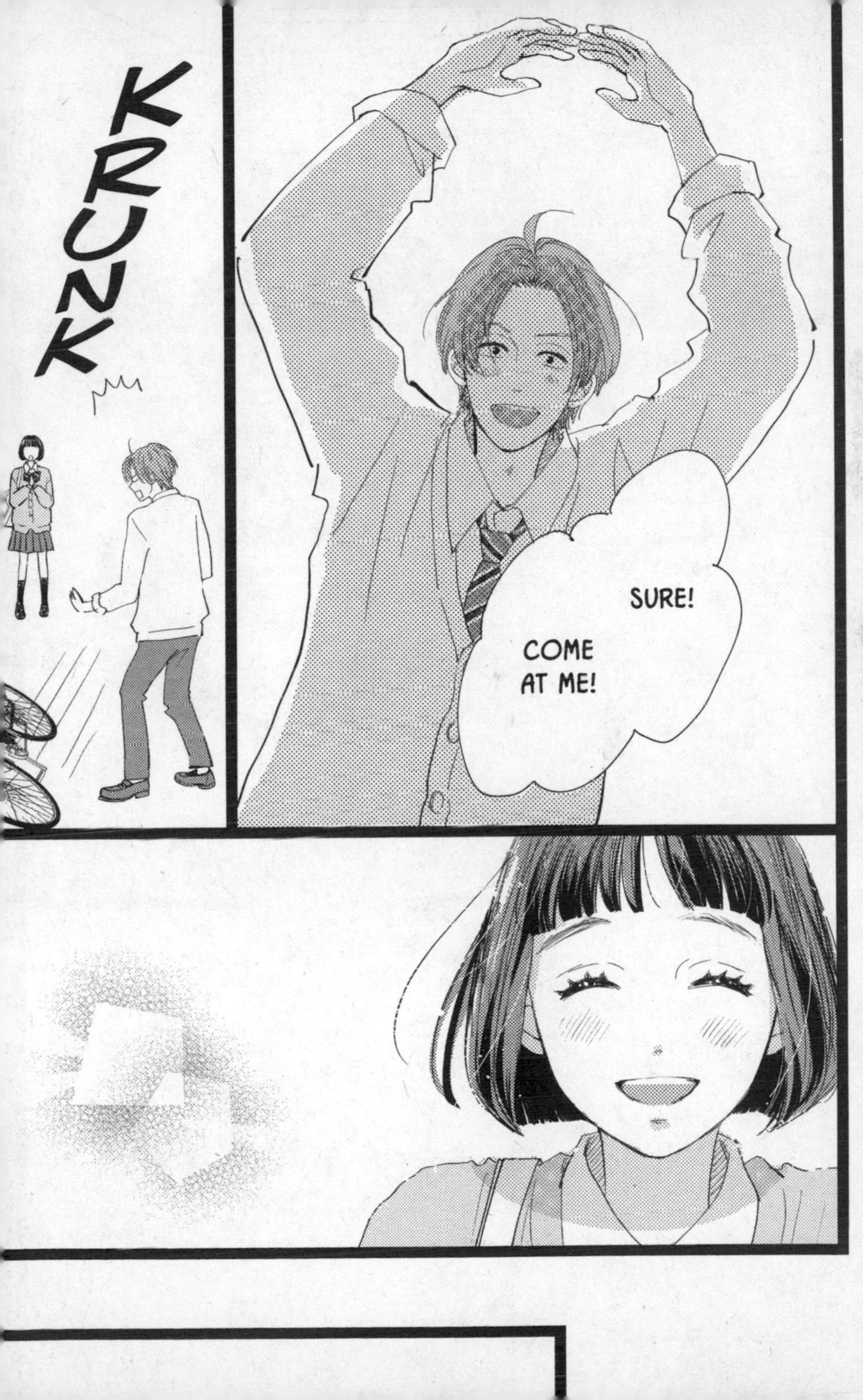
SURE!
COME AT ME!
KRUNK

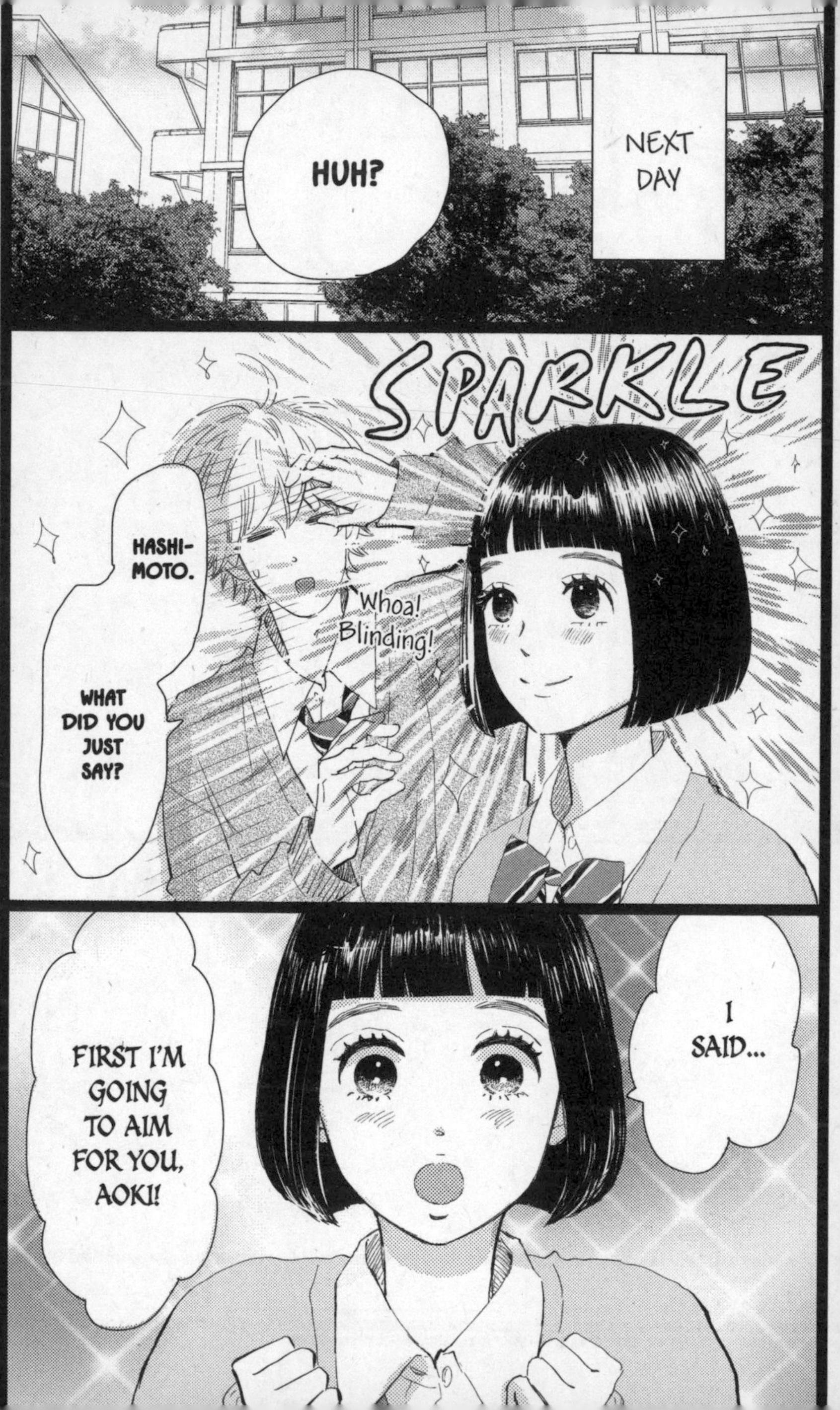
NEXT DAY
HUH?
SPARKLE
Whoa! Blinding!
HASHI-MOTO.
WHAT DID YOU JUST SAY?
I SAID...
FIRST I'M GOING TO AIM FOR YOU, AOKI!

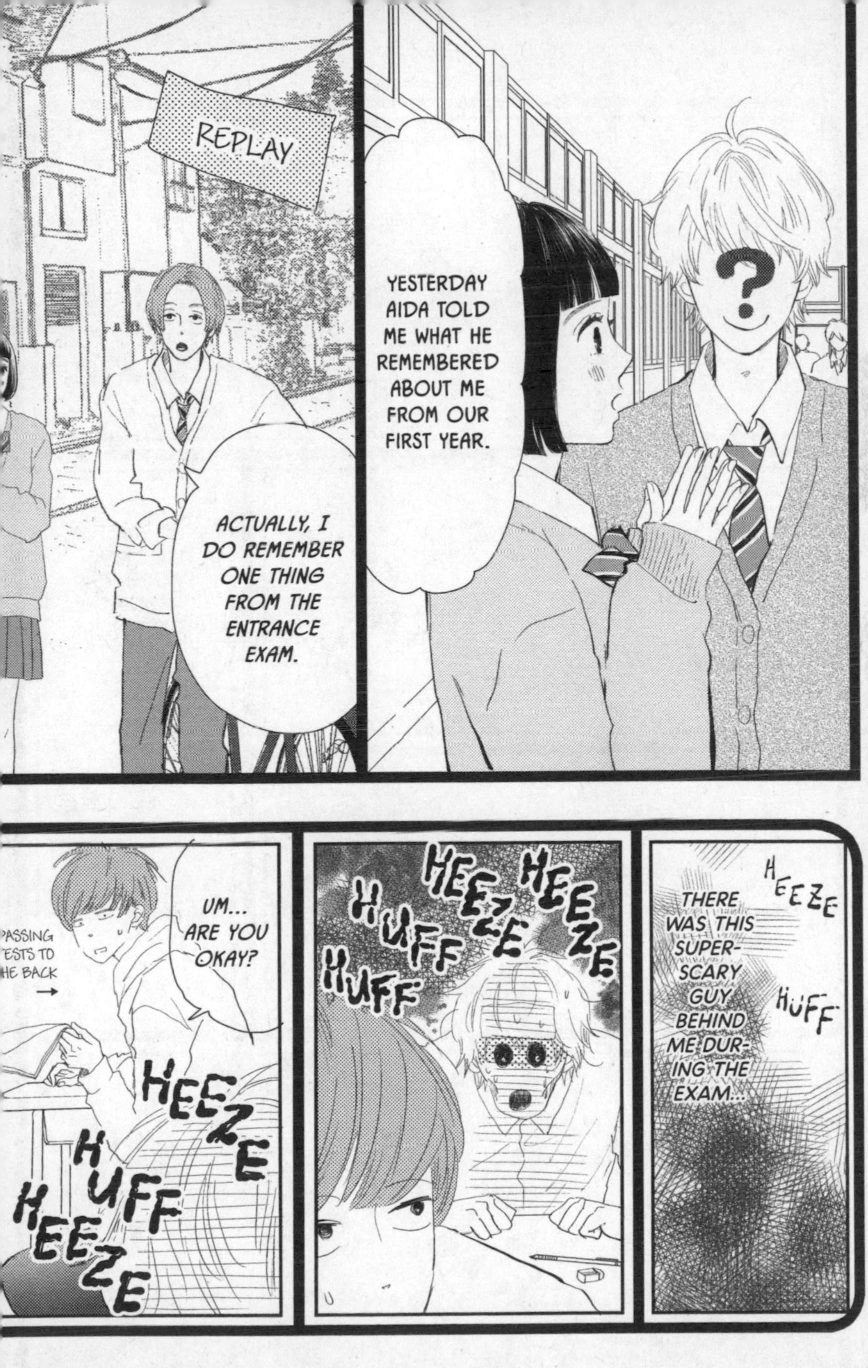
YESTERDAY AIDA TOLD ME WHAT HE REMEMBERED ABOUT ME FROM OUR FIRST YEAR.
REPLAY
ACTUALLY, I DO REMEMBER ONE THING FROM THE ENTRANCE EXAM.
HEEZE
THERE WAS THIS SUPER-SCARY GUY BEHIND ME DURING THE EXAM...
HUFF
HEEZE HEEZE
HUFF HUFF
UM... ARE YOU OKAY?
PASSING
ESTS TO
HE BACK
HEEZE
HUFF
HEEZE

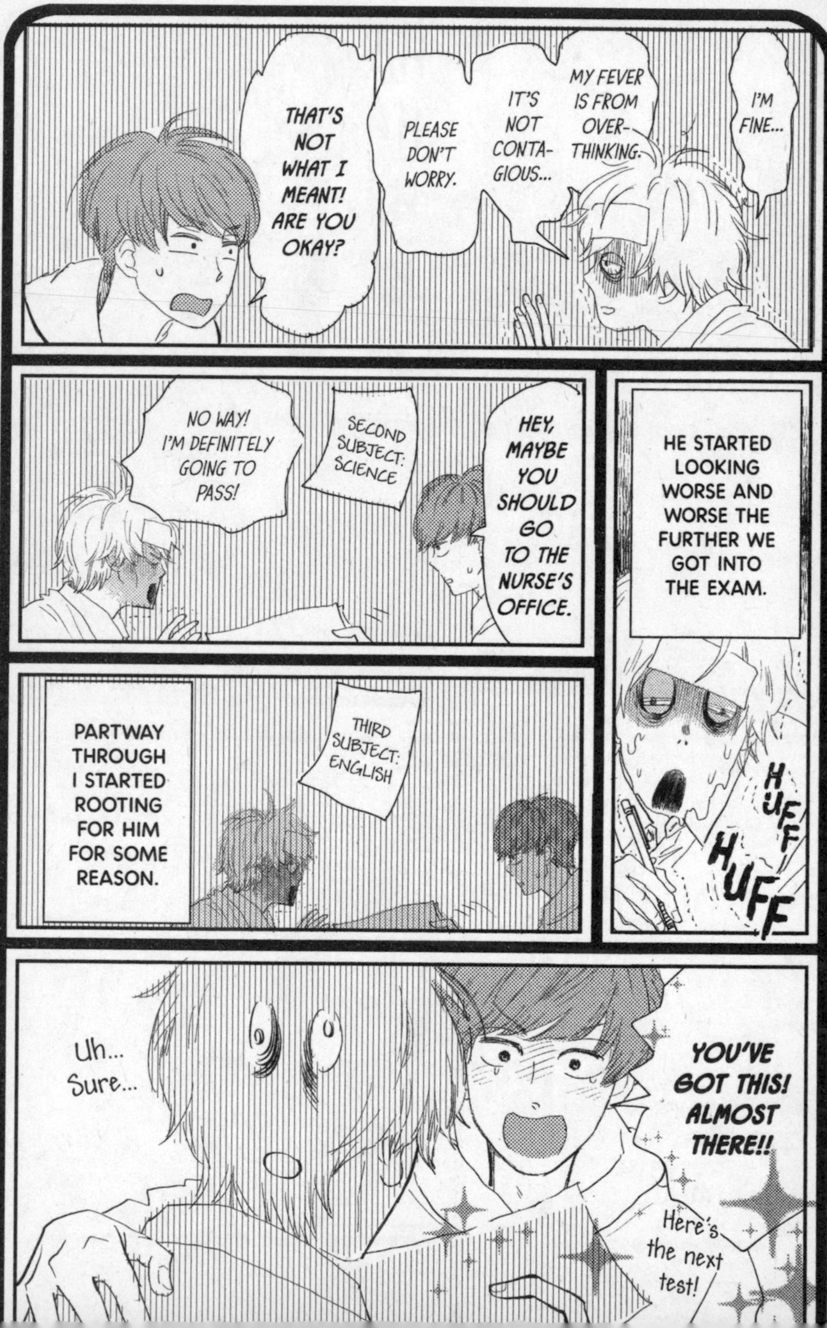
I'M FINE...
MY FEVER IS FROM OVER-THINKING.
IT'S NOT CONTA-GIOUS...
PLEASE DON'T WORRY.
THAT'S NOT WHAT I MEANT! ARE YOU OKAY?
HE STARTED LOOKING WORSE AND WORSE THE FURTHER WE GOT INTO THE EXAM.
HUFF
HUFF
HEY, MAYBE YOU SHOULD GO TO THE NURSE'S OFFICE.
SECOND SUBJECT: SCIENCE
NO WAY! I'M DEFINITELY GOING TO PASS!
THIRD SUBJECT: ENGLISH
PARTWAY THROUGH I STARTED ROOTING FOR HIM FOR SOME REASON.
YOU'VE GOT THIS! ALMOST THERE!!
Here's the next test!
Uh... Sure...

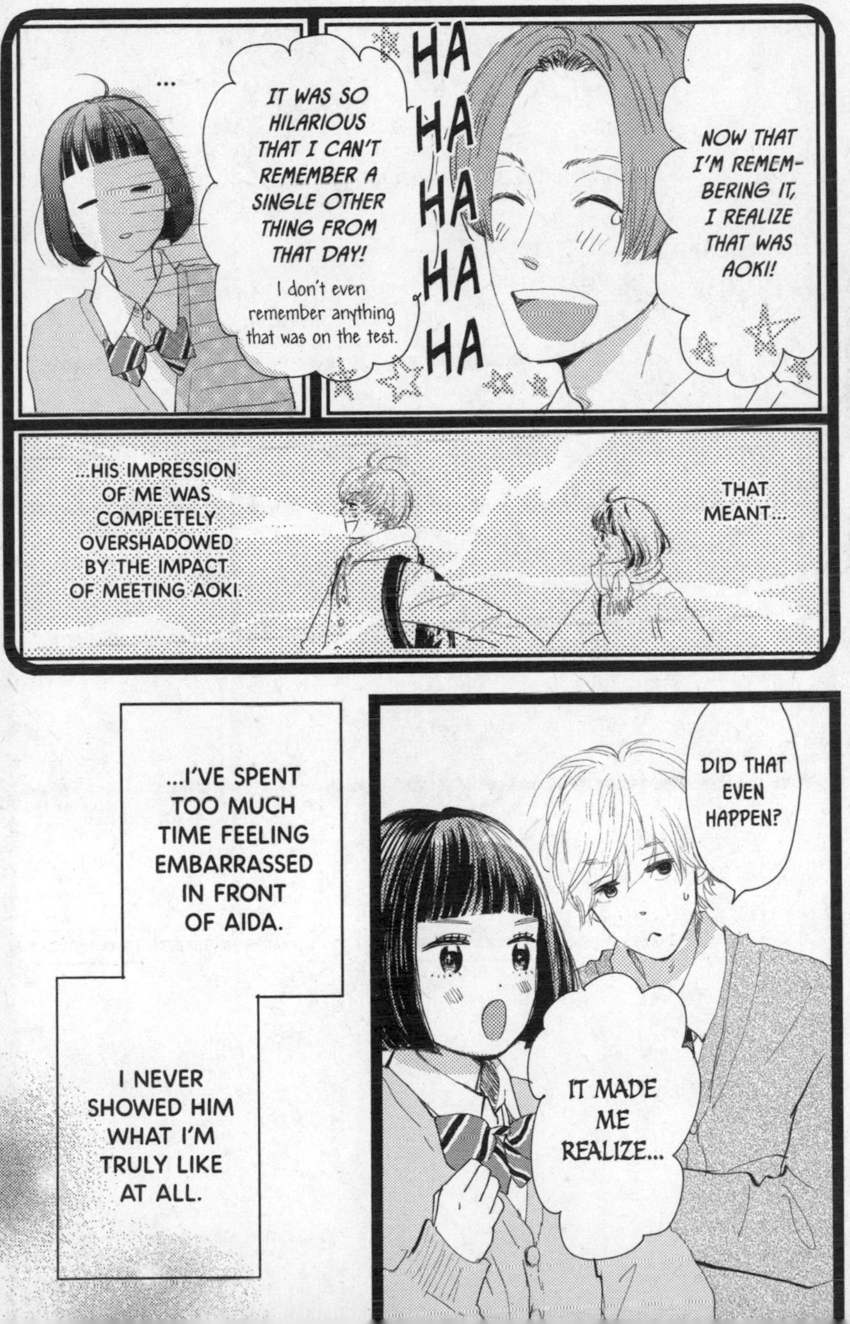
NOW THAT I'M REMEMBERING IT, I REALIZE THAT WAS AOKI!
HA HA HA HA HA HA
IT WAS SO HILARIOUS THAT I CAN'T REMEMBER A SINGLE OTHER THING FROM THAT DAY!
I don't even remember anything that was on the test.
...
THAT MEANT...
...HIS IMPRESSION OF ME WAS COMPLETELY OVERSHADOWED BY THE IMPACT OF MEETING AOKI.
DID THAT EVEN HAPPEN?
IT MADE ME REALIZE...
...I'VE SPENT TOO MUCH TIME FEELING EMBARRASSED IN FRONT OF AIDA.
I NEVER SHOWED HIM WHAT I'M TRULY LIKE AT ALL.

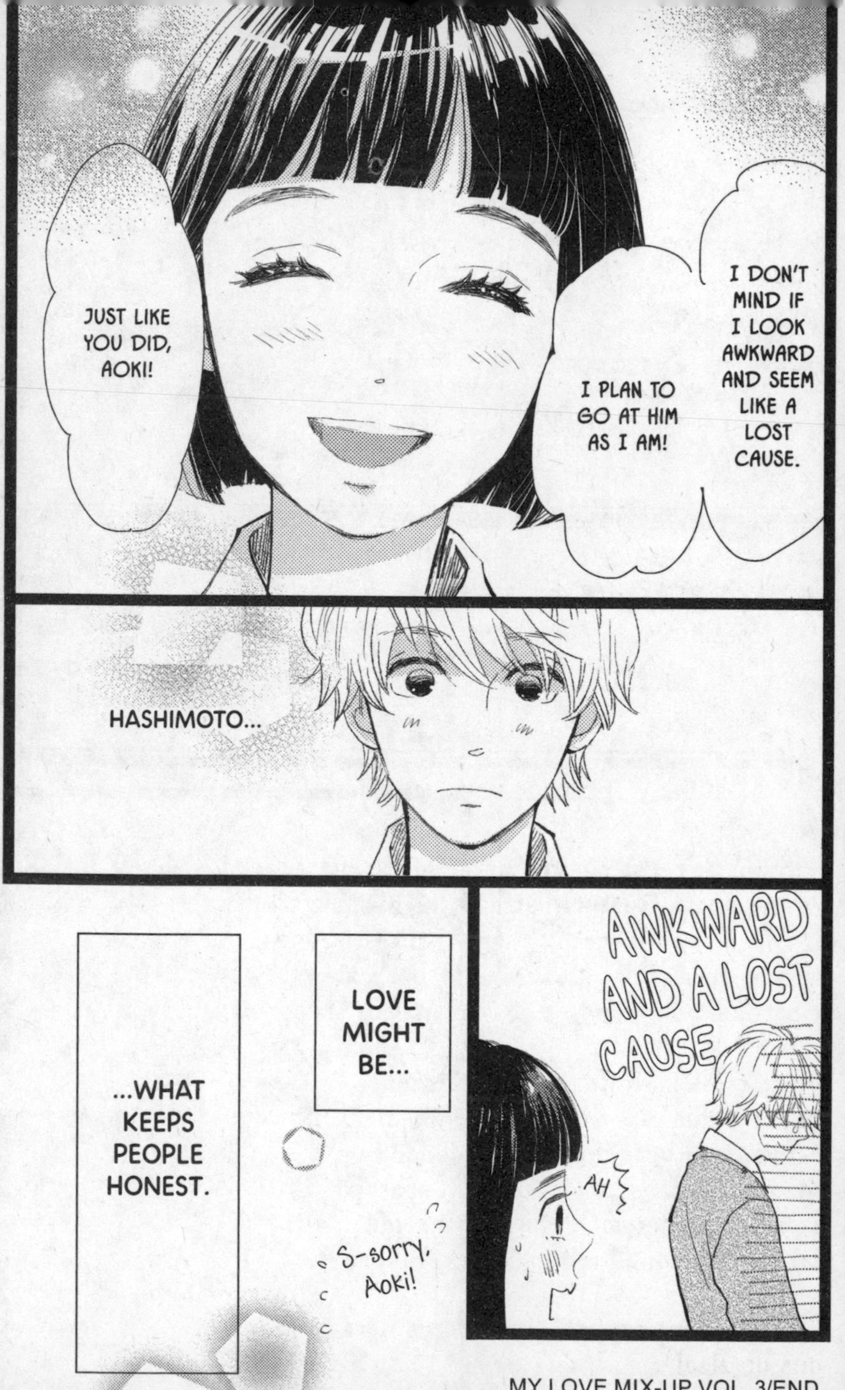
I DON'T MIND IF I LOOK AWKWARD AND SEEM LIKE A LOST CAUSE.
I PLAN TO GO AT HIM AS I AM!
JUST LIKE YOU DID, AOKI!
HASHIMOTO...
AWKWARD AND A LOST CAUSE
AH
S-sorry, Aoki!
LOVE MIGHT BE...
...WHAT KEEPS PEOPLE HONEST.

MY LOVE MIX-UP VOL. 3/END

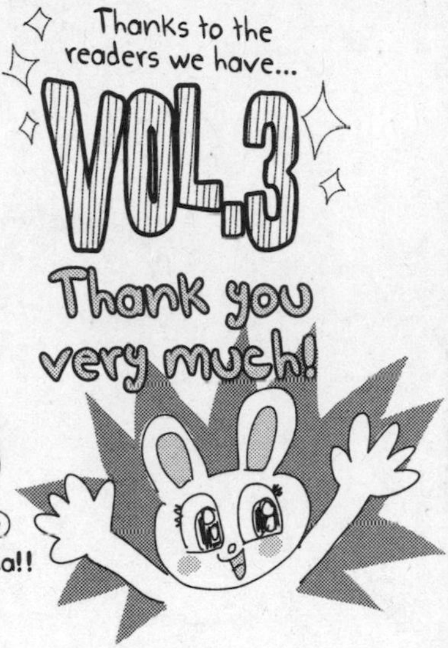
Thanks to the readers we have...
VOL.3
Thank you very much!

The longer I've been with the characters, the more affection I feel for them. That's how it's been these days. I'm looking forward to working with you more in the future, Hinekure. I'm so excited to see what comes next!! ♡

6/2020 Aruko

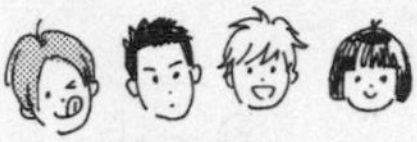

Thank you to my assistants, Amane Oyama ☺ and Yuuko Hishida ☺ , and my editor Sawada!! I'm grateful to everyone involved! ✧✧

My Love Mix-Up! Vol. 3
Thank you very much!

I'm Hinekure, the one in charge of the manuscript. We're at the third volume. Basically that means a whole year has passed since we started serialization. Thanks to Aruko, our editor, and especially the readers, we've been able to see Aoki and the other characters full of life. Thank you so very much!

Volume 3 was in full swing with scenes full of skiing and dating, all of which Aruko drew beautifully. As a reader I thought, "It's so cute!! Wow!!" It sparked so much joy for me. Aruko, thank you for everything. I'll work hard on volume 4.

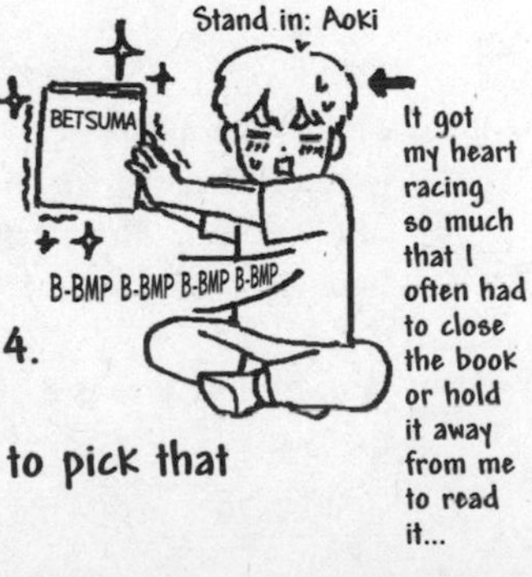
Stand in: Aoki
BETSUMA
B-BMP B-BMP B-BMP B-BMP
It got my heart racing so much that I often had to close the book or hold it away from me to read it...

I'd be so very happy if the readers were to pick that one up also!

We did it! Thank you for making the third volume happen. A lot sure happened in 2020. I hope that we stay healthy!

Aruko

The third volume's cover is so lovely that I keep looking at it! It almost looks like it's from Mametaro's perspective, and I can't help but let my imagination run wild thinking about how cute it is.

Wataru Hinekure

Aruko is from Ishikawa Prefecture in Japan and was born on July 26 (a Leo!). She made her manga debut with *Ame Nochi Hare* (Clear After the Rain). Her other works include *Yasuko to Kenji*, and her hobbies include laughing and getting lost.

Wataru Hinekure is a night owl. *My Love Mix-Up!* is Hinekure's first work.

My Love Mix-Up!

Vol. 3
Shojo Beat Edition

STORY BY
Wataru Hinekure

ART BY
Aruko

Translation & Adaptation/Jan Cash
Touch-Up Art & Lettering/Inori Fukuda Trant
Design/Yukiko Whitley
Editor/Nancy Thistlethwaite

KIETA HATSUKOI © 2019 by Wataru Hinekure, Aruko
All rights reserved.
First published in Japan in 2019 by SHUEISHA Inc., Tokyo.
English translation rights arranged by SHUEISHA Inc.

The stories, characters, and incidents mentioned in this publication are entirely fictional.

Printed in the U.S.A.

Published by VIZ Media, LLC
P.O. Box 77010
San Francisco, CA 94107

10 9 8 7 6 5 4 3 2 1
First printing, April 2022

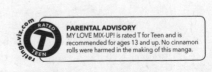

PARENTAL ADVISORY
MY LOVE MIX-UP! is rated T for Teen and is recommended for ages 13 and up. No cinnamon rolls were harmed in the making of this manga.

viz.com

shojobeat.com

An unexpected love quadrangle comes between a group of friends!

Blue Flag

story and art by
KAITO

Love is already hard enough, but it becomes
an unnavigable maze for unassuming high
school student Taichi Ichinose and his shy
classmate Futaba Kuze when they begin to fall for
each other after their same-sex best friends have
already fallen for them.

Honey So Sweet

Story and Art by Amu Meguro

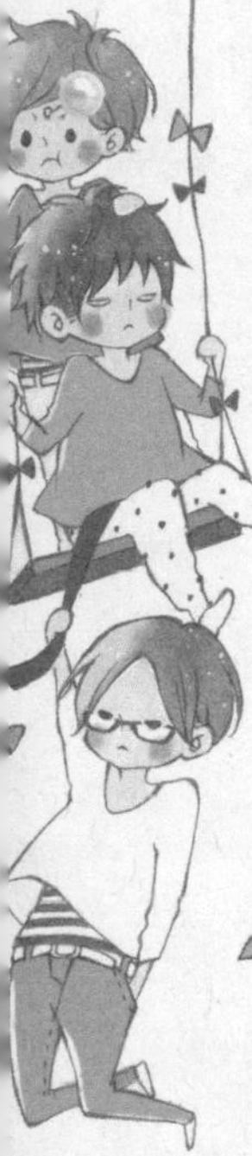

Little did Nao Kogure realize back in middle school that when she left an umbrella and a box of bandages in the rain for injured delinquent Taiga Onise that she would meet him again in high school. Nao wants nothing to do with the gruff and frightening Taiga, but he suddenly presents her with a huge bouquet of flowers and asks her to date him—with marriage in mind! Is Taiga really so scary, or is he a sweetheart in disguise?

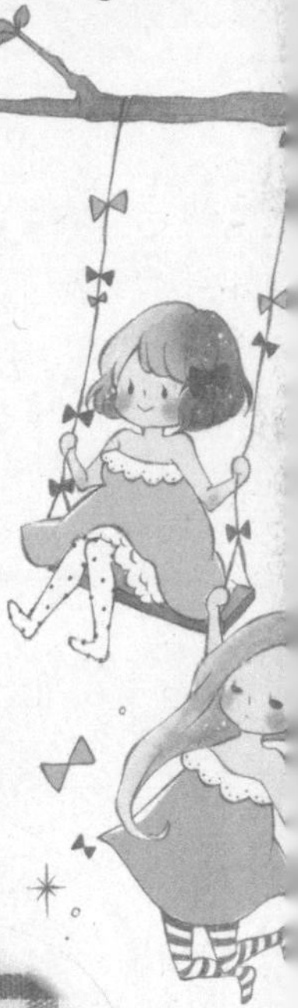

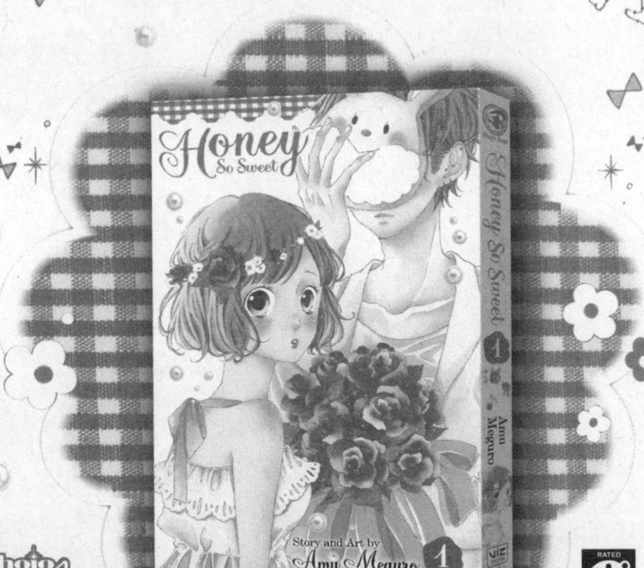
Honey So Sweet
Honey So Sweet 1
Amu Meguro
Story and Art by
Amu Meguro 1

SHORTCAKE CAKE

STORY AND ART BY
suu Morishita

An unflappable girl and a cast of
lovable roommates at a boardinghouse
create bonds of friendship and romance!

When Ten moves out of her parents' home
in the mountains to live in a boardinghouse,
she finds herself becoming fast friends with
her male roommates. But can love and
romance be far behind?

VIZ

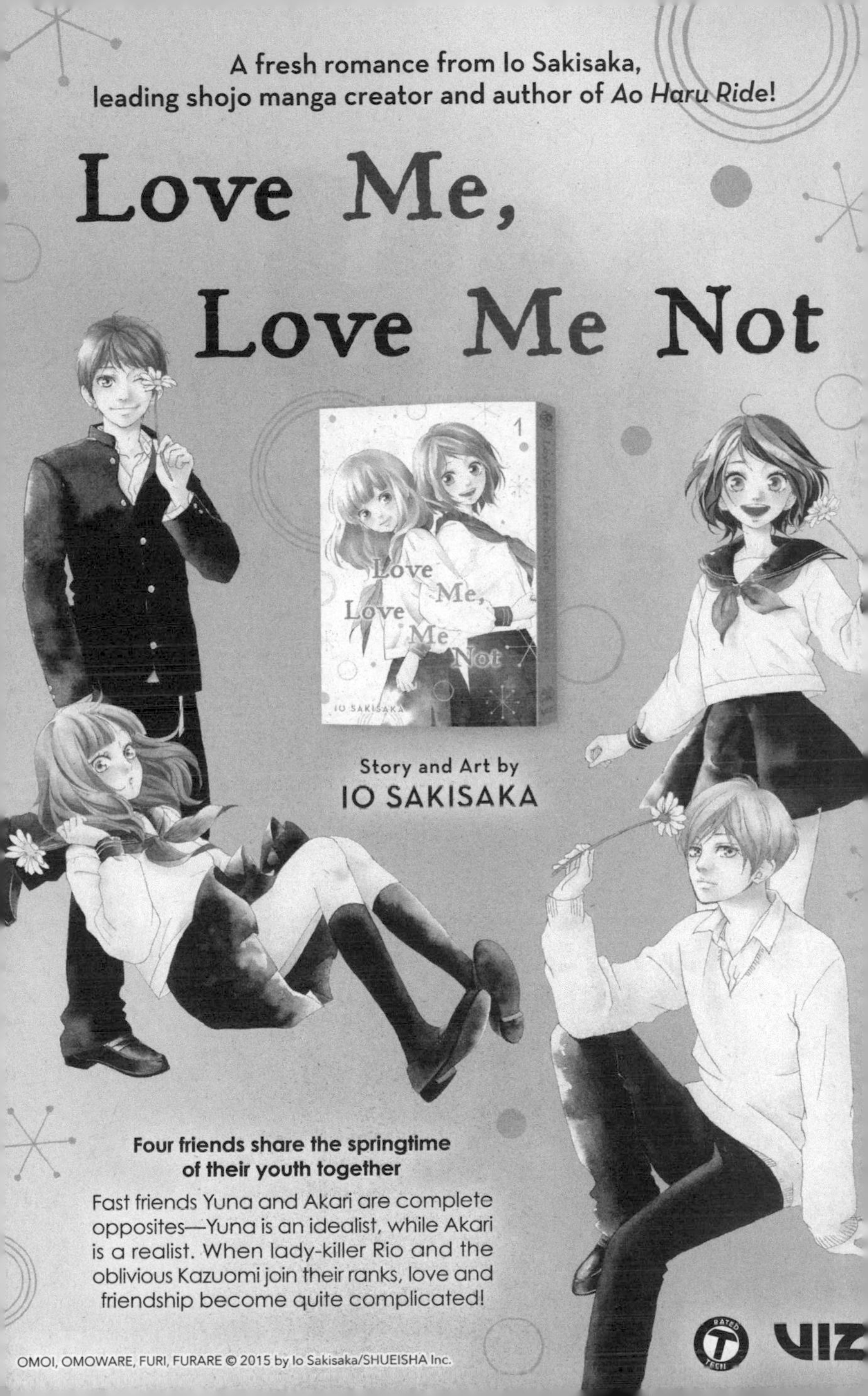
A fresh romance from Io Sakisaka,
leading shojo manga creator and author of Ao Haru Ride!
Love Me,
Love Me Not
1
Love Me, Love Me Not
IO SAKISAKA
Story and Art by
IO SAKISAKA
Four friends share the springtime
of their youth together
Fast friends Yuna and Akari are complete opposites—Yuna is an idealist, while Akari is a realist. When lady-killer Rio and the oblivious Kazuomi join their ranks, love and friendship become quite complicated!
OMOI, OMOWARE, FURI, FURARE © 2015 by Io Sakisaka/SHUEISHA Inc.
RATED T TEEN
VIZ

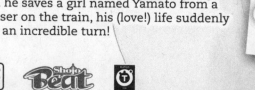